THE PATRIOT OPPOSITION TO WALPOLE

THE PATRIOT OPPOSITION TO WALPOLE

Politics, Poetry, and National Myth, 1725-1742

CHRISTINE GERRARD

CLARENDON PRESS · OXFORD

1994

Oxford University Press, Walton Street, Oxford OX2 6DP

Oxford New York
Athens Auckland Bangkok Bombay
Calcutta Cape Town Dar es Salaam Delhi
Florence Hong Kong Istanbul Karachi
Kuala Lumpur Madras Madrid Melbourne
Mexico City Nairobi Paris Singapore
Taipei Tokyo Toronto
and associated companies in
Berlin Ibadan

Oxford is a trade mark of Oxford University Press

Published in the United States
by Oxford University Press Inc., New York

British Library Cataloguing in Publication Data
Data available

Library of Congress Cataloging in Publication Data
Gerrard, Christine.
The patriot opposition to Walpole: politics, poetry, and national myth,
1725–1742 / Christine Gerrard.
Includes bibliographical references.
1. English poetry—18th century—History and criticism.
2. Politics and literature—Great Britain—History—18th century.
3. Walpole, Robert Earl of Orford, 1676–1745—In literature.
4. Political poetry, English—History and criticism. 5. Great
Britain—Politics and government—1714–1760. 6. Opposition
(Political science) in literature. 7. Great Britain—
Civilization—18th century. 8. Prime ministers in literature.
9. Myth in literature. I. Title.
PR555.H5G47 1994   821'.509358—dc20   94–12039
ISBN 0–19–812982–3

1 3 5 7 9 10 8 6 4 2

Typeset by Hope Services (Abingdon) Ltd.
Printed in Great Britain
on acid-free paper by
Bookcraft Ltd.,
Midsomer Norton, Bath

TO

GEORGE AND ELSIE

Preface

FEW HISTORICAL periods have received such intense scrutiny as the Walpole era. Politics and poetry were more closely intertwined in this period than they were (arguably) ever to be again: and this relationship has inspired an impressive body of scholarship. Recent years have yielded new individual studies of the literary 'giants' who directed their formidable talents against Walpole—Fielding, Pope, Swift, Gay, Thomson. Other literary historians have turned a fresh eye on those authors who wrote for, not against the administration, wielding the 'venal pen' on Walpole's behalf. This study began life some years ago, prompted by a curiosity about the very different kinds of political writing produced by poets who opposed Walpole. Why did some writers turn to patriotism and others to satire? Why did James Thomson write 'Rule, Britannia' and Pope *The Dunciad*? The generic distinction Goldgar describes in his *Walpole and the Wits* (1976) between the 'Wits' and the 'Patriots' was in some senses predicated on a political distinction between the Tory element and the dissident Whig element in the opposition to Walpole.

My pursuit of the Patriots—not just Thomson, but other Whig writers who attacked Walpole and celebrated their political figurehead, the dissident Frederick, Prince of Wales—was subsequently overtaken by new developments in historical scholarship. One was the challenge which recent historians have posed to the assumption that Whig and Tory opponents of the administration were absorbed into an ideologically homogeneous 'Country' party. Most of their scholarship has concentrated on reconstructing a distinctive Tory party identity. Very little has yet been done to address the question of where, and how, Patriot Whigs differed from their Tory counterparts, or indeed from the Court Whigs. These are issues which, in the absence of the more detailed historical study which yet remains to be written, I have attempted to explore in Chapters 1 and 2.

I have also been inspired by the new wave of scholarship which has restored patriotism from its long-standing academic moratorium to a central role in eighteenth-century studies. Historians such as Linda Colley, Gerald Newman, Nicholas Rogers, and Kathleen Wilson, to name but a few, have done much to enrich our understanding of the eighteenth century, not least the heady decade of the 1730s, in which popular patriotism flourished in the vocal campaign leading up to the declaration of the War of Jenkins' Ear. Much of this book is concerned with exploring, in its broadest sense, the patriotism of the Walpole period—a task begun by political historians but which still requires a fuller reappraisal of its literary and cultural manifestations. Patriotism was not, of course, simply the property of the opposition, and some of this study has invaded a territory explored from a political perspective by Reed Browning's *The Political and Constitutional Ideas of the Court Whigs* (1982). There is far more to Court Whig literary propaganda than Colley Cibber's birthday odes. Goldgar's *Walpole and the Wits* does not conceal its author's preference for the '*gay*, the *polite*, and *witty*' over the effusive and patriotic. Patriotism and the Patriot poets occupy a relatively minor role in his account of the literary opposition to Walpole. Recent historical work has demonstrated that the dominant concerns of Thomson, Mallet, Glover, Lillo, and numerous other Patriot Whig writers, those who were most vocal in their poetic rallying cries for war with Spain, were not marginal. Nor did they seem marginal to either Alexander Pope or Samuel Johnson, whose involvement with the Patriot campaign is explored from a rather different perspective in Chapters 4 and 8.

The patriotism of the Patriot poets was not mere jingoism. It was also a sensitive response to some of the deeper intellectual and artistic movements of the period seeking a reassertion of British identity in the artistic as well as the commercial sphere. Literary critics have long been familiar with the notion that the fall of Walpole in 1742 represented some kind of literary watershed, with poets adopting a new agenda, one which rejected Pope's 'wit and satire' for a romantic engagement with the explicitly British, and often very distant British past. An active engagement with the British past, with its patriotic glories and its historical myths, was one of the distinctive features of Patriot writing of the Walpole period. In Part II (Chapters 5, 6, and 7) I have explored the wealth of historical myth-making prompted by the political conflicts of the Walpole era as well as its relationship with the literary movements of the mid-eighteenth century. The mid-century fascination with the Gothic, the Elizabethan, and the Spenserian, the world of chivalry and romance, is not as divorced from the party-political writing of the previous decades as is often assumed.

I recently had a tutorial with an undergraduate grappling for the first time with the literary and historical background of the Walpole period. After immersing herself in recent studies on popular patriotism and the creation of British national identity, she turned to some traditional studies of the 'Augustan' age, with their emphasis on a literature that was stylistically decorous and socially conservative, dependent on notions of ordered literary and social hierarchy. How, she asked, could one reconcile such very different eighteenth centuries? Was there really such a gap between the world-view of the poets and the broader movements of eighteenth-century national consciousness? This book is, in part, an attempt to answer her question.

Acknowledgements

I AM indebted to many friends and colleagues who have been willing to share their time, enthusiasm, and ideas with me while I was writing this book. John Stevenson and Paul Langford both read drafts of an earlier and rather different version. Stephen Taylor, David Armitage, Richard Holmes, Ruth Smith, and Robert Harris have discussed with me their own work in progress and offered invaluable information. If I have plundered their findings, I hope that this acknowledgement will be some form of recompense. The staff of the Bodleian Library have been unfailingly helpful and tolerant of reserve shelves groaning under the weight of my extra volumes. Graham Haslam enabled me to find my way round the Duchy of Cornwall Record Office. I am especially grateful to Lord Cobham for permitting me to consult the Hagley MSS and for allowing me to use his library under the inspiring gaze of Pope's own busts of the great English poets. My colleagues at Lady Margaret Hall enabled me to take a term's sabbatical leave—enough to absorb myself in the rewriting of earlier drafts, but not enough to complete the book in its entirety. I am even more grateful to them for tolerating their undeniably distracted colleague in the weeks that followed. My greatest debt is to my husband Duncan Anderson whose own immersion in military history and the pragmatic environment of Sandhurst usefully tempered some of my wilder literary ideas. His unflagging support and patience, especially in recent months, deserve a medal.

Contents

List of Illustrations   xii

Abbreviations   xiii

PART I: POLITICIANS, POETS, AND THE PRINCE

1. Patriots and Patriotism   3

2. Whigs in Opposition   19

3. Cultural Patriotism: Frederick and the Arts   46

4. Pope, Politics, and Genre   68

PART II: MYTHOLOGIZING HISTORY

Prologue   99

5. Patriot Gothic   108

6. Political Elizabethanism and the Spenser Revival   150

7. Mythologizing the Monarch: Ideas of a Patriot King   185

8. Jacobites and Patriots: Johnson and Savage   230

Bibliography   248

Index   261

List of Illustrations

(between pp. 114–115)

1. *The Voice of Liberty* (1738). Reproduced by permission of the Trustees of the British Museum.

2. *Admiral Hosier's Ghost* (1740). Reproduced by permission of the Trustees of the British Museum.

3. Van der Gucht's engraved frontispiece to Aaron Hill's *Progress of Wit: A Caveat* (1730). Reproduced by permission of the Bodleian Library.

4. The Gothic Temple at Shotover, Oxon. Reproduced by permission of *Country Life*.

5. James Gibbs, Design for the Temple of Liberty, Stowe, Bucks (1741), front elevation. Ashmolean Museum, Oxford, Gibbs Collection II.100. Reproduced by permission of the Ashmolean Museum.

6. Engraved frontispiece to Jane Brereton's *Merlin: A Poem Humbly Inscrib'd to Her Majesty* (1735). Reproduced by permission of the Bodleian Library.

7. George Vertue's engraved frontispiece to William Oldys's edition of Sir Walter Ralegh's *A History of the World* (1736). Reproduced by permission of the Bodleian Library.

8. *The Treacherous Patriot Unmask'd* (1742). Reproduced by permission of the Trustees of the British Museum.

Abbreviations

(Unless otherwise indicated, place of publication is London.)

BJECS	*British Journal for Eighteenth-Century Studies*
BL	British Library
BMC	Frederick George Stephens, *Catalogue of Prints and Drawings in the British Museum: Division I, Political and Personal Satires*, vol. iii, parts 1 and 2, 2 vols. (1877)
Bolingbroke, *Works*	*The Works of Lord Bolingbroke*, 4 vols. (1844)
Boswell, *Life of Johnson*	James Boswell, *The Life of Samuel Johnson LL.D.*, ed. G. B. Hill, rev. L. F. Powell, 6 vols. (Oxford, 1934–50)
Carlisle MSS	*The Manuscripts of the Earl of Carlisle*, HMC 15th Report, Appendix, part vi (1897)
Coxe, *Walpole*	William Coxe, *Memoirs of the Life and Administration of Sir Robert Walpole, Earl of Orford*, 3 vols. (1798)
ECS	*Eighteenth-Century Studies*
Egmont Diary	*Diary of Viscount Perceval, Afterwards First Earl of Egmont*, HMC, 3 vols. (1920–3)
GM	*Gentleman's Magazine*
Hervey, *Memoirs*	*Some Materials towards the Memoirs of the Reign of King George II, by John Lord Hervey*, ed. Romney Sedgwick, 3 vols. (1931)
HMC	Historical Manuscripts Commission
Johnson, *Lives of the Poets*	Samuel Johnson, *Lives of the English Poets*, ed. G. B. Hill, 3 vols. (Oxford, 1905)
Lyttelton, *Persian Letters*	George, Lord Lyttelton, *Letters from a Persian in England to His Friend at Ispahan* (1735)
Marchmont Papers	*A Selection from the Papers of the Earls of Marchmont*, ed. George Henry Rose, 3 vols. (1831)
N&Q	*Notes and Queries*
OED	*Oxford English Dictionary*
OET *Liberty*	James Thomson, *Liberty, The Castle of Indolence, and Other Poems*, ed. James Sambrook (Oxford, 1986)
OET *Seasons*	James Thomson, *The Seasons*, ed. James Sambrook (Oxford, 1981)

PMLA   *Publications of the Modern Language Association of America*

Pope, *Corr.*   *The Correspondence of Alexander Pope*, ed. George Sherburn, 5 vols. (Oxford, 1956)

PQ   *Philological Quarterly*

RES   *Review of English Studies*

Rundle, *Letters*   *Letters of the late Thomas Rundle, LLD., Lord Bishop of Derry in Ireland, to Mrs. Barbara Sandys,* 2 vols. (Gloucester, 1789)

SP   *Studies in Philology*

Spence, *Anecdotes*   Joseph Spence, *Observations, Anecdotes, and Characters of Books and Men*, ed. James M. Osborn, 2 vols. (Oxford, 1966)

TE   *The Twickenham Edition of the Poems of Alexander Pope*, gen. ed. John Butt, 11 vols. (London and New Haven, Conn., 1939–69)

Thomson, *Letters*   *James Thomson (1700–48): Letters and Documents*, ed. A. D. McKillop (Lawrence, Kan., 1958)

TLS   *Times Literary Supplement*

Walpole Correspondence   *The Yale Edition of Horace Walpole's Correspondence*, ed. W. S. Lewis *et al.*, 48 vols. (London and New Haven, Conn., 1937–83)

Yale Johnson   *The Yale Edition of the Works of Samuel Johnson*, 16 vols. (New Haven, Conn., Oxford, and London, 1958–90)

Part I

Politicians, Poets, and the Prince

Patriots and Patriotism

THIS IS a book about patriotism, politics, and poetry in the age of Robert Walpole. It is especially concerned with the activities and writings of the dissident, or 'Patriot' Whigs, Walpole's most vigorous critics in parliament and the press in the years after 1725. Part of its task is to explore the broader currents of national feeling enshrined in their distinct brand of oppositional poetry and drama: a body of literature which played a vital role in shaping the way in which poets (and, indeed, less elevated mortals) from the 1740s onwards conceived of themselves as uniquely British. It was James Thomson, one such poet, who produced 'Rule, Britannia' for his royal masque, *Alfred*, written for Frederick, Prince of Wales, the Patriots' political figurehead. When *Alfred*'s venerable British Bard, ancient and blind, first stepped across an open-air stage to Arne's swelling tune and spoke those memorable lines one warm night in August 1740, Britain was basking in Admiral Vernon's recent victory at Porto Bello. National pride was at its height, and 'Rule, Britannia', which began life as a potent piece of opposition propaganda, soon became the unofficial national anthem.[1]

But even 'Rule, Britannia'—an apparently straightforward expression of patriotism—proves resistant to analysis. The Walpole era witnessed not one, but a number of complex, interrelated forms of patriotism. If at one level—the party-political—patriotism was, in Hugh Cunningham's words, a 'legitimation of opposition', then government writers fought back in kind.[2] Court Whig pamphlets such as Arnall's *Opposition No Proof of Patriotism* (1735) challenged the opposition's claim to be opposing the government out of principled public-spiritedness by equating opposition with faction, and 'true' patriotism with loyalty to the government. The Court Whigs, especially their poets, created more imaginative forms of patriotism through an iconography which embroidered national myths upon the unpromising fabric of the Hanoverian royal family.

[1] See A. D. McKillop, 'The Early History of *Alfred*', *PQ* 41 (1962), 311–24. Vernon was in the throes of preparing a second fleet after his first victory. *Alfred* was first privately performed at Cliveden but in 1741 (at the Prince's behest) it opened at Drury Lane.

[2] Hugh Cunningham, 'The Language of Patriotism', in R. Samuels (ed.), *Patriotism: The Making and Unmaking of British National Identity*, 3 vols. (1989), i. 57–89, p. 58. See also his 'The Language of Patriotism, 1750–1914', *History Workshop*, 12 (1981), 8–33. The fullest account is Quentin Skinner, 'The Principles and Practice of Opposition: The Case of Bolingbroke versus Walpole', in Neil McKendrick (ed.), *Historical Perspectives: Studies in English Thought and Society in Honour of J. H. Plumb* (1974), 93–128, though his sole focus on Bolingbroke and the neo-Harringtonian tradition now requires readjustment. See also Linda Colley, 'Radical Patriotism in Eighteenth-Century England', in Samuels (ed.), *Patriotism*, i. 169–87; Betty Kemp, 'Patriotism, Pledges and the People', in M. Gilbert (ed.), *A Century of Conflict* (1966).

Since Prince Frederick was part of that family, Court–opposition rivalry over national myths was rife. The opposition credo of patriotism in itself contains tensions and inherent self-contradictions which invite further scrutiny. If the patriotism to which Lord Bolingbroke gave a shape and name in the 1720s became a 'mid-century variant of country ideology',[3] an opposition platform calling for the subordination of Whig–Tory party identity in the 'national good', how did it happen that it was the *Whig* opponents of Robert Walpole who were generally known as 'Patriots'? Is there a subtle difference between 'Patriots' and the doctrine of patriotism? Furthermore, what is a dissident Whig Patriot opposition which uses the language of liberty to attack, among other things, the influence of Crown power on the Commons, doing with a royalist cult of monarchy at its centre, the cult of the Patriot King?

One of the catch-phrases which some historians and many literary critics use to define opposition to Walpole is the 'politics of nostalgia': nostalgia for a simpler, 'traditional' rural England threatened by Walpolian modernity, urban complexity, credit, commerce, and proto-capitalism.[4] Yet, arguably, the 'politics of nostalgia' is a phrase far more applicable to Britain in the late twentieth century than it was to Britain in the 1730s. Like the inhabitants of Walpole's Britain, we too are bombarded with the signs and symbols of Britishness and visions of 'Old England'. The plethora of recent academic studies which make patriotism part of their title (this is yet another) testifies to our urge to pin down our national identity before it is lost in the ambiguous embrace of a larger Europe. In both Walpole's time and our own, images of the past are used to reinforce the sense of what it means to be British. Yet whereas we may find ourselves drawn to a fantasy of rural Victorian or Edwardian England fabricated by the soft-focus camera of a Merchant–Ivory film, Walpole's critics invoked historical myth in a far more energetic way. Their appeal to past periods of British strength or greatness—gritty Saxon solidarity, seafaring Elizabethan enterprise—aimed to inspire active emulation rather than armchair idylls. Pressure for war and for British commercial and colonial expansion made opposition patriotism in the 1730s aggressive and jingoistic. Yet the ideological legacy to which this was married was, in its origins, a far more benevolent creed.

Country-Party Patriotism

'PATRIOTISM has, in all Ages, and among all Nations, been acknowledged a glorious virtue.'[5] So opened Bolingbroke's stirring 1727 appeal in the *Craftsman*,

---

[3] Robert Harris, *A Patriot Press: National Politics and the London Press in the 1740s* (Oxford, 1993), 5, 48.

[4] Isaac Kramnick, *Bolingbroke and His Circle: The Politics of Nostalgia in the Age of Walpole* (Cambridge, Mass., 1968). Kramnick's nostalgic declining country gentry still exert a powerful hold in literary studies.

[5] *Craftsman*, 15 July 1727. Identified as Bolingbroke's in *Lord Bolingbroke: Contributions to the 'Craftsman'*, ed. Simon Varey (Oxford, 1982), 18–22.

the leading opposition journal he established the previous year with the dissident Whig William Pulteney. Although 'patriotism' was almost certainly a new-coined word (first recorded the previous year, 1726),[6] the ideology upon which Bolingbroke drew heavily was not: a civic-humanist tradition of Commonwealth thought and argument which had supplied a platform for Country oppositions to the Court since the 1670s.[7] Patriotism was civic virtue, an ideal of selfless public activity which found its noblest embodiment in the classical republican hero Cato. It was the duty of citizens to place public interest before private self-interest, to sacrifice 'their own particular ease and enjoyment of Pleasure . . . to the more general Concerns of the Publick'.[8] The neo-Harringtonian tradition which perpetuated the Patriot ideal in the seventeenth century harnessed Machiavellian corruption theory to emphasize the fragility of Britain's 'balanced' constitution of king, Lords, and Commons. Corruption, once it had gained entrance, would eventually lead to national ruin if unchecked. Patriotism, or Country doctrine, thus entailed constant vigilance, a suspicion of anything that threatened the independence of the Commons. It translated itself into a parliamentary programme pressing for frequent parliaments, a militia, and a blue-water naval policy which stressed England's defensive and mercantile role as a sea power. It was opposed to expensive continental entanglements, standing armies, and high land taxes. This body of arguments had rallied 'Old Whigs' and Tories in the Harley–Foley Country opposition to William's Whig Junto ministry of the 1690s.[9] It came to embrace a deep suspicion of the consequences of the late seventeenth-century financial revolution: the credit systems established to fund William's costly Nine Years War, the Bank of England, the National Debt, and large City finance houses such as the South Sea Company. This ideological platform subsequently evolved through various transmutations. Harley, heading the Tory administration of Anne's last four years, used it to attack the Marlborough–Godolphin Junto Whigs to bring pressure for peace to its con-

---

[6] The *OED* cites as its earliest source Nathan Bailey's *Universal Etymological Dictionary* (3rd edn. 1726).

[7] For the classic formulations of the civic-humanist tradition, see Caroline Robbins, *The Eighteenth-Century Commonwealthmen* (Cambridge, Mass., 1959), and esp. the work of J. G. A. Pocock: 'Machiavelli, Harrington and English Political Ideologies in the Eighteenth Century', in his *Politics, Language, Time* (1972), 104–47, and *The Machiavellian Moment* (Princeton, NJ, 1975).

[8] *Craftsman*, 15 July 1727.

[9] The Harley–Foley group was an alliance of Tory and Whig back-bench members linked by suspicion of William's Court management and government mishandling of the war. There is much debate over whether this constituted a 'Country party'. See e.g. B. W. Hill, *The Growth of Parliamentary Parties, 1689–1742* (1976), 52–7; David Hayton, 'The "Country" Interest and the Party System, 1689–c.1720', in Clyve Jones (ed.), *Party and Management in Parliament, 1660–1784* (Leicester, 1984), 37–85; D. A. Rubini, 'Party and the Augustan Constitution, 1694–1716: Politics and the Power of the Executive', *Albion*, 10 (1978), 193–208. The Harley–Foley group may have been known as 'Patriots'. See David Ogg, *England in the Reigns of James II and William III* (Oxford, 1955), 129: 'They were "Patriots" . . . before they were Whigs or Tories.' Dryden's emphatic repetition of the word 'Patriot' in his pro-Harley 'To My Honour'd Kinsman, John Driden' (1700) suggests the identification.

clusion in the Treaty of Utrecht of 1713. In the early 1720s the 'Old Whigs'
Thomas Gordon and William Trenchard's famous *Cato's Letters* used similar
arguments to attack the corruptions of the Sunderland–Stanhope Whig ministry after the South Sea Bubble débâcle.[10]

The 'Patriot' platform which the *Craftsman*, and subsequent opposition
journals such as *Common Sense*, promoted thus echoed 'Cato' in both its call
for a burial of party labels and its attacks on ministerial corruption, coupled
with a gloomy prognosis of Britain's imminent decline in a malaise of luxury
and selfishness. Yet oppositional patriotism in the Walpole period was not simply the Country doctrine of previous years refurbished. The 'Country' label
was by now far less descriptive of the demographic basis or outlook of its
adherents. Country-party patriotism had expanded to accommodate new, often
urban elements, with a particular emphasis on trade and commerce and popular extraparliamentary participation in the political process.[11] The neo-
Harringtonian tension between the property-owning 'landed' (therefore
independent) Patriot and the unreliable man of credit and commerce was no
longer relevant—if indeed such a polarity had ever really existed.[12] The active
'Patriot' opposed to Walpole was now less likely to be a rural squire than a
tradesman living in London, Manchester, or Bristol, one who defined his
patriotism through defence of a 'national interest' in which Britain's commercial enterprise and potential colonial expansion played a central role. By the
early 1730s, the two issues which defined his opposition to Walpole most
clearly were hostility to Walpole's projected general Excise tax on wine and
tobacco, and—most important for this study—his support for the campaign for
a war with Spain which would open up new prospects for British merchants in
the expanding Atlantic markets.

Popular Patriotism and the War with Spain

The campaign for war developed out of the increasing tension which the com-
petition for the Atlantic markets generated between Britain and her trade rivals

[10] See J. G. A. Pocock, 'The Varieties of Whiggism from Exclusion to Reform', in his *Virtue,
Commerce, and History* (Cambridge, 1985), esp. 234–41.

[11] For major contributions to this field, see Nicholas Rogers, 'Resistance to Oligarchy: The City
Opposition to Walpole and his Successors', in John Stevenson (ed.), *London in the Age of Reform*
(Oxford, 1977), 1–19; id., *Whigs and Cities: Popular Politics in the Age of Walpole and Pitt* (Oxford,
1989); Kathleen Wilson, 'Empire, Trade and Popular Politics in Mid-Hanoverian Britain: The
Case of Admiral Vernon', *Past and Present*, 121 (1988), 74–109; Gerald Jordan and Nicholas
Rogers, 'Admirals as Heroes: Patriotism and Liberty in Hanoverian England', *Journal of British
Studies*, 28 (1989), 201–44; Linda Colley, 'Eighteenth-Century English Radicalism before Wilkes',
Transactions of the Royal Historical Society, 5th ser. 31 (1981), 1–19.

[12] Pocock, *Virtue, Commerce, and History*, 108–15, opposes the 'Patriot' to the 'man of commerce'. But J. R. Goodale, 'J. G. A. Pocock's Neo-Harringtonians: A Reconsideration', *History of
Political Thought*, 1 (1980), 257–9, argues that Pocock and Kramnick greatly underestimate the
original place of trade and commerce in Commonwealth thought.

France and Spain. Since the seventeenth century, British merchant ships had been conducting a fast-growing illegal trade with Spanish Central America. During the 1720s the Spanish authorities clamped down, using private hired coastguard ships to retaliate, with notorious severity, on British seamen. Stories of depradations, tortures, and 'insults' filtered home alongside the legends of martyred British naval heroes. One was Captain Jenkins, whose severed ear gave the war which finally ensued its lacklustre name. Another was Admiral Hosier, who in 1726 had waited in vain for ministerial permission to strike down a Spanish gold fleet in the West Indies. When Hosier and most of his crew died of yellow fever, the blame was laid at Walpole's door. Spain declared war on Britain in 1727. Walpole, who consistently claimed to support British trade interests best through the maintenance of peace, negotiated the Treaty of Seville in 1729. This ultimately served only to fan rather than quench war fever. During the 1730s, relations between Britain and Spain continued to deteriorate as pressure mounted, culminating in parliamentary petitions signed and presented by merchants from major cities between March 1738 and March 1739. Walpole's attempts during this period to negotiate the Treaty of Pardo broke down when the South Sea Company withdrew support, and in October 1739 he was forced to declare war. The triumphalism which followed Admiral Vernon's celebrated victory at Porto Bello in November proved short-lived. The following months witnessed a series of British reversals, notably the disastrous siege of Cartagena (1741), all of which fuelled the pressure for Walpole's resignation in early 1742.

If the patriotism Bolingbroke derived from the civic republican legacy was originally 'a doctrine of universal libertarian benevolence . . . universalist rather than specific in its reference to the English', it soon lost its more generous internationalist spirit.[13] In 1727 Bolingbroke had claimed that the *Craftsman*'s brand of patriotism was 'actuated by the noble Principles of universal and unconfin'd Benevolence', conducive to 'the Peace and Prosperity of Mankind'.[14] By 1730, Bolingbroke himself had become, if not xenophobic, then certainly nationalistic. His opening letter in the *Craftsman*'s 'Remarks on the History of England' describes 'a revival of the true old English spirit, which prevailed in the days of our forefathers, and which must always be national, since it has no direction but to the national interest'. The Bolingbroke of the 'Remarks' is first and foremost a 'Brit'. 'I feel a secret pride in thinking that I was born a Briton.'[15] The patriotism which pressure for war generated often went with the crudest of slogans and a bigoted bellicosity which put the anti-Argentine 'Gotcha' slogans of the early 1980s to

---

[13] J. C. D. Clark, *The Language of Liberty: Political Discourse and Social Dynamics in the Anglo-American World, 1660–1800* (Cambridge, 1993), 54.

[14] *Craftsman*, 15 July 1727. Here he asserts that the 'more generous the Genius of a People', the more patriotism they display.

[15] 'Remarks on the History of England', Letters 1 and 4 (Bolingbroke, *Works*, i. 295, 316).

shame.[16] 'Britons Strike Home!' was the tabloid-like title of one popular song. Other prints such as 'The Naked Truth' depicted the sturdy Cromwell exposing his arse for France and Spain to kiss.[17]

One of the distinctive features of the opposition patriotism of the 1730s was its injection of overt war fever into the Country party programme. The opposition's blue-water naval policy which now actively promoted agitation for a trade war in the national interest had indeed always been a staple feature of the Country platform. Under both William and Anne, Gordon and Trenchard and subsequently the Tory Swift had voiced the traditional arguments against squandering Britain's resources on continental entanglements when she could be using the same resources to expand her trade and empire by sea.[18] Yet under both William and Anne, Country critics of Whig Juntos had ultimately used Country doctrine to martial a successful peace campaign against a national war effort. Swift's *Conduct of the Allies* (1711), for all its veiled threats to the Spanish empire, was, above all, propaganda for peace.[19] By 1713 nearly a quarter of a century of virtually continuous continental warfare—the Nine Years War (1689–97), then the War of Spanish Succession (1702–13)—had led to general war-weariness, especially among the trading community, as the National Debt and land tax soared. Marlborough's triumphs in 1704 and 1706 at Blenheim and Ramillies may have prompted patriotic victory parades through London, but by 1713 the Treaty of Utrecht which the Tory Pope celebrated in *Windsor-Forest* equated the patriotic with the irenic. It was a Whig poet of that year, Samuel Croxall, who voiced his opposition to the Utrecht Treaty through a patriotic allegory of Spenser's Britomart (symbolizing Britain's warlike spirit) tied up and taunted by Catholic cur-dogs.[20] In 1713 Pope's patriotism expressed itself in a profound messianic vision of 'Peace and Plenty'.[21] This sounds like Horace Walpole's 1788 lament for his father's golden 'era . . of prosperity and peace' which a band of 'wretches'—the Patriots—threw away in 1739 by agitating for an unnecessary war.[22] But by the late 1730s, a significant part of the nation saw Walpole as a symbol not of peace and prosperity but of pusillanimity and corruption. Even Pope turned

[16] The best accounts are Rogers, *Whigs and Cities*; Wilson, 'Empire, Trade and Popular Politics'.

[17] See Herbert Atherton, *Political Prints in the Age of Hogarth: A Study of the Ideographic Representation of Politics* (Oxford, 1974), esp. 167–90.

[18] See David Armitage, 'The British Empire and the Civic Tradition, 1656–1742' (Cambridge Ph.D. thesis, 1991), esp. ch. 5.

[19] Swift, *The Conduct of the Allies* (1711) (*The Prose Works of Jonathan Swift*, ed. Herbert Davis, 16 vols. (Oxford, 1939–74), vi). His praise for some buccaneering Bristol merchants 'inflamed by a true spirit of Courage' who seized an Acapulco galleon 'and are lately returned laden with unenvied Wealth' became an overt strain in war propaganda under Walpole.

[20] See [Samuel Croxall], *An Original Canto of Spencer* (1713) and *Another Original Canto of Spencer* (1714). The *Craftsman* later used the same allegorical figures to criticize Walpole's pacificism. See below, Ch. 6.

[21] Pope, *Windsor-Forest* (1713), l. 42.

[22] *Walpole Correspondence*, xxv. 6.

from a peace poet into a war poet. The reassertion of Britain's pride at sea and abroad lay behind even the most pragmatic financial arguments for war.

Past periods of British greatness supplied a potent stimulus to national hubris. The Patriot opposition's most effective contribution to the prevailing spirit of patriotism lay in its recourse to, and recovery of, British history— whether Saxon, medieval, Elizabethan, or more recent. Part II of this book is devoted to examining specific forms of historical myth-making in which opposition, as well as some ministerial journalists, pamphleteers, and poets engaged. The Roman 'Patriot-heroes' Cato and Brutus never lost their exemplary appeal: they had been Anglicized by Addison, Gordon, and Trenchard and countless others, and strode across the English stage not in togas but in knee-breeches.[23] Yet these legendary classical figures were joined by other heroes long enshrined in British legend and resurrected in response to the demands of the 1730s. The images of the naval heroes Ralegh, Drake, and Blake were superimposed on to the figure of Admiral Edward Vernon to form a composite part of the widespread 'Vernon cult' which seized the public imagination in this period.[24] All this was part of a much broader valorization of the Elizabethan age, a phenomenon not unique to the Walpole era but given extraordinary vigour by the campaign for war.

Opposition pamphleteers pursuing the tradition of trade and empire which Elizabeth was credited with initiating traced its progression to the Commonwealth period, recalling Cromwell's Western Design and the English capture of Jamaica from the Spanish in 1655.[25] Historians were active in recovering and reprinting state papers and documents from both the Elizabethan age and the Protectorate, pressing the past into the service of the present.[26] Thomas Birch and Andrew Millar were responsible for producing new editions of Milton's prose and Harrington's works in 1738, and the young Patriot Mark Akenside modelled his cry for war, *The Voice of Liberty; or a British Philippic* (1738), on Milton's verse. Yet Cromwell himself proved too dangerous a figure to be widely invoked by a patriotic opposition, especially one that centred on a prince. Government critics were all too ready to draw the parallel between the regicides and radical opposition which Samuel

[23] For Cato in popular debate, see esp. Reed Browning, *The Political and Constitutional Ideas of the Court Whigs* (Baton Rouge, La., 1982), 1–20.

[24] The Vernon cult is admirably well documented. See Rogers, *Whigs and Cities*, esp. 235–40, 374–8; Wilson, 'Empire, Trade and Popular Politics'; Jordan and Rogers, 'Admirals as Heroes'.

[25] David Armitage, 'The Cromwellian Protectorate and the Languages of Empire', *Historical Journal*, 35 (1992), 531–55, esp. 553–4. This lists much material from the Protectorate reprinted in the late 1730s.

[26] See Thomas Carte (ed.), *A Collection of the Original Letters and Papers, Concerning the Affairs of England. From the Year 1641 to 1660*, 2 vols. (1739); Thomas Birch (ed.), *A Collection of the State Papers of John Thurloe, Esq.*, 7 vols. (1742); John Nickolls (ed.), *Original Letters and Papers of State, Addressed to Oliver Cromwell, Concerning the Affairs of Great Britain from . . . MDCXLIX to MDCLVIII* (1743); Dr [P.] Forbes (ed.), *A Full View of the Public Transactions in the Reign of Queen Elizabeth; or, A Particular Account of all the Memorable Affairs of that Queen. Transmitted in a Series of Letters and other Papers of State*, 2 vols. (1740–1).

Johnson later made explicit in his attack on the Wilkite radicals of the 1770s, baying for Spanish blood like 'Cromwell's patriotick tribes'.[27] Admiral Blake's memory may have inspired almost as much adulation as Ralegh's, but there was no real Cromwell cult in the 1730s. The Whig Patriot poet Richard Glover praised 'Unconquerable Blake' for 'perfecting at once | What by Eliza was so well begun', but depicted 'perfidious Cromwell' as a mere 'ruffian'.[28]

The Patriot Label

The most vocal parliamentary spokesmen for war and the merchants' cause were the Patriot Whigs: men such as Chesterfield and Carteret, Samuel Sandys, William Pulteney, and especially the 'Boy Patriots' Hugh Polwarth, George Lyttelton, and his cousin William Pitt—the future 'Patriot Minister'.[29] The qualification of 'Patriot' with 'Whig' leads one into deeper waters. Bolingbroke's patriotism was a non-party credo, and the *Craftsman*'s constant refrain unambiguous—'Let the very names of Whig and Tory be for ever buried in oblivion'.[30] Yet (as will be argued in the next chapter) still active party distinctions prevented the amalgamation of Whigs and Tories in opposition: a separateness symptomized by the still divisive application of the term 'Patriot'.

'Patriotism' may have been given political currency in the 1720s, but 'Patriot' had long possessed something of both the positive and the negative political connotations later captured by Johnson's primary and secondary definitions of a Patriot: 'One whose ruling passion is the love of his country' and (subsequently) 'a factious disturber of the government'.[31] The association between the 'Patriot' or 'Modern Patriot' and anti-monarchist, libertarian atti-

---

[27] Johnson, *Thoughts on Falklands Islands* (1771) (*Yale Johnson*, x. 346–86).

[28] Richard Glover, *London; Or, The Progress of Commerce* (1739), ll. 378–405. Armitage, 'Cromwellian Protectorate', 553 n. 88, lists Cromwellian works which augment the 'Whig canon' at the turn of the 1730s. But Cromwell's example could easily be turned against the opposition: e.g. *Popular Prejudices Against the Convention and Treaty with Spain* (1739); and in *GM* 5 (1735), 194–5, an essay parodying the *Old Whig*'s 'Alarm to Rebellion': 'Here's your Oliver! . . . Here's your Leader to Liberty!' Blake appears frequently in opposition works, e.g. Thomson's *Britannia* (1729), but there are no images of Cromwell in any opposition Patriot pantheons such as Stowe's Temple of British Worthies, which houses Milton and Hampden among its Patriot-heroes. The republication in *GM* 1740 of a modernized version of an obscure 1660 pamphlet, *Monarchy Asserted To be the best most Ancient and Legall form of Government, in a conference . . . with Oliver late Lord Protector*, may have been a contribution to the debate.

[29] For their role, see Wilson, 'Empire, Trade and Popular Politics', 106–7. Lyttelton's *Considerations upon the Present State of Affairs, at Home and Abroad* (1739) was one of the most influential pamphlets of that year.

[30] *Craftsman*, 24 Apr. 1727.

[31] The ironic definition was added in 1773 to Johnson's straightforward description of 1755. Cunningham, 'The Language of Patriotism', in Samuels (ed.), *Patriotism*, i. 61, claims that the second was a direct response to the growing 'radicalisation' of patriotism. But Johnson had used the term ironically for opposition Whigs in the Walpole period. See below, Ch. 8.

tudes and anticlerical zeal dates back to at least the 1640s.[32] Dryden harnessed it for his attack on the Shaftesbury Whigs in *Absalom and Achitophel* (1691), where a 'Modern' Patriot is 'one that would by Law supplant his Prince'. Shaftesbury (Achitophel) has 'usurped a Patriott's All-attoning name' to 'cancel private Crimes' with 'publick Zeal'. Yet in 1700, after Dryden's hostility to William and the Junto Whigs led him into sympathy with the aims of Harley's Country opposition, he described his ideal Patriot in very different terms: 'A Patriot, both the King and Country serves; | Prerogative, and Privilege preserves.'[33] A 'Patriot' was not invariably a Whig of radical or republican tendencies; he could also (as Dryden shows us) be a moderate back-bench Country party supporter like his 'honoured kinsman' John Driden. But the prototype of the demotic Wilkite 'Patriot' caricatured in Johnson's 1774 pamphlet attack of that title, those orators for lawless liberty who 'rant and rail', could be traced back through the eighteenth to the seventeenth century.[34]

The Whiggish provenance of the Patriot title seems significant. As B. W. Hill observes of the Walpole period, 'if the patriot philosophy was the polemical contribution of Bolingbroke, the soubriquet of Patriots settled down largely to denote Whig dissidents'.[35] The recent disagreement over the extent to which patriotism as a doctrine united opposition Whigs and Tories in a Country opposition to the Court throws the Patriot label itself under renewed scrutiny.[36] Reed Browning argues that 'this united Opposition usually called itself "Patriotic" and its members "Patriots". And this adoption of a single self-designation for all wings of the opposition was not misdirected. The same basic political ideals were credible to all.'[37] The willingness of the Tories to identify themselves as 'Patriots' might prove the acid test: and yet the evidence for it in

---

[32] In 1644 the High-Church John Maxwell, one of Charles I's Laudian bishops, stigmatized the 'specious and spurious pretences of our glorious Reformers, and zealous Patriots today'. See *OED* under 'Patriot'.

[33] *Absalom and Achitophel*, ll. 965–6, 179–81 (*The Poems of John Dryden*, ed. James C. Kinsley, 4 vols. (Oxford, 1958), i. 241, 221); 'To My Honour'd Kinsman, John Driden, of Chesterton', ll. 171–2 (*Poems*, iv. 1534). Mercury in Dryden's *Amphityron* (1690) identifies Patriots as 'Grumbletonians', 'meer Country Gentlemen' still 'rayling at the Government' (i. i. 138–43)—a parody of the government view. Dryden's conception of the Patriot changed after 1688. See J. A. Levine, 'John Dryden's *Epistle to John Driden*', in Bruce King (ed.), *Dryden's Mind and Art* (Edinburgh, 1969), 114–42.

[34] *Yale Johnson*, x. 391.

[35] Hill, *The Growth of Parliamentary Parties*, 196.

[36] See esp. Harris, *A Patriot Press*, ch. 2. Few historians seem to discriminate between the older term 'Patriot' and the far more recent derivation, 'patriotism'—a distinction that might profitably be pursued. Revisionist historians who stress the survival of Whig–Tory differences in the opposition tend to use 'Patriot' or 'Whig-Patriot' to describe opposition Whigs. See Linda Colley, *In Defiance of Oligarchy: The Tory Party 1714–60* (Cambridge, 1982); Hill, *The Growth of Parliamentary Parties*, esp. ch. 11, 'Walpole Whigs, Tories and Patriots 1724–34'; J. C. D. Clark, 'The Politics of the Excluded: Tories, Jacobites and Whig Patriots, 1715–1760', *Parliamentary History*, 2 (1983), 209–22. The distinction was one made by Walpole in 1741 defining the opposition as 'Tories, Jacobites and Patriots'. See Colley, *In Defiance of Oligarchy*, 45.

[37] Browning, *Court Whigs*, 22.

this period is not compelling.[38] Bolingbroke was the first to call himself a Patriot, but by this stage his political career had gone through so many transmutations that most Tories would have hesitated to identify him as a Tory. Many Tories remained suspicious of Whig dissidents, and were almost as ready as the Court Whigs to stigmatize them ironically as 'Patriots'—that is, mock-patriots or proclaimers of libertarian principles for selfish reasons. When the Tory Edmund Lechmere refused to support the opposition City Whig Sir John Barnard's bill to reduce the interest on the National Debt in 1737 he wrote: 'I am in hopes now t'will not succeed, which will be a prodigious baulk to the worthy Patriots.' In 1736 the Tory Edward Harley shrank from the anticlerical implications of the opposition Whig-sponsored Mortmain Bill, one which would damage the basis for Anglican corporate charity. He condemned 'the Warmth & Bitterness of their Speeches to the poor clergy, & to the Clergy in General. None more forward in these Invectives than Mr. Sandys & the Patriots (as they are termed).'[39] The only Tories in the Walpole period who earn from the Tory Alexander Pope the tribute of 'Patriot sighs' are William Wyndham and his son-in-law Henry Hyde, Viscount Cornbury, both working in close alliance with the Patriot Whigs. Pope was capable of using the Patriot epithet both approvingly and (as suspicion set in) ironically, especially for William Pulteney and his partner John, Lord Carteret. By 1740, for Pope a 'Patriot' was, primarily, a frustrated Whig politician.[40] After Walpole's fall in 1742 Pulteney and most of the Patriot Whigs dropped their patriotic masks in their scramble for power. The Whig betrayal of patriotism (the identification between Whigs and Patriots became thoroughly discredited) meant that the Tories were now far readier to refurbish themselves with the language of patriotism and the name of Patriot.[41] But in the Walpole era the angry Patriots were nearly always angry opposition Whigs.

Royal Patriotism

But if 'Patriots' were usually opposition Whigs, it does not mean that they were necessarily radicals. Walpole's journalists discredited and divided the

---

[38] Archibald Foord, *His Majesty's Opposition 1714–1830* (1964), 154, argues that '"patriots" never included the Tories, who persistently rejected identification with the dissident Whigs'. Browning, *Court Whigs*, 22, cites Bolingbroke (a very unrepresentative Tory) and 'various Tory pamphleteers' (unnamed).

[39] Cited in Colley, *In Defiance of Oligarchy*, 347, 109. Lechmere successfully opposed the Patriot Whig Lyttelton in the Worcestershire County contest in 1741.

[40] 'Verses on His Grotto' (Pope, *Corr.* iv. 262). Pope later substituted the less politicized 'British Sighs'. For Pope's usage, see *TE* vi. 882–3; *Ep. Satires*, i. 24 n. (*TE* iv. 299); *1740* l. 4 (*TE* iv. 332); Pope, *Corr.* iv. 250.

[41] This point is convincingly made in Harris, *A Patriot Press*, who argues that, after Walpole's fall and William Pulteney's 'betrayal' of patriotism, Tory writers took over and identified with Patriot principles. But for a different view, see M. Peters, '"Names and Cant": Party Labels in English Political Propaganda *c.*1753–1763', *Parliamentary History*, 7 (1984), 103–27.

Craftsman's claims to Country unity by identifying its disparate authors by their style. If 'every *Period* ring with *Liberty*; if every *Prince* be represented as a *Claudius* or a Nero, it is only the *Ravings* of a *Discontented Whig*'.[42] Yet 'discontented Whigs' were less prone to seek satisfaction in a republican than in a royalist solution—national salvation through a Patriot King. J. C. D. Clark has argued that Bolingbroke's patriotism, derived from the civic republican tradition, was not in itself conducive to a collective sense of national identity: 'no alternative matrix of group identity arose before 1776 to challenge the monarchical one. This was true even of a system of ideas which appears on the surface to be an obvious candidate for that role . . . "patriotism".'[43] The evaporation of oppositional patriotism at times of external threat was apparent to both its advocates and its critics: on the eve of the Seven Years War 'the almost universal language is, opposition must be wrong, when we are ready to be eat up by the French'. There was 'not a mob in England now capable of being the dupe of patriotism'.[44] In both 1715 and 1745, journals which carried the 'Patriot' title always defined patriotism in explicitly dynastic terms—loyalty to the House of Hanover.[45] Jacobites such as the poet Richard Savage defined their 'Patriots' differently: supporters of the exiled Stuarts. 'See how the Patriots of Land become | Martyrs, if here, or Exiles from their Home.'[46] The Patriot platform which the *Craftsman* promoted in the 1720s and 1730s did not, of course, acknowledge this deeply divisive language of patriotism. But the opposition campaign, harnessing anti-Catholic aggression against Spanish insults and French imperial ambitions, took a defiantly Protestant, pro-Hanoverian form, especially in the extraparliamentary community. It was for this reason that Vernon, redoubtable critic of Walpolian corruption, proved a more powerful public symbol of Patriot virtue than the Jacobite-tainted Bolingbroke. Vernon's speeches proclaimed: 'We have for years past betrayed our king by strengthening France to put on us the son of a whore; while our fleets lay idle.'[47] Poems celebrating his victories at Porto Bello were dedicated

---

[42] *The Crafts of the Craftsman: Or the Detection of the Designs of the Coalition* (1735), 6. The 'coalition' is the opposition to Walpole.

[43] Clark, *The Language of Liberty*, 54. He (inevitably) dismisses the civic-humanist Commonwealth notion of patriotism as 'never more than a minor tradition in English public discourse'.

[44] Thomas Potter writing to William Pitt; Horace Walpole. Both cited in Marie Peters, *Pitt and Popularity: The Patriot Minister and London Opinion during the Seven Years War* (Oxford, 1980), 45.

[45] See e.g. *Patriot* [ed. John Harris], 22 and 29 Mar. 1714, calling for a 'burial of the Appellations of Whig and Tory' and such 'insignificant disputes' for 'the Honour of Her Majesty, the safety of her People, and the Succession in the House of Hanover'; and Henry Fielding's *True Patriot*, the anti-Jacobite organ he edited between Nov. 1745 and July 1746.

[46] Savage, 'Britannia's Miseries' (*Poetical Works*, ed. Clarence Tracy (Cambridge, 1962), 22). Country-party patriotism was highly flexible. 'Commonwealth' arguments were used by Charles Edward Stuart drumming up support for the '45. See Eveline Cruickshanks, *Political Untouchables: The Tories and the '45* (1979); W. A. Speck, *The Butcher: The Duke of Cumberland and the Suppression of the '45* (Oxford, 1981), 23–4.

[47] *Egmont Diary*, ii. 17.

to 'Glory, Liberty and VERNON's Name . . . | [The day] which gave t'Immortalize a Brunswick's Reign'.[48]

Yet the reigning Brunswicks, George II and Caroline, were not personally popular. By the 1730s most people's Hanoverianism may have depended more on sense than sentiment. It was for this reason that their alienated son Frederick, Prince of Wales, who went into open opposition to the ministry in 1737, could be proferred as a Patriot King. If the Patriot programme inherited from the Commonwealth Country tradition remained inherently suspicious of the abuse of Crown power, it was not immune to idealizing a monarch.[49] The most Whiggish of opposition supporters were the keenest promoters of the cult of Patriot kingship. Patriot kingship was an eschatology of opposition which prophesied an end to all opposition. It looked forward to an era of government above party, a renovated national monarchy 'when patriotism fills the throne and faction is banished from the administration'.[50] A renovated or 'restored' monarchy had, of course, other connotations. Political expedience may have prompted Bolingbroke to leave the hero at the centre of his 1738 tract *The Idea of a Patriot King* without a name or a family in order to fit both Princes of Wales, the Stuart and the Hanoverian one. Yet most declarations of Patriot kingship—literary and propagandistic—were conducted within a Hanoverian framework, and not just by secret Jacobites trying to conceal their subversion behind a cloak of legitimacy. The Patriot opposition's capture of the heir to the throne was, in a very obvious sense, a 'legitimation of opposition'. The patriotism described in this study is primarily an oppositional variant of Hanoverian loyalism. Like the agitation for war, the Patriot campaign harnessed and exploited underlying sentiments which the current regime did not foster: British self-assertion in the international sphere, and a latent sense of royalism.

Certain aspects of the Patriot campaign of the 1730s foreshadow the blend of the mercantile, popular, and royal that Linda Colley has explored in the reign of George III.[51] 'Poor Fred' was the 'people's prince': and (despite a subsequent bad press) a more obvious focus for Hanoverian sentiment than either of his parents. His son George III became something which his grandfather had not been and which Frederick might have become had he not died in 1751—a 'Patriot King' in the national, British, rather than political sense of

---

[48] Cited Wilson, 'Empire, Trade and Popular Politics', 82.

[49] Betty Kemp points out that 'the phrase "patriot king" has often been regarded as a contradiction in terms. The patriot programme meant, in practice, place bills, short parliaments, free elections, the destruction of the king's influence over Parliament' ('Frederick Prince of Wales', in A. Natan (ed.), *The Silver Renaissance* (1961), 38–56). This view requires readjustment in light of recent work on Whigs, kingship, and patriotism. See below, Ch. 7.

[50] *Of the State of Parties at the Accession of King George the First* (1739) (Bolingbroke, *Works*, ii. 438).

[51] Linda Colley, 'The Apotheosis of George III: Loyalty, Royalty and the British Nation, 1760–1820', *Past and Present*, 102 (1984), 94–129, and *Britons: Forging the Nation, 1707–1837* (New Haven, Conn., 1992).

the term. During his period in opposition Frederick displayed a keen sense of the merchant and trading communities' role and significance.[52] While George II had by 1734 managed to offend representatives of the City of London, 'the obvious arena for royal display',[53] by refusing the Mayor and Aldermen permission to kiss his hand, Frederick showed a singular talent for publicity.[54] So closely did he court the mercantile and trade sectors of London and Bristol, hosting banquets for dignitaries and being hosted in turn at civic festivals, that he was the first Prince of Wales to be granted the Freedom of either city. 'The city was exceedingly pleased and said to one another they now have a Prince of their own.'[55] The City of London Saddler's Company made him their Perpetual Master and altered their audit days to commemorate the respective birthdays of Frederick and his popular wife Augusta.[56] Unlike Walpole, who made the mistake of referring to the tradesmen petitioning outside Westminster during the Excise Crisis as 'a parcel of sturdy beggars', Frederick pronounced to the Aldermen and Mayor of London that 'he knew their importance in this kingdom and the value of their friendship and should never look upon them as beggars'.[57] As late as 1748 Frederick's court at Leicester House maintained a strictly protectionist British trade attitude, banning entry to anyone wearing 'French stuffs' or foreign manufactures.[58]

Two poetic prophecies written by Frederick's supporters in the late 1730s capture the essential flavour of at least one of the varieties of patriotism in the Walpole period. Thomson and Mallet's *Alfred* gave 'Rule, Britannia' its first airing. Yet the Hermit's closing vision of Britain's future imperial greatness is even more unabashedly triumphalist.

> I see thy Commerce, *Britain*, grasp the world:
> All nations serve thee: every foreign flood
> Subjected, pays its tribute to the *Thames*.
> Thither the golden south obedient pours
> His sunny treasures; thither the soft East
> Her spices, delicacies, gentle gifts;
> And thither his rough trade the stormy North.
> See, where beyond the vast *Atlantic* surge,
> By boldest keels untouch'd, a dreadful space!

[52] Frederick's role in City politics has not yet been fully explored. Rogers, *Whigs and Cities*, 373, notes the City's celebration of Frederick's birthday in 1741 but not the 1730s.

[53] Colley, 'The Apotheosis of George III', 96.

[54] *Egmont Diary*, ii. 67; Hervey, *Memoirs*, i. 281.

[55] *Egmont Diary*, ii. 321–2. For the Bristol celebrations, see *GM* 8 (1738), 602–4.

[56] J. W. Sherwell, *The History of the Guild of Saddlers* (1937), 93–6.

[57] *Egmont Diary*, ii. 836–7. Wilson, 'Empire, Trade and Popular Politics', 101, cites Pulteney's view of Walpole's error. Frederick made his speech after he had been turned out of St James's in 1737.

[58] For Frederick's 'Buy British' edict, see *Remembrancer*, 26 Nov. 1748. The *Remembrancer* was edited by James Ralph, Frederick's publicist and propagandist for the Leicester House opposition in the 1747–51 period.

Shores, yet unfound, arise! in youthful prime,
With towering forests, mighty rivers crown'd!
These stoop to *Britain's* thunder. This new world
Shook to its centre, trembles at her name:
And there, her sons, with aim exalted, sow
The seed of rising empire, arts and arms.

Britons, proceed, the subject Deep command,
Awe with your navies every hostile land.
In vain their threats, their armies all in vain;
They rule the balanc'd world, who rule the main.[59]

The previous year, Richard Powney had also envisioned the reign of the future
King Frederick:

When Time shall Fame to *British* Annals bring,
When all the Prince shall brighten in the King;
He shall o'er subject Seas extend his Reign,
And claim in Storms the Empire of the Main;
His Fleets command, where e'er the Ocean roars,
And Nations tremble from a thousand Shores.
So, when the rocking Battlements above
Denounce in Thunder the high Will of *Jove*,
And pointed Lightenings sudden Vengeance pour,
The Sons of Earth fall prostrate and adore.[60]

Patriot Poetry

This brief sample of Patriot poetry should give pause for thought to readers
accustomed to a different kind of opposition verse—the Poetry of
Conservatism, the country-house tradition of Swift or Pope. This tradition
represents neither the widely divergent forms of opposition verse nor the
equally diverse social outlook of its authors.[61] Several recent studies have
acknowledged the complex relationship of 'politics to literature, 1722–1742', to
use the subtitle of the most wide-ranging of these, B. A. Goldgar's *Walpole*

---

[59] James Thomson and David Mallet, *Alfred: A Masque* (1740), III. v (p. 43).

[60] [Richard Powney], *The Stag Chace in Windsor Forest* (1739), 16.

[61] The tradition is described in Maynard Mack, *The Garden and the City: Retirement and Politics in the later Poetry of Pope, 1731–1743* (Toronto, 1969); Howard Erskine-Hill, *The Social Milieu of Alexander Pope: Lives, Examples and the Poetic Response* (New Haven, Conn. and London, 1975); Isabel Rivers, *The Poetry of Conservatism* (Cambridge, 1973). Kramnick, *Bolingbroke and His Circle*, extended this literary tradition to supply a socio-economic explanation for all 'Country' opposition to Walpolian Whiggery. The view prevails in many works, e.g. W. A. Speck, *Society and Literature in England 1700–1760* (Dublin, 1983); J. A. Downie, '1688: Pope and the Rhetoric of Jacobitism', in David Fairer (ed.), *Pope: New Contexts* (Hemel Hempstead, 1990), 9–24; B. W. Last, *Politics and Letters in the Age of Walpole* (1987).

and the Wits.[62] Yet the myth of a monolithic rural back-bench opposition to Walpole's urban 'money men' and the forces of modernity still lingers on in the purlieus of literature, if not of history. Undergraduates are still comfortable with the undemanding equation of conservatism, Toryism, and opposition to Walpolian Whiggery, recently leavened with a pinch of Jacobitism.

Two of the Patriot poets featured in this study, Richard Glover and George Lillo, were (literally and figuratively) streets away from Kramnick's nostalgic gentry-orientated 'Bolingbroke and his Circle', a 'circle' which no longer existed in any recognizable form by the 1730s.[63] Lillo was a Dissenting London Whig jeweller-cum-dramatist of Dutch descent, Richard Glover a prosperous City merchant from a family of Hamburg merchants.[64] Their opposition to Walpole was expressed not in laments for the old order but in the hindering of the new. Glover, a well-known figure in city politics, was at the forefront of the merchants' campaign, as well as an intimate of Prince Frederick.[65] His most enduring Patriot poem was not the pseudo-classical epic *Leonidas* (1737) but the sentimental seafaring ballad *Admiral Hosier's Ghost* (1740), a timely reminder of Walpole's former pusillanimity. James Thomson, the Low-Church pro-Union Scottish Whig at the centre of this book, epitomizes many aspects of the Patriot campaign. His continued poetic refashioning of an ever-evolving figure of Britannia, in 1729 distraught and weeping, in 1735 hopeful yet uncertain, in 1740 triumphantly ruling the azure main, is perhaps the clearest expression we have of the way in which poetry can mirror national sentiment.[66] Thomson's disappointing experiences during the Grand Tour may have ingrained within him a 'rough English love for liberty' unquestioningly confident of British superiority.[67] Yet his more sensitive

---

[62] Bertrand A. Goldgar, *Walpole and the Wits: The Relation of Politics to Literature, 1722–1742* (Lincoln, Nebr., 1976), 219, argues that Bolingbroke's 'Country ideology' fails to acknowledge the difference between Swift and Thomson, or Glover and Pope. Recent work on Jacobitism suggests more diverse ideological motivations. See also Thomas R. Cleary, *Henry Fielding: Political Writer* (Waterloo, Ont., 1984); J. A. Downie, 'Walpole, "The Poet's Foe"', in Jeremy Black (ed.), *Britain in the Age of Walpole* (1984), 171–88, for some ministerial writers.

[63] John Gay died in 1732; his *Beggar's Opera* (1728) and *Polly* (1729) were his only substantial contributions to the literary assault on Walpole. Swift's *Gulliver's Travels* (1726) was his last real contribution to opposition polemic. By the 1730s Swift was concerned less with attacking Walpole than in brooding on Ireland and the last years of Anne's reign. After 1735 Bolingbroke departed to France and made only sporadic visits to England (other than in 1738–9). Kramnick includes Lyttelton among the gathering of the nostalgic élite presumably on the grounds of his aristocratic birth, and makes no mention of his speeches and pamphlets on the London merchants' behalf.

[64] For a forthcoming study of Lillo in a political context, see Kathleen Wilson, 'Empire of Virtue: The Imperial Project and Hanoverian Culture, c. 1720–1785', in Lawrence Stone (ed.), *The British State and Empire in War and Peace*.

[65] See Peters, *Pitt and Popularity*, *passim*; Rogers, *Whigs and Cities*, 62, 67, for Glover's role in this period. See also Glover's *Memoirs of a Celebrated Literary and Political Character from the Resignation of Sir Robert Walpole, in 1742* . . . (1873).

[66] Cf. 'Rule, Britannia' (1740), and *Britannia* (1729) (OET *Liberty*, 21–30); *Liberty* (1735–6), iv. 464–516 (OET *Liberty*, 103–5).

[67] Rundle, *Letters*, ii. 164–5. The phrase was applied to Thomson's ward Charles Talbot, but the sentiment was certainly shared by his tutor.

response to the meditative and even mystical penumbra of the British past—
the Gothic, the Spenserian, the bardic and Druidic—emerges even in his
overtly political verse. That the Patriot poetry of the Walpole years provided
an enduring legacy for a subsequent generation of poets such as Thomas Gray
and William Collins says much about the transmutations of patriotism in the
mid-eighteenth century. Linda Colley has recently suggested that 'the patriotism of the past requires flexible, sensitive and above all, imaginative reconstruction'.[68] This is the aim of this book.

[68] Colley, *Britons*, 372.

2

Whigs in Opposition

EIGHTEENTH-CENTURY patriotism once seemed a relatively straightforward phenomenon. Recent cultural and historical research has rendered it more interesting and (inevitably) infinitely more complicated. The same may be said of the transformations which revisionist historians of the last two decades have made to the landscape of early Hanoverian party politics. The two fields of scholarship are not distinct: one of the areas where they intersect, as the last chapter has shown, is the debate over how far the ideology of patriotism and the Patriot label can be equated with a united Country opposition to the Court. Since at least one of the definitions of a Patriot in the Walpole period was an out-of-office *Whig*, the simple identification of 'Patriot' with 'Country party' or 'opposition to Walpole' may not be adequate. In both Parliament and the press, Walpole faced a heterogeneous body of political adversaries, a 'hybrid' opposition. The Tories, consigned to near-permanent opposition after the Hanoverian accession in 1714 and the onset of single-party Whig government, formed the largest and most consistent opposition element in the Commons. They were joined by a number of 'independents' (though their number is debatable) and by a series of dissident Whigs who switched from supporting to opposing the Whig administration. Between 1717 and 1720 Walpole himself had followed his colleague Townshend into opposition to the Stanhope–Sunderland administration as a calculated political gambit. He exploited the grievances of the disaffected Prince George, who (in a pattern which his own son Frederick adopted in 1737) set up a rival 'alternative' court. The Prince proved a useful bargaining counter, enabling Walpole to help engineer a reconciliation between father and son in 1720, thereby returning himself and Townshend to office.

The dissident Whig element became a consistent feature of opposition politics only after Walpole achieved a virtual monopoly on power in the early 1720s. Walpole's political acumen and a series of fortuitous events (the deaths of Sunderland and Stanhope, the opportunities offered by the South Sea Bubble crash and the Atterbury Jacobite scare) enabled him to forge a prime-ministerial role from his combined offices of Chancellor of the Exchequer, Leader of the Commons, and king's adviser. The Whig 'haemorrhage' began in 1725 when Walpole's former ally William Pulteney (furious at being passed over as Secretary of State) resigned office and joined the former High-Tory Bolingbroke to harangue Walpole from the *Craftsman*. Pulteney at first took few Whig dissidents with him but after 1730 their numbers steadily

increased.[1] Contentious issues such as ministerial foreign policy, the abandonment of Dunkirk to the French, the retention of the Hessian troops, and especially the Excise Crisis and its repercussions, precipitated others into
opposition. In June 1733 Walpole purged the Lords of seven factious Whig
peers (Stair, Cobham, Clinton, Bolton, Montrose, Marchmont, and
Chesterfield) who pressed for an enquiry into the uses made of the forfeited
estates of South Sea Company directors. They took with them into opposition
a considerable group of supporters, notably the 'Boy Patriots' fostered by
Cobham, and Marchmont's young Scottish followers. Prince Frederick went
into open opposition in 1737, taking with him most of the MPs attached to
him through his Duchy of Cornwall and Leicester House patronage.[2] In 1740
the Duke of Argyll and a large group of Scottish Whigs moved into opposition. Although the Tories always constituted the majority of the opposition in
the Commons, by the eve of Walpole's fall in January 1742, 276 ministerial
Whigs faced a combined opposition of 135 Tories and 124 opposition Whigs.

Court and Country vs. Whig and Tory

But just how 'combined' had this opposition really proved to be? How
effectively did the *Craftsman* unite behind its rallying-cry of patriotism both
Tories and dissident, or Patriot, Whigs? Since this book is concerned primarily
with the latter group, it is based on the premiss that they were in some senses
distinct from both Court Whigs and their Tory counterparts in opposition.
Many historians have claimed (and still claim) that after 1720 the old party
labels of Whig and Tory were largely irrelevant, subsumed into the fundamental conflicts between the Country opposition and the Court.[3] Revisionist historiography has, however, persuasively argued that Whig and Tory identities
remained strong until at least the 1750s. A united 'Country' opposition was an
illusion based on *Craftsman*-style rhetoric and the highly partial evidence of
opposition-printed division-lists for a selective number of debates in which
dissident Whigs and Tories voted in concert. The relationship between Tories
and opposition Whigs was at best a marriage of convenience marked on both

[1] For the 'Second Whig Opposition', see Romney Sedgwick (ed.), *The History of Parliament:
The House of Commons 1715–1754*, 2 vols. (1970), i. 19–61.
[2] A. N. Newman, 'The Political Patronage of Frederick Lewis, Prince of Wales', *Historical
Journal*, 1 (1958), 68–75.
[3] Two major proponents of this view are H. T. Dickinson and W. A. Speck. See esp.
Dickinson, *Liberty and Property: Political Ideology in Eighteenth-Century Britain* (1977); Speck,
Stability and Strife: England 1714–1769 (1977); and his *The Butcher: The Duke of Cumberland and
the Suppression of the '45* (Oxford, 1981). The case is reiterated and defended in John Cannon
(ed.), *The Whig Ascendancy: Colloquies on Hanoverian England* (1981), esp. Speck, 'Whigs and
Tories Dim their Glories: English Political Parties under the First Two Georges', 67–71, discussion 71–6.

sides by suspicion and mistrust.[4] Most revisionist historians have been predominantly historians of the Tory party, more concerned with establishing the survival of Tory party identity through the long years of political proscription than in paying close attention to the identity of their uneasy political bedfellows, the dissident Whigs. Linda Colley writes of the fragmented opposition that it was 'the survival of distinctly Tory attitudes [that] prevented the party's amalgamation with dissident Whiggery'. Yet some dissident Whigs may themselves have had certain principled reasons for not amalgamating with Tories in the Commons, as was sometimes the case. Colley hints that 'the motives of the leading Patriots were more complex than ministerial pamphleteers, with their endless jibes at frustration, allow'.[5] But any history which views Patriot Whigs from the reconstructed Tory perspective is likely, however unconsciously, to reflect Tory prejudices against careerist out-of-office Whigs whose professed patriotism was a cover to court Tory votes, eject Walpole, and replace him with themselves.

As yet we await a full study of the Whigs in opposition, their principles and practice.[6] Such a study might prove fragmentary and unrewarding. The documentation for William Pulteney, the leading Patriot Whig in the Commons, is very thin: brilliant speeches but few letters or personal papers.[7] The relatively small band of Patriot Whigs with whom this study is primarily concerned—those closely associated with the Cobham circle—offers more to work from, and certainly far more for the literary historian.[8] But the problems are far more intransigent. As W. A. Speck observes, any argument that Whigs and Tories in opposition retained their separateness as *parties* 'raises problems of definition which, in the case of the dissident Whigs, above all, appear to be insuperable'.[9] Proscription gave the excluded Tories a strong sense of party identity, one which Colley shows remained extremely strong both in Westminster and in the provinces. The Jacobite element which some historians (controversially) have seen as vital to Tory identity provides another kind of

---

[4] See esp. J. C. D. Clark, *The Dynamics of Change: The Crisis of the 1750s and the English Party System* (Cambridge, 1982); id., 'A General Theory of Party, Opposition and Government, 1688–1832', *Historical Journal*, 23 (1980), 295–325; Linda Colley, *In Defiance of Oligarchy: The Tory Party 1714–60* (Cambridge, 1982); Eveline Cruickshanks, *Political Untouchables: The Tories and the '45* (1979); B. W. Hill, *The Growth of Parliamentary Parties, 1689–1742* (1976). An excellent recent summary of the debate which sides with the revisionist view can be found in Geoffrey Holmes and Daniel Szechi, *The Age of Oligarchy: Pre-Industrial Britain 1722–1783* (1993).

[5] Colley, *In Defiance of Oligarchy*, 101, 212.

[6] The effective 'exclusion' of the Patriot Whigs from J. C. D. Clark's 'The Politics of the Excluded: Tories, Jacobites and Whig Patriots, 1715–1760', *Parliamentary History*, 2 (1983), 209–22, seems telling. Most accounts are conducted from a neo-Harringtonian Country-party perspective. The best account of individuals is supplied by Colley, *In Defiance of Oligarchy*.

[7] There is no collected edition of the correspondence of Pulteney, his later ally Carteret, or any of their followers. Pulteney's letters are scattered throughout other volumes. See Archibald Foord, *His Majesty's Opposition, 1714–1830* (1964), 143 n. 3. There are few records for other prominent opposition Whigs such as Samuel Sandys, Walter Plumer, and Sir John Rushout.

[8] See *Marchmont Papers*, esp. vol. ii.   [9] Speck, 'Whigs and Tories Dim their Glories', 76.

'touchstone' which separates the Tory party from Patriot Whigs. But Patriot Whigs, like their Court Whig counterparts, were almost entirely Hanoverian to a man, loyal adherents of the Protestant Succession. Like them, they would probably also have broadly declared their Whiggery in terms of a commitment to 'Revolution principles' centring on a mixed monarchy of king, Lords, and Commons and the supremacy of Parliament.

The Whigs who went into opposition were nothing like a political party. They were individuals or alliances of individuals motivated by a variety of factors: some by the frustrated ambition which had led Walpole himself into opposition, others (undoubtedly) by principles and convictions. On certain occasions these principles led them to vote alongside the Tories on a range of traditional 'Country' issues such as taxation, standing armies, and Hessian troops; on others to vote alongside the administration against the Tories, and on a few occasions to vote against an unusual concurrence of Tory and administration. Many Patriot Whigs placed their allegiance to the Whig party above any schemes for a shared Whig–Tory Patriot administration, some more frankly than others. Pulteney may have strenuously promoted the Country party ideal in both his Commons speeches and the *Craftsman*, yet many other Patriots suspected he never intended to convert his principles into practice. His part in engineering the narrow Old Corps-style Whig administration which replaced Walpole came as no surprise. Sturdy Patriot Whig elders such as Joseph Jekyll and Walter Plumer carried with them into the 1730s a sense of party loyalty forged in the Whig–Tory conflicts of Anne's reign and the precarious security of the Hanoverian succession threatened by a Tory-supported Jacobite invasion. They may have attacked Walpole for betraying his Whig legacy but refused to ally closely with the Tories in opposition. Jekyll opined that 'A Country Party will not do'. The independent Whig Robert Vyner denounced the Country programme as 'cant'.[10] The anticlerical opposition Whig journal the *Old Whig* was as rude about the unprincipled former Tory Jacobite Bolingbroke's efforts to inveigle 'true' Whigs into a coalition as it was about the Walpole administration. Yet other opposition Whigs felt differently. The younger Patriots or 'Cubs' who emerged after 1733, taking up Bolingbroke's ideology and working alongside the Tory William Wyndham and Prince Frederick, were almost certainly more sincere in their commitment to a broad-bottom administration formed from a Patriot or Country coalition.

Thus generalizations become dangerous: a study of Patriot Whiggery perforce becomes, like this one, primarily a study of certain Patriot Whigs. This chapter is as much historical narrative—the events and dramatis personae which form the vital context for subsequent chapters—as it is political interpretation. Yet recent historical debate has begun to place the 'Whig tradition' under close scrutiny and to view both its origins and its transmission during the eighteenth century in a new light. The broader revisionist trends towards

---

[10] Cited by Colley, *In Defiance of Oligarchy*, 96.

the study of religion and royalty rather than liberty and property have interesting implications for opposition Whigs.

Few accounts of either Court or opposition Whigs in the Walpole period have been positive in approach.[11] The Walpole administration represented the corrupt nadir of Whiggism, an abandonment of 'Old Whig' principles which began with the self-protective oligarchic juntos of William and Anne's reigns and which rapidly accelerated after the onset of single party dominance in 1714. The Septennial Act of 1716, the suspension of Habeas Corpus, and a succession of punitive penal laws showed that the Whigs had become 'oligarchic and mercenary, with no thought for reform, toleration, or popular participation'.[12] The radical tradition of 'Old Whig' or 'Commonwealth' principles which Caroline Robbins and others traced from the mid-seventeenth century through to the Wilkite radicalism of the 1760s and the American Revolution hit a dry patch in the Walpole era.[13] The schism in Whig political culture—which had led successive 'Old' or 'True' Whigs to attack the 'Modern Whigs' from a neo-Harringtonian, Commonwealth tradition which fostered notions of political democracy and parliamentary reform—was less apparent in the 1730s than it had been in even the early 1720s. The Whig radical Thomas Gordon, co-author of *Cato's Letters* (1720–1), sold out in 1727 after his partner John Trenchard's death to become Walpole's press officer and Commissioner of Wine Licences. Meanwhile the Country platform advanced by the *Craftsman* was (according to Robbins) only 'pseudo-Whig'. Its Saxonist rhetoric invoking Gothic liberty lacked the focus of the seventeenth-century Parliamentarian debates over the ancient rights of the Commons, or the radical thrust of the later Wilkite 'Norman Yoke' polemic.[14] The Commonwealth legacy still remained a potent source of inspiration to the Patriot Whigs of the Walpole era, especially to the poets. They erected monuments to Milton, Algernon Sidney, and John Hampden, read Molesworth, Tyrell, and Moyle. Yet even though William Pitt, a leading young Patriot, immersed himself in Sidney, Ludlow, and May, he later remained immune to the radical Thomas Hollis's pressure for parliamentary reform. During the 1730s, Tory motions to repeal the Septennial Act and reinstate frequent parliaments (an 'Old Whig' ideal) received little support from opposition Whigs.[15] The frequent ministerial accusation that Patriot Whigs, especially those of the younger generation

[11] Notable exceptions are Dickinson, *Liberty and Property* and Reed Browning, *The Political and Constitutional Ideas of the Court Whigs* (Baton Rouge, La., 1982). An account of some of the complex transmutations of Whig thought in the 18th century is supplied by J. G. A. Pocock, 'The Varieties of Whiggism from Exclusion to Reform', in his *Virtue, Commerce, and History* (Cambridge, 1985), 215–310.

[12] J. P. Kenyon, *Revolution Principles: The Politics of Party, 1689–1720* (Cambridge, 1977), 203.

[13] See esp. Caroline Robbins, *The Eighteenth-Century Commonwealthmen* (Cambridge, Mass., 1959); Bernard Bailyn, *The Ideological Origins of the American Revolution* (Cambridge, Mass., 1967).

[14] Robbins, *Eighteenth-Century Commonwealthmen*, 284. For a fuller discussion of the Saxon constitution, see below, Ch. 5.

[15] See Colley, *In Defiance of Oligarchy*, 94–5; Kenyon, *Revolution Principles*, 181–7.

such as Lyttelton and Pitt, were dangerous radicals bent on overthrowing the government and establishing a democracy, had no substance. Government spies were less likely to find reds under opposition Whig beds than they were to find Jacobites under Tory ones. But the simple fact that opposition Whigs were not interested in initiating a radical campaign for political reform does not mean that they were devoid of principle or even hostile to certain different forms of Whig radicalism.[16] The 'Varieties of Whiggism from Exclusion to Reform' are far more complex.

Shaking the Pillars of Priestcraft

One issue which split the Whigs in the 1730s—religious policy—reveals one strand of opposition Whiggism to which most previous political and (especially) literary accounts of the Walpole era have paid insufficient attention.[17] It may be here that we can discern the bones of a strong and active 'Whig tradition' which could not and did not link opposition Whigs and Tories behind the *Craftsman*'s Country programme drawn from a secularized civic-humanist critique of ministerial corruption. J. A. I. Champion, J. C. D. Clark, and Mark Goldie have in different ways shown the complexity of the theological strands underpinning Whig thought, more complex than the historical alliance between Whiggism and Dissent.[18] Clark suggests that the prevalence in the Hanoverian period of various forms of anti-Trinitarian heterodoxy within the Anglican Church itself (Arianism and Socinianism) represented a radical challenge to ministerial oligarchy. Attacks on 'priestcraft' were a well-established part of the language of opposition Whiggery. Gordon and Trenchard edited not only the civic republican *Cato's Letters* but also the violently anticlerical *Independent Whig* (1720–1), directed against the alliance of Whig politicians with the Established Church.[19] English Whiggism, notes Goldie, 'was born as much in anticlericalism as in constitutionalism, and church history was as natural a

[16] For a questioning and redefinition of the 'radical' tradition, see J. C. D. Clark, *Revolution and Rebellion: State and Society in England in the Seventeenth and Eighteenth Centuries* (Cambridge, 1986).

[17] A notable exception was Norman Sykes, *Church and State in the Eighteenth Century* (Cambridge, 1934) and *Edmund Gibson, Bishop of London, 1669–1748* (1926). Attacks on Walpole's religious policy are not mentioned at all in B. A. Goldgar's otherwise full *Walpole and the Wits: The Relation of Politics to Literature, 1722–1742* (Lincoln, Nebr., 1976).

[18] See esp. J. A. I. Champion, *The Pillars of Priestcraft Shaken: The Church of England and its Enemies 1660–1730* (Cambridge, 1992); J. C. D. Clark, *English Society, 1688–1832: Ideology, Social Structure and Political Practice during the Ancien Regime* (Cambridge, 1985), esp. 277–315; Mark Goldie, 'Priestcraft and the Birth of Whiggism', in Nicholas Phillipson and Quentin Skinner (eds.), *Political Discourse in Early Modern Britain* (Cambridge, 1993), 209–31. Many of the themes outlined here, especially those concerning the nature of Whig kingship, are surprisingly relevant to the 1730s.

[19] See Marie P. McMahon, *The Radical Whigs, John Trenchard and Thomas Gordon* (Lanham, Md., 1990).

stamping ground for Whig polemicists as was parliamentary history'.[20] Anticlericalism was not synonymous with deism or secularism; a profound Whig Erastianism could lie behind Whig attacks on tyrannical Anglican prelates exercising control over civil jurisdiction. Calls for a purged or reformed Church led by a Protestant king untrammelled by priestcraft recur repeatedly in Whig pamphlets of the Restoration period, later (perhaps unconsciously) echoed in the messianic opposition Whig language of Patriot kingship during the 1730s.

Although there is some truth behind the traditional caricature of a theologically somnolent early Hanoverian Britain, religion as a source of heated political dispute did not end with the Bangorian Controversy of 1717 to 1719. The political rumpus in the first half of the 1730s over the Excise Crisis has often overshadowed a concurrent area of hostile opposition to Walpole, one created by Walpole's Court Whig alliance between 1723 and 1736 with his ecclesiastical adviser, the High-Church Bishop of London, Edmund Gibson. The stripe of true Whiggism emerged in Patriot attacks on Walpole which some ministerial Whigs but no Tories could share. Opposition Whig cries for 'liberty' in these years had far more to do with freedom of thought, conscience, and speech than they did with freedom of property or parliamentary freedom. It is no coincidence that selected speeches from the affrays of the 1730s found their due place in the radical republican Richard Barron's classic *Pillars of Priestcraft Shaken* (1768), designed to 'emancipate the minds of men, and to free them from those chains in which they have long been held'.[21]

Walpole's choice of Gibson to administrate ecclesiastical patronage was politically calculated. Gibson attempted to ensure that advancement was given only to clerics who could prove both their theological orthodoxy and their total loyalty to the Hanoverians and the Whig government, thereby cementing a closer alliance between Church and State. This tightly controlled policy of advancement was designed to give Walpole the support of a growing number of Whig clergy, especially loyal Whig bishops essential for maintaining his majority in the Lords. Another benefit (supposedly) would be an absence of religious controversy, since the presence of the High-Church Gibson would allay Tory restiveness about 'the Church in danger'.

But the alliance with Gibson posed Walpole some major difficulties. Gibson's High-Churchmanship and his intolerant views towards religious dissent and forms of Anglican heterodoxy such as anti-Trinitarianism made him deeply unpopular with many lay Whigs, including a number of Court Whigs. His famous *Codex Juris Ecclesiasticae* of 1713, which earned him the nickname 'Dr Codex', had argued for an extension of ecclesiastical authority into civil affairs markedly different from the more tolerant Erastianism favoured by George I's foremost bishop Benjamin Hoadly. Gibson was known to favour the revival of the traditional jurisdiction of ecclesiastical courts and the prosecution of laws

---

[20] Goldie, 'Priestcraft and the Birth of Whiggism', 214.
[21] Richard Barron, *The Pillars of Priestcraft Shaken*, 4 vols. (1768), i, p. vi.

against vice and irreligion. His adversaries compared him to Bishop Laud and stigmatized his policies as sinister and oppressive. Norman Sykes noted that the latter half of the Parliament of 1727–36 'recalled the Reformation Parliament of Henry VIII in its zeal to attack the stronghold of clerical privilege and abuse'.[22] A series of anticlerical measures were put forward, beginning in 1730 when opposition Whigs moved a motion to undermine the clergy's power to collect tithes and to prevent the translation of bishops. In 1733 an opposition bill attacking the jurisdiction of ecclesiastical courts passed the Commons and was only narrowly defeated in the Lords. Within this climate of revived anticlericalism the Dissenters embarked on a campaign for the repeal of the Test and Corporations Act. The motion was introduced in 1736 by a prominent opposition Whig Walter Plumer and backed by some other notable opposition Whigs such as Lord Polwarth, but defeated by a majority of Court Whigs voting alongside the Tories, the traditional defenders of the Church Establishment.[23] The controversy culminated in the debate over the Quaker Tithe and Mortmain Bills in 1736, the former drafted by the opposition Whig Jekyll. The first was designed to relieve Quakers of undue harassment in their conscientious stand against paying tithes to the Anglican Church. The second, which was to prohibit the bestowal of estates by will in Mortmain, was intended, so thought the Tories, to hit at the very structure of Anglican charitable and educational institutions. Both measures had considerable Court Whig as well as opposition Whig support. Walpole used the debate to exploit the fundamental differences between opposition Whigs and Tories, who angrily attacked the anticlerical implications of the Quaker Tithe and, especially, the Mortmain Bill. It was this which led the Tory Edward Harley bitterly to denounce Samuel Sandys and his zealous 'Patriot' supporters who attacked the 'poor clergy'.

Such tensions in the opposition could not comfortably be glossed over by the tenets of a secular 'Country' ideology. The *Craftsman* was unable to exploit the issue to embarrass the government because it so clearly divided the opposition along Whig–Tory lines. When it did briefly mention Dissenting pressure for Test Act repeal in 1733 it was with extreme caution, appealing to the Dissenters to make their religious concerns subservient to more 'important' secular matters: 'that you will make the Preservation of our Constitution your first Care, and consider any Ease to yourself only as a secondary Point'. Not until the movement for Test Act repeal had been defeated in 1736 did the

[22] Sykes, *Edmund Gibson*, 169. This subject is discussed ibid. 83–182; N. C. Hunt, *Two Early Political Associations: The Quakers and Dissenting Deputies in the Age of Sir Robert Walpole* (Oxford, 1961); T. F. J. Kendrick, 'Sir Robert Walpole, the Old Whigs and the Bishops, 1733–6: A Study in Eighteenth-Century Parliamentary Politics', *Historical Journal*, 11 (1968), 421–5; Stephen Taylor, 'Sir Robert Walpole, the Church of England and the Quaker Tithe Bill of 1736', *Historical Journal*, 28 (1985), 51–78.

[23] See Colley, *In Defiance of Oligarchy*, 220. The *Daily Gazetteer*, 15 May 1736, estimated that only 20 Patriots supported the bill, but this was probably a deliberate underestimate.

Craftsman briefly summarize the debate, non-committally describing itself as 'neuter according to a former Engagement'.[24] B. W. Hill ascribes Pulteney's parliamentary absence during the three stormy sessions of 1736 to his reluctance to become involved in issues which would alienate the Tories whose support he had gone out of his way to court. His ally the Tory William Wyndham was 'unusually subdued'.[25] The House was polarized at this stage into Whig and Tory groups, Walpole signalling his own ultimate sympathy to religious toleration by voting for the Quaker Tithe Bill, a move which effectively, though probably not intentionally, signalled the end of his alliance with Gibson, who resigned in disquiet in 1736.[26] Walpole transferred the control of ecclesiastical patronage at this stage to the less controversial charge of the Duke of Newcastle.

The Rundle Crisis and its Aftermath

During this period, Whig anticlericalism flared up with particular vehemence over one specific episode—the so-called 'Rundle Crisis' of 1733–5—'the most serious ecclesiastical controversy since the banishment of Atterbury', coming at a time when Walpole faced growing criticism on the Excise Bill and needed the support of the clergy for the forthcoming election.[27] The crisis was the unforeseen result of Walpole's appointment of Charles Talbot, his former Solicitor-General, to a peerage and the office of Lord Chancellor in November 1733. Talbot, who had remained loyal to Walpole during the Excise Crisis, filled one of the gaps in the Lords created by Walpole's recent purge of the factious Whig peers. Talbot may have been a loyal Court Whig but he was also a man of independent views and high principle who, when Solicitor-General, had headed the 1729 Jail Committee enquiring into alleged corruptions in the Fleet prison. This 'patriot-band', as James Thomson described them, had remained a standing rebuke to other Walpolian corruptions in the 1729–30 session.[28]

Charles Talbot was the son of William Talbot, the well-known latitudinarian Bishop of Durham. His father's former chaplain, the Arian divine Thomas Rundle, remained a close family friend. In December 1733 Talbot attempted

[24] See Hunt, *Two Early Political Associations*, App. F, 208–10.

[25] Hill, *The Growth of Parliamentary Parties*, 212–13. But Pulteney spent much of 1736 in Holland in a state of general fatigue and depression.

[26] Hunt, *Two Early Political Associations*, 92, argues that Walpole deliberately engineered the breach with Gibson. This is questioned by Taylor, 'Sir Robert Walpole, the Church of England and the Quaker Tithe Bill'.

[27] Sykes, *Edmund Gibson*, 155. Account of Rundle crisis, pp. 155–9. There is little special scholarship devoted to the affair. But see Stephen Bland, 'The Affair of Dr. Rundle: An Examination of Ecclesiastical Patronage under Walpole' (Cambridge BA dissertation, 1985).

[28] For Thomson's account of this committee, see *Winter*, ll. 359–88 (OET *Seasons*, 220; A. D. McKillop, 'Thomson and the Jail Committee', *SP* 48 (1950), 62–71.

to use his new Lord Chancellor's powers of ecclesiastical patronage to promote Rundle to the vacant see of Gloucester, but was at once blocked by Gibson on the grounds of Rundle's unorthodox and apparently heretical religious views. An unholy row broke out between Talbot and Gibson, accompanied by a flood of pamphlets accusing and defending Rundle. A major contributor on the ministerial side was the *Weekly Miscellany*, a pro-Gibson paper of extreme High-Church orthodoxy edited by William Webster, designed to 'defend the Church of *England* against the united Efforts of Infidels and Sectaries to destroy it'.[29] Gibson backed a smear campaign conducted by his clerical henchmen—the High-Church Tory Henry Stebbing, one of the King's chaplains, and the City cleric William Venn—to vilify Rundle's morals and conduct, accusing him of being a Socinian, a free-thinker, a deist, even an atheist. Talbot expressed his opposition to Gibson in no uncertain terms, hiring Thomas Gordon to write in Rundle's defence.[30] Gordon may by this stage have 'sold out' to Walpole, but had little trouble in reviving the strong anticlericalism of his *The Independent Whig* of the early 1720s for his attacks on Gibson, who by this stage was also the target of numerous vehement squibs and satirical prints showing the State riding on an ass's back led by the Church. Gibson, according to Hervey, was 'pelted with all the opprobrious language that envy and malice ever threw at eminence and power'.[31] Many onlookers, including Egmont, who revised his initial prejudices against Rundle's fitness for the Gloucester see, believed that the real issue at stake was not Rundle's heretical religious views but the conflict between the supremacy of ecclesiastical or civil power.[32] Walpole prolonged the Gloucester vacancy for a whole year until the 1734 general election was safely past, then at the end of 1734 promoted the less controversial Archdeacon Martin Benson to Gloucester. In July 1735 Rundle was given the consolation prize of the lucrative but remote see of Derry. This piece of ministerial tact fuelled rather than quenched the flames of anticlerical opinion pronouncing 'the State in danger'. As Sir Thomas Robinson remarked, 'if this doctrine of the Bench be allowed as an established maxim, 'twill be adding an Ecclesiastical independent power in the State, which might prove more dangerous to Liberty than even a Military One; as of all tyranny that practised by those in black have [*sic*] in all ages and nations been most destructive of Liberty'.[33]

Charles Talbot remained Chancellor, despite having considered resigning over the Rundle affair; he registered his disgust by a marked coolness towards Walpole and a studied rudeness towards the King.[34] His son William took a

---

[29] Cited in Michael Harris, *London Newspapers in the Age of Walpole: A Study of the Origins of the Modern English Press* (1987), 183.

[30] See Kendrick, 'Sir Robert Walpole, the Old Whigs and the Bishops', 427. Gordon's 'A Letter to the Rev. Dr. Codex' appeared in *GM* 4 (1734), 152–3.

[31] Hervey, *Memoirs*, ii. 401.

[32] *Egmont Diary*, ii. 151.   [33] HMC *Carlisle MSS*, 131.

[34] *Egmont Diary*, ii. 137.

more extreme line. In 1734 he entered Parliament as opposition Whig MP for Glamorgan and took the first possible opportunity to vote against the administration. His move into opposition, a radical departure from the Court Whig loyalism which had previously characterized his family, was almost certainly prompted by the Rundle affair. To his famous definition of a 'Real Whig', one made along *Craftsman*-style Country-party lines—attacks on ministerial corruption, standing armies, the defence of trade and commerce—he added an important, often overlooked, tenet: that 'the freedom of the press is the bulwark of religious and civil liberty;—that as religion is of the utmost consequence to every man, no person ought to suffer civil hardships for his religious persuasion'.[35] The Rundle controversy entered the political poetry of the period. Swift, whose own theological views were quite otherwise, got to know and admire Rundle in Ireland and passed ironic comment on the affair.

> Make *Rundle* Bishop; fye for Shame!
> An *Arrian* to usurp the Name!
> A Bishop in the Isle of Saints!
> How will his Brethren make Complaints?
> Dare any of the mitred Host,
> Confer on him the HOLY GHOST;
> In Mother Church to breed a Variance,
> By coupling *Orthodox* with *Arrians*?
>
> . . . . . .
>
> For Liberty a Champion stout,
> 'Though not so Gospel-ward devout.
> While others hither sent to save us,
> Came but to plunder and enslave us;
> Nor ever own'd a Pow'r Divine,
> But *Mammon*, and the *German* Line.[36]

James Thomson was a close friend of Rundle; it was almost certainly Rundle who introduced him to the Talbot family, who remained Thomson's patrons until Chancellor Talbot's death in 1737. Thomson had accompanied William's short-lived older brother Charles on the Grand Tour. Thomson himself was a staunch Erastian whose liberal views emerge in his praise for Hoadly's 1735 *Plain Account of the . . . Lord's Supper*, noting that 'All Bigots roar against it'.[37] He almost certainly supported the opposition agitation for the repeal of the Test Act. Thomson publicly revealed the depth of his feeling about Rundle's victimization after Chancellor Talbot's death in 1737; his elegy on his former patron depicted the exiled Rundle wandering the Derry shores,

---

[35] The definition appears in Talbot's letter to Sir John Dutton, printed in Rundle, *Letters*, ii. 243–4.
[36] 'On Mr. Rundle, Bishop of Derry' (1735) (Swift, *Poetical Works*, ed. Herbert Davis (Oxford, 1967), 596–8).
[37] Thomson, *Letters*, 95.

'Driven from your Friends, the Sun-shine of the Soul, | By Slanderous Zeal, and Politics infirm, | Jealous of Worth'.[38]

The Rundle controversy may have done as much as Walpole's ignominious foreign policy to precipitate Thomson into opposition. It was undoubtedly a factor which helped confirm Thomson's friend Richard Savage in his hostility to the Walpole administration. The case of Savage is complex, as we shall see in Chapter 8. In his youth he had been a Jacobite propagandist and supporter of Sacheverell and the High-Church Tories; strong elements of Jacobite nostalgia colour some of his later verse. By the early 1730s he was a member of opposition Whig and Dissenting circles, especially friendly with the famous Arian Dissenting preacher James Foster.[39] His involvement in the anticlerical controversy of this period was certainly imprudent, leading him into direct conflict with the administration. In March 1735 Savage published a short poem in praise of his friend Foster, whose heated dispute with Henry Stebbing on the subject of heresy brought him into collision with Gibson. Savage's *The Character of the Reverend James Foster*, albeit a tribute to Foster's modesty and simple piety, contained an overt criticism of Gibson, Stebbing, and Venn. The following month (27 April) he published a more controversial poem, *The Progress of a Divine*, a far more vitriolic exposure of Gibsonian turpitude. Dr Johnson deplored this poem for its attacks on the clergy, but *The Progress of a Divine* is one of the most spirited and accomplished political satires of the period.[40] Taking his cue from the recent accusation that Gibson had used his power to protect an unmarried clergyman on trial for 'unnatural sin', Savage portrayed the fictional career of a remarkably deviant cleric who was intended as an amalgam of Stebbing and Venn, and the epitome of ecclesiastical abuses and sinister Church powers. The cleric progresses through various forms of peculation, paedophilia, and fornication to high preferment under Gibson:

> A *Spy*, he aims, by other's Fall to rise;
> Vile as *Iscariot V*[en]*n*, betrays; belies;
> And say, what better recommends than this?
> Lo, CODEX *greets* him with, a *holy kiss*.

The Judas kiss is, of course, for the betrayal of Rundle: 'Wou'd now the *Mitre* circle *Rundle*'s Crest? | See *him*, with *Codex*, ready to *protest!*'[41]

---

[38] Thomson, *A Poem to the Memory of the Right Honourable the Lord Talbot*, ll. 244–6 (OET *Liberty*, 156).

[39] Clarence Tracy, *The Artificial Bastard: A Biography of Richard Savage* (Toronto, 1953), 121–2. Foster arranged to have Savage's poems published in the *London Magazine*.

[40] *The Character of the Reverend James Foster* was printed in *GM* Apr. 1735. The longer poem (*The Progress of a Divine*) was obviously known about at this stage since the editor claimed (erroneously) that the *Character of Foster* was an extract from 'an Epistle not yet published'. For Johnson's dislike of the *Progress*, see his *An Account of the Life of Mr. Savage*, ed. Clarence Tracy (Oxford, 1971), 389–90.

[41] *The Progress of a Divine*, ll. 335–8, 415–16 (Savage, *Poetical Works*, ed. Clarence Tracy (Cambridge, 1962), 191–203).

The poem provoked a storm of protests as well as defences of Savage, suggesting the politically sensitive nature of the issue. On 29 April a whole issue of the ministerial *Hyp-Doctor* was dedicated to fulminating (as only its oratorical author Henley knew how) against that 'Mad Animal' Savage. On 2 May the *Daily Courant* trumped up the charge that Savage was currently being prosecuted for raising a riot in the Flintshire elections. *The Progress of a Divine* almost certainly led to threats of ministerial prosecution; however, there is no evidence to prove Johnson's report that Savage was hauled before the King's Bench on obscenity charges, then acquitted.[42] The April 1735 issue of the *Gentleman's Magazine* printed a poem from the Gibsonite *Weekly Miscellany*, a nasty attack on Savage's recent last-minute pardon on a murder charge, 'For cruel Murder doom'd to Hempen Death'. The May issue printed a poem by an anonymous 'Wiltshire Correspondent' rushing to Savage's defence. To attack clerical corruption was the task of a 'Patriot'. Even Savage's prosecution for murder was not as heinous as the crimes against freedom of conscience committed by Gibson.

> Not half so fierce, his *midnight sword*, or rage,
> As *Codex* zeal or W-bst-r's high church page
> The mitred *Fury*, and the *cassock'd* imp,
> To *hell* an *agent* and to *Rome* a pimp.
> Bloated with *priestly* rage, and holy spite,
> Consign to flames the wretch, *that Thinks not right*.[43]

A more tempered but essentially similar view was supplied by the significantly titled *The Old Whig; or, The Consistent Protestant*, a journal established by the Dissenting minister Samuel Chandler which ran between 13 March 1735 and 30 March 1738, stirred into being by the Rundle crisis and as a riposte to the ministerialist *Weekly Miscellany*.[44] Its title, like William Talbot's definition of 'Real Whig' principles, proclaimed the inextricable link between politics and religion, the first issue (13 March 1735) setting out a definition of patriotism, establishing that *'Britons* and *Protestants* . . . are born ourselves to Liberty'. It championed a wide variety of heterodox Low-Church clergymen, including Rundle, Foster, Hoadly, Samuel Clarke, even the deist William Chubb. Much of its political thrust was aimed at supporting the campaign for the repeal of the Test Act, though its chief vigour was reserved for attacks on Gibson, comparing him to the overweening Laud. The paper offered 'evidence' of clerical interference in the daily lives of the laity, alluding to ominous historical precedents such as men being hanged for stealing hares from clergymen's grounds. Part of its 'Old Whig' idiom was a pervasive

---

[42] *Hyp-Doctor*, 23 Apr. 1735; *Daily Courant*, 2 May 1735; for the story of Savage's prosecution, see Johnson, *Account of the Life of Savage*, 389–90.

[43] *GM* 5 (1735), 213, 252.

[44] For a brief account, see Harris, *London Newspapers*, 121, 183, 186. He may underestimate the *Old Whig*'s political content.

anti-Catholicism, almost a revival of Exclusion Crisis Whiggery in its efforts to unearth a Popish plot in the London parishes, citing endless examples of smells, bells, and images, absurdly estimating that 10,000 Catholic priests now lived in London and over 60,000 Catholics in Britain as a whole—about four times the real number.[45] This was partly inspired by the decade's growing anti-Spanish, anti-French sentiment: even Gibson in December 1734 had circulated a letter to his clerics warning them to be on their guard against the increased activities of Catholic priests. The *Old Whig*, however, makes little distinction between Catholicism and the High-Church Anglicanism espoused by Gibson, having no truck with 'C-d-x, nor Monks, nor Popes, nor Bishops'.[46]

The paper did not confine itself to religious disputes. It supplied a coherent running commentary on Westminster politics in its 'A Letter to a Friend in the Country' column. It would be hard to think of an oppositional journal which stood in such sharp contrast to the *Craftsman*. As we have seen, the conciliatory 'Country' platform of the *Craftsman* remained singularly silent on religious issues. In one sense the *Craftsman* 'theologized' secular politics in a quite different way, clothing its civic-humanist Commonwealth arguments in quasi-religious metaphor and symbolism: the Satanic archetypes invoked, for example, by its account of the 'TREE OF CORRUPTION, which bears a very near Resemblance to the *Tree of Knowledge*, in the Garden of *Eden*'.[47] The *Old Whig*'s oppositional idiom was by contrast sharply distinguished by real Protestant zeal. In 1735 it was extremely dismissive of the role Bolingbroke had played in the opposition, approving heartily of his recent departure to France after being 'unmasked' by Walpole's late denunciation of him as an anti-minister: 'May this Resentment be a Memento to All others.' If Bolingbroke's recent political writings such as *A Dissertation on Parties* had had any good effect, argued the *Old Whig*, it was to inculcate some Whig principles into his former Tory friends. But the role played by a man impeached for Jacobitism who had injured his country could be at best nugatory. 'But 'twas impossible, by any thing he could say, by the most artful and delicate Addresses and Apologies, to reconcile the People to himself.'[48] A further issue addressed the problem of an oppositional Country coalition but saw it as only a temporary and tactical expedient.

The *Coalition of Parties* seems indeed a Thing very *capable* of being effected. Interest or Conviction may cause Men to lay aside their *peculiar* Differences, and may make them unite in some *common* Maxims and Designs. But Principles are invariable: and as Truth and Falshood, Liberty and Slavery, true *Whiggism* and staunch *Toryism* are necessarily and immutably different, and quite irreconcilable with each other; it is impossible they can ever *coalesce*, or be brought into a real Union and Friendship.[49]

[45] *Old Whig*, 13 Mar. 1735.   [46] Ibid., 8 May 1735.
[47] *Craftsman*, 25 Mar. 1732.   [48] *Old Whig*, 8 May 1735.
[49] Ibid., 11 Sept. 1735.

Although we have no record of its circulation, the *Old Whig* clearly enjoyed nothing like the *Craftsman*'s wide readership. However, it would probably be wrong to dismiss it as an extremist Dissenting journal. The 'liberty' it champions encompasses freedom of conscience, of speech, and especially of the press—very much in line with traditional Whig tenets. Its staunch Protestant Hanoverianism (according special praise to Prince Frederick) would have been central to the political identity of most opposition Whigs. The *Old Whig* makes little mention of Pulteney, and, as we have seen, dismisses Bolingbroke. All its political praise is reserved for the young 'Boy Patriots' who first appeared on the parliamentary scene in the middle of its publication, 'several New Members of Parliament, who are very worthy ingenious Men, Lovers of Liberty, and who have a passionate Zeal for the Common Welfare . . . The General Attention is much fixed upon them; and great Things are expected from their future Conduct.' The political correspondent talks much about a political club to which he belongs where we 'generally have a large Company'.[50] One might speculate that this was the recently formed Liberty or Rumpsteak Club, given that he alludes to the presence of a number of opposition Whig peers, including Cobham and especially the new young Patriots who had just entered Parliament. The Rumpsteak Club, chaired by Cobham, was formed in January 1734 primarily by opposition Whigs who had lately shared the honour of having the 'Royal Rump' turned in disfavour on them.[51] Lord Cobham, recently dismissed for attacking Walpole's cover-up over the forfeited South Sea Directors' estates, becomes the *Old Whig*'s ideal of 'Country' Protestant Whiggery. Cobham's nephew George Lyttelton warrants the paper's particular attention: it defends his recent *Persian Letters* against the ministerial attacks in the *Persian strip'd of his Disguise*, rejecting the latter as a disgusting work defending priestcraft and divine right theory.

That the *Old Whig* should single out these figures for political approval is not odd. Cobham was a renowned anticlerical. He barred his sister from his estates after she married a High-Anglican clergyman and attempted to bribe his nephew Gilbert West from reading divinity at Oxford by offering him a cornetcy in his own regiment.[52] The assertively Protestant thrust of Cobham's pantheon of British worthies at Stowe, including Milton and Locke and an Elizabeth I who 'took off the Yoke of Ecclesiastical Tyranny', says much.[53] Although Lyttelton was later converted (probably by West) to devout Anglican orthodoxy, during the Walpole period he certainly entertained other views about both scriptural authority and the authority of the Anglican Church.[54]

[50] Ibid., 1 May 1735.

[51] Account of the Rumpsteak Club and a list of members in *Marchmont Papers*, ii. 19–20. The list seems to have included a few moderate Tories as well as opposition Whigs.

[52] Rose Mary Davis, *The Good Lord Lyttelton* (Bethlehem, Pa., 1939), 34.

[53] G. B. Clarke (ed.), *Descriptions of Lord Cobham's Gardens at Stowe, 1700–1750* (Buckingham, 1990), 138.

[54] Johnson, *Lives of the Poets*, iii. 449–50; *Annual Register*, 25 (1782), 55–7.

One of the features which distinguished Lyttelton's *Persian Letters* of 1735 from the Country-party platform of Bolingbroke's recent *Dissertation on Parties* (1734) was a strong strain of Whig anticlericalism which a ministerial critic was quick to detect. *The Persian strip'd of his Disguise* claimed that Lyttelton was arguing that ' "the *Bishops* ought not to be admitted to sit and vote in the *House of Lords.*" In this he excells and goes beyond his *Master* the *Dissertator* [Bolingbroke], who has us'd a little more Caution, than to assert this Doctrine in express Terms.'[55] His neighbour Richard Graves thought that Lyttelton's anticlericalism, much disliked by the 'country gentlemen', was largely responsible for his losing his seat at Worcester to his Tory rival Lechmere in the 1741 election: 'his Persian Letters, which were written with a freedom to which we were then less accustomed, disgusted the clergy and made them his adversaries'.[56] Lyttelton's personal tutor Francis Ayscough, who later married his sister Anne, had very strong Low-Church latitudinarian leanings. He 'suffered at Oxford as a Whig & a Hoadlian' to the extent that his election to a fellowship at Corpus Christi was initially blocked by the President and Fellows and secured only by an appeal to the Visitor.[57]

Thomson, Savage, William Talbot, Ayscough, Cobham, and Lyttelton were all associated (with varying degrees of intimacy) with Prince Frederick's circle, some occupying household positions. Lyttelton and Pitt introduced Ayscough to the Prince. He became Frederick's clerk of the closet and preceptor to the future George III, also responsible for managing Frederick's privy purse and electoral affairs.[58] Savage was the Master of the Richmond Lodge of Masons of which Frederick, Thomson, and other opposition sympathizers became members. William Talbot became one of Frederick's political agents for the Leicester House alliance. The Patriot poet David Mallet, Frederick's under-secretary, enjoyed a reputation for radical free-thinking. The poet Paul Whitehead, connected with this circle, came in for savage ministerial attack, not merely for writing a eulogistic poem on Frederick but as a 'public Disputant against Religion'. 'Religion in General he declaims against, as Priest-craft, and a Burthen on Society . . . From levelling the Church he at Length proceeds to an Attack on the State.'[59] The associations between Patriot Whiggery and anticlericalism deserve fuller exploration.

---

[55] *The Persian strip'd of his Disguise* (1735), 11–13.

[56] Richard Graves, *Recollections of Some Particulars in the Life of the Late William Shenstone Esq.* (1788), 80–1.

[57] Albert Hartshorne (ed.), *Memoirs of a Royal Chaplain 1729–1763: The Correspondence of Edmund Pyle D.D.* (1905), 282.

[58] See R. Harris (ed.), *A Leicester House Political Diary 1742–3*, Camden Miscellany, 4th ser. 44 (1992), 373–408.

[59] *Observations on the Present Taste for Poetry; with Remarks . . . on Manners* (1739), 11.

Cobham and his Cubs

1736 was the last year in which religious disputes occupied any major parliamentary role during the Walpole period. Gibson's resignation and the sympathy Walpole had shown for religious dissent in his support of the Quaker Tithe Bill defused the situation. The *Old Whig*'s clear discrimination between the patriotism of the Cobham circle and the dubious claims to patriotism made by the Jacobite-tainted Bolingbroke was not, of course, reflected in this circle's own dealings with Bolingbroke. After his return to France in 1735, Bolingbroke was largely responsible for supplying the new alliance between the Whig Patriots of the Cobham circle and the Tory followers of William Wyndham with the ideological tenets for their new opposition platform.

The Boy Patriots and their allies are interesting for rather different reasons. They were widely perceived as reinvesting Patriot Whiggery with an unimpeachable moral validation, one which Walpole's former associate William Pulteney could never quite convincingly claim. The chief event which led to this 'second wave' of Whig Patriots was Walpole's dismissal between April and June 1733 of Cobham, Clinton, Bolton, Marchmont, Montrose, Stair, and Chesterfield from their government places. Walpole needed to command a majority in the House of Lords and had little room for disloyal Whig peers. But the cleansing of the Augean stables was an extremely unpopular measure, largely because Walpole simultaneously deprived both Cobham and Bolton of their regimental posts. Richard Temple, Viscount Cobham, was a loyal Whig Hanoverian with a long and distinguished military career. His impeccable service record as one of Marlborough's colonels at Flanders had been enhanced by his superb leadership of the capture of the Gallician port of Vigo in 1719 during the War of the Quadruple Alliance. The regiment of which he was now deprived—the colonelcy of the King's own Horse—had been George I's personal reward to him for his bravery at Vigo. Walpole added insult to injury by transferring Cobham's regimental post to his supine son-in-law Cholmondley, a man who had never seen active service. Three years later Walpole stoked the furnace of military martyrdom when he deprived Cobham's nephew the young William Pitt of his cornetcy of horse for his inflammatory speeches in the Commons.[60]

Before 1733 Cobham, whose abilities were better suited to the battlefield than the cabinet, had never enjoyed a high political profile. His stand on South Sea Company corruption, which left him much to lose and nothing to gain, was evidently motivated by principle. His political 'retirement' to the family seat at Stowe proved anything but politically retired. Cobham channelled his energies into building up a formidable array of opposition support

---

[60] *Egmont Diary*, ii. 34. For the widespread resentment over the subsequent cashiering of Stair and Pitt, see *Carlisle MSS*, 133, 136, 172.

by cultivating his young nephews by birth or marriage (he himself was child-less). He used his vast wealth to secure some of them parliamentary seats during the 1734 election. By 1735 Richard Grenville, Thomas Pitt, William Pitt, and George Lyttelton had all entered the Commons. George Grenville came in after the general election of 1741.[61] Lyttelton's cousin and fellow poet Gilbert West played a less politically active role, though he lent his support through his Patriot poetry. It was at this stage that the gardens of Stowe began to acquire the dimensions of an overtly political landscape, an allegory of Patriot Whig principles manifest in the architectural design of buildings such as the Gothic Temple of Liberty; the Temple of British Worthies with its formidable array of Protestant Whig thinkers, heroes, and monarchs; the Temple of Ancient Virtue with its pantheon of ancient Greek patriots; and the corresponding and ironic Temple of Modern Virtue, whose headless bust of a recognizably Walpolian figure graphically embodied the recent decline in modern civic virtue.[62] In 1735 Cobham called a grand oppositional meeting of his nephews and political supporters to formulate stratagems for attack. It may be misleading however to argue, as has Lewis M. Wiggin, that this was the master-plan for the establishment of the Temple–Bedford–Grenville dynasty, the 'Faction of Cousins' which came to dominate British politics in the 1750s and 1760s. In 1735 the downfall of Robert Walpole rather than long-term political dynasty-building was Cobham's pressing concern.[63]

Cobham's newly formed 'Cubs' rapidly made alliances with other opposition Whigs such as the young lawyer William Murray, the young members of the Scottish Roxburgh Squadrone (the dismissed Marchmont's talented twin sons Lord Polwarth and Alexander Hume Campbell), as well as the young Tory Viscount Cornbury. Walpole, unable to boast similar youthful recruits to the Court Whig side, publicly mocked the political naïvety of the 'Boys' but evidently feared their new presence in the Commons. He offered Thomas Pitt, who controlled several seats in the House, 'any terms' to keep his brother-in-law Lyttelton and his younger brother William out of it. He also tried to stop Marchmont, a powerful speaker, from serving in the Lords as a representative Scottish peer.[64] Youth was in fact the Boy Patriots' chief asset. In 1735 they were all under 30 (George Lyttelton was 26, William Pitt 27, Richard Grenville 24, George Grenville 23, Cornbury 25, Murray, the oldest, just 30) and, unlike the older generation of opposition Whigs, untainted by any former attachment to the Walpole ministry. Ministerial writers attacking Bolingbroke

---

[61] Richard Grenville was elected for Buckingham in the general election of 1734; in 1735 Old Sarum returned William Pitt; and at a by-election in 1735 George Lyttelton was returned for the Pitt family borough, Okehampton in Devon, joining Thomas Pitt in representing the town. George Grenville was brought into Parliament for Buckingham by Cobham in 1741.

[62] Stowe's iconography is discussed in fuller detail below, Ch. 5.

[63] Lewis M. Wiggin, *The Faction of Cousins: A Political Account of the Grenvilles, 1733–1763* (New Haven, Conn., 1958), 10–50. This is a very Namierite account.

[64] Lord Rosebery, *Chatham* (1910), 147.

and Pulteney's mock-patriotism played on the gap between Patriot rhetoric and political practice by pointing to Bolingbroke's untrustworthy past and Pulteney's former association with Walpole. The same charges could not be levelled at either Cobham, dismissed for his principles, or the Boy Patriots. The *Old Whig* now countered the familiar ministerial definition of 'Patriot' as one who 'only cloaths his private Views with the imaginary rhetoric of a Lover of his Country' with the confident assertion that 'Men decry Public Virtue, and endeavour to bring it into Contempt, just in proportion to the Want of it they are conscious of in themselves'.[65] Pope adopted the same line in his *Epilogue to the Satires*, Dialogue II. His pusillanimous Court Whig 'friend' attempts to undermine opposition credibility by remarking 'I think your Friends are out, and would be in'. The poet tartly responds: 'If merely to come in, Sir, they go out, | The way they take is strangely round about'.[66] The young Boy Patriots had of course never been 'in' at all. George Lyttelton, who followed the politics of his uncle Richard rather than those of his staunch Court Whig father Sir Thomas, a leading supporter of Walpole's Excise Bill, was credited with an even higher degree of patriotic self-denial. Rumour circulated that his father was threatening to cut him out of his will, and the *Old Whig* of 10 April 1735 remarked that

Amidst all the Complaints of Corruption and Degeneracy, there is a Spirit in many of Our young Men, that rises almost to Enthusiasm. Some despise Frowns and Disgrace; and even the Threat of Disinheriting has been unattended to by Others. The old *Greek* and *Roman* virtue, perhaps, if inquired into, had not a little of this Tincture.[67]

William Pitt distinguished himself during his first parliamentary session in April 1735 in a maiden speech supporting an opposition motion for a place bill. But it was during the next summer that he, Lyttelton, and Grenville created a major stir in their 'remarkable' speeches congratulating Frederick on his recent marriage. They combined daring sallies on the King and Walpole with the insinuation that the long-awaited marriage had finally been enforced by popular demand. Pitt's speech, which led to loss of his military post, reputedly prompted Walpole to remark, 'We must muzzle this terrible young Cornet of Horse'.[68] It is hard to assess whether they ever matched up to the forceful eloquence of William Pulteney. More cynical commentators sneered at a classical rhetoric drawn from the university rather than the hustings, no one more efficiently than the staunch Court Whig satirist Sir Charles Hanbury Williams. His well-known satire on Lyttelton, *A Political Eclogue* (1740), a poem much concerned with driving home the wedge between the Patriot cant of an opposition Whig and the staunch High-Church Toryism of his successful Tory rival Lechmere, unseats Lyttelton in more ways than one. Lyttelton's Patriot speechifying, head in the clouds as he trips through the Worcestershire

---

[65] *Old Whig*, 8 May 1735.   [66] Pope, *Ep. Satires*, ii. 122–5 (*TE*, iv. 320).
[67] *Old Whig*, 10 Apr. 1735.   [68] Hervey, *Memoirs*, ii. 553.

cow-pats with the blunt Tory squire Lechmere, shows how absurd the language of liberty could sound to the politically pragmatic:

> 'Think of the high employment that I bear,
> 'I write in verse, and have my Prince's ear.
> 'The glorious talent to declaim is mine:
> 'In Council and in Parliament I shine.
> 'Have you not heard me? Yes, you must have heard,
> 'When Tully's spirit in each word appear'd;
> 'When the still senate on each accent hung,
> 'And oratory dwelt upon my tongue;
> 'When I, great Liberty, thy standard bore
> 'And Walpole pale sat trembling on the floor;
> 'When all th'applauding patriot band allow'd
> 'That I myself appear'd their leading god.'[69]

But the Boy Patriots won many genuine admirers. Their youthful vigour injected a new dimension into Commons debates hitherto much dominated by staged battles between those political old-timers Walpole and Pulteney; the outspokenness of their speeches led one critic to describe them as 'young gentlemen who took great personal liberties'.[70] Both Pope and Johnson, the former by no means politically naïve by the 1730s, found much to admire as well as, ultimately, to reject in the Patriot cause. In both cases their disillusionment corresponded in its bitterness to the higher hopes they had previously entertained for these young Patriots, with whom Pope 'would never fear to hold out against all the Corruption of the world'.[71] A good example of the response which their appearance prompted from more idealistic opposition Whigs is indicated by Robert Craggs Nugent's *Political Justice*, an encomium on 'those young Patriots who have lately appeared upon the Scene of Business, and are the Glory and Honour of the present Age'. The poem first appeared in the oppositional *Fog's Weekly Journal* on 17 April 1736 and was reprinted in the June issue of the *Gentleman's Magazine*.

> While *Greece* and *Rome* record an hoary Train,
> Who dar'd the Cause of Liberty maintain,
> The *British* Senate boasts a youthful Band,
> Form'd for th'exalted Task by Nature's Hand,
> She gave their Souls with early Charms to shine,
> And Love of Arts these Beauties to refine;

---

[69] Charles Hanbury Williams, *Works*, 3 vols. (1822), i. 61–70, at p. 65. The poem has been much discussed by historians refuting the Court/Country argument: see Colley, *In Defiance of Oligarchy*, 98; Eveline Cruickshanks (ed.), *Ideology and Conspiracy: Aspects of Jacobitism 1689–1759* (Edinburgh, 1982), 7–8. A less convincing reading is supplied by W. A. Speck, *Society and Literature in England, 1700–1760* (Dublin, 1983), 39–40.

[70] Coxe, *Walpole*, iii. 516.

[71] Pope, *Corr.*, iv. 178.

She gave those Thoughts which she alone inspires,
And deck'd them out in all that Care acquires,
Wisdom unclog'd by Years, by Pain unbought
A Zeal by Vigour kindl'd, rul'd by Thought.

   .   .   .

While you, brave Patriots! from each Tongue receive,
A glorious Tribute for the Joys you give,
While all the Good your deathless Praise proclaim;
And, higher Praise! while all the Bad defame,
Be this your Pride! in Youth's unsully'd Minds,
Her fittest Mansion heavenly Virtue finds.[72]

George Lyttelton, despite a physically unprepossessing appearance, occupied the politically dominant role in this group, even though it was later William Pitt who rose to political eminence. Pitt's real 'popularity' came far later, not for another twenty years. Though in 1735 he was described as 'a very pretty young speaker, one the Prince is particular to', Pitt was never as close to Frederick as his cousin Lyttelton.[73] The extreme anti-Hanoverianism which only seven years later distinguished Pitt's offensive speeches to both George II and Frederick himself (by this stage a supporter of the new administration) was probably latent in his oppositional speeches of the 1730s.[74] Lyttelton added literary parts to his oratory. His 1735 *Letters from a Persian in England to His Friend at Ispahan* probably owed more to Bolingbroke than to their model Montesquieu, although their attack on the bishops was clearly independently motivated. Their readable format, which combined a disingenuously chatty style with more pointed oppositional commentary, was in large measure responsible for their extraordinary popularity. The *Persian Letters* were cited, praised, parodied and attacked for weeks by the opposition and government press.[75] Lyttelton also contributed, alongside Chesterfield, to the new weekly opposition journal *Common Sense, or, the Englishman's Journal*, started in February 1737. This was one of the most significant opposition journals to emerge in the period following the *Craftsman*'s demise. The quality of its writing was virtually unrivalled, as one might expect from a journal to which Chesterfield, Lyttelton, and other accomplished writers contributed. The political ideas it advances are essentially a reworking of Bolingbroke's Patriot platform, though its outspokenness is signalled by its inclusion of the scurrilous print and allegorical satire on Walpole and George II, the *Vision of the Golden*

---

[72] This poem was published in 1737 as *An Epistle to the Right Honourable the Lord Viscount Cornbury*. When it appeared in vol. ii of Dodsley's *Collection* (1748) it had lost much of its earlier partisan thrust.

[73] *Carlisle MSS*, 172.

[74] Rosebery, *Chatham*, 188.

[75] Goldgar, *Walpole and the Wits*, 140–1. Lyttelton was not the first to turn Montesquieu's *Lettres Persanes* to political purposes. *Mist's Weekly Journal*, 24 Aug. 1728, carried the Jacobite Duke of Wharton's 'Persian Letter', an attack on George I and II disguised in fairy-tale format.

Rump. The paper's political provenance is complicated by the fact that its founder Charles Molloy had been approached by an agent, sent by the Pretender, aiming to set up a new weekly paper to give support to English Jacobites. According to the agent's report back, Molloy was apparently ready to start the paper with the help of both Pope and Chesterfield. It is hard to determine, however, whether Molloy ever received funds from Jacobites or only from opposition Whigs. The Machiavellian Lord Chesterfield may well have been capable of playing a double game, though it is very doubtful whether Lyttelton, at this stage Prince Frederick's secretary, was.[76]

Prince Frederick and the Patriots

The Boy Patriots may have been new to the political scene in 1735 but Prince Frederick was not. In 1728 he had arrived in England under a cloud of parental disapproval for his recently thwarted attempts to elope with the Prussian princess Sophia: a long-planned marriage alliance from which George II had recently reneged owing to worsening relations with King Frederick Wilhelm. Prince Frederick had been left in the Hanoverian court when his father came to Britain in 1714 and his family were virtual strangers to him. He continued to cause trouble even under the parental eye. Lord Hervey's insider accounts from the Hanoverian court in the early 1730s present a squalid tale of domestic squabbles and personal slights taken. Frederick clearly went out of his way to annoy his parents but the provocation was mutual. The pattern for his oppositional role had of course already been set by his father's own earlier period in opposition to George I.

Frederick had two valid sources of grievance which his parents would have been wise to remedy earlier. One was his frustrated desire to find a suitable wife. His sister Anne, the Princess Royal, was married amid much pomp and circumstance to the Prince of Orange in 1734. Frederick and his supporters interpreted the reverse priority of royal marriages as a deliberate slight, especially Anne's acquisition of the separate allowance denied her elder brother. Frederick's major complaint was his apron-string financial dependence on his father. Frederick pressed for independent quarters and, more importantly, for an independent allowance from the Civil List. The provisions of the large Hanoverian Civil List had envisaged that Frederick should received £100,000 per annum as Prince of Wales, as had his father. At first he received £34,000; by 1737 his total income with the addition of Duchy of Cornwall revenues probably amounted to £59,000. But this was manifestly insufficient to cover all the salaries in the Prince of Wales's household and, as we shall see, to permit

---

[76] G. H. Jones, 'The Jacobites, Charles Molloy, and *Common Sense*', *RES* NS 4 (1953), 144–7. The paper's 'ideological capitulation to Whiggism' is described by Robert Harris, *A Patriot Press: National Politics and the London Press in the 1740s* (Oxford, 1993), 45 n.

him to cultivate his active cultural interests. Frederick was always short of money, borrowing heavily from some of his wealthier courtiers. George Bubb Dodington's early intimacy with the Prince may have been determined as much by his vast wealth as by his advisory skills. Opposition politicians had been competing keenly for Frederick's favours since his arrival in England. One was Lord Essex, an intimate of Pulteney's and Bolingbroke's, who soon renounced his connections when he realized that Frederick would not guarantee him a household post were he dismissed from the King's service—an imminent possibility for all those who courted Frederick's favour and opposed the ministry.[77] James Pelham, Frederick's secretary since 1728, tried to tread the same tightrope but gave up in 1737, voting with the ministry on the parliamentary debate over the Prince's allowance.

By 1734 George Lyttelton had found considerable personal favour with the Prince, partly because of their shared cultural interests. He persuaded Frederick to dismiss Dodington, who was having trouble reconciling his services to the Prince with his loyalty to the court, and to replace him as his political adviser with Chesterfield, who had just been ejected from his ministerial post in the Excise Crisis purge. In 1735 Lyttelton became Frederick's equerry and unofficial secretary, in early 1737 his secretary—a move widely read as a signal for Frederick's open move into opposition.[78] The rivalry between the Cobhamite Patriots and the new Pulteney–Carteret alliance of Patriot Whigs seems to have emerged as early as January 1735 in competing bids for management of Frederick.[79] That October, shortly after Lyttelton had contrived an audience between Pope and Frederick, he wrote to the Prince at length, advising him against the idea of pressing in Parliament for an increase in his allowance from the Civil List and arguing that it would cause 'a universal discontent . . . rendering the family more unpopular than ever' and would play into Jacobite hands as well as alienating potential Tory support. Lyttelton hinted at the ill advice given the Prince on this issue by some designing ministers, by which he may well have meant Pulteney.[80] It was Pulteney who moved the motion for an increased allowance in February 1737 with an eloquent but also offensive speech citing a series of historical precedents for the increased allowance.[81] At this stage Pitt and Lyttelton spoke in favour of the motion but Lyttelton's earlier doubts about its advisability were confirmed by the notable lack of Tory support it received. Wyndham was alone among the Tories in speaking on the Prince's behalf and the motion was defeated, albeit

---

[77] For Essex, see Hervey, *Memoirs*, i. 96–7.   [78] Ibid. iii. 850–1.

[79] *Marchmont Papers*, ii. 67–8.

[80] See *Memoirs and Correspondence of George, Lord Lyttelton*, ed. Robert Phillimore, 2 vols. (1845), i. 74–8. Phillimore claimed that the idea was originally Bolingbroke's and that the ministers Lyttelton alludes to are Jacobites. This seems unlikely. Bolingbroke was always chary of Frederick making any manœuvres that would damage his popularity. He much disapproved of the row over the birth of the Princess Augusta.

[81] Hervey, *Memoirs*, iii. 684–92.

narrowly.[82] During the summer of 1737 relations between father and son rapidly deteriorated; by September, after a much-publicized row over Frederick carrying off his wife Augusta in the pangs of labour from Hampton Court to St James's to give birth to their first child away from parental interference, the point of no return had been reached. George II expelled Frederick and Augusta from St James's, and they went on to set up their separate court, first in Norfolk House then in Leicester House.

A Centre of Union

Chancellor Hardwicke noted that Frederick's move into opposition would prove dangerous to the ministry.

Before this, the Whigs in opposition wanted a head: became liable to the disagreeable imputn of constantly acting with the Jacobites: & had no prospect of ever coming into any share of power, but by reuniting with their old friends. They will now find a head in the Prince, & he being an immediate successor in the Protestant line, will be an irrefragible answer to the reproach of Jacobitism.[83]

By February 1738 Bolingbroke was urging the Prince to take a leading role in uniting the opposition. He would prove 'a centre of union among yourselves, under whose influence men of different characters and different views will be brought to draw better together'.[84] Frederick's appeal to the Tories may well initially have been limited, not least by his refusal in early February 1738 to join in a 'Treaty' with the Tories to support the annual motion for a cherished tenet of Tory (but not Hanoverian) thought, a reduction in the standing army. But the increasing extraparliamentary support for the campaign pressing for war with Spain seemed perceptibly to threaten Walpole's political position, and the summer and autumn of 1738 witnessed revived opposition hopes and a stepped-up campaign which the Patriots centred on the Prince. William Wyndham, who by this stage had overcome some of his earlier doubts about the Prince, played a leading role in advising Frederick and attempting alongside Chesterfield, Lyttelton, and other Patriots of the Cobham circle to forge links with the Tories. *Common Sense* took up where the *Craftsman* had left off in its advocacy of a unified Country opposition. In the three sessions of 1738 Wyndham and Chesterfield made concerted efforts to conciliate the Tories, a campaign which has been described as 'broad-bottom' in the sense that it seemed based on the recognition that an alliance of separate Whig–Tory groupings, rather than an unrealistic expectation of a complete merging of Whig–Tory identity, was a more plausible key to success. Bolingbroke himself

---

[82] For Tory intransigence, see Colley, *In Defiance of Oligarchy*, 221–2.
[83] George Harris, *The Life of Lord Chancellor Hardwicke*, 3 vols. (1847), i. 377–8.
[84] Coxe, *Walpole*, iii. 506.

returned from France in the period July 1738 to April 1739 to play a more active behind-scenes role in the campaign. It was at this stage that he wrote the exhortatory *Idea of a Patriot King*—not such a defeatist or nostalgic work as is sometimes assumed, as I shall argue in Chapter 7.

The Cobhamite Patriots were linked not only in their support for the Prince, their efforts to work with the Tories, and the idealizing mode of political thought which emerges throughout the Patriot poetry described in the second part of this study. Deep suspicion of the machinations of Pulteney and Carteret led to a distinction which they themselves made between 'real Patriots' and 'mock-Patriots' whose only aim was to commandeer the Prince's favours in order to strengthen their own political ambition. The Cobhamite Patriots remained in uneasy alliance with Pulteney and Carteret; but as early as 1737 Chesterfield wrote to Lyttelton that Pulteney, who 'despises me too much to talk about business', would almost certainly 'get as much power and as much money as soon as he can, and on any terms'.[85] In February 1739 'Lord Cobham told Lord Marchmont of a project of Lord Carteret and Mr. Pulteney having been formed to get the Prince of Wales into their hands, by which they might make a property out of him . . . But as soon as the Earl of Chesterfield and Lord Cobham heard of it, they went and prevented it.'[86]

The pressure for war with Spain dominated the parliamentary sessions of 1738. In the heated debate over the Pardo Convention in March the opposition was narrowly defeated by 28 votes. But the staged protest planned by the opposition, the withdrawal or secession from further business, showed the damaging extent of their disunity. Some Tories refused to follow the lead taken by opposition Whigs, and Pulteney subsequently advocated a return by the absentees, claiming that the Tories should take responsibility for approving the secession lest it should damage the Whig party. Pulteney's wish to reunite the 'whole body of the Whigs' revealed his own underlying agenda which by this stage did not include plans for an opposition Whig–Tory coalition. The Cobhamite Patriots' cause was further damaged, irreparably, as Lyttelton surmised, by the death of Sir William Wyndham in June 1740, signalling an end to any hopes of a real alliance with the Tories and leaving the way clear for those 'without any regard to the coalition, or to any material reformation of Government' who intend to 'build a new fabrick on Sir Robert's narrow and rotten foundations'.[87] The death of Wyndham, the one statesman who had enjoyed the trust of both opposition Whigs and many Tories, threw the Tories under the influence of the Jacobite sympathizer Sir Watkins William Wynn. The loss of contact between opposition Whigs and Tories was overtly symbolized in the division which took place over the opposition Whig Samuel Sandys's famous motion of 13 February 1741 to remove Walpole 'from the king's counsels and presence for ever'. The motion failed, partly because some

---

[85] *Marchmont Papers*, ii. 92.   [86] Ibid. ii. 107–8.

[87] Cited in H. T. Dickinson, *Bolingbroke* (1970), 268.

opposition Whigs who thought it unjust refused to lend their support; even more through the refusal of a large group of back-bench Country Tories. Their refusal may have been prompted by both a traditional Tory dislike of challenging the royal prerogative as well as their having 'too much pride to be the tools of the discontented Whigs, and put their hand under the stirrup to mount them into the saddle' to be later 'swept away with the rest of the rubbish'.[88]

The Demise of Patriotism

Walpole's parliamentary majority was narrowed in the May 1741 general election; sufficiently, it was thought, for an agreement between Tories and opposition Whigs acting in concert to bring him down. But Pulteney's lack of enthusiasm for the plan, as Chesterfield suspected, was based on the fact that he and his followers 'reason quite differently, desire to get in a few, by negotiation, and not by victory with numbers'.[89] In the event this proved the case. Later that summer the Cobhamite Patriots' hopes revived with the support of a large body of the Tories hoping for a new broad-bottom war office. It has been argued that Tory support was engineered via Chesterfield's acquisition of a letter written by the Pretender in September 1741, urging the Tories to ally with the Patriot Whigs for their own reasons.[90]

In the new parliamentary session of January 1742 Walpole was finally unable to command a working majority and was forced to resign office. But in the preceding weeks he had been negotiating behind scenes to ensure that were he forced to go, any new administration would keep the Whig party intact. His chief agents in this were Newcastle and Hardwicke on the one hand and Pulteney and Carteret on the other. A large and angry meeting of broad-bottom supporters took place at the Fountain Tavern on 13 February 1742, denouncing Pulteney and his narrow plans. Pulteney defended his conduct by repeatedly claiming that he ultimately intended to bring Tories into the ministry 'but this must be done gradually, and the Party must allow time for it'—a promise which of course proved empty.[91] In the list of the new administration drawn up in March neither Tories nor Cobhamite broad-bottom Patriot Whigs were included. The political confusion surrounding Walpole's fall and the subsequent reconstruction of the ministry, as new evidence suggests, does not present even the patriotism of Lyttelton and the Boy Patriots at this stage in a commendable light. Pulteney's later self-justification for his own desertion of patriotism included the accusation that Lyttelton, Pitt, and

---

[88] Colley, *In Defiance of Oligarchy*, 228; cited in Eveline Cruickshanks, 'The Political Management of Sir Robert Walpole, 1720–42', in Jeremy Black (ed.), *Britain in the Age of Walpole* (1984), 41.   [89] Cited in Hill, *Growth of Parliamentary Parties*, 222.
[90] Cruickshanks, *Political Untouchables*, 27.   [91] *Egmont Diary*, iii. 252.

the Grenvilles had also entered negotiations with the ministry before February 1742. The Ayscough diaries for this period confirm the charge that Lyttelton, acting with Frederick's approval, had negotiated with Walpole before his imminent fall. Walpole's 'Security and Protection' from impeachment were to be guaranteed in return for ministerial places—though the hurried negotiations fell through.[92] Frederick refused Walpole's offer of an increase in his allowance in return for his support in January; he was unambiguous about the fact that Walpole had to go. But after Walpole's fall, Frederick, despite his initial attacks on Pulteney's conduct, agreed on a reconciliation with his father and the new Pulteneyite administration in return for the promised raise of his allowance. Although Pitt and Lyttelton remained in opposition after 1742, they retained an ambiguous position as members of the Prince's household. By 1744 Lyttelton had entered the Whig Pelham administration as Lord of the Treasury, an administration which also in time came to incorporate other oppositional Patriots of 1730s vintage.

The demise of the Patriots' high ideals led to widespread cynicism, and it is often hard to extrapolate an account of the Patriot ideal from this period which is not tainted by a knowledge of subsequent events. From one perspective the conduct of all the Patriot Whigs might seem a more prolonged version of the manœuvres conducted by Townshend and Walpole between 1717 and 1720, when their promise to accommodate the Tories was never more than an illusion barely concealing a Whig-based power struggle governed by 'that old, ridiculous question that even divided the disciples of Christ, who should be greatest?'[93] Yet from another perspective it could be argued that the frequently articulated ethos of a Patriot administration above party, even though it crumbled in 1742, supplied the rationale for Frederick's more thoroughgoing attempts to win Tory support in the programme of government above faction which underpinned his more broad-based Leicester House alliance of the 1747–51 period. The optimistic note of patriotic regeneration which characterized both the Patriot campaign of the late 1730s and Frederick's Leicester House campaign of the late 1740s—each campaign harnessing the idealistic language of Bolingbroke's *Idea of a Patriot King*—finally materialized in the reign of Frederick's son George III. His accession in 1760, welcomed by many Tories for whom the '45 had put paid to any alternative form of political renewal, inaugurated an administration drawn from both Whigs and Tories, an end to the narrowly Whig ministries of the previous forty-six years. This may not have been quite the untroubled fulfilment of Bolingbroke's messianic vision of a time when 'patriotism fills the throne, and faction be banished from the administration', but it came pretty close.[94]

[92] Harris (ed.), *A Leicester House Political Diary*, 385 (6 Jan. 1742); see editor's discussion, 379–80.

[93] *The Old and Modern Whig Revived in the Present Divisions at Court* (1717), 32.

[94] Bolingbroke, *Works*, ii. 438.

3

Cultural Patriotism: Frederick and the Arts

IN 1740 the *Gentleman's Magazine* supplied a readers' guide to the members of the 'Lilliputian Senate' or British Parliament. Prominent among them was the 'Urg Lettyltno' (George Lyttelton). 'He is highly in favour with the Prince Imperial, and all the Virtuosi and Ingenious in the Liberal Arts, particularly in poetry, expect to see the Golden Age revive when he shall come into Court.' The 'Prince Imperial' is, of course, Prince Frederick. 'His court', the writer had reported the previous month, 'tho' small, is reckon'd the most polite and elegant in all *Degulia* [England]; it being composed wholly of Men who have distinguished themselves by their Service in the State, or the Figure they have made in Learning, particularly the liberal Arts. The Prince himself has given some instances of a fine Genius for Poetry and Music.' Two years earlier the *London Magazine*'s rival parliamentary reports had featured Lyttelton under the pseudonym 'Maecenas'.[1]

Was this mere wishful thinking? Was Frederick really an embryonic Augustus who, aided by his budding young Maecenas Lyttelton, would bring about a cultural version of the 'golden age' which Swift in Ireland claimed by 1739 everyone 'in both kingdoms' was expecting from his future reign?[2] Or was this simply a flattering gloss on a situation which, after September 1737, had left Frederick and his Leicester House followers forced into fabricating myths of cultural superiority to compensate for the chilly realities of political proscription from St James's? This chapter will be devoted to unravelling the controversial myth of Frederick as a patron of the arts and letters. The word controversial is used advisedly. By 1737 ministerial critics were accusing Lyttelton of exploiting his proximity to the Prince and his network of literary connections in order to create an opposition propaganda machine by dangling the promise of patronage to hungry writers.[3] All the Patriot poets whose works are to be discussed in the second half of this book—writers such as James Thomson, David Mallet, Richard Glover, Gilbert West, Henry Brooke, George Lillo, William Somervile, and Richard Powney—were associated with Lyttelton's literary circle, linked in their professed admiration for the Prince. This fact has been largely responsible for relegating the Patriot poets to the margins of modern critical scholarship. Not only was their poetry dull and 'patriotic', a poor cousin to the audacious satire of a Swift or a Pope—but

---

[1] *GM* 10 (1740), 229, 100; *London Magazine*, 7 (1738), 237.
[2] Swift–Lyttelton, 5 June 1739 (*The Correspondence of Jonathan Swift*, ed. Harold Williams, 5 vols. (1963), v. 158–9).
[3] *Daily Gazetteer*, 14 Apr. 1737.

worse still, they committed the cardinal sin of royal sycophancy. Goldgar writes that

Lyttelton, who became an influential favourite of Frederick in 1732 and his secretary in 1737, certainly thought of himself as a patron and urged the silly and ineffectual prince to give to men of letters the rewards they could not obtain from Walpole. . . . Some of the poets thus patronised, like Thomson, had been hostile to Walpole well before 'Cobham's Cubs' came into opposition; and others, like Glover, found their meager talents well suited to express the spirit of patriotism which then seemed to pervade the literary world as the most popular of themes.[4]

One of the chief problems here is the need to unpick an intellectual consensus which has, until recently, been both uncomfortable with literary expressions of patriotism and intrinsically sympathetic towards the 'independent' writer outspoken in his attacks on the Establishment. For most modern readers it is not Thomson the Patriot patronized by a prince, but Pope the financially independent satirist who symbolizes the spirit of political opposition—Pope, who always professed his indisposition to kings and courts and his refusal to be bought. Furthermore, our views on the contentious issue of literary patronage are still very much Johnson-shaped—a Johnson whose outspoken letter to the former Patriot Chesterfield in 1755 'proclaim[ed] . . . to the listening world, that patronage should be no more!'[5] Johnson's own account of the Patriot writers under consideration here has done much to shape later critical views. In Volume 3 of the *Lives of the English Poets* he made continual sidesweeps at Frederick and Lyttelton's 'pretences' to patronage and did not disguise his contempt for those such as Thomson whose royal pension 'obliged' him to write on the Prince's behalf. 'Rebellious Samuel Johnson' was Thomas Carlyle's literary hero for an age when patronage was 'wellnigh *necessarily* polluted by sycophancy'.[6] Two classic accounts of the state of letters in the eighteenth century, Alexandre Beljame's *Men of Letters and the English Public in the Eighteenth Century* and A. S. Collins's *Authorship in the Days of Johnson* enshrined both Pope and Johnson as literary heroes; both studies depicted the eighteenth century as a steady advance from the bad old days of literary dependence on royal or aristocratic patronage to the new enlightened age of the liberated author and his 'reading public'.[7]

---

[4] Goldgar, *Walpole and the Wits: The Relation of Politics to Literature, 1722–1742* (Lincoln, Nebr., 1976), 139–40.

[5] Thomas Carlyle, 'Boswell's *Life of Johnson*', *Critical and Miscellaneous Essays: Collected and Republished by Thomas Carlyle*, 5 vols. (1840), iv. 73.

[6] Ibid. 72.

[7] Alexandre Beljame, *Men of Letters and the English Public in the Eighteenth Century*, trans. E. O. Lorimer, ed. B. Dobrée (1st Eng. edn., 1948), 366–81; A. S. Collins, *Authorship in the Days of Johnson* (1927), esp. 123–7, 193–9. See also J. W. Saunders, *The Profession of English Letters* (1964).

There is something odd about finding these views resurfacing in Goldgar's *Walpole and the Wits*, a study dominated by the assertion that most writers were driven into opposition to Walpole by their anger at Walpole's, and George II's, refusal to patronize the arts. Goldgar almost certainly overstates this factor at the expense of some of the more complex political motives which led writers to move into opposition.[8] Nevertheless, he supplies compelling evidence from newspaper attacks as well as famous literary works like Pope's *Dunciad* to show the pervasiveness in opposition writing of images of a new cultural 'dark age' brought about by a Hanoverian dynasty which refused to patronize artists, and by a minister notorious for his contempt for 'wits'. The growing commercialization of the arts in the Grub-Street market-place was reinforced by the pragmatic Sir Bob who 'pays his Workmen on the Nail' for writing pamphlets in his defence without regard to the verdict that posterity would make on his ministry.[9] Opposition writers attacked George and Walpole as antitypes of Augustus and Maecenas.[10] Goldgar's study ought thus logically to be more sympathetic to the preoccupations of a group of opposition writers who could sincerely hope, as did one in praising the Patriot Whig William Somervile in 1735, '*A Georgic Muse awaits* AUGUSTAN *Days,* | *And* Somerviles *will sing, when* FREDERICS *give the Bays*'.[11]

Patriotism and the Arts

Frederick was not a lavish patron of poets. He could not afford to be. His finances were always in a highly precarious position, his expenses far exceeding his limited income—a fact endlessly and publicly acknowledged by opposition motions to increase his allowance from the Civil List. The poets who gravitated towards him (some of them, as we shall see, far too old to benefit from the distant prospect of a reversionary interest) may have had other and less immediately pecuniary aims in praising the Prince for his cultural inclinations. The 'patriotism' of the Patriot poets stemmed not simply from the fact that they supported the 'Patriot opposition' or even that they wrote patriotic poems about war with Spain. At its core lay a strong sense of *cultural* patriotism: an

---

[8] For a corrective view, see J. A. Downie, 'Walpole, "The Poet's Foe"', in Jeremy Black (ed.), *Britain in the Age of Walpole* (1984), 171–88.

[9] Swift, 'On Poetry: A Rapsody', ll. 187–90 (*Poetical Works*, ed. Herbert Davis (Oxford, 1967), 574).

[10] For the pervasiveness of the George/Augustus and Walpole/Maecenas parallel, both affirmative and subversive, see Goldgar, *Walpole and the Wits*, 14–15; Howard D. Weinbrot, 'History, Horace and Augustus Caesar', *ECS* 7 (1974), 391–414. For the complex manipulations of the political and literary aspects of the Augustan myth, see Weinbrot, *Augustus Caesar in 'Augustan' England: The Decline of a Classical Norm* (Princeton, NJ, 1978); Howard Erskine-Hill, *The Augustan Idea in English Literature* (1983).

[11] John Nixon, 'To Mr. William Somervile, Esq; On his Poem called The Chace', preface to Somervile, *The Chace* (1735).

acute anxiety about Britain's role and future as a model of artistic achievement. Both Thomson and Aaron Hill, two of the writers who will feature prominently in this and the following chapters, were, like Pope, filled with gloomy prognostications about the decline of the arts in England, sacrificed to the commercial market-place and that 'vast Temple of *Corruption*, under which this Generation, more than any other, worships the dirty, low-minded insatiable Idol of Self-interest'.[12] Thomson had a habit of quoting from *The Dunciad*'s apocalyptic ending when he claimed that 'a new Gothic Night seems to be approaching, the Great Year the Millenium of Dulness'. 'Happy he! who can comfort himself amidst this general night.'[13] Yet mingled with the gloom was a fierce sense that British culture, rooted in free-born English genius, was still, or at least should be, innately superior to anything that other nations had to offer. As Gerald Newman points out, the most assertive pronouncements of British cultural patriotism (or what he defines as nationalism) were stimulated by the threat of the cultural pre-eminence of absolutist France.[14] Thomson's *Liberty* exclaims 'Oh shame to think! shall BRITONS, in the Field | Unconquer'd still, the *better Laurel* lose?' Shall 'BRITONS . . . | In FINER ARTS, and PUBLIC WORKS, shall *They* | To *Gallia* yield?—yield to a Land that bends, | Deprest, and broke, beneath the Will of *One*?'[15] Yet such rallying-cries were underscored by an unease and uncertainty about the practical means by which a British cultural renaissance might be engendered or sustained. The '*Eternal Patron*, LIBERTY', however inspiring in theory, might in practice prove both insubstantial and evanescent.[16]

This sense of insecurity pervades Aaron Hill's intriguing dramatic opera, *The Muses in Mourning*, almost certainly written in the 1730s.[17] Apollo and the nine Muses preside over a literary version of the Judgement of Paris, asked to choose between the respective literary geniuses of Spain, Italy, France, Holland, and England. The Genius of France claims to be both the leader and arbiter of other nations' tastes: ''Tis my fame, | To lend my lights, and glitter among nations: | To guide their learning, fashions, thought and taste, | And, oft to change, and to be follow'd, ever.' The Genius of England can make no such claims. He bases England's entitlement to Apollo's favour on the fact that she is above all a writing nation with a copious if untrammelled talent: 'All England writes; | Learn'd, and unlearn'd, each sex, all ages, *write*!' But Eng-

---

[12] Thomson–Hill, 23 Aug. 1735 (Thomson, *Letters*, 98).

[13] Thomson–Cranstoun, 7 Aug. 1735; Thomson–Munbee, 27 Oct. 1730 (*Letters*, 95, 76). Thomson uses similar phrases on both occasions concerning the approaching 'Millenium of Dulness'.

[14] Gerald Newman, *The Rise of English Nationalism: A Cultural History, 1740–1830* (1987), *passim*.

[15] Thomson, *Liberty*, v. 441–6 (OET *Liberty*, 139).

[16] Thomson, *Castle of Indolence*, II. xxiii (OET *Liberty*, 205).

[17] *The Muses in Mourning*, in Hill, *Dramatic Works*, 2 vols. (1760), ii. 5–17. No date is given, but the references to 'Will' and 'Bob' and the parallels with Hill's 1736 *Tears of the Muses* point firmly to the 1730s. All quotations from pp. 10–12.

land's latent literary potential remains unfulfilled, still dominated by party-political scribbling; he hopes to see '*Will* [William Pulteney] to treat *Bob* [Robert Walpole], like a brother and friend | . . . And the Muses be married to parliament men'. In confessing England's 'want', the modest Genius of England earns Apollo's approval; yet his appearance and his final plea speak volumes. He is dressed '*like a gentleman-commoner, with a square cap: in one hand a pen in an inkhorn; in the other, a few roll'd sheets of blank paper*' and exclaims, 'O, take these sheets, ye Muses! harmless, yet, [*Presents the blank paper, and pen and ink, on the altar*] | And blank.' The echoes of book I of *The Dunciad* are unmistakable—Tibbald's altar piled with bad writing dedicated to the Goddess Dulness. Yet where Tibbald's invocation ends in conflagration, Hill's Genius of England pleads for new direction and inspiration. Who will guide his pen, and what will be written on the blank sheets?

The same uncertainty underscores Thomson's prophecy of British cultural supremacy in Book V of *Liberty*, 'The Prospect' (1736). Thomson claims that liberty is the only true basis for an enduring national cultural achievement: Corneille, Racine, and Molière would have been 'Superiour' had their talents 'branch'd luxuriant to the Skies, | In BRITAIN planted, by the potent Juice | Of *Freedom* swell'd'. But Thomson's inability to envision a similar renaissance of talent in Britain points to the unspoken conclusion that the arts can flourish only under the kind of encouragement given to them by a strong monarch such as Louis XIV. The 'FINE ARTS and PUBLIC WORKS' of Britain are to be modelled on the recent success of France: '*The Encouragement of These urged from the Example of* France, *tho' under a Despotic Government*'.[18] As Thomson later exclaimed in *The Castle of Indolence*, 'Is there no Patron to protect the Muse, | And fence for her *Parnassus*' barren Soil?'[19] The same conclusion is implicit in Pope's footnote to Book II, l. 314 of *The Dunciad* criticizing Walpole's wasted expenditure on ministerial pamphleteers.

Which shews the Benevolence of One Minister to have expended, for the current dulness of ten years in Britain, double the sum which gained Louis XIV. so much honour, in annual Pensions to Learned men all over Europe. In which, and in a much longer time, not a Pension at Court, nor Preferment in the Church or Universities, of any Consideration, was bestowed on any man distinguished for his Learning separately from Party-merit, or Pamphlet writing.[20]

Writers such as Thomson, Mallet, and Hill, members of the so-called Hillarian circle of the mid-1720s, had long hoped for a reformation of the arts in England under the enlightened patronage of a 'great man' or royal figurehead. What they wanted was not stifling patronage linked to political despotism (Thomson accuses both Augustus and Louis XIV of disguising imperialist

---

[18] *Liberty*, v. 526–9; 'The Contents of Part V' (OET *Liberty*, 141, 126).

[19] *Castle of Indolence*, II. ii (OET *Liberty*, 199). Cf. Thomson's complaints about false patrons who wear 'MAECENAS' Name' in II. xii–xiii.

[20] *Dunciad*, ii. 314 n. (*TE* v. 311–12).

ambitions under the cloak of cultural benevolism) but the authority and support which an eminent public figure might lend to a number of public-spirited projects.[21] As early as 1726 Thomson's idealistic preface to *Winter* had called for 'POETRY, once more, [to] be restored to her ancient Truth, and Purity . . . and POETS, yet, become the Delight and Wonder, of Mankind'. Such a reformation would take place only under the aegis of a Patriot patron 'of equal Power, and Beneficence' who would 'rise on the Wintry World of Letters: One of a genuine, and unbounded, Greatness, and Generosity, of Mind; who, . . . stretching his Views into late Futurity, has the true Interest of Virtue, Learning, and Mankind, intirely, at Heart'.[22] It is not odd then to find Thomson looking to Prince Frederick in 1732 and hoping to see 'the fine arts flourish under a Prince of his so noble equal humane and generous dispositions', or that he chooses Frederick as the royal figurehead in *Liberty* who may preside over Britain's cultural renaissance, 'added give | The Touch, the *Graces* and the *Muses* owe. | For BRITAIN's Glory swells his panting Breast'.[23] It was Aaron Hill who gave the fullest and clearest articulation to these views throughout the 1730s, much inspired by the parallel movements towards a nationalistic reformation of the Italian theatre under the influence of the eminent Italian writer Scipione Maffei, whose own initiative was prompted by the active interest taken in the arts by prominent men such as Cardinal Borromeo in Italy and Richelieu in France.

Aaron Hill and the Reformation of the Arts

Aaron Hill is a fascinating figure whose reputation has unjustly suffered from the excesses of literary enthusiasm which led him into copious correspondence with writers such as Pope and Samuel Richardson. It is only recently that his really enlightened views on a range of important cultural issues such as theatrical training, funding, and musical education are being explored.[24] Hill may have been one of Pope's many thorns in the flesh, and a poet and playwright whose prolific output was only sporadically matched by genuine talent, but he

---

[21] Accounts of the activities of the Hillarian circle in the 1720s are to be found in Dorothy Brewster, *Aaron Hill: Poet, Dramatist, Projector* (New York, 1913), 153–208; Clarence Tracy, *The Artificial Bastard: A Biography of Richard Savage* (Toronto, 1953), 54–79. For the religious strand in their reformist ideas, much influenced by the critic John Dennis, see David B. Morris, *The Religious Sublime* (Lexington, Ky., 1972), and James Sambrook, *James Thomson, 1700–1748: A Life* (Oxford, 1991), 43–4.

[22] OET *Seasons*, 304. Thomson's preface was indebted to the preface to Hill's *The Creation* (1720).

[23] Thomson, *Letters*, 83; *Liberty*, i. 372–3 (OET *Liberty*, 54).

[24] The standard biography is Brewster, *Aaron Hill*. I am currently preparing a new biography. For more recent discussions of various aspects of Hill's work, see Sambrook, *James Thomson*, 38–44, *passim*; Tracy, *The Artificial Bastard*, 54–79; Rosamund McGuinness, 'The *British Apollo* as a Source of Musical Information', *BJECS* 14 (1991), 61–73; Ruth Smith, *Handel's Oratorio Librettos and Eighteenth-Century Thought* (Cambridge, forthcoming).

was a tireless campaigner for the arts. Not the least of his achievements were befriending and supporting Handel, setting up the first theatre journal (the *Prompter*), and offering disinterested patronage and encouragement to a number of writers such as Gay, Mallet, Thomson, and Savage. Hill was not an opposition factotum. Although he was closely associated with opposition circles and in sympathy with their views, especially where the future of the arts was concerned, he maintained a sufficient degree of political detachment to enable him to correspond on gardening with Lady Walpole as well as to address some rather more admonitary letters to her husband.[25] In 1731 Hill prefaced his *Advice to the Poets*, a poem primarily directed at Pope, with a significant 'Epistle Dedicatory to the Few Great Spirits of Great Britain'. Like Thomson, Hill asserts that poetry and drama in England will never flourish unless aided by a 'qualified *Judge* of the *Art*; Great, and Powerful, by his Rank in Life'. Hill was looking over his shoulder to France: Richelieu's encouragement of France's poetry and theatre strengthened both her cultural confidence and her imperialist ambitions. The interweaving of the bays and the laurels stirred the French with 'an ambition of enlarging their Glory; *This* taught them to conceive Themselves superior to the Nations round them'. Enlightened patronage should thus be the patriotic duty of a minister or monarch, a 'noble (and indeed a *National*) Part, of [his] Discharge of the Publick Trust'.[26] In this preface Hill is aiming for nothing less than a National Theatre: a '*tragic academy*' for 'instructing and educating *actors*' (an eighteenth-century version of RADA) as well as a playwrights' school.[27] Hill wanted his academy to be set up by subscription, with a royal fund established to give annual drama prizes to young writers. It was a favourite project of Hill's: one at least partly inspired by the ideas in the preface to Maffei's influential *Teatro Italiano* (1723–5), an essay concerned with reforming the stage, reviving native Italian

---

[25] Hill's political alignments have been subject to some debate. Goldgar, *Walpole and the Wits*, 153, claims for him only a loose alliance with the opposition and evidence of ministerial sympathies in his joint editorship with William Popple of the *Prompter* (1734–6), a paper attacked by the oppositional *Fog's*. Popple was accused of supporting the administration and may have done so, though Frederick gave him a gift of £21 for dedicating to him *The Ladies Revenge* of 1734 (see below, n. 78); even at this stage Frederick was at odds with his parents, so the pro-government nature of the play cannot have been very pronounced. He and Hill seem to have alternated in their editorship of each issue, giving the paper a politically schizophrenic quality. The 14 Feb. 1734/5 issue warmly praised Thomson's *Liberty* for its attacks 'against Corruption'; the previous issue, by Popple, 11 Feb. 1734/5, had attempted to answer the accusation in Budgell's *Bee*, 8 (1735), that 'the *Prompter* would at last turn out to be a ministerial paper'. But Hill was very closely associated with Patriot circles; his *Caesar* (published as *An Enquiry into the Merit of Assassination: with a View to the Character of Caesar*, 1738), edited by Pope and Bolingbroke, was intended as one of the Patriot dramas for the winter season of 1738/9.

[26] Aaron Hill, *Advice to the Poets. A Poem. To which is Prefix'd, An Epistle Dedicatory to the Few Great Spirits of Great Britain* (1731), pp. iv, vii, ix. The positive example of Richelieu in France had previously been cited in the leader article of *Fog's*, 1 Aug. 1730.

[27] Hill–Thomson, 5 Sept. 1735 (*Works of the Late Aaron Hill*, 4 vols. (1753), ii. 128–9). See *Advice to the Poets*, p. xiii, and *Prompter*, 21 Mar. and 4 Apr. 1735.

drama, and improving the quality of acting by proper training in speech and gesture.[28]

In 1730 Hill was angling for the support of both Queen Caroline and Walpole. Caroline had recently extended patronage to Milton's daughter and to Stephen Duck. Hill refers to the by this stage politically loaded precedent of Augustus and Maecenas, coyly alluding to the latter as the 'ROMAN SIR ROBERT', but the preface and accompanying verses sound a minatory rather than a flattering note. 'If we had, in *England*, a *Prime Minister*, I should be glad to hear *Him* ask'd, *why* He thought *Himself* less able, than *Mecaenas*, to find, or produce, such poets.' Unless Walpole does something soon the neglected Muse will 'his Pow'r defie; | And bid his blacken'd Mem'ry *never die*'.[29] Walpole probably greeted Hill's plea and his accompanying letter on the same subject with the amused contempt he usually reserved for idealistic poets. Caroline also failed to respond. Hill takes a more humorous line on Walpole's indifference to the arts in his 'Humble Petition of PEGASUS to the White Horse of H———R' in which the winged Pegasus asks his 'fair *Cuz*' to give him some oats. Since 'S—R R———T's too busy, to mind, what I say', the white horse must 'tell your *owner*, who loves to *aspire*, | He must cherish *our stud*, if he means to *ride higher*'.[30] Frederick may have been the new Hanoverian 'owner'. By 1735 he was certainly the focus for Patriot expectations. When the arts 'do find such patronage in *England*', remarks Hill, 'the manly genius of our nation will exert itself, and carry on, to future times, the honour of that prince, who cherished it'.[31] A more auspicious sign was Frederick's reception of the great reformer Maffei himself during his three-month visit to England in 1736. Maffei was fêted by Oxford and Cambridge alike and hosted by Burlington and Pope; but it was Frederick alone who paid him the honour of addressing him warmly in his native Italian and asking to read his poetry. He liked Maffei's modern Italian translation of the first book of the *Iliad* so much he immediately paid for it to be published.[32]

Hill publicly addressed the Prince on the patronage issue in the dedications to plays such as *Zara* and *Alzira*; he had hoped that Frederick would advance the cause of a 'protected stage' by heading the list of subscribers for his projected tragic academy.[33] In 1737 he also addressed to him an updated version of Spenser's *Tears of the Muses* (1590), a work which had articulated Spenser's own anxieties over the decay of literature and learning under the Burghley

---

[28] Both Hill and Thomson knew Maffei's work: Thomson owned a copy of his *Teatro Italiano*, whose preface contains arguments very similar to Hill's. Hill's *Merope* (1749) was based on Voltaire's translation of Maffei's own *Merope* (1743). See George Dorris, *Paolo Rolli and the Italian Circle in London, 1715–44* (The Hague, 1967), 232–5; J. G. Robertson, *Studies in the Genesis of Romantic Theory in the 18th Century* (Cambridge, 1923), 152–61.

[29] *Advice to the Poets*, pp. xi, v, 38. See Hill–Walpole, 12 Mar. 1731 (*Works*, i. 50–1).

[30] Hill, *Works*, iv. 149–50.

[31] Hill–[?], undated letter (*Works*, ii. 120–1).

[32] See Dorris, *Paolo Rolli*, 232–3.

[33] Hill, *Dramatic Works*, ii. 21–3.

administration and which married both praise and pleading in its portrait of an Elizabeth who 'with rich bountie and deare cherishment, | Support[s] the praise of noble Poësie'.[34] Hill depicts Frederick as 'Prince Germanicus' (the Roman republican hero whose popularity made him odious to his adoptive father the emperor Tiberius), one 'whose Heart | Inly confess'd the Pow'r of cherish'd Art'. This is by no means an unqualified panegyric on the Prince, as Hill implies by his rather nervous defence of his allegorical satirical procedures in the 'Advertisement to the Reader'. Germanicus, the 'sparkling PRINCE', is not as effectual as he might be in his support for the arts: too preoccupied, hints Hill, with party politics. After the Muses address to him, one by one, their complaints about artistic decline in England, he advises them to go underground and disguise themselves as politicians in the 'Nine *Cornish* Boroughs' (the hotly contested seats controlled by Frederick's political patronage in the Duchy of Cornwall) until the times are more propitious. When the Prince wakes from his allegorical dream-vision he finds himself alone in an empty street, when 'ev'ry empty *Muse* was lost in Air'.[35]

The Society for the Encouragement of Learning

Hill's *Tears of the Muses* may have been addressed to Frederick but it was also dedicated to the 'Right Honourable, and Publick-spirited' members of the newly formed Society for the Encouragement of Learning. The Society's title and founding charter of 1735 anticipate the terms of the subscription-based 'oeconomical societies' which flourished under George III's reign with the help of royal premiums. It aimed ambitiously to 'supply the want of a regular and publick encouragement of learning; . . . to institute a republick of letters, for the promoting of arts and sciences, by the necessary means of profit, as well as by the nobler motives of praise and emulation'.[36] In this it sounds very like William Shipley's proposals in 1754 for the seminal Society of Arts where 'a body of generous and public-spirited persons' should 'form themselves into a body by the name of a Society for the Encouragement of Arts, Sciences and Manufactures' and be given a charter of incorporation and royal patronage.[37] The Society for the Encouragement of Learning, despite its rather grandiose title and its ambitious charter, was in reality a modest philanthropic venture to aid deserving authors by publishing their works without requiring them to sell

[34] Spenser, *Minor Poems*, ed. Charles Osgood, 2 vols. (Baltimore, Md., 1947), ii. 79.

[35] Hill, *The Tears of the Muses: in a Conference between Prince Germanicus and a Male-Content Party* (1737, 2nd edn. 1738), 22, 38, 40.

[36] The Society's records are contained in 9 vols. (BL Add. MSS 6184–6192). The citations are taken from Clayton Atto, 'The Society for the Encouragement of Learning', *Library*, 4th ser. 19 (1938–9), 263–88.

[37] D. G. C. Allan, 'The Society of Arts and Government, 1754–1800: Public Encouragement of Arts, Manufactures, and Commerce in Eighteenth-Century England', *ECS* 7 (1974), 434–52. Shipley's quotations are on p. 438.

their copyright to the booksellers. The project was doomed to failure since its publications were deliberately sabotaged by the bookselling mafiosi, and the enthusiasm of its founder members dwindled over the first four years after its original meeting in the Rainbow Coffee House in May 1736. It lasted for only thirteen years. But its real interest lies less in its failure than in its potential—or at least the spirit which prompted its inception. James Thomson was one of the members of the original committee; he chose for its symbol William Kent's patriotic 'Device and Motto', engraved by George Vertue, which bore the optimistic Latin motto 'RESURGES',

being the figure of Knowledge in a declining appearance, with that of Britannia leaning on a Shield, wheron are the crosses of St. George and Saint Andrew. Britannia is in an attitude of raising Knowledge from the Ground, behind, is the view of an ancient Temple, or ye Temple of Art. and through the openings of the pillars, of the Portico is a rysing Sun, in the center is Seen, in a perspective view and at a distance a Columna Rostrata, on wch rests Britannia's Spear.[38]

In 1736 the list of founder members, although clearly not dictated solely by political allegiance and including a number of prominent antiquarians such as Richard Mead, seems to have had a distinctively oppositional cast.[39] Although Thomson did not receive a pension from Frederick until 1737, he had already openly shown his commitment to the Patriots in the dedication to *Liberty* of 1735–6. Other members were Charles Seymour, William Wyndham's father-in-law; the Tory Edward Harley; Hugh Smithson, the future earl of Northumberland and a close friend and gentleman of the bedchamber to Frederick; the radical opposition Whig MP William Talbot, Chancellor Talbot's son, who had gone into open opposition on gaining his seat at Glamorgan in 1734; Lord Chesterfield; Benjamin Martyn, a close friend of Thomson's and the author of *Timoleon* (1731), one of the first Patriot dramas; William Paterson, another of Thomson's friends and the future author of *Arminius* (1740), one of the opposition plays banned by the Stage Licensing Act; the opposition satirist Paul Whitehead, later arrested for his *Manners* of 1739 but who had already got into trouble for his anti-Walpole *The State Dunces* of 1733; Samuel Strutt, a radical free-thinker who had already contributed to the *Craftsman*; and George Lewis Scott, a close friend of Bolingbroke's, better known for his role as George III's preceptor and for his friendship with Bute. It is not surprising that the staunch Court Whig Richard Bentley refused to allow his *Manilius* to head the Society's publications list.[40]

---

[38] Atto, 'The Society for the Encouragement of Learning', 268. Cf. Thomson, *Liberty*, iv. 501–3. For the Society's failure, see James Ralph, *The Case of Authors by Profession or Trade* (1758), 59–60.

[39] The list of members is in John Nichols, *Literary Anecdotes of the Eighteenth Century*, 9 vols. (1812–15), ii. 90–7.

[40] Harley and Bentley were sworn enemies. But it was probably Strutt's and Whitehead's reputation for atheism that affronted Bentley. Both were reputedly members of the Hellfire Club. Strutt

We do not know whether Frederick was ever asked, either formally or informally, to lend his support and patronage to the Society, but Hill's linkage of his name and the Society's in the dedication to the *Tears of the Muses* suggests its likelihood. D. G. C. Allan and, more recently, Linda Colley have described the social and political context for the new voluntary associations which arose in the 1750s for the attainment of national aims: societies whose initiative came not from the Crown or the government but from the impetus of patriotically spirited Englishmen preoccupied with national trade and national culture.[41] Colley suggests that these enterprises were one of the most striking examples of active patriotism, the social range of their philanthropic subscribers a standing rebuke to ministerial oligarchy. The drawing-master William Shipley's Society of Arts, founded in 1754, encouraged not only commercial and scientific enterprises, but also the creative arts, awarding annual prizes to promising young artists and sculptors. Royal patronage was eminently desirable, as a way of influencing others to lend their support. This was, in essence, the ethos behind Aaron Hill's own enlightened plans for a National Academy of Drama outlined in his 1731 'Epistle Dedicatory' which had been addressed, significantly, to 'the Few Great Spirits of *Great Britain*'. It was to be established by public subscription and with a '*Royal Fund* for its Encouragement . . by Annual Allotment of Rewards to the Authors of a stated Number of *Prize Tragedies*, in gradual Proportion to their Merit, or Success'.[42]

George II took no interest in the creative side of such enterprises. But his son Frederick did, and, had he not lived most of his life under the shadow of massive debts, would almost certainly have contributed more than moral support to them. When the Irish Patriot Samuel Madden (whose own Patriot drama of 1729, *Themistocles, the Lover of His Country*, was dedicated to Frederick) drew up his plans for a Dublin Society for Promoting Husbandry and other Useful Arts in 1731, he wrote to Frederick requesting an association. That year Madden wrote the dedicatory preface to his extraordinary and subversive utopian satire, *Memoirs of the Twentieth Century*, published on 24 March 1733 but suppressed almost immediately. This futuristic vision of England and Europe conveyed through letters dated from the 1990s, functions, like *Gulliver's Travels*, as a satiric mirror for Walpole's Britain as well as describing some genuinely modern projects at work. Madden's long dedication to Frederick is sincere. Frederick is praised for his learning and enterprise,

was the 'leader and oracle' of a sect of Cambridge atheists. In 1739 Bentley stripped one of Strutt's followers of his degree. See J. H. Monk, *The Life of Richard Bentley DD*, 2 vols. (2nd edn. 1883), ii. 391–5.

[41] See D. G. C. Allan, 'The Society of Arts and Government', and his *William Shipley: Founder of the Royal Society* (1968); D. G. C. Allan and John L. Abbott (eds.), '*The Virtuoso Tribe of Arts and Sciences': Studies in the Eighteenth-Century Work and Membership of the London Society of Arts* (Athens, Ga., 1992). Linda Colley, *Britons: Forging the Nation, 1707–1837* (New Haven, Conn., 1992), 90–6.

[42] Hill, *Advice to the Poets*, p. xiii.

and called on 'to encourage the Improvement of the rising Arts, and patronize the Learned Sciences, till they gain new Life among us, and grow in proportion cultivated as our Manufactures, and extended as our Trade'.[43] In 1757, many years later, when Madden sent an encouraging letter to William Shipley about his own plans for an English version of the Dublin Society, he stressed the value of attaining royal patronage from Frederick's widow Augusta. He told Shipley that he had once submitted a plan for giving premiums in England to his 'dear and ever honoured Master the late Prince of Wales, but I am sorry to say, though the Prince approved it and my zeal, he told me his finances would not bear such a burden'.[44] This, as we shall see, was all too true. But Leicester House was the seed-bed for Shipley's Society of Arts: the zeal for artistic and scientific patronage developed during Frederick's own lifetime lived on after his death. Stephen Hales, a close friend of George Lewis Scott and Lord Bute, Chaplain to the Princess Dowager and a veteran scientist and botanist, became the vice-president of the infant Society of Arts when officers were first chosen in 1755. Some of the founder members of the Society for the Encouragement of Learning—notably Richard Mead—were later involved in setting up classes for painting and drawing which came under the aegis of the newly formed Royal Society of Arts. George Vertue recorded that in the late 1740s Frederick himself 'spoke much concerning the settlement of an Accademy for drawing and painting'. He discussed in detail with Vertue his plans for establishing separate schools for technical and creative drawing in London, Oxford, and Cambridge, as well as many more junior provincial drawing schools under the supervision of 'An Accademy settled by Publick Authority'.[45] The talented group of artists associated with the St Martin's Lane Academy, with whom Frederick was closely involved, often discussed plans for a Royal Academy when they met at Slaughter's Coffee House.[46] Had Frederick lived longer the Royal Academy might have been founded earlier and along different lines.

[43] Samuel Madden, *Memoirs of the Twentieth Century, Being Original Letters of State, under George the Sixth: Relating to the most Important Events in Great-Britain and Europe*, 6 vols. (only 1 published) (1733), p. ix. The edition was suppressed on the day of publication, and all copies unsold nine days later were withdrawn and destroyed.

[44] Cited in Allan, *William Shipley*, 16–17; 'Society of Arts and Government', 439. For Madden's *Themistocles*, see John Loftis, *The Politics of Drama in Augustan England* (Oxford, 1963), 107–8.

[45] *The Notebooks of George Vertue*, 7 vols., Walpole Society Annual Volumes 18, 20, 22, 24, 26, 29, 30 (numbered *Vertue Notebooks* i–vi; vol. 29—the index vol.— is unnumbered) (Oxford and London, 1930–55) i. 10.

[46] For Frederick's association with this group, which included Roubiliac, Hayman, Hogarth, Gravelot, Moser, Henry Fielding, and David Garrick, see Mark Girouard, 'Coffee at Slaughters: English Art and the Rococo—I', *Country Life*, 139 (1966), 58–61. Shipley also had many associations with Frederick's circle. See Allan and Abbott (eds.), *'The Virtuoso Tribe of Arts and Sciences'*, 93–5. William Chambers, whose sketches for the Society of Arts's building included sculptors' pavilions and art galleries, in 1751 prepared several designs for a mausoleum for Frederick.

Frederick and the Arts

We are racing ahead here. But it should already be clear that the Patriots were not labouring under a misapprehension when, in the 1730s, they focused on Frederick as a potential figurehead for a patriotic cultural regeneration. Regrettably no one has as yet written a scholarly biography of Frederick—a task that awaits its historian.[47] Opinions of the Prince have always fluctuated wildly; even one historian, Linda Colley, could claim in one place that Frederick was 'an empty space', 'vacillating in his politics and his resolution, limited in his intelligence', and in another that Frederick, 'so often dismissed as just another puny princeling', was 'one of the great might-have-beens of British history'.[48] Judged on his political track record alone, most historians would shade towards the former view, one endorsed by the recent publication of Francis Ayscough's diaries for the period 1742–3.[49] Most princes of Wales from the long-living German line manage to blot their copy-books at some stage during their long wait in the wings occupying an ill-defined public and political role. Frederick's support for a Patriot opposition whose chief tenet was the formation of a non-party administration says much in his favour; the Leicester House alliance of the period 1747–51 certainly anticipates the mood of optimism which enabled the long-awaited reconciliation between Tories and the Hanoverians at George III's accession in 1760. However, the Ayscough diaries suggest that Frederick was often pushed along by forces over which he had little control. In the murky confusion surrounding Walpole's fall in 1742 he was clearly bargaining hard for ministerial accommodations for his own favourites, and vacillated between opposing and supporting the new Pulteney–Carteret administration. In 1749 Frederick may have identified himself once again, as he had ten years previously, with Bolingbroke's newly published description of the morally unimpeachable Patriot King; but this rather glosses over his activities in the period 1742–6. Frederick's support for a broad-bottom Patriot administration was by no means unwavering.

But Frederick's political skills are not the issue under discussion in this chapter. In cultural terms there is no doubt whatsoever that his reputation as a

[47] Most more recent studies belong to the popular 'royal biography' genre, based largely on secondary sources such as Lord Hervey, Horace Walpole, and Lord Egmont. See Captain Henry Curtis, *A Forgotten Prince of Wales* (1912); Sir George Young, *Poor Fred: The People's Prince* (1937); Morris Marples, *Poor Fred and the Butcher* (1970); John Walters, *The Royal Griffin* (1972). Averyl Edwards, *Frederick Louis, Prince of Wales 1707–1751* (1947), is probably the best, esp. its documentation of Frederick and the arts. A more recent short balanced appraisal is Betty Kemp, 'Frederick Prince of Wales', in A. Natan (ed.), *The Silver Renaissance* (1961), 38–56.

[48] Colley, *In Defiance of Oligarchy: The Tory Party 1714–60* (Cambridge, 1982), 222; *Britons*, 206. This apparent inconsistency reflects, however, the discovery in recent years of new material which places Frederick in a better light than many former accounts.

[49] Robert Harris (ed.), *A Leicester House Political Diary 1742–3*, Camden Miscellany, 4th ser. 44 (1992), 373–408.

pretentious dunderhead of 'limited intelligence' is a complete fiction: a fiction widely promoted by the malicious testimonials of his critics and enemies such as Lord Hervey, Horace Walpole, and the pseudonymous 'Parson Etoffe'.[50] It was Henry Etough's damning *Free and Impartial Reflexions* (written *c.*1751, published 1862–3) which did most to confirm the myth that Frederick's 'professions of esteem' for artists and writers were all 'mere pretence and a false shew' and that his 'whole mein and manner indicated an absence of every valuable intellectual endowment'. 'He had no patience, taste or capacity for the improvement and entertainment resulting from the ardours of the studious and impartial searchers for truth.' 'So unfixed were his thoughts, so unexercisd his mental powers', claimed Etough, that he only ever bothered to read the first and last pages of any book presented to him. Etough, however, had no personal knowledge of the Prince; his poor reputation among his contemporaries as a 'pimping, tale-bearing dissenting preacher', one of Walpole's spies and scandal-mongers, suggests that his account was likely to be anything but impartial.[51]

As many recent historians working in the area of eighteenth-century art history, theatre, opera, and Italian scholarship have shown, Frederick was an exceptionally cultured Prince of Wales: a view easy to recover from many contemporary accounts such as the notebooks of his great friend and admirer, the engraver George Vertue, and even the impartial John Perceval, Lord Egmont. Egmont was taken aback to find Frederick quoting Longinus and Boileau in a conversation he had with him in 1736 over Tillotson and Clarke's sermons: 'I was extremely pleased to find the Prince had read so much, and had so good a memory.'[52] A prince who did not bother with reading books would scarcely have written to his children, 'I have allways wished you would come to like reading, it is only by that one forms ones-Self'.[53] George Vertue, walking with him through the King's Gallery at Hampton Court, observed his use of 'proppr & significant Termes & expressions which is a plain evidence of his application to knowledge & skill in these historys & works of eminent Masters—and their merit to be thoroughly acquainted with them. a strong memory whilst thus engaged.' Frederick was 'to Arts and Sciences a great Lover and admirer. had a taste for the belles Letters and a lover of paintings and works of fine taste.'[54] Kimerly Rorschach's recent Yale doctoral dissertation on

---

[50] The most widely read is Hervey's *Memoirs* which makes extended comparisons between Frederick and Nero and ridicules Frederick's intellectual and artistic pursuits as well as his popularity with his future subjects. It is odd how many later accounts reflect Hervey's version of events and echo his patrician sneer.

[51] 'Parson Etoffe', *Free and Impartial Reflexions on the Character, Life and Death of Frederick Prince of Wales*, repr. in *Miscellanies of the Philobiblon Society*, vii/9 (1862–3), 2, 70–1. Henry Etough was rector of Therfield, Herts. He was reputed to have officiated at the marriage ceremony between Walpole and his former mistress Maria Skerrett. Thomas Gray satirized him in his *Tophet* (1749). See Nichols, *Literary Anecdotes*, viii. 262–3; *The Poems of Gray, Collins and Goldsmith*, ed. Roger Lonsdale (2nd edn. 1976), 100–3.

[52] *Egmont Diary*, ii. 245.   [53] Undated letter, cited in Edwards, *Frederick Louis*, 164.

[54] *Vertue Notebooks*, i. 10–11; v. 156.

Frederick's patronage of the visual arts has shown just how extensive and independent his tastes were.[55] As Oliver Millar long since noted, Frederick was the most important and intelligent royal collector between Charles I and George IV.[56] He modelled his own collection on the tastes of his famous predecessor Charles I and attempted to recover some of his breathtaking collection of Rembrandts, Titians, and Mantegnas which had been sold off during Cromwell's Protectorate.[57] He was also a notable patron of new artists in the French rococo style such as Philip Mercier and Charles Phillips, whose paintings of Frederick and his family have a lightness of touch and an informal pastoral quality absent from the stolid heroic portraiture of the Kneller school commissioned by his less enterprising parents. One of the most famous portraits of Frederick is the 1735 Jacopo Amigoni painting depicting Frederick holding in his right hand a copy of Pope's *Homer* and pointing with his left to two flying putti hovering in the background, representing the arts and sciences—a signal indication that Frederick was anxious to present himself publicly as patron of the arts.[58] He patronized a wide variety of artists and craftsmen in different media who were commissioned in projects ranging from William Kent's expensively beautiful royal barge through to silver work and picture frames, works of art in themselves, to large-scale building projects such as the redesigning of Kew, Norfolk House, and Cliveden.[59]

Kent assisted him in redesigning Kew Gardens: Frederick's keen interest in botany and exotic plants formed the basis for the gardens which flourished under his widow Augusta's directions.[60] He converted part of the top storey of Kew House into a planetarium and commissioned the popular astronomer and natural philosopher J. T. Desaguliers to give a series of lectures on astronomy for the members of his household in 1737.[61] Frederick's love for music is captured in Philip Mercier's charming 1733 painting, *The Music Party*, depicting the Prince and his sisters in rehearsal for a concert. We know from Hervey's scornful accounts that Frederick wrote songs and accompanied himself on the

[55] Kimerly Rorschach, 'Frederick, Prince of Wales (1707–51) as a Patron of the Visual Arts: Princely Patriotism and Political Propaganda' (Yale Ph.D. thesis, 1985). This contains a full list of articles and studies on various aspects of Frederick's artistic patronage. A good short account is Stephen Jones, *Frederick, Prince of Wales and His Circle* (Sudbury, Suffolk,1981). See also Christopher Lloyd, *The Queen's Pictures: Royal Collectors through the Centuries* (1991), 117–42.

[56] Oliver Millar, *Tudor, Stuart and Early Georgian Pictures in the Royal Collection*, 2 vols. (1963), i. 28.

[57] He commissioned Vertue to catalogue these in *A Catalogue and Description of Pictures, Limnings, Statues, Bronzes, Medals and other Curiosities*, pref. by Horace Walpole (1757).

[58] Millar, *Tudor, Stuart and Early Georgian Pictures*, no. 256 (i. 175–6), plate 198. The picture was commissioned for George Dodington.

[59] See esp. Michael Wilson, *William Kent: Architect, Designer, Painter, Gardener, 1685–1748* (1984), 127–5, 161–2.

[60] Ronald King, *Royal Kew* (1985), 53–4; see also *The Political Journal of George Bubb Dodington*, ed. J. Carswell and L. A. Drake (Oxford, 1965), 59. Dodington did not share Frederick's enthusiasms.

[61] *Carlisle MSS*, 191.

cello, holding late-night public concerts for his informal audiences in the courtyards of Kensington.[62] His patronage of the Opera of Nobility between 1733 and 1737 against the rival Handelian Royal Opera Company patronized by George and Caroline gave birth to the Tweedledum–Tweedledee rhyme and Hervey's allegation that he was bent on ruining Handel to vex his parents. As Carole Taylor and others have pointed out, Frederick's reputed slight of Handel is not based on the evidence supplied by his account books in the Duchy of Cornwall Office.[63] Frederick did indeed patronize the Opera of Nobility and its famous leading singer the castrato Farinelli: on Christmas Day 1735 his household hosted a dress rehearsal, with full audience, of the Opera of Nobility's *Arianna*. But he was also an enthusiastic attender and patron of Handel's oratorios. In 1736 Handel's superb *Atalanta* was commissioned for Frederick's marriage to Augusta. Several of Handel's librettos, notably Newburgh Hamilton's *Samson* of 1741, dedicated to Frederick, were themselves the musical analogies to the Patriot King drama of the same period.[64]

As we have seen, Frederick spoke fluent Italian to Scipione Maffei on his visit to England in 1736. Maffei noted that he was 'expert in our language, in which his teacher was the celebrated Rolli'.[65] Paolo Rolli, one of the leading members of London's Italian circle during the 1720s and 1730s, was also an Italian tutor to other members of the royal family. But it was Frederick who took an especial interest in Italian literature, especially Tasso and Ariosto. He also gave Rolli £100 in 1734 to enable him to publish in full his Italian translation of *Paradise Lost*—the first ever. Rolli's important prefatory life of Milton was a pioneering work of critical appreciation which did much to spread Milton's popularity in Italy. The work rapidly gained a European reputation; Rolli's account of the 'Questo Clementissimi Prince di Vallia' in the fulsome dedicatory preface must have established Frederick's reputation as a patron of the arts in the drawing-rooms of Europe.[66] Frederick's own literary efforts have not survived in any extensive form, though we know that he wrote pastoral poetry in French to his wife under her pseudonym 'Sylvia'. He was almost certainly, however, the author or co-author of a rather less innocent form of literary fiction, the satirical *Histoire du Prince Titi* of 1736 (twice translated into English that year) which contained a flagrant attack on his parents.[67]

---

[62] Millar, *Tudor, Stuart and Early Georgian Pictures*, no. 522 (i. 174–5), plate 184; Hervey, *Memoirs*, i. 309–10.

[63] For Hervey's version, see his *Memoirs*, i. 273–4; Carole Taylor, 'Handel and Frederick, Prince of Wales', *Musical Times*, 125 (1984), 89–92; Dorris, *Paolo Rolli*, 114–19.

[64] Smith, *Handel's Oratorio Librettos and Eighteenth-Century Thought*.

[65] Dorris, *Paolo Rolli*, 332.   [66] Ibid. 149–50.

[67] Frederick's French poems repr. in John Heneage Jesse, *Memoirs of the Court of England from 1688 to the Death of George the Second*, 3 vols. (1843), iii. 149–52. The *Histoire du Prince Titi*, *A. R.* is sometimes attributed to a minor French author, Themiseul de Saint-Hyacinthe, but the journalist James Ralph (Frederick's subsequent publicist) may have had a hand in it. (See Edwards, *Frederick Louis*, 158–9.) Frederick was almost certainly either author or co-author. Its interest lies less in its caricature of George II as Ginguet (shabby, sour), and Caroline as Tripasse,

His association with a long series of theatrical and musical entertainments at Leicester House probably places his literary interests in a better light. Under Lyttelton's guidance he became interested in the careers of two of the most famous actors of the day, James Quin and David Garrick. It was Quin who was employed to give speech-training to the future George III. All Frederick's children were encouraged to take speaking parts in Leicester House performances of plays such as Rowe's *Lady Jane Grey* and Addison's *Cato*. Frederick almost certainly wrote the Prologue for the performance of *Cato* in which his son George uttered the memorable claim to Patriot kingship which his German-born father could never fully make—'A boy in *England* born, in England bred'.[68]

Perhaps the most revealing sign of Frederick's cultural inclinations lay in his choice of friends, advisers, and household staff. In 1729 he took with him to England the artist Philip Mercier, who became both his principal painter as well as his librarian, responsible for purchasing books for his library. George Bubb Dodington was one of Frederick's early political advisers, always treading the tightrope between St James's and Leicester House and sometimes falling off midway. Dodington's vast wealth undoubtedly proved useful to the impecunious prince; however, he was also one of the most notable artistic patrons of his day, whatever Pope may have said about him as the vulgar 'Bufo'.[69] In 1734 Dodington was replaced by Lord Chesterfield, a leading opposition politician but also the age's most famous arbiter of literary taste. George Lyttelton was, as Pope noted, 'the Man, so near | His Prince, that writes in Verse, and has his Ear'.[70] Although Smollett later caricatured Lyttelton as the skinny and naïve 'Sir Gosling Scragg', easy touch for devious Grub-Street indigents, Lyttelton was a genuinely committed patron of poets and a competent albeit unoriginal writer himself.[71] He was undoubtedly in large measure responsible for steering authors in Frederick's direction, although it is wrong to assume, as does his biographer Rose Mary Davis, that 'he was decidedly the intellectual superior of the rather ineffectual Prince'.[72] Even before he got to know Lyttelton in 1732 Frederick had shown ample evidence of his independent artistic tastes. Lyttelton had been Frederick's equerry since 1733;

alluding to her stoutness, than in its account of the king's efforts to exclude his heir from the title. The people subsequently rise up in a successful rebellion to place the prince on the throne. There are close parallels with the fairy-tale atmosphere of the Jacobite 'Persian Letter' printed in *Mist's*, 24 Aug. 1728, where the popular prince is held, victimized by an oppressive and evil king. In the winter season 1736/7 Fielding's Little Theatre in the Haymarket advertised 'a new Farce of two Acts, call'd THE. KING AND TITI; or, The MEDLARS'.

[68] The performance took place in 1749. See Edwards, *Frederick Louis*, 161–2.

[69] See Pope, *Ep. Arbuthnot*, ll. 230–50 (*TE* iv. 113–14).

[70] Pope, *Ep. Satires*, i. 45–6 (*TE* iv. 301).

[71] Tobias Smollett, *Peregrine Pickle* (1751), ch. 102 (ed. J. L. Clifford, rev. P.-G. Boucé (Oxford, 1983), 658–9).

[72] Rose Mary Davis, *The Good Lord Lyttelton* (Bethlehem, Pa., 1939), 48. This study supplies the fullest account so far of Lyttelton and Frederick's literary circle.

on his elevation to the role of secretary in 1737, replacing James Pelham, his former post was given to the young James Hammond, a lyrical love-poet patronized by Chesterfield and a member of the Stowe circle who died there in 1741.[73] In May 1742 David Mallet was appointed to the post of Frederick's under-secretary.[74] By that time the cultural ambience of Frederick's court was well known, as we can see from the opening citation from the *Gentleman's Magazine*. It received its best advertisement from the writers passing freely through its doors, including Thomson, Pope (albeit rarely), Bolingbroke, Mallet, Chesterfield, and Glover. In 1739, a tailor from Halesowen imagined that he had caught sight of 'the Prince of Wales and all his nobles walking by the river's side'.[75] The 'nobles' accompanying Frederick in the grounds of Richmond Park were none other than Thomson and Mallet. All this was in marked contrast to the 'alternative court' set up by Frederick's father during his own brief period in opposition between 1717 and 1720. Even as a young man, George II was no patron of the arts. His rival court, as Ragnild Hatton notes, 'made a sorry and dull impression and could in no way compete with that which George I kept up'.[76]

But of course the moot question raised by literary historians is whether, for all his professed esteem for poets, Frederick matched his words with his deeds. Rose Mary Davis points out that during the period of his connection with Frederick, Lyttelton's efforts brought material reward only to Thomson, West, and Mallet.[77] There is no proper record of Frederick's patronage of poets. His Household Accounts in the Duchy of Cornwall Office, while ample in their documentary evidence for sums paid out on the musical and visual arts, are notably thin on the literary side; even Glover is mentioned primarily in his role alongside John Barnard in raising a loan for Frederick on the Cornish stannaries.[78] Frederick reputedly gave Glover 'a complete set of all classics elegantly bound'; in 1843 John Jesse claimed that when Glover was 'in embarrassed circumstances he sent him a present of 500 l'.[79] In the latter part of 1737 Frederick, under Lyttelton's guidance, rewarded Thomson's overtly loyal poems, *Liberty* and the *Ode to His Royal Highness*, with a pension of £100 per annum after he had lost his sinecure as the Chancellor's Secretary of Briefs following Charles Talbot's death earlier that year.[80] After 1742 David

[73] Johnson, *Lives of the Poets*, ii. 312–16.

[74] Reported in *GM* 12 (1742), 275.

[75] Johnson, *Lives of the Poets*, iii. 291 n.

[76] Ragnild Hatton, *George I, Elector and King* (1978), 209.

[77] Davis, *The Good Lord Lyttelton*, 58.

[78] See Duchy of Cornwall Office, Bound MSS, Household Accounts of Frederick Louis, Prince of Wales, 30 vols. (1728–49), xii. 574–7. The accounts reveal other one-off gifts, including one to William Popple for dedicating to him *The Ladies Revenge* (gift made Dec. 1733) and one to Lewis Theobald for his edn. of Shakespeare. See iv. 139.

[79] Jesse, *Memoirs of the Court of England*, iii. 148.

[80] For Frederick's patronage of Thomson, see Sambrook, *James Thomson*, 168–71.

Mallet received an annual salary of £200.[81] James Sambrook claims that Frederick also bestowed a pension or place on the Patriot dramatist Henry Brooke.[82] Frederick had apparently at one time considered Gilbert West for the appointment of governor to Prince George, a post which was in the event given to Lyttelton's former tutor Ayscough. But we know that he gave an annual pension of £100 to West in 1743.[83] The documentary evidence for this in Ayscough's diaries does nothing to dispel the notion that Frederick was a reluctant patron of poets. On 9 January 1743 Ayscough records:

With the Prince—who settled a Pension on G.W. [Gilbert West] of 100 per ann.—but much out of humour about it—bid me tell Lyttelton that there must be an end to these things—That he had already put *M.* [Mallet] upon him, and now another—He never designed it as a Pension, but only a gift of £100—They called him stingy—He did not know what they might call him—bid me look into his Cash—but one Salisbury Bill of £20 said he was poor—He paid £20,000 a year towards his debts—10000 Interest and 10400 Pensions and Bounties—The list of Chaplains to be reduced no more to be added till they were brought to 36.[84]

Ayscough clearly caught Frederick on a bad day when he had been going through his account books and discovering just how empty his coffers were. There are two points which emerge from his diary entry. The first is Frederick's increasingly dire financial situation. Although poor management may have been partly responsible, Frederick's cultural tastes and ambitions, which far outstripped his limited finances, cannot have helped. It is remarkable that he achieved as much in the way of artistic patronage as he did. As A. N. Newman has demonstrated, Frederick's discontent over his allowance from the Civil List was not merely a political ploy but rooted in a genuine financial difficulty.[85] While single and living in St James's he had an allowance of £25,000 from his father; this was increased on his marriage to Augusta in 1736 to £50,000, but it still depended on his father's pleasure—and was only half the sum which his father had enjoyed as Prince of Wales, a father who had no

[81] In Apr. 1748 Thomson wrote to William Paterson that he had been 'struck off from a certain hundred Pounds a Year which you know I had. West, Mallet and I were all routed in one day' (*Letters*, 195). Frederick and Lyttelton had been on opposing political sides since Frederick's move back into opposition in 1746. The termination of the pensions was almost certainly prompted by the row between Lyttelton and Frederick in the 1747 election when Lyttelton was re-elected for Okehampton; the Prince wanted to nominate one of his servants for the seat (see Romney Sedgwick, *The History of Parliament: The House of Commons 1715–1754*, 2 vols. (1970), i. 228). Thomson's letter gave rise to the misunderstanding that Mallet may have had a 'pension' of £100 like Thomson and West, but the ref. probably alludes to the loss of Mallet's salary as under-secretary.

[82] Sambrook, *James Thomson*, 171. He does not list a source for Brooke's pension.

[83] Lord Marchmont's Diary, *Marchmont Papers*, i. 63, dated 15 Oct. 1744, records Chesterfield's remark that 'when Lyttelton hinted his old promise to Mr. West, the Prince ordered a pension of 100l a-year for Mr West'. But the pension seems to have been settled 21 months previously.

[84] Harris (ed.), *A Leicester House Political Diary*, 398.

[85] A. N. Newman, 'The Political Patronage of Frederick Lewis, Prince of Wales', *Historical Journal*, 1 (1958), 68–75. The following figures taken from this source.

aspirations to be an artistic patron. Frederick did not get the £100,000 until after Walpole's fall in 1742. Horace Walpole's well-known remark at this point—'We may indeed hope a little better to the declining arts. The reconciliation between the royalties is finished, and £50,000 a year more added to the Heir Apparent's revenue. He will have money now to tune up Glover, and Thomson, and Dodsley again'—albeit ironic, does say something about what were widely perceived to be the Prince's priorities.[86] But by this stage Frederick had fallen heavily into financial debt and was having trouble keeping up with even essential payments. In March 1737 his treasurer John Hedges laid out to the House of Commons the bare fact that Frederick's total income (including the revenue from Cornish tin) amounted to £58,000 and that the running costs of the establishment the King had made for him in salaries, tables, and stables amounted to £63,000 per annum: a very Micawberish situation. Frederick tried to get round it by borrowing heavily from every possible source, including his followers, and by taking out large loans against Cornish tin revenues. But by 1738 over £25,000 of the loan went to pay immediate debts. By 1743 he was paying food bills nine months after supplies had been delivered, by 1749 the delay had risen to a year and a half. A more sensible prince would not have attempted any form of artistic patronage in such circumstances.

The second point which emerges from the Ayscough diaries—in the remark 'He never designed it as a Pension, but only a gift of £100'—is that Frederick was understandably reluctant to commit himself to annual and repeated payments such as pensions, preferring one-off gifts. The former would tie him to unlimited expense dependent on the longevity of the recipient whereas gifts were a means of controlling his expenses while at the same time suggesting his approval and support of the arts: a token of the things to come when he finally became king. Many of his payments to artists were thus a kind of 'advance' on his future reign. In 1729 he told Mercier that 'tho' he could not settle 200 [pounds per annum] yet he should do as much business for him yearly as the amount of that sum'.[87] One-off grants and payments were the norm, as we can see from his £100 gift to Rolli for the publication of his translation of *Paradise Lost*. Frederick's gifts were tokens of personal esteem, such as his present of a fine-bound edition of the classics to Glover; his gift in 1735 of 100 guineas and a bejewelled snuffbox and kneebuckles to the opera singer Farinelli; the gold medal (valued at 40 guineas) he gave to Nicholas Tindal, the translator of Rapin's *History of England*, and the urns and busts of the poets he gave to Pope.[88]

Technically, then, Goldgar is right to claim that 'the significance of [Frederick's] role as patron can be easily overstated'.[89] But this misses the more

---

[86] Walpole–Richard West, 4 May 1742 (*Walpole Correspondence*, xiii. 249).

[87] *Vertue Notebooks*, iii. 37.

[88] For Farinelli, see *Grub-Street Journal*, 10 Apr. 1735; for Tindal, see Jesse, *Memoirs of the Court of England*, iii. 148; for Pope, see Pope, *Corr.* iv. 170, 178.

[89] Goldgar, *Walpole and the Wits*, 139.

significant symbolic implications of a Prince of Wales who gave every sign that
he would prove a true patron of the arts. It was for this reason that many
artists and writers were drawn into Frederick's court, clearly knowing meanwhile that his finances were overstretched, some of them even lending money
to him themselves, like the family of the Tory Patriot poet Richard Powney.[90]
George Lillo was on his deathbed when he requested that his last unpublished
play, *Elmerick*, a study of Patriot kingship, be dedicated to the Prince.[91]
William Somervile was also well advanced in years when he dedicated to Frederick his late and last work, *Field Sports*.[92] Most plans for cultural projects of a
larger kind were directed towards the Prince's future reign. The shock of Frederick's unexpected early death in 1751 reverberated throughout the artistic
community. Vertue lamented that 'No Prince since King Charles I took so
much pleasure nor observations in works of arts and artists—and in all proba-
bility, had he lived, been an ornament to this Country—but alass. Mors ultima
rerum. O Gd thy will be done.'[93] Joshua Reynolds, writing from Italy in 1751,
said 'we are all extremely afflicted for the loss of the Prince of Whales [*sic*] who
would certainly have been a great Patron to painters'.[94] The poems written on
Frederick's death by both Oxford and Cambridge scholars and by independent
poets rehearse one dominant theme—the extinction of artistic hopes in a barren
age, 'The Muses's darling patron dead'.[95] Richard Rolt's *Monody* is an extraordinary *Dunciad*-like allegory showing 'The BRITISH prince' dispelling the 'RUNIC
cloud'. The forces of dullness then unite with the pestilential figures of sick-
ness, 'Pleurisia', to snuff out Frederick's life, and, with it, a patriotic regeneration of the Arts. The 'slighted ARTS' were Frederick's 'peculiar care', the hope
pinned on him, 'Shall BRITONS ever see | Their island, with indignant pride, |
Scorn the inferior world beside?'[96] In 1751 the botanical gardener Peter
Collinson wrote to the famous American naturalist John Bartram:

The death of our late excellent Prince of Wales has cast a great damp over the nation.
Gardening and planting have lost their best friend and encourager; for the Prince had
delighted in that rational amusement a long while; but lately he had a laudable and
princely ambition to excell all others. But the good things will not die out with him;
for there is such a spirit and love of it amongst the nobility and gentry, and the pleasure and profit that attends it, will render a lasting delight.[97]

[90] See Newman, 'The Political Patronage of Frederick Lewis', 71. Peniston Powney, Richard's
nephew, estimated in 1784 that his family had lost £20,000 from the association.
[91] The Prologue and Epilogue to *Elmerick* were written by Hammond. See *The Works of Mr.
George Lillo; with some Account of His Life*, ed. Thomas Davies, 2 vols. (1775), i, pp. xxxix–xli.
[92] Somervile was a friend of Shenstone's, who introduced him to Lyttelton. See Davis, *The
Good Lord Lyttelton*, 63–4.   [93] *Vertue Notebooks*, i. 14.
[94] Reynolds–Miss Weston, Rome, 30 Apr. 1751, in *Letters of Sir Joshua Reynolds*, ed. F. W.
Hilles (Cambridge, 1929), 11–12.
[95] *The English Poems collected from the Oxford and Cambridge Verses on the Death of His Royal
Highness Frederick Prince of Wales* (Edinburgh, 1751), 26. See also the remarks by F. Montagu,
117; L. Blackwell, 18; F. Gower, 35.
[96] Richard Rolt, *A Monody on the Death of His Royal Highness Frederic-Louis, Prince of Wales*
(1751), 16–17.   [97] Cited in King, *Royal Kew*, 60.

It was into this princely circle of gardeners, poets, and artists that Lyttelton tried to draw the gardening, painting, and poetry-loving Alexander Pope. Pope's refusal to become anything more than an occasional and aloof visitor will be explored in the next chapter.

4

Pope, Politics, and Genre

POPE would have been annoyed by Johnson's dismissive account of his political role during the 1730s. Pope was 'then entangled in the opposition', remarked Johnson, 'a follower of the Prince of Wales'.[1] Pope had himself pre-empted the accusation of royal sycophancy. In the *Epilogue to the Satires*, Dialogue II, he pronounced himself proud to count Chesterfield, Lyttelton, Cobham, Bolingbroke, and other Patriots his friends; even Prince Frederick could ask no more: 'And if yet higher the proud List should end, | Still let me say! No Follower, but a Friend.'[2] Pope was neither a Patriot cipher nor (in the words of the inscription he wrote for the collar of the puppy he gave Frederick) 'His Highness' Dog at *Kew*'.[3] But the extent of Pope's involvement with Patriot Whig politics and the Hanoverian Frederick raises questions about the traditional equation of Pope with Toryism, and more recently Toryism of a discernibly Jacobite flavour. There is something incongruous about finding the Catholic poet's bust enshrined in Stowe's Whiggish Temple of British Worthies alongside Milton, Hampden, Locke, Algernon Sidney, William III (Pope's unfavourite king), and an Elizabeth who had 'restored Religion from the Corruptions of Popery'.[4] Pope's close friendships with Patriot Whigs such as Lyttelton, Chesterfield, Cobham, and Marchmont cannot be attributed merely to the political influence of his mentor Bolingbroke. Yet the fluctuating pattern of his commitment to their campaign, alternating between idealism and mistrust, tells us much about broader Tory attitudes towards Patriot Whiggery in this period as well as hinting at more complex and deep-seated sources of ambivalence in the poet himself. Was Pope so committed to the House of Stuart, in either nostalgic or possibly more active ways, that he could never quite bring himself to admire Prince Frederick or write patriotic panegyrics on his behalf? Of did the deepening pessimism so many critics have discerned in his later years make any form of optimistic patriotism impossible? Why, to address that much-vexed question, did Pope in his last years sketch out detailed plans but no more than a few lines of a patriotic blank-verse epic, *Brutus*? The apparent anomaly of Pope the satirist planning the *Brutus* project while at work on the final book of *The Dunciad* raises a further issue, one fore-

---

[1] Johnson, *Lives of the Poets*, iii. 179.

[2] *Ep. Satires*, ii. 92–3 (*TE* iv. 318).

[3] 'Epigram. Engraved on the collar of a dog which I gave to his Royal Highness' (*TE* vi. 372). Probably the most pithy summary of Pope's political attitudes.

[4] G. B. Clarke (ed.), *Descriptions of Lord Cobham's Gardens at Stowe, 1700–1750* (Buckingham, 1990), 138. As M. J. Gibbon points out in *The Stoic*, 24 (1970), 62, the theme of the Temple was '1688 . . . anti-Stuart and anti-clerical'.

grounded by the Patriot poets' outspokenly critical attitude to Pope's 'sacred Weapon' of satire. Is there a correlation between politics and genre? How do we account for the widely divergent forms which oppositional writing assumed in this period, from the witty rhyming-couplet satires produced by Pope and other so-called 'Tory wits' to the heroic tragedies and blank-verse 'dissident Whig panegyrics' produced by opposition Whig Patriots?

Pope and the Patriots

Pope's friendship with Lord Cobham went back to the days when Cobham was still a staunch Court Whig—a further testament to the ecumenical nature of the poet's friendships. But in 1733 Cobham's recent dismissal from his government posts prompted Pope to welcome him into the ranks of the truly patriotic: metaphorically (if not literally) one of those who 'dare to love their Country & be poor'.[5] In the *Epistle to Cobham* Pope even attributed to Cobham the same imagined dying wish, 'O save my Country Heav'n!', with which he had only recently honoured his deceased friend the Jacobite Atterbury—a singularly suggestive indication of Pope's shifting sense of political interests.[6] Pope spent the summer of 1735 in Lyttelton and Gilbert West's company at the absent Bathurst's seat at Cirencester. It was around this time that Frederick paid him a personal visit. Pope first mentions the Boy Patriots in a letter to Swift of 25 March 1736: 'Here are a race sprung up of young Patriots who would animate you.' In December he added that his 'few chance-acquaintance of young men . . . look rather to the past age than the present, and therefore the future may have some hopes of them'.[7] In personal terms, the past, present, and future were very much in Pope's thoughts at this time. Bolingbroke's recent departure to France had deprived Pope of his dearest friend and the close contact with the currents of political life which had begun to inspire and shape his satire. Arbuthnot's death in February 1735, following Gay's in 1732, virtually depleted the remaining rump of the Scriblerus Club. Swift wrote gloomy letters from Ireland, brooding over the former golden age

---

[5] 'Verses on a Grotto', Pope, *Corr.* iv. 262.

[6] Pope's use of the same line for the Jacobite Atterbury and the Hanoverian Whig Cobham was probably not mere forgetfulness. Norman Ault, *New Light on Pope* (1949), 281–5, suggests that, when it dawned on Pope he had used the line before, he cancelled the Atterbury epitaph from vol. ii of his *Poems* (1735) at the last minute to avoid embarrassment. Such absent-mindedness is improbable. Howard Erskine-Hill, 'Life into Letters, Death into Art: Pope's Epitaph on Francis Atterbury', *Yearbook of English Studies*, 18 (1988), 200–20, points out that in 1735 Pope may have been warned of the political imprudence of publishing a patriotic epitaph to a Jacobite, hence the cancellation. But this does not explain why Pope chose to apply the line to Cobham. There can be none of the residual Jacobitism he suggests in Pope's transferral of the line to the Whig anti-Stuart Cobham.

[7] Pope, *Corr.* iv. 6; iv. 51. The first remark is omitted from Pope's authorized text of the 1741 quarto edn. of his letters—a sign of his desire to dissociate himself from previous Patriot enthusiasms.

of Scriblerus and Queen Anne Toryism rather than producing anything new for the opposition to Walpole. Swift, whose account-book mentality evidently extended to balance sheets of friendships past and present, may have been envious of Pope's new friends. In December 1736 he pointedly asked Pope: 'Have you got a Supply of new friends to make up for those who are gone? and are they equall to the first?'[8] Pope assured him that Lyttelton and his peers could not supplant former loyalties. When Pope's *Correspondence* appeared in 1741 some of the Patriots were understandably upset by Pope's unflattering metaphors:

But as when the continual washing of a river takes away our flowers and plants, it throws weeds and sedges in their room; so the course of time brings us something, as it deprives us of a great deal; and instead of leaving us what we cultivated, and expected to flourish and adorn us, gives us only what is of some little use, by accident.[9]

Pope was clearly playing up to Swift's nostalgia. But the Boy Patriots were lively and above all young: an insurance against future emotional loss. 'I'm weary of Loving & taking Leases when the Life is almost run out', Pope complained in 1735.[10] Pope's feelings towards these young men—George Lyttelton, William Murray, William Pitt, the young Viscount Cornbury, especially the Scottish Patriot Hugh Polwarth (Lord Marchmont)—ran deeper than mere politics. Pope pretended to Swift that he was more courted than courting, that Lyttelton was always 'more prompt to catch, than I to give fire'.[11] Yet his correspondence with Lyttelton and, especially, Marchmont suggests instead romantic enchantment, the seduction of youth and idealism embodied in the golden boys of Britain's future 'with whom I would never fear to hold out against all the Corruption of the world'.[12] When he first wrote to Marchmont, Pope was tongue-tied by more than his lordly status: 'I esteem you so much, I can't tell what to say to you.'[13]

This was not just a mutual admiration society. Lyttelton, as a budding poet, admired Pope enormously. But as literary leader of the Patriots, Lyttelton also saw Pope as a potentially valuable asset to the Patriot campaign. Pope's close friendship with Bolingbroke was in this respect a mixed blessing. In 1735 Bolingbroke had broken with Pulteney; back in France he was conducting an active correspondence with the leading members of the Cobham circle and their Tory ally William Wyndham. Bolingbroke's attention was now focused on this group, and his writings of this period shaped their political platform. Pope's interests were likely to follow those of his 'Guide, Philosopher, and Friend'. But the Patriots were also aware that Bolingbroke's reputation for Jacobitism remained an Achilles heel; it alienated many opposition Whigs who

[8] Swift–Pope, 2 Dec. 1736 (*Corr.* iv. 45).

[9] Pope–Swift, 30 Dec. 1736 (ibid. 50). For the hostile reaction, see *Pope's Works*, ed. Joseph Warton, 9 vols. (1797), ix. 291.

[10] Pope–Orrery, 12 July 1735 (*Corr.* iii. 470).   [11] Pope–Swift, 17–19 May 1739 (ibid. iv. 178).

[12] Pope–Swift, 17 May 1739 (ibid.).   [13] Pope–Marchmont, 10 Jan. 1739 (ibid. 217).

preferred to follow the unquestionably Hanoverian Pulteney as well as exposing Pope in particular to ministerial slurs.[14] Pope's friendship with
Bolingbroke, rooted as it had been in the last years of the Tory ministry and
continuing through the dangerous days of the Atterbury crisis, supplied ministerial critics with powerful ammunition when Pope began his outspoken
attacks on the Walpole administration. In 1738 Pope drew down much government fire for continuing his unqualified expressions of admiration for
Bolingbroke.[15] Lyttelton and other Patriot writers clearly hoped to draw Pope
more closely into the unquestionably legitimate company of Prince Frederick
as well as attempting to persuade him to renounce satire and turn his hand to
writing patriotic opposition verse. They conducted a campaign of persuasion
on both fronts, and met with only partial success. Before moving on to discuss
the first of these issues—Pope's role in Frederick's life and the Patriot campaign—I shall focus on the second, since it raises important questions about
whether the Patriots had a literary, as well as political, agenda. If so, how were
the two connected?

Politics and Genre

Throughout the 1730s criticisms of Pope's satires came from two distinctive
quarters. There were the customary attacks from ministerial critics who not
only impugned Pope's personal motives but pontificated high-mindedly about
the dubious ethical value of 'Satyr and Libelling': 'I'd be glad to know what
Vices do they really prevent.'[16] Similar arguments, more surprisingly, were
voiced by Patriot Whigs, though for different reasons. Unlike ministerial writers (whose own readiness to resort to satire and ridicule patently undermined
the sincerity of their arguments), Patriot Whigs did not want to silence Pope;
they wanted only to redirect his talents into a vein of writing more appropriate
(so they thought) both to his natural genius as well as to the 'Service of
Virtue', so that 'The Moral Song may steal into our Hearts'.[17] Lyttelton and
his peers believed that their political cause would be better served by more
uplifting and patriotically spirited poetry which would (unlike Pope's) not only
attack the degeneracy of the present age but also look forward to a regenerated
Britain, a renewal to political health with a Patriot ministry and under a
Patriot King: positive goals rather than merely negative attacks.

---

[14] See *The Letters of Lord Chesterfield*, ed. Bonamy Dobrée, 6 vols. (1932), ii. 467–70.
[15] See Bertrand A. Goldgar, *Walpole and the Wits: The Relation of Politics to Literature,
1722–1742* (Lincoln, Nebr., 1976), 167–8. Attention was focused primarily on Pope's compliments
to Bolingbroke in the *Epistle to Bolingbroke* and his earlier praise of him in the *Essay on Man*.
[16] *London Journal*, 14 Sept. 1738. For ministerial attitudes to satire, see Goldgar, *Walpole and
the Wits*, 20–7.
[17] Lyttelton–Pope, 7 Nov. 1741 (*Corr.* iv. 369).

Bertrand Goldgar's *Walpole and the Wits* draws some helpful distinctions between opposition writing of the kind produced by the 'wits' of his title and the literary campaign conducted by the Patriot poets, who were (he notes) 'neither very gay nor very witty'. Patriot literature is 'a fusion of chauvinism and sentimentality'. 'Hortatory rather than satirical, rhetorical rather than realistic, [the Patriots'] poetic campaign against the government seems far removed from the acerbic wit of *Gulliver's Travels* or *The Beggar's Opera*.'[18] Goldgar aligns Patriot poetry with the tradition of Whig panegyric verse described by C. A. Moore in an important seminal article of 1926 and redefined by A. D. McKillop for Thomson and other oppositional Whig poets in the Walpole period as 'dissident Whig panegyric'.[19] Whig panegyric dealt with 'principles rather than personalities'—principles such as liberty, empire, commerce, Britain's naval supremacy, the Revolution settlement, a socially 'benevolist' credo, and the blessings of Protestant enlightenment. It was expansive, patriotic, and intensely earnest rather than satirical, humorous, critical, or personal. Many of the examples proffered by Moore (and these include works by Court Whig and opposition Whig poets alike) are written in lofty Miltonic blank verse, a form with its own political implications. Miltonics came to be associated with British freedoms—a line of argument developed by writers and critics from the Restoration through into the eighteenth century who militated against the shackles of the rhyming couplet, particularly when it was associated with a French-inspired school of neo-classical correctness. British poets were enjoined to 'reassume | The free-born right of Greece and Rome' while leaving 'slavish France in jingling strain' to 'hug the servile chain'.[20]

Louis M. Bredvold's 'The Gloom of the Tory Satirists' (whose title has become almost a critical commonplace in accounts of Swift, Pope, and Johnson) offers the classic definition of a contrasting 'Tory' form. Satire was fundamentally a 'Tory' genre: its pessimistic roots lay in the Anglican conviction of man's essential depravity rather than the 'Whig perfectibilitarian's' faith in man's capacity for progress and enlightenment. 'Tory satire' operated through the highly disciplined rhyming couplet form, a form which mirrored Tory faith in universal order, degree, and social hierarchy: a form which could

---

[18] Goldgar, *Walpole and the Wits*, 137.

[19] C. A. Moore, 'Whig Panegyric Verse, 1700–1760: A Phase of Sentimentalism,' *PMLA* 41 (1926), 362–401. James Thomson, *The Castle of Indolence and Other Poems*, ed. A. D. McKillop (Lawrence, Kan., 1961), 162–3. See also O. H. K. Spate, 'The Muse of Mercantilism: Jago, Grainger and Dyer', in R. K. Brissenden (ed.), *Studies in the Eighteenth Century* (Canberra, 1968), 119–31.

[20] Quotation from Brockhill Newburgh's *Essay Poetical* (1769), 39. For discussions of the arguments about Miltonic blank verse, see Eric Rothstein, *Restoration and Eighteenth-Century Poetry 1660–1780* (1981), 63–8; Dustin Griffin, *Regaining Paradise: Milton and the Eighteenth Century* (Cambridge, 1986), 7, 81; R. D. Havens, *The Influence of Milton on English Poetry* (1922), chs. 2 and 4. Both Thomson and Hill were strongly influenced by John Dennis, whose preface to *Britannia Triumphans* (repr. in *The Critical Works of John Dennis*, ed. E. N. Hooker, 2 vols. (Baltimore, Md., 1939), i. 374ff.) contains the strongest endorsement of the freedoms of blank verse. These arguments are rehearsed in Hill's *Advice to the Poets* (1731), esp. p. 31.

also ironically frame (as in Pope's case) a vision of modern social disintegration.[21]

There are inherent dangers in any attempt to formulate generalizations about the correlation between political ideology and aesthetic form (whether literary or architectural) as we shall see with the problem of 'Whig Gothic' in Chapter 5. There are certainly many opposition Whig poems which fit into the 'dissident Whig panegyric' pattern, especially those concerned with the issue of war with Spain such as Thomson's *Britannia*, Glover's *London: Or the Progress of Commerce*, or Akenside's *The Voice of Liberty; or a British Philippic*. But Patriot verse does not always announce itself by interminable Miltonics, with (as one government critic complained), 'every *Period* ring[ing] with *Liberty*'.[22] The Patriot verse discussed in this book comes in a wide variety of forms and styles: many Pindaric odes (also associated with political liberty) but also a series of allegorical critiques of the ministry veiled in intricate Spenserian stanzas. There are heroic-couplet *Windsor-Forest* style poems which bear more than a passing resemblance to the royalist forms of Denham and Waller; heroic tragedies and also masques which bear traces of both Milton's radical *Comus* and Carew's royalist *Coelum Britannicum*. Richard Glover's most successful oppositional poem was not his pseudo-epic *Leonidas* but his popular sentimental ballad *Admiral Hosier's Ghost*, 'To the tune of, Come and listen to my ditty'.

Nor are there easy discriminations to be made on grounds of ideological content between the 'gloom of Tory satire' and the optimistic 'Psychology of Whiggism'. Liberty may be a constant refrain of Patriot Whig verse, but trade, commerce, and empire were never, of course, exclusively 'Whiggish' property, as we can see from the presence of a powerful urban commercial strain in a series of 'royalist' works from Denham's *Coopers-Hill* through to Dryden's *Annus Mirabilis* and Pope's *Windsor-Forest*. As J. A. Downie has observed, Pope's poem affirming the blessings of a Stuart reign sounds at times remarkably 'Whiggish': 'Fair *Liberty*, *Britannia*'s Goddess, rears | Her chearful Head, and leads the golden Years.'[23] The Prologue to Gay's Spenserian *Shepherd's Week*, similarly extolling Queen Anne, the Tory leaders, and the Treaty of Utrecht, exhorts Britain's rustic swains to dedicate their labours to Britain's commercial advancement and thriving foreign trade.[24] Before the mercantile community grew increasingly disaffected with Walpole's apparent contempt for

---

[21] See Louis M. Bredvold, 'The Gloom of the Tory Satirists', in J. L. Clifford (ed.), *Eighteenth-Century English Literature: Modern Essays in Criticism* (New York, 1959), 3–20. Margaret Doody, *The Daring Muse: Augustan Poetry Reconsidered* (Cambridge, 1986), 232–3, equates the couplet and its binary oppositions with the rise of the two-party political system.

[22] *The Crafts of the Craftsman: Or the Detection of the Designs of the Coalition* (1735), 6.

[23] J. A. Downie, '1688: Pope and the Rhetoric of Jacobitism', in David Fairer (ed.), *Pope: New Contexts* (Hemel Hempstead, 1990), 17.

[24] John Gay, *Poetry and Prose*, ed. V. A. Dearing and C. Beckwith, 2 vols. (Oxford, 1974), i. 95.

their interests, commerce and naval greatness were indubitably Court Whig themes. There is, as A. D. McKillop observes, little essential difference between the tenets of Young's *Imperium Pelagi* (1730) and Thomson's oppositional *Britannia* (1729).[25] The 'Country' theme of rural retirement, albeit a hallmark of the 'Poetry of Conservatism', could also find expression in poems written by opposition Whig poets throughout the Walpole period, notably Thomson's *Seasons* or William Somervile's *The Chace*, whose nostalgic evocation of the British countryside also incorporates a vision of Frederick as a protector of Britain's commerce and liberty.[26] The years 1738–9 were distinguished by what would seem to be (according to Goldgar's distinctions) a hybrid genre of Patriot satire, mingling Juvenalian castigation of British degeneracy with a patriotic romanticization of past political golden ages such as 'ALFRED's golden Reign', Edward III at Crécy, and the Armada victories of Elizabeth.[27]

Thus far the argument would seem to suggest that there is little clear distinction between Tory and opposition Whig verse in the Walpole period; the shared language of corruption, luxury, and national decline points rather to the broader 'Country' ideology propounded in the *Craftsman* and other opposition journals.[28] Yet there are distinguishable features. The romanticization of the British past is, as we shall see in Part II, the most salient quality of Patriot verse, one by no means shared by satirists since it is always coupled with an optimistic sense of national future—a vision of future greatness which derives from a broadly affirmative vision of Hanoverian dynastic continuity. Patriot Whig verse often looks surprisingly royalist, the monarch (Prince Frederick) at its centre occupying the place once taken by figures such as Dryden's Charles or Pope's 'Great ANNA'. The difference between Pope and the Patriots lies less in the fact that Pope wrote satire and they did not (for there are some exceptions, as we shall see) than in the factors which informed their conscious decision to avoid satire.

This difference becomes clear when we compare two pairs of poems, two by Pope and two by different Patriot Whig writers, James Thomson and Paul Whitehead, a friend of Pope's who also moved in Frederick's circle. The gap between Thomson's *Liberty* (1735–6) and Pope's four-book *Dunciad* (1743) at first seems considerable. *Liberty* looks like the quintessential dissident Whig panegyric, a hortatory long Miltonic blank-verse poem dedicated to a perennially popular Whig theme. *The Dunciad* is a brilliant satirical dissection of an

---

[25] Thomson, *The Castle of Indolence*, ed. McKillop, 162–3. But as he notes, Thomson qualifies and subverts the praise of peaceful imperialism.

[26] William Somervile, *The Chace* (1735), esp. Book I, ll. 20–31.

[27] Goldgar, *Walpole and the Wits*, 173–85. Johnson's *London* (quotation l. 248) is a classic example.

[28] This is the argument advanced by W. A. Speck, *Society and Literature in England, 1700–1760* (Dublin, 1983), esp. pp. 14–40. But ministerial critics thought it possible to tell the difference between the writings of Tories, Jacobites, and 'discontented Whigs'. See *The Crafts of the Craftsman*.

urban landscape of corruption and decay located in the specificities of time and place—dozens of named and half-hinted-at individuals inhabiting the murky world of Grub Street. Yet there are also close parallels. Both *Liberty* and *The Dunciad* are political reappropriations of the epic form, both lacking a coherent narrative action. In both cases the 'epic hero' has been replaced by a personification of spiritual or moral force: in Thomson's case the Goddess Liberty, the active and outwardly motivating spirit of public virtue, in Pope's case the Goddess Dulness with her magnetic attraction of 'self-love' and solipsistic dullness. Both works owe something to the 'progress poem' genre which traces the rise and historical progress of a particular theme—in Thomson's case, liberty, in Pope's, dullness.[29] Both poems are also deeply indebted to a model which in Thomson's case militates against the notion of 'progress' though one eminently suited to Pope's vision of decline: the Polybian or Machiavellian concept of the historical cycle of the birth, rise, and ultimate fall of nations, based in both cases on the underlying model of imperial Rome. Both are informed by a strong awareness of civic and cultural decline: Thomson's Goths, Vandals, and Huns are confined to a period in past history whereas Pope's barbaric swarms function as metaphors for modern vandalism. Curiously, both poems dwell on the evils of divine right theory—in Thomson's case the Stuarts' slavish doctrines of divine right and passive obedience, in Pope's the Hanoverians' claims to divine hereditary right.[30] But for Pope the final 'imperial vision' unfolded by a shabby Grub-Street dunce can only predict the fulfilment of a prophecy rooted in twenty years of Hanoverian and Walpolian dullness; whereas for Thomson, the 'Prospect' of Part V of *Liberty*, albeit filled with stern admonitions about the need to guard British liberties jealously from the fate that befell imperial Rome, is none the less an optimistic account of Britain's future recovery and unconquerable cultural and national greatness. Such contrasting prophetic visions also distinguish Paul Whitehead's 1739 *Manners*, an imitation of the *Epilogue to the Satires*, from its Popeian original. Unusually for a Patriot supporter of Frederick, Whitehead was an accomplished satirist whose excursions in the Popeian vein got him arrested—some thought to warn off Pope.[31] Whitehead follows Pope in concluding that satire is 'pointless' in these 'Iron Times'. But where Pope's pair of dialogues end in sombre apocalypse, Whitehead's *Manners* ends in a rhapsodic (albeit unconvincing) millennium of 'future Glories'.

> Wrap'd into Thought, Lo! I *Britannia* see
> Rising superior o'er the subject Sea;
> View her gay Pendants spread their silken Wings,

[29] See R. H. Griffith, 'The Progress Pieces of the Eighteenth Century', *Texas Review*, 5 (1919–20), 218–33; Aubrey M. Williams, *Pope's 'Dunciad': A Study of its Meaning* (1955), 42–8.
[30] See *Liberty*, iv. 970 n. (OET *Liberty*, 118). Cf. *Dunciad*, iv. 188 (*TE* v. 360).
[31] See Goldgar, *Walpole and the Wits*, 175–6.

> Big with the Fate of Empires and of Kings:
> The Tow'ring Barks dance lightly o'er the Main,
> And roll their Thunder thro' the Realm of *Spain*.
> *Peace*, violated Maid, they ask no more,
> But waft her back triumphant to our Shore;
> While buxom *Plenty*, laughing in her Train,
> Glads ev'ry Heart, and crowns the Warriour's Pain.
> On Fancy, on, still sketch the pleasing Scene,
> And bring fair *Freedom* with her golden Reign;
> Chear'd by whose Beams ev'n meagre want can smile,
> And the poor *Peasant* whistles 'midst his Toil.
>
> SUCH Days, what *Briton* wishes not to see?
> And such each *Briton*, FREDERICK, hopes from Thee.[32]

A ministerial critic accused Whitehead of plagiarism. 'The Prophecy at the End, is also stolen from Mr. *Pope's Messiah*! . . . he has borrow'd, not to improve but prejudice Ideas'.[33] The 'prejudice' was clearly political— Whitehead's association of Prince Frederick with the prophetic vein long since lost from Pope's own poetry but which is a staple feature of Patriot verse. Without a genuine commitment to and confidence in the redemptive role of the *princeps*, that vision loses conviction. Maynard Mack shows that Pope's satires frequently suggest 'in various versions . . . intimations of a throne usurped, or a throne occupied by shadows'.[34] Pope's apparent reluctance to comply with Mrs Caesar's suggestion (*c.*1739) that he write another *Windsor-Forest* for James III and the Jacobite cause suggests a lack of faith even in the 'logical' alternative to Hanoverian decline.[35] As we shall see in Chapter 6, both Patriot verse and Jacobite verse might in some sense be seen as parallel and overlapping forms, both predicating a national regeneration through the agency of a redemptive Patriot prince. None of Pope's poetry of the 1730s, not even (as I shall go on to argue) the fragmentary *One Thousand Seven Hundred and Forty*, corresponds with this pattern.

Satire, Epic, and Tragedy

Lyttelton and the Patriots tried to persuade Pope of both the inadequacy of satire and the superiority of Prince Frederick. In 1739 the Patriot dramatist

---

[32] Paul Whitehead, *Manners: A Satire* (1739), 17.

[33] *Observations on the Present Taste for Poetry; with Remarks . . . on . . . Manners* (1739), 46.

[34] Maynard Mack, *The Garden and the City: Retirement and Politics in the later Poetry of Pope, 1731–1743* (Toronto, 1969), 234–5.

[35] See Howard Erskine-Hill, 'Under Which Caesar? Pope in the Journal of Mrs Charles Caesar, 1724–1741', *RES* NS 33 (1982), 436–44, pp. 441–2. See also Valerie Rumbold, *Women's Place in Pope's World* (Cambridge, 1989), 247.

Henry Brooke told Pope that he was 'heartily angry' with him: 'I wish all the profits of Homer were sunk in the sea, provided you had never improved him, but spent your time excelling him in his own way. Is it yet too late?'[36] *The Dunciad* was not the epic Pope's friends and admirers had anticipated after ten years' toil on Homer. As early as 1730 Lyttelton mustered all the moral indignation of youth to reprimand Pope for wasting his talents. In *An Epistle to Mr. Pope, from a Young Gentleman at Rome*, written on the Grand Tour, Lyttelton takes advantage of Pope's early claims to Virgilian inspiration, to 'wait inspiring dreams at *Maro*'s Urn'. Here he turns Virgil's ghost against Pope.[37] Virgil's ghost warns Pope that 'meaner Satire' can only 'taint thy Bays, | And stain the Glory of thy nobler Lays'. Pope must instead attempt to 'raise | A lasting Column to thy Country's Praise' and 'join the PATRIOT's to the POET's Praise'.[38] In the same year Aaron Hill also sent Pope a piece of poetic 'advice': *The Progress of Wit*, subtitled 'A Caveat: For the Use of an Eminent Writer'. Hill, notorious for his bizarrely 'high sublime' poetic style, was deeply offended that Pope should have included him in both *Peri Bathous* and *The Dunciad* as a 'flying fish' and high diver who sinks to unfathomable depths.[39] Yet Hill was too good-tempered to harbour a Pope-like grudge: *The Progress of Wit*, not without humour, was written more in sorrow than in anger. Both the preface and the poem itself ingeniously appropriate and then subvert the very techniques of *The Dunciad*, turning them back on the poet. Hill supplies a Scriberian-style bogus provenance for his manuscript (discovered in the bottom of a hackney carriage) as well as a heavy-handed pedantic interpretation of its meaning from a fictional critic, one Gamaliel Gunson, close cousin to Pope's Esdras Barnivelt. In the poem itself Hill reworks the symbolic features of *The Dunciad*'s landscape of dullness, dramatizing Pope as 'Tuneful ALEXIS', steering a light boat along the great Stream of Life with the great void of Death's 'dark *Profound*' looming in the distance. As Alexis approaches a fitting resting-place in the green islands of immortal fame, he cannot resist turning his boat round to do one last battle with flies and insect witlings. The poem leaves him on the point of disappearing down the vortex of death and '*Oblivion*' with his undistinguished subject-matter: 'Contempt's cold Vale had caught him, wak'd, and stunn'd, | And deep intomb'd him, in his own PROFUND.'[40]

---

[36] Brooke–Pope, Nov. 1739 (*Corr.* iv. 199).

[37] Pope, 'An Epistle to Mr. Jervas', l. 28 (*TE* vi. 157).

[38] George Lyttelton, *An Epistle to Mr. Pope, from a Young Gentleman at Rome* (1730), 5–6.

[39] The quarrel originated in 1718 out of Pope's negative remarks on the MS of Hill's *Northern Star*. Hill showed his resentment in the preface, though he publicly apologized in his preface to *The Creation* of the same year (1720). But Pope then went on to ridicule Hill as 'A. H.' in *Peri Bathous* (1728). Hill retaliated with an epigram in the *Daily Journal* (16 Apr. 1728) and in May Pope included 'H——' in the mud-diving hack writers in *Dunciad*, ii. 273. A snide note to this line in the 1729 quarto edition removed all doubts as to Hill's identity. The letters which followed between the two show Hill in a far better light than Pope. For a full account, see Pope, *Works*, ed. W. Elwin and J. W. Courthope, 10 vols. (1871–89), x. 8–23.

[40] Aaron Hill, *The Progress of Wit: A Caveat. For the Use of an Eminent Writer* (1730), 15, 19, 31. The work is discussed interestingly by Doody, *The Daring Muse*, 177–9.

The following year (1731) Hill's *Advice to the Poets* contained an apology for *The Progress of Wit* and a new compliment to Pope's genius. Even though early, its important prefatory 'Epistle Dedicatory' contains the closest we can find to a carefully worded agenda behind the Patriots' choice of literary modes. Although the preceding discussion suggests that there are no easy generalizations to be made about politics and genre, there were two genres much favoured or attempted by the Patriots—epic poetry (or versions thereof) and heroic tragedy. Hill supplies a rationale for both. Satire, he writes, unless Juvenalian in its loftiness, debases the poet. Epic and tragedy are more appropriate to the 'true Poet [who] is a *Patriot*'.[41] Heroic poetry, which inflamed the Athenians with 'lofty Sentiments', can stir nationalistic, even xenophobic feeling in its readers: '*This* taught them to conceive Themselves superior to the Nations round them' (p. vii). Hill's account is characterized by a strongly chauvinistic strain, a response to the mounting pressure for war which also led him to note in the *Prompter* of 1735 that 'Taste for *Epic Poetry* being One of the natural Consequences of a *Martial Disposition*, and as there seems a Time approaching, when the TRUMPET will be *fashionable Musick*, It can neither be a useless nor unseasonable Entertainment'.[42] There is a curious anticipation of Burke's hostile recognition that 'Sir Robert Walpole was forced into the war by the people who were inflamed to this measure . . . by the greatest poets of the time' in Hill's lines, 'These are the Seasons, O, ye Muse-inspired! | When *states, unwarlike,* may, to War, be *fir'd*' (p. 35).[43] Hill thought tragic drama could be even more useful: 'there is no Part of Learning, in its own Nature, so capable, as *This* Branch of Poetry, to serve the Wise, and the National, Views, of a Great, and Able, Politician' (p. xii).

Hill's conception here of tragic drama pressed into service by a politician with 'national views' anticipates the campaign of Patriot drama of 1738–40.[44] Patriot tragedy was an even more effective form of opposition writing than Fielding's satirical burlesques. As John Loftis remarks: 'Tragedy took as its ostensible subjects affairs of monarchs, nobles and generals in remote times and places and avoided literal social comment, but the superficial distance from contemporary concerns notwithstanding, tragedy was in even closer touch with the currents of political thought than comedy.'[45] Robert D. Hume has

---

[41] Aaron Hill, *Advice to the Poets. A Poem. To which is Prefix'd, An Epistle Dedicatory, to the Few Great Spirits of Great Britain* (1731), p. viii. All further citations inc. in text.

[42] *Prompter*, 15 July 1735.

[43] Edmund Burke, *Two Letters . . . on the Proposals for Peace with the Regicide Directory of France* (1796), 71–2.

[44] Hill's lofty language seems distant from party politics. But the tragic dramatist he praises (Mallet and his *Eurydice*, 1731) had recently been attacked as a factotum of Bolingbroke and a Jacobite (which he was not). See *Remarks on the Tragedy of Eurydice* (1731).

[45] John Loftis, *The Politics of Drama in Augustan England* (Oxford, 1963), 5. Fielding's satirical burlesque comedies were very different in kind from Patriot drama. Though Thomas Cleary's *Henry Fielding: Political Writer* (Waterloo, Ont., 1984) depicts Fielding as one of the leading writers championed by Lyttelton and committed to 'broad-bottom principles', he cannot be described

usefully distinguished between 'topical allusion' plays and 'application' plays, the former, mainly comedies, referring openly to current events, the latter, mainly tragedies, inviting the audience to draw parallels and see connections between the distant dramatic action and contemporary affairs.[46] Patriot tragedies, of course, had an inbuilt satirical and applicational dimension; yet they also stirred up a strain of idealistic self-righteousness in their enthusiastic audiences, as anyone could attest who had watched theatre-goers wildly applauding Prince Frederick at the 1739 revival of Addison's *Cato* or any of the many Patriot dramas he attended. They had the double virtue of inspiring patriotic sentiment while simultaneously proclaiming their own innocence. After *Gustavus Vasa* fell victim to the stage licensers, Brooke asserted injured innocence; he claimed that he was unfamiliar with party politics but 'liked our Constitution, and zealously wish'd that the Religion, the Laws, and the Liberties of *England* might ever be sacred and safe. I had nothing to fear or hope from Party or Preferment. My Attachments were only to Truth, I was conscious of no other Principles, and was far from apprehending that Such could be offensive.'[47] The subscription edition of the banned *Gustavus Vasa* proved a sell-out success. As opposition sympathizers greeted each other by clapping their hands to their breasts and declaiming (in a new version of Brooke's line), 'O B[ritain], O my country, yet I'll save thee', ministerialists must have despaired of finding a foothold on the smoothly unimpeachable surface of Patriot literature.[48] Unlike topical satire, it did not expose its authors to accusations of personal spleen or to prosecution: and government proscription (as in the case of Brooke's play) only further fuelled the martyrology of opposition. Moreover, there was clearly some validity in Hill's argument that the stirring strains of patriotism appealed to wider audiences than political satire. Satiric prints and ballads depicting Sir Robert in numerous familiar disguises, from Screen of Brass to Robin Blue-String, were of course perennially popular, especially among London audiences; and from these Pope derived some of his own satiric iconography.[49] But Pope's satires may have presented a political world too self-enclosed and a web of innuendo too subtle to be grasped by audiences unfamiliar with the affairs of Westminster or St James's.

as a Patriot writer. He did not move closely in Frederick's circle even though Frederick attended his plays. Fielding took satirical swipes at Walpole but it is hard to imagine him praising a prince or engaging in historical myth-making. It is also difficult to believe that Frederick could have forgiven Fielding for satirizing him as the fumbling, stupid, randy Master Owen Apshinken of the *Welsh Opera* as recently as 1731.

[46] Robert D. Hume, *Henry Fielding and the London Theatre 1728–1737* (Oxford, 1988), 78.

[47] Henry Brooke, *Gustavus Vasa: or, The Deliverer of His Country* (1739), Prefatory Dedication, p. iv.

[48] The scene described by Johnson, *A Compleat Vindication Of the Licensers of the Stage*, in *Yale Johnson*, x. 67. For Brooke's subscribers, see W. A. Speck, 'Politicians, Peers, and Publication by Subscription 1700–1750', in Isabel Rivers (ed.), *Books and their Readers in Eighteenth-Century England* (Leicester, 1982), 47–68.

[49] See Mack, *The Garden and the City*, 128–62.

Patriot literature, with its broad historic sweep, did not demand an intimate knowledge of court intrigue. Middle-class readers may have found Pope's 'filthy similes' and 'beastly lines' less engaging than sentimental appeals to British patriotism.[50]

Patriot poets found dramatic tragedy more amenable than epic poetry. It involved less effort with more immediate political rewards, and was not hemmed in by the thorny thicket of critical guides, rule-books, mock rule-books, and mock-epics which by this time had rendered the 'serious' epic poem unapproachable to any but the thick-skinned.[51] Even though Thomson had planned a Patriot epic, *Timoleon*, in 1731, his friend Benjamin Martyn had already used the subject for his early Patriot drama of the same title. After exclaiming that such a project would need to be 'the work of years, and one in an epic situation to execute it. My heart both trembles with diffidence and burns in ardour at the thought', Thomson abandoned the task.[52] He clearly saw *Liberty* as his own version of the epic: in *The Castle of Indolence* he imitates Spenser's announcement of his epic ambitions to sing of 'greater things' to allude to his own succession of 'high heroic' Patriot poems and plays of the 1730s.[53] But the young City merchant Richard Glover (like William III's City-bred physician Richard Blackmore) had fewer literary inhibitions. By 1734 he was well advanced on *Leonidas*, a nine-book epic on the heroic Spartan defence of the bridge at Thermopylae, a singular moment in the history of patriotic self-sacrifice. Prince Frederick was the inspiration for the hero. *Leonidas* appeared in April 1737, dedicated to Lord Cobham as one to whom 'a poem, founded on a character eminent for military glory, and love of liberty, is due from the nature of the subject'.[54]

The critical reception Glover's epic enjoyed now seems hard to fathom. Some of the acclaim came from critics such as Henry Pemberton, delighted to find a new full-length modern epic from which he could extrapolate 'rules' for his 1738 *Observations on Poetry, especially the Epic*—just the kind of prescriptive manual Pope had satirized in his 'Receipt to Make an Epick Poem'.[55] Most of the attention, from both the opposition and the government, was political and had little to do with the work's intrinsic literary merit. Thomas Rundle, who married Glover to the beautiful and wealthy heiress Henrietta

[50] Pope, *Ep. Satires*, ii. 168–82. Many middle-class audiences preferred the mixture of sentiment, piety, patriotism, and mercantilism embodied in the opposition plays of George Lillo.

[51] See esp. H. T. Swedenberg, *The Theory of Epic in England, 1650–1800* (Berkeley, Calif., 1944); Dustin Griffin, 'Milton and the Decline of Epic in the Eighteenth Century', *New Literary History*, 14 (1982), 143–54; Doody, *The Daring Muse*, 63–7.

[52] Thomson, *Letters*, 74.

[53] *Castle of Indolence*, I. xxxii (OET *Liberty*, 184).

[54] Richard Glover, *Poetical Works*, in R. Anderson (ed.), *A Complete Edition of the Poets of Great Britain*, 13 vols. (1795), xi. 485. See Lyttelton, 'To. Mr. Glover, On His Poem of Leonidas' (1734), *The Poetical Works of George, Lord Lyttelton* (1801), 137–8.

[55] Henry Pemberton, *Observations on Poetry, especially the Epic, Occasioned by the Late Poem upon Leonidas* (1738). Cf. Pope's 'Receipt to Make an Epick Poem', *Guardian*, 10 June 1713.

Nunn just a month after the poem was published, offered a measured literary appraisal. He thought *Leonidas* strong on moral sentiment but short on anything approximating 'the agreeable wildness of a young imagination', its tersely laconic style 'inspired rather by reason than fancy'.[56] Its fame reached Swift in Ireland, who asked about Glover and his 'Epic Poem called Leonidas, which is re-printing here and hath great vogue'.[57] Richard Savage, whose recent efforts to inveigle himself into Frederick's literary circle were meeting with indifference, greeted Glover's instant success with ill-concealed jealousy. Glover's double good luck—an epic and an heiress, all by the age of 25—prompted Savage's cruelly funny letter on the 'sublime Leonidas Glover', whose honeymoon night placed him in the same predicament as his epic hero, 'a second time crushed in the Streights of Thermopyle. "Ah, cruel fate!—that wounds must bleed afresh!"'[58] It was Lyttelton's puff for the poem that really annoyed Savage—and probably a number of other opposition writers.[59] Two pages of *Common Sense* were devoted to the eighteenth-century equivalent of a feature article on *Leonidas*.[60] The 'old man' advertising the work's merits found it so gripping he was unable to sleep until he had finished it (a long night, as Savage probably remarked). Lyttelton's puff was clearly framed to deter ministerial imputations of its subversive political content: 'none can say that he meant it *against them*, unless by declaring that they are *against Liberty*, to improve a general love of *which* is the sole Aim and Intention of this poem.' But behind Lyttelton's extravagant praise of Glover, now placed in the poetic pantheon of Homer, Virgil, and Milton, lay an ulterior target—Pope. The final lines make a provocative comparison between the great Bard of Twickenham and the young City poet, conceding second place to Pope as the 'elegant and extensive' translator of other men's epics, but crowning Glover, an original genius, as the heir apparent to the epic bays. Pope's epic translations had cleared the thorny paths of Parnassus to make way for Glover's ascent; nothing could now be 'of such Advantage to a rising Genius as *the Praise of Mr. Pope*'.

Pope and Prince Frederick

Pope was unlikely to be goaded by Lyttelton's remarks. Glover may have been the opposition's current literary darling, but he could scarcely have eclipsed Pope's poetic supremacy. Pope was very much his own man. When he did finally turn to plans for a blank-verse epic in the early 1740s they were far from a straightforward response to Lyttelton's pleas. Lyttelton kept up the

---

[56] Rundle, *Letters*, ii. 234–5.   [57] Swift–Pope, 31 May 1737 (*Corr.* iv. 72).

[58] Savage–Solomon Mendez, 26 May 1737 (Thomson, *Letters*, 110–11).

[59] See James Sambrook, *James Thomson, 1700–1748: A Life* (Oxford, 1991), 161.

[60] *Common Sense*, 9 Apr. 1737. For ministerial responses see *Daily Gazetteer*, 25 Jan. 1738 and Henley's *Hyp-Doctor*, 12 Apr. 1737. Henley turned Lyttelton's championship of Spartan 'liberty' back on the opposition by pointing out that Sparta was a slave-owning aristocratic oligarchy where blank verse would probably have been high treason.

pressure on Pope in a series of letters throughout the late 1730s and early 1740s. One, a long letter of 25 October 1738, steeped in Bolingbrokean rhetoric, urges Pope to take an active role in supplying moral guidance and support of a more literary kind for Frederick: 'he can not be too often in your company . . . One *in his Station* may draw the greatest services, as well as the greatest delight from One *in Your's*. Be therefore as much with him as you can, Animate him to Virtue.' Lyttelton throws out a heavy hint: Pope is the age's 'Greatest Dispenser of Fame', so if Frederick 'wou'd Immortalise himself, the only way he can take, is to deserve a place by his conduct in *some writings*, where he will never be admitted only for his Rank'.[61] Three years later Lyttelton was still dropping hints: deep in his labours on his history of Henry II, he described it as a 'Work of some Instruction and Pleasure to my Countrymen, and I hope to the Prince my Master, for whose service I chiefly design it' but thought that Pope could produce something superior in the same vein, 'out of these Gothick Ruins, rude as they are, Raise a new Edifice, that wou'd be fitt to Enshrine the Greatest of our English Kings, and Last to Eternity'.[62] That November, when the Cobham circle's prospects were looking increasingly gloomy, Lyttelton again urged Pope for a 'Moral Song' for the young men of his country: 'some Sparks of Publick Virtue are yet Alive, which such a Spirit as Your's might blow into a flame.'[63]

Why was Pope so reluctant to commit himself? His reticence is only too apparent from his reply to Lyttelton's October 1738 letter, neatly sidestepping the issue of his own direct personal involvement as Frederick's moral tutor. Pope regretted that he had missed the chance to send Bathurst a letter of instruction 'in what manner a Great Man should treat a Prince'—i.e. an unwritten letter of advice to a would-be adviser.[64] Lyttelton had complained how hard he found it to drag Pope into Frederick's company: 'I was almost forced to compell You to go and dine at Kue the last time you was there. And yet there never was a morning better spent by you.'[65] Even at the high point of his involvement in Patriot politics, Pope couldn't bring himself to see Frederick as a wellspring of national regeneration: he hints that Frederick is more than 'a little Short sighted' and his closing obeisance is not untinged by irony. 'Pray assure your Master of my Duty & Service; They tell me he has every body's love already. I wish him Popular, but not Familiar, and the Glory of being beloved, not the Vanity of endeavouring it too much.'[66] Even though Frederick may have been superior to his parents, Pope, like many Tories, remained mistrustful of Hanoverian princes in opposition and in the hands of ambitious out-of-office Whigs. In the end Frederick might well renege on his

---

[61] Lyttelton–Pope, 25 Oct. 1738 (*Corr.* iv. 138–9).
[62] Lyttelton–Pope, 13 June 1741 (ibid. 348–9).
[63] Lyttelton–Pope, 7 Nov. 1741 (ibid. 369).
[64] Pope–Lyttelton, *c.*1 Nov. 1738 (ibid. 142–4).
[65] Lyttelton–Pope, 25 Oct. 1738 (ibid. 139).
[66] Pope–Lyttelton, *c.*1 Nov. 1738 (ibid. 142–3).

previous promises to Tory supporters just as George II in 1727 had turned his back on the loyal Bathurst, when Pope had ruefully remarked: 'Bathurst Lements the truth the Psalmist sings | And finds that Princes are the Sons of Kings.'[67] Such doubts may have informed Pope's response to Frederick's enquiry as to how the poet managed to reconcile his love for a prince with his professed indisposition to kings: Pope claimed to like the lion best before his claws had had time to grow.

Pope was rather proud of this *bon mot*. As Johnson pointed out, Pope's much-vaunted 'disesteem' of kings and courts concealed a strong streak of upward mobility and personal vanity.[68] Even though Pope may have been rude about Frederick's early sexual escapades among his mother's ladies-in-waiting—the 'Six Maidens' of an early squib he wrote on the Prince—none the less he was undoubtedly flattered by being visited by Frederick at his home in October 1735.[69] There is a studied casualness behind Pope's brief mention of the occasion in a letter to Bathurst: 'suprised by a Favour of his R. Highness, an unexpected Visit of 4 or 5 hours'—as if the heir to the throne dropping in for tea and chat were nothing very remarkable.[70] The conversation obviously went well for both parties: Pope may have discovered more common ground than he had anticipated in their shared tastes in gardening and literature. That year Frederick commissioned the Amigoni portrait described in the previous chapter showing him deeply engrossed in a copy of Pope's Homer translation; he later presented Pope with some urns for his garden and four marble busts of Spenser, Shakespeare, Milton, and Dryden for his library.[71] In May 1736 Pope came the closest to the reverence due to Hanoverian princes with his *Bounce to Fop: An Heroick Epistle from a Dog at Twickenham to a Dog at Court*, commemorating his own recent gift to the Prince: the uncommon honour of a puppy from his celebrated dog Bounce.[72] The poem's genially comic tone is worlds apart from the harsh political satire of the *Epistle to Bathurst*

[67] Mrs Caesar's Journal, Bodleian MS Film 740, v. 2. See Erskine-Hill, 'Under Which Caesar?', 442. Bathurst's subsequent courtship of Frederick prompted Charles Caesar later to add: 'Bathurst forgetts that what the Psalmist Writ | Is strictly True, and he'll Again be Bitt'.

[68] Johnson, *Lives of the Poets*, iii. 209–10. For different versions of Pope's 'royal lion' anecdote, see Owen Ruffhead, *The Life of Alexander Pope* (1769), 535; Spence, *Anecdotes*, no. 591 (i. 245–6); Boswell, *Life of Johnson*, iv. 50; Pope, *Imit. Horace*, I. i. 115–19. The conversation may have taken place during Frederick's Oct. 1735 visit.

[69] The 'Six Maidens' is in *TE* vi. 341–3. See Ault, *New Light on Pope*, 276–80. In 1732 Frederick acknowledged his fathership of a child by his mistress Harriet Vane, one of the ladies-in-waiting. Swift also satirized his affairs in 'On Poetry: A Rapsody' (*c*.1733).

[70] Pope–Bathurst, 8 Oct. 1735 (*Corr.* iii. 500).

[71] For the portrait, see Oliver Millar, *Tudor, Stuart and Early Georgian Pictures in the Royal Collection*, 2 vols. (1963), no. 526 (i. 175–6), plate 198. For Frederick's gift, see *Corr.* iv. 170, 178. The busts now line the walls of the library at Hagley.

[72] For Pope and his dogs, see Maynard Mack, *Alexander Pope: A Life* (New Haven, Conn., 1985), 676–80. *Bounce to Fop* was issued in May 1736 as being by 'Dr. S[wift]' and reissued in Dublin soon after by Swift's printer Faulkner. Swift may have had a hand in some original version of the text, but it was not until May 1739 that Swift himself first seems to have realized Frederick's full significance for the opposition. (See Pope, *Corr.* iv. 175–6.)

and other recently reprinted poems of the previous year. Bounce, a dog who congratulates herself on her moral independence and keen nose for sniffing out any whiff of court corruption, becomes an (almost) absurd symbol of Pope the morally self-aggrandizing opposition satirist. Bounce's heartfelt desire to see two of her sons accompanying 'Iülus' (Frederick) to ward off 'Flatt'rers, Spies, and Panders', including the ubiquitous 'Lord *Fannys*' (Hervey—Lord Fanny—was now an enemy to both Pope and Frederick), is both funny yet possibly sincere:

> Then might a Royal Youth, and true,
> Enjoy at least a Friend—or two:
> A Treasure, which, of Royal kind,
> Few but Himself deserve to find.[73]

But the following year, 1737, caught Pope in a different mood. Although Frederick's popularity reached new heights during George II's protracted visit to Hanover between July 1736 and January 1737, the widening rift with his father did not endear him to everyone. Pulteney's parliamentary motion of 22 February 1737 demanding an increase in the Prince's allowance alienated many Tories, to whom the measure smacked of forcing the King's hand.[74] Pope was on his summer rambles when Frederick carried off Augusta from Hampton Court on 31 July to give birth to a daughter in St James's. The royal pair were expelled from the court just before Pope wrote to Hugh Bethel in September, commenting on the royal wrangles with wry detachment.

I am glad by my rambles, to have escaped much of the disagreable noise, & the impertinent chatter of this place, about the late Difference of the Courts. To the other reasons I gave you in my last, of my Joy in the *Sex* of the Child, I may add this one more, now, That we may have no prospect in the next Generation, of a Third Quarrel between a Father & a *Son*.[75]

Pope went on to report the spread of a brain fever in the south of England and observed ironically: 'You may be sure there can be no such thing at Hampton Court.' The row over the birth of the Princess Augusta reminded Pope of the row between George I and the future George II over the christening of George II's second son in 1717. It revived all his old prejudices about disagreeable foreign kings who, unlike the dignified Stuart Anne, insisted on airing their dirty domestic linen in public.

---

[73] *Bounce to Fop*, ll. 77–80 (*TE* vi. 369).
[74] See Linda Colley, *In Defiance of Oligarchy: The Tory Party 1714–60* (Cambridge, 1982), 221–2. A total of 45 Tory MPs absented themselves from the division.
[75] Pope–Bethel, 25 Sept. 1737 (*Corr.* iv. 86).

Pope and Jacobitism?

Pope's contempt for George II and Caroline is a dominant feature of much of his political poetry between 1728 and 1742. Recent critics have explored the extent to which Pope's anti-Hanoverian frustrations may have found an outlet in continued support for the House of Stuart.[76] Disaffection with the Hanoverians is not necessarily a symptom of Jacobitism. Swift never disguised his dislike of the Hanoverians but did not seek a Stuart restoration after the death of the Protestant Anne. Pope as a Catholic may have had a different set of loyalties. Given the treasonable nature of Jacobitism, the evidence for Pope's Jacobitism has to be constructed from other sources—notably his close friendships with known Jacobites such as Bolingbroke, Orrery, and Atterbury, and the rhetorical signposts in his poetry which suggest the hidden 'rhetoric of Jacobitism'.

The arguments advanced by a number of critics, notably John Aden, Howard Erskine-Hill, and Douglas Brooks-Davies, seem most convincing when applied to Pope's early literary career and to the events surrounding the trial and impeachment of his close friend the Jacobite Atterbury in 1722. Placed in the context of other Jacobite writings of this period, *The Rape of the Lock* and *Windsor-Forest* seem to resonate with the Jacobite imagery of rape and illegal seizure as a metaphor for William III's usurpation of the English Crown.[77] Pope, like many Tories, would undoubtedly have preferred a restoration of James III to the ascent of the 58th-removed Hanoverian elector King George. But there is no evidence that he was in any way supportive of Bolingbroke's spell in the Pretender's service during the 1715 rebellion. Pope may have known about Atterbury's Jacobite activities: it is possible that he perjured himself while defending Atterbury during his trial. Letters from this period reveal the depths of Pope's emotion over the affair.[78] But Atterbury's banishment, as G. V. Bennett remarks, was a 'turning point in British politics and a decisive blow to the Tory cause'. One by one the former leading Tory

---

[76] See esp. John M. Aden, *Pope's Once and Future Kings: Satire and Politics in the Early Career* (Knoxville, Tenn., 1978); Howard Erskine-Hill, 'Literature and the Jacobite Cause: Was There a Rhetoric of Jacobitism?', in Eveline Cruickshanks (ed.), *Ideology and Conspiracy: Aspects of Jacobitism, 1689–1759* (Edinburgh, 1982), and his 'Alexander Pope: The Political Poet in His Time', *ECS* 15 (1981–2), 123–48; Douglas Brooks-Davies, *Pope's 'Dunciad' and the Queen of the Night: A Study in Emotional Jacobitism* (Manchester, 1985); Brean Hammond, *Pope* (Brighton, 1986). Dissenting views advanced esp. by Vincent Carretta, *The Snarling Muse: Visual and Verbal Satire from Pope to Churchill* (Philadelphia, Pa., 1983), 173–4; Chester Chapin, 'Pope and the Jacobites', *Eighteenth-Century Life*, 10 (1986), 59–73; Downie, '1688: Pope and the Rhetoric of Jacobitism', 9–24.

[77] See esp. Aden, *Pope's Once and Future Kings*, and his '"The Change of Scepters and impending Woe": Political Allusion in Pope's Statius', *PQ* 52 (1973), 728–38; and Erskine-Hill, 'Literature and the Jacobite Cause'.

[78] Erskine-Hill, 'Alexander Pope: The Political Poet', 133. But Chapin, 'Pope and the Jacobites', 62, argues that Pope's value as a witness lay precisely in his lack of awareness.

peers who had been involved in Jacobite negotiations '"declared themselves weary of the situation they were in, and ready to enter into measures"'.[79] These included Pope's friends Wyndham, Gower, Bathurst, and Orrery. George Granville, Lord Lansdowne, had strong Jacobite sympathies in the period prior to 1725 but by the early 1730s was writing embarrassingly fulsome panegyrics to Caroline as the true focus for Tory loyalty.[80] Pope seems to have distanced himself from politics after the Atterbury affair. His apparent friendliness with Walpole and his political silence between 1722 and 1728 have been construed as evidence that Walpole 'muzzled' Pope by holding his brother-in-law Charles Rackett as a kind of poetic ransom.[81] But Pope was also very busy during this period translating Homer, an arduous task, and wrote little of his own poetry, political or not, until 1728 and *The Dunciad*, with its anti-Hanoverian innuendo. It is hard, however, to be convinced that the web of alchemical Stuart symbolism one critic has extrapolated from this poem points to anything like Jacobitism, emotional or not.[82]

Bolingbroke, a man of known Jacobite associations, was in large measure responsible for 'emboldening' Pope to play a more active political role in his poetry in the 1730s. Bolingbroke dabbled in Jacobitism in 1731–3 and again after his return to France in July 1739, depressed by the opposition's failure to make any headway. He and Sir William Wyndham were excluded from the Jacobite negotiations leading up to the '45.[83] It seems evident from the very ambiguity of the *Patriot King* that Bolingbroke, always a political opportunist, was prepared to entertain the possibility of a Jacobite restoration when the united Patriot opposition for which he was a chief ideologue failed to materialize; and Pope's own *1740*, as we shall see, echoes something of this rhetorically open-ended ambiguity. But more often than not Bolingbroke lamented the Tory proclivity towards Jacobitism as one of the chief causes of the opposition's lack of unity.[84] Most of Bolingbroke's political energies were invested in trying to create an oppositional alliance between Whigs and Tories; after 1735 and his rift with Pulteney he was most closely associated with the members of the Cobham–Wyndham circle, trying to promote Frederick as a 'centre of union, a superior authority among yourselves, under whose influence men of

---

[79] G. V. Bennett, 'Jacobitism and the Rise of Walpole', in Neil McKendrick (ed.), *Historical Perspectives: Studies in English Thought and Society* (1974), 70–92, p. 91.

[80] Granville was arrested on the accession of George I and put in the tower for Jacobite conspiracy but finally released in 1717. By his last years he seems to have been very pro-Hanoverian. His 'The Muses' Last Dying Song', discussed in Ch. 6, transferred Tory aristocratic loyalism and language to Caroline and the Hanoverians. See Elizabeth Handasyde, *Granville the Polite* (Oxford, 1933).

[81] See E. P. Thompson, *Whigs and Hunters: The Origin of the Black Act* (1975), 287. But see Aden, *Pope's Once and Future Kings*, 170–5.

[82] See Brooks-Davies, *Pope's 'Dunciad' and the Queen of the Night*. This study is far more convincing in its earlier accounts of the Queen Anne period, 1–45.

[83] See Romney Sedgwick, *The History of Parliament: The House of Commons, 1715–1754*, 2 vols. (1970), ii. 564.

[84] See Coxe, *Walpole*, iii. 524.

different characters and different views will be brought to draw better together'.[85] The period between July 1738 and April 1739, when the *Patriot King* was first calculated, showed both Bolingbroke and Pope busy on Frederick's and the Patriots' behalf. The fact that Pope maintained friendships at this time with known Jacobite sympathizers proves little. His determination to preserve friendships *despite* party politics is demonstrated by his continued familiarity with both William Fortescue, one of Walpole's most loyal henchmen, and the former Old Whig Thomas Gordon, now Walpole's press supervisor. In July 1738, while Bolingbroke was staying at Twickenham but absent for the day in London, Pope even invited Gordon round to toast Walpole's health.[86] It may well be that Pope's political satires of the late 1730s, with their attacks on pervasive degeneracy and corruption and their invocation of the spirit of 'Old England', are written in an idiom which overlaps with Jacobite rhetoric: much other opposition writing shared the same language.[87] But it cannot be forgotten that both Dialogues of the *Epilogue to the Satires* are specific in their praise of named Patriot Whigs. Pope's high level of activity in the Patriot campaign and in his oppositional writing in this period was not simply a 'cloak' to enable him to express underlying Jacobite sentiments with impunity.[88]

One Thousand Seven Hundred and Thirty-Eight

1738 was the *annus mirabilis* of Pope's opposition career: a renewed commitment to the Patriots prompted in large measure by news of Bolingbroke's return, which he heralded in March by the controversial *Epistle to Bolingbroke*. Dialogues I and II of the *Epilogue to the Satires* appeared in May and July. Their Juvenalian loftiness prompted even Aaron Hill to revise his former opinions

[85] Bolingbroke–Wyndham, 3 Feb. 1738 (Coxe, *Walpole*, iii. 506).

[86] See Pope–Fortescue, 31 July 1738 (*Corr.* iv. 114). Pope's tone and his mention of Bolingbroke, Gordon, and Walpole suggest a conscious satisfaction in flaunting friendships with such political incompatibles. Erskine-Hill's representation of Pope's Jacobite friendships ('Pope: The Political Poet', 127–9) has come under severe attack by Downie and Chapin. Erskine-Hill also misrepresents Cobham listing him as 'Tory and Protestant', failing to mention his impeccable Whig credentials. Cobham may have expressed some admiration for Charles Stuart the man in 1743, but baulked at his Papism. See Eveline Cruickshanks, *Political Untouchables: The Tories and the '45* (1979), 91. Erskine-Hill's list also omits Pope's many friendships with opposition Whigs other than Lyttelton.

[87] It is hard to know what can be proved by the fact that a 1745 pamphlet in support of Charles Stuart quoted a line about corruption from Pope's *Epilogue to the Satires* (Erskine-Hill, 'Pope: The Political Poet', 148). The Young Pretender at this stage was also using opposition-Whig Patriot-style language about constitutional liberty. Both cases suggest the readiness of Jacobites to use any political rhetoric to serve their turn.

[88] Erskine-Hill, 'Pope: The Political Poet', 135, suggests that the Patriot campaign of the 1730s did not 'necessarily involve a current Jacobite commitment' but that it offered 'a new sort of protection' for Pope's expression of Jacobitism—a misrepresentation of Pope's political activities in this period.

about satire: the second contains 'something, inexpressibly daring and generous
. . . it reaches *heights* the most elevated without seeming to design any soaring. It
opposes just *praise* to just *censure*. . . . It places the *Poet* in a light for which
nature and *reason* designed him.'[89] Never before had Pope been so outspoken in
his support for opposition leaders; the second Dialogue reads like a roll-call of
Patriot worthies, including the tribute to Frederick quoted at the start of this
chapter. However, that tribute was a qualified one—Frederick may be honoured
with Pope's friendship, but Pope is not Frederick's follower. When Pope draws
up his own personal 'honours list' to set against the court's now corrupted honours, the Garter and the Bath, George II and even Frederick are excluded: 'Far
other Stars than * and ** wear.'[90] And even in these poems, written at the
height of his involvement, Pope is flexible about the word 'Patriot'.[91] In the first
Dialogue, ll. 37–44, he invests it with all the best meanings against the cynical
Friend's 'Horse-laugh' for 'Some odd *Old Whig*' (the independent Whig Joseph
Jekyll). The Patriot's old-fashioned integrity stands out against his denouncer's
'modern' political morality. 'A Patriot is a Fool in ev'ry age.' They 'keep their
Fashion still, | And wear their strange old Virtue as they will'. For some reason
Pope praises Pulteney's 'Roman Spirit' in Dialogue II, l. 85, even though in
Dialogue I he had hinted at Pulteney and Carteret's career gambits under the
'mock-patriot' cloak: '*Patriots* there are, who wish you'd jest no more' (l. 24).
More surprising is the apocalyptic vision of the triumph of Vice in the same
poem, which excludes Pope, the one who 'held it in disdain', but includes
Patriots among the 'thronging Millions' who follow in her path dragging 'Old
England's Genius' down into the dirt (ll. 157, 152). 'In Soldier, Churchman,
Patriot, Man in Pow'r, | 'Tis Av'rice all, Ambition is no more!' (ll. 161–2). Pope
doesn't discriminate here between one kind of Patriot and another: the 'Patriot'
walks alongside the 'Man in Pow'r'.

   The sombre mood of these poems, contrasting with Pope's real-life activities
during the period of their composition, shows that poetic self-dramatization is
not the same as autobiography. The summer of 1738 was one of Pope's happi-
est and busiest on the Patriots' behalf. He spent much of his time with
Bolingbroke editing the manuscripts of Thomson, Mallet, Hill, and Brooke's
Patriot dramas, planned for an onslaught on the London theatres' winter season.[92] Twickenham became a meeting-place for the disaffected: in November

---

[89] Hill–Pope, 31 July 1738 (*Corr.* iv. 112).

[90] *Ep. Satires*, ii. 236 (*TE* iv. 326). The names to fit the gaps were supplied by Marchmont.

[91] For a check-list of Pope's use of the term 'Patriot' see Emmett G. Bedford and Robert J.
Dilligan, *A Concordance to the Poems of Alexander Pope*, 2 vols. (Detroit, 1974), ii. 89. Pope's epitaph on the Jacobite John Caryll (1711) described him as 'An honest Courtier, and a Patriot too'.
In 1717 Pope used almost exactly the same phrase for an epitaph on the Whig William Trumbull;
and, after this, nearly all his references to Patriots apply to opposition Whigs, or to a very small
number of Tories working with them. An exception was his reluctant epitaph to the Duchess of
Buckingham's short-lived son (1735).

[92] See Malcolm Goldstein, *Pope and the Augustan Stage* (Stanford, Calif., 1958), 46–64. But he
trivializes Pope and Bolingbroke's role as editors, suggesting it was little more than a parlour-
game.

Pope entertained Cornbury, the Marquess of Queensberry, Lyttelton, Bolingbroke, and Chesterfield. The manuscript of Bolingbroke's *Idea of a Patriot King* was probably circulated around this time. Pope's activities were uncharacteristic on two scores; both testify to a rapid quickening of his political pulse. He had never previously been much of a theatre-goer, but his customary winter visits to the town were dominated by his new interest in theatrical affairs. In April 1738 he had made a much noted and applauded personal appearance on the first night of Thomson's *Agamemnon*, even (according to one source) cutting the play between performances to improve it.[93] He also appeared at the opening night of Mallet's *Mustapha* on 13 February 1739, and his correspondence of this period, particularly his letters to Hill, are full of detailed references to the staging of these plays and Frederick's role in selecting them.[94] Pope's appearances may have been prompted by curiosity for his own literary progeny; they also signalled a public commitment to the cause they promoted. Pope told Hill he had 'no objection' for his and Bolingbroke's names to be used to sell the plays to Fleetwood, stage-manager at the Haymarket, 'for it is what both of us will speak in the gates, as the scripture expresses it; and to all mankind'.[95]

The second role Pope played at this time was in working out the tactical details of the new broad-bottom alliance—a role which shows just how uncharacteristically involved he had become in Westminster affairs. By the autumn of 1738 Pope was in the thick of high politics. The letter he sent Lyttelton on 1 November may have been evasive about playing moral tutor to the Prince but it is brisk and pragmatic in its attention to 'something . . . more material' than Lyttelton's vague idealizing.[96] Pope seems to have known more about tactical details than Lyttelton: the letter fills him in on the political instructions he had received from a conference with Wyndham on the stratagems to be adopted by the Cobhamite Patriots to undermine Pulteney and Carteret's power-base. It contains a detailed programme for broad-bottom policies: in this 'New Opposition . . . (or rather the old one reviv'd)', as Pope accurately describes it, Whigs and Tories should no longer be 'applyd to in the *Collective Body*' but privately, 'in seperate Conversations & Arguments'. Frederick should be enjoined to back this 'New Measure: who, the moment it takes place, will be Head of the Party, and Those two Persons cease to be so at that instant'.

---

[93] See Benjamin Victor (a usually reliable source), *Original Letters, Dramatic Pieces and Poems*, 3 vols. (1776), ii. 11.

[94] See *Corr.* iv. 110–12, 120–3, 126–7, 128–9, 131–3, 145–6, 151–3, 158–60, 161–2, 165–6, 167–8.

[95] Pope–Hill, 22 Jan. 1739 (ibid. 159).

[96] Pope–Lyttelton, 1 Nov. 1738 (ibid. 142–4). For the significance of this, see Colley, *In Defiance of Oligarchy*, 223.

'The most dirty, rascally Race on Earth'

But Bolingbroke's departure to France the following April (1739), after the opposition's disastrously divided attempts in March at a mass secession from the government motion for the Convention Treaty with Spain, seems to have been the point at which Pope began to have grave misgivings about Patriot politics.[97] In March he curtly refused Richard Nash's request for an inscription for the monument commemorating the honours heaped on Frederick by the City of Bath, retreating into his usual pose of unfamiliarity with 'the great' and their affairs. When he did finally agree he insisted on anonymity. It hardly mattered, since the inscription was so plain and short anyone could have written it.[98] Pope still maintained an active political correspondence with Lyttelton and other Patriots throughout the months of 1739 and 1740, but his growing absorption with his Twickenham grotto symbolizes an underlying impulse to seclude himself from the opposition's increasingly gloomy prospects. By 1740 Pope had become strangely infatuated with Marchmont (or what he thought he saw in him). Pope focused on the 32-year-old Scot as an impossibly idealized political hero. His urgent and emotional letters to Marchmont suggest a loss of detachment; they alternate between profound pessimism and disgust with English politics and the unrealistic hope that Marchmont might somehow 'keep Virtue & Honour alive . . . and . . . dash the Forehead and shake the soul of Guilty Wretches, who else would intail their Profligacy on all future generations'. Marchmont represents a desperate last hope: 'you can animate, you can supply, you can better, a better Age than this, & prepare happier Scenes for the Coming Generation.'[99] Trying to find the source of Marchmont's imagined greatness, Pope enquires 'I wish I knew what it is? that I may admire you less, & understand you better'.[100]

Pope's admiration for Marchmont certainly unbalanced his literary judgement. When in March 1740 Robert Craggs Nugent sent Pope a series of third-rate odes on the Patriots, Pope singled out the ode to Marchmont, implausibly comparing Nugent's performance to those of the celebrated Greek lyric poet, Alcaeus.[101] Marchmont's elevation to the Lords on inheriting the family title

---

[97] Critics disagree about the extent of Pope's active commitment to politics after this period. Sherburn (Pope, *Corr.* iv. 214) claims that 'at this time there is little doubt of Pope's political bias', and Chapin, 'Pope and the Jacobites', 67, sees Pope's disillusion setting in only after Walpole's fall in 1742. But Pope's letter to Swift of 17–19 May 1739 (*Corr.* iv. 176–80) suggests less enthusiasm for Frederick and Lyttelton—a detachment prompted partly by ill health but also by a withdrawal from his previous level of activity. Pope mentions his own poetic and political silence after *Ep. Satires*, Dia. ii. By 12 Dec. 1739 Lyttelton was complaining that Pope had forgotten about him. In May 1740 Lyttelton wrote him a very formal note asking to be introduced to Pope's new favourite friend, William Warburton.   [98] *Corr.* iv. 170, 176.

[99] Pope–Marchmont, Oct. 1740 (ibid. 273); 29 Feb. 1740 (ibid. 228).

[100] Pope–Marchmont, 10 Jan. 1740 (ibid. 217).

[101] Pope–Nugent, 27 Mar. 1740 (ibid. 231).

in February 1740, followed by Wyndham's unexpected death on 17 June, represented a double, critical loss to the Patriots. Pope recorded Bolingbroke's reaction: '"What a Star has our Minister? Wyndham dead, Marchmont disabled! The loss of Ma: & Wy: to our Country . . ."'.[102] Wyndham's death hit Pope very hard: a long letter to Marchmont written five days later is undisguisedly bitter about so-called 'Patriots' who go about business as usual, not even bothering to put on a decent mask of sorrow. 'Our Great Men & Patriots . . . hate Honour openly, & pray devoutly for the Removal of all Virtue. Their prayers have been pretty well heard.' Carteret and Pulteney are hinted at, but an ampersand links 'Great Men [i.e. Walpole] & Patriots' in the same breath. There is little to choose between them in a land cursed by these 'Scourges': we are 'not to imagine the most dirty, rascally Race on Earth are the Favorite People of God'.[103]

This is the tone of the unpublished satiric fragment, *One Thousand Seven Hundred and Forty*, written (as the reference to the loss of Wyndham and Marchmont shows) some time soon after June 1740.[104] Critics who have seen this etiolated but finished poem as either Pope's projected third Horatian dialogue or his considered response to Lyttelton's promptings for a Patriot King poem glorifying Frederick have misread his political frame of mind in 1740: Pope's pessimism—'grieved at [Britain's] present state, & unable to help her'—could have produced neither.[105] Editorial reconstruction of the lacunae shows that *1740* extends well beyond the easy Cobhamite targets of the 'firm' of Pulteney and Carteret to attack Pope's own friends, the Patriot and Tory stalwarts Chesterfield, Cobham, Gower, Bathurst, and Cornbury.[106] Chesterfield, previously admired for his '*Attic* Wit', is now a mere wiseacre who finds Britain 'at best, the butt to crack his joke on' (l. 28). Gower, Cobham, and Bathurst's patriotism is governed by personal self-interest. They will pay Britain their 'due regards, | Unless the ladies bid them mind their cards' (ll. 23–4). Cornbury's sins of omission (he 'hopes, and candidly sits still' (l. 18)) are almost as bad. The Jacobite leader William Shippen and the independent Patriot Samuel Sandys come under fire; so too do the easily manipulated illiterate Tory country squires, a flock of silly geese. Pope's satirical

---

[102] Pope–Marchmont, Oct. 1740 (ibid. 272).

[103] Pope–Marchmont, 22 June 1740 (ibid. 249).

[104] See *1740*, ll. 79–80 (*TE* iv. 336). All further quotations inc. in text.

[105] Pope–Marchmont, Oct. 1740 (*Corr.* iv. 272). This letter (271–3) supplies the best context for a reading of *1740*. Butt, *TE* iv, pp. xl–xli, suggests that *1740* was written as a direct response to Lyttelton's pleas and perhaps as the fulfilment of his 31 July promise to Fortescue to write a third Horatian dialogue (see *TE* iv. 320–1). But the poem is not a dialogue. Nor is it the enthusiastic Patriot King poem described by Brean Hammond, *Pope and Bolingbroke: A Study of Friendship and Influence* (Columbia, Mo., 1984), 104–5; Isaac Kramnick, *Bolingbroke and His Circle: The Politics of Nostalgia in the Age of Walpole* (Cambridge, Mass., 1968), 219; and Chapin, 'Pope and the Jacobites', 67, where 'Bolingbroke's dream had become Pope's'. Chapin also misrepresents the poem by implying that Pope condemns only Pulteney and Carteret.

[106] The gaps were mostly filled in by Pope's 19th-cent. editors F. H. Bowles and J. W. Croker. See Pope, *Works*, ed. W. Elwin and J. W. Courthope, 10 vols. (1871–86), iii. 500–1.

scatter-gun leaves no political group untouched. This is the most cynical poem he ever wrote. Over it hangs a spirit of political torpor which makes *The Dunciad*'s kingdom of dullness seem energetic by comparison. Walpole lingers on in power only because his opponents are unable to summon the effort and united will to oust him from power. 'Rise, rise, great W[alpole] fated to appear, | Spite of thyself a glorious minister!' (ll. 43-4). Pope's half-ironic 'third compliment' to Walpole—'At length to B[ritain] kind, as to thy [whore] | Espouse the nation, you [debauched before]' (ll. 47-8)—might well correspond in mood with the cavalier bumper with which he had previously toasted Sir Robert in the company of Thomas Gordon.[107] A twenty-year enforced intimacy had wed Walpole to Britain as firmly as to Maria Skerrett, recently elevated from long-suffering mistress to second wife.

There is no hint of the patriotic optimism central to Bolingbroke's *Patriot King*. The poem opens with a desperate jeremiad on Britain's corrupt ministers *and* Patriots.

> O wretched B[ritain], jealous now of all,
> What God, what mortal, shall prevent thy fall?
> Turn, turn thy eyes from wicked men in place,
> And see what succour from the Patriot Race.
>
> (ll. 1-4)

This is scarcely a positive piece of Patriot propaganda. The poem's final appeal, 'Alas! on one alone our all relies, | Let him be honest, and he must be wise' (ll. 85-6), is indeed a statement of Patriot King ideals—national salvation by one miraculous monarch. Pope's assertion that neither religion nor blood should debar a prince whose 'public virtue makes his title good' (l. 96) certainly leaves open the possibility that either a Hanoverian or a Stuart might fill that role.[108] But the appeal comes at the end of a poem whose deeply disillusioned view of politics exposes such ideals as absurdly unworkable. By 1740, even if honesty were a relevant quality in public life, would 'one man's honesty' be sufficient to 'redeem the land' (l. 98)? Almost certainly not. In the face of ambiguity, one thing is clear. *1740* was never intended for publication. Its lacunae may have been prompted either by fear of prosecution at a time when satire was 'as unsafe as it was ineffectual', or by Pope's reticence to satirize his once-admired opposition friends so openly. The poem is less a satire on the ministry than a betrayal of the opposition. It is no coincidence that its only

---

[107] Pope's second 'compliment' to Walpole is in *Ep. Satires*, i. 27-36. Pope mentions it and raises the possibility of a third compliment in a letter to Fortescue, 31 July 1738 (*Corr.* iv. 114-15), when he was drinking with Thomas Gordon.

[108] Suggested by Croker but refuted by Butt, *TE* iv. 337; subsequently raised again by Erskine-Hill, 'Pope: The Political Poet', 139, and Simon Varey, 'Hanover, Stuart and the *Patriot King*', *BJECS* 6 (1983), 163-72; refuted again by Chapin, 'Pope and the Jacobites', 67, and Downie, '1688: Pope and the Rhetoric of Jacobitism', 20. My 'Pope and the Patriots' in Fairer (ed.), *Pope: New Contexts*, 35, sides with the argument that *1740* is dynastically ambiguous.

extended metaphor—the opposition as a carriage stuck fast in the mud, rendered even more immobile by its quarrelling drivers—also lies at the centre of
Fielding's cynical political allegory *The Opposition: A Vision* of 1741: a work
which, like *1740*, satirizes not only Pulteney and Carteret but also Fielding's
own political patrons the Cobhamite Patriots.[109] On 13 February 1741 Sandys
put forward his disastrously divisive motion to remove Walpole. In the opposition gloom and ministerial triumph which followed, print-makers had a field
day with 'The Motion' series of prints, which portrayed various distraught
opposition leaders (including Chesterfield, Lyttelton, and Pulteney) spurring
on or lagging behind a Whitehall-bound stagecoach exclaiming 'Lost it!' or 'O!
my P[lac]e'.[110] Pope's gloomy prognostications had crystallized into the same
metaphor some six months earlier.

When Pope wrote to Sarah, Duchess of Marlborough shortly after
Walpole's fall it was as one political old-trooper to another. The former Queen
Anne Tory and the widow of the famous Whig general had at least one thing
in common—a dislike of Walpole and an even greater dislike of false Patriots.

Madam,—I said nothing to your Grace of Patriots, & God forbid I should. If I did, I
must do as they do, & Lye: for I have seen none of 'em, not even their Great Leader
[Pulteney], nor once congratulated any one Friend or Foe, upon his Promotion, or
New Reveal'd Religion . . . call it which you will; or by the more distinct & intelligible
Name, his New Place or Pension. I'm so sick of London, in her present State.[111]

The fourth book of Pope's *Dunciad* came out soon after Walpole's fall. Here
Pope invested his vision of Britain's political and cultural decline with an
unprecedently powerful vein of satiric mythology, not least its central figure of
Walpole, the 'WIZARD OLD' with his all-potent cup of 'Self-love'. It was as if
Pope had poured all his imaginative myth-making energy into this poetic 'cup'
alone; there seems to have been little left for the plans for the blank-verse
Brutus epic, also mapped out at around the same time.[112] Curiously, the handful of blank-verse lines Pope penned as his invocation carry echoes of
Lyttelton's 1730 *Epistle to Mr. Pope* calling on him to write a national, patriotic epic. Just as Lyttelton had advised Pope, 'No more let meaner Satire taint
thy Bays | And stain the Glory of thy nobler Lays', Pope here renounces
'meaner Care or meaner Song' for the 'Holy Hill of Spotless Bay'. So too, just

[109] Critics are in considerable disagreement about whether or not this work symbolized
Fielding's 'defection' from the opposition. Cleary, *Henry Fielding: Political Writer*, 152–67, tortu-
ously claims it shows Fielding still loyal to his 'broad-bottom' patrons the Cobhamites; Goldgar,
Walpole and the Wits, 203–8, discusses the case and supplies a convincing argument for Fielding's
total disenchantment. Fielding openly satirized his former allies; Pope kept his similarly sceptical
1740 unpublished.

[110] *BMC* nos. 2478–92. Captions from no. 2490.

[111] Pope–Sarah, Duchess of Marlborough, 19 Jan. 1742 (*Corr.* iv. 382).

[112] For dating and discussion of the plans in both Owen Ruffhead's description of a now lost
version in his 1769 *Life of Pope* and in BL Egerton MS 1950, see Miriam Leranbaum, *Pope's
'Opus Magnum' 1729–1744* (Oxford, 1977), 131–74.

as Lyttelton had once urged Pope to 'join the PATRIOT's to the POET's Praise'
in raising a 'lasting Column to thy Country's Praise', Pope presents himself
here as 'My Countrys Poet, to record her Fame'.[113]

But if this was indeed a response to Lyttelton's promptings for Pope to
raise an edifice out of 'Monkish Annals', in this case Geoffrey of Monmouth's
Historia Regum Britanniae, formerly ridiculed by Pope, it came too little too
late. Donald Torchiania observes that the plans abound with many of the com-
monplaces of Patriot literature: the heroic prince, the scheming minister, even
(most pertinently) a Druid bard, a key figure in the Patriots' poetic pantheon,
who prophesies the decline of Britain and its subsequent regeneration—the
Machiavellian call for a *ritorno* which is the central feature of not only the
Patriot King but nearly all Patriot poems and plays.[114] The *Brutus* plans may
seem to contain all the right ingredients, bar one, the most important—a sense
of patriotism in both its British and its heroic sense. Chester Chapin has
asserted that 'Brutus, Pope's final hero, is every inch a political hero, a patriot
king in the Bolingbroke mold', that 'he represents in Pope's imagination the
longed-for truly national ruler' and that solely 'the Love of his Country'
induces his arduous voyage to England.[115] But Britain is not Troy—a small
quibble, perhaps, but Brutus is undoubtedly a foreign prince, albeit one who
conquers by kindness, ensuring that 'the whole island submits to good
Government'.[116] His similarities to the 'pius Aeneas' suggest that he is an
unmistakably classical hero. Pope's plans show that it is the Trojan Brutus
who first introduces 'Love of Liberty . . . the Martial Spirit, and other Moral
Virtues' to the 'good and gentle dispositions' of the early inhabitants of
Britain: qualities which become supine 'in an age or two' and need to be
reaffirmed by 'a Descendant of his Family out of Italy, Julius Caesar'.[117] As
we shall see in Chapter 5, the Patriot poets had very different ideas about
native British liberty and moral toughness. The early Britons' defiance of
Julius Caesar was repeatedly celebrated as a triumph of the British patriotic
spirit over foreign imperial tyranny. Pope had his own independent, rather
than political agenda in mind when he planned *Brutus*, and it shows—interests
in primitive religions and noble savages, most of all ideas for a work which
would fit into his larger ethical *opus magnum* to demonstrate the 'establishment

[113] The fragment printed *TE* vi. 404. Lyttelton, *Epistle to Mr. Pope*, 5–6.

[114] Donald T. Torchiana, 'Brutus: Pope's Last Hero', repr. in Maynard Mack (ed.), *Essential
Articles for the Study of Alexander Pope* (Hamden, Conn., 1968), 705–23, advances a strong case for
the work as a potential contribution to the Patriot campaign.

[115] Chapin, 'Pope and the Jacobites', 69.

[116] BL Egerton MS 1950, cited in Leranbaum, *Pope's 'Opus Magnum'*, 158.

[117] BL Egerton MS 1950, cited ibid. 172. Although Pope planned to 'mythologize' his Cornish
landscapes with giants and fables, the rationalist tone of the plans dismisses these fables as savage
superstitions; Ruffhead thought Pope intended to 'moralize' them. Brutus himself is not a mythol-
ogized British figure: other Patriot and Hanoverian works of this period were using the
Troynovant myth in a far more full-blooded way.

of civil government'.[118] Brutus may correspond with Pope's idealized model of good kingship but he is not in its most basic sense a national 'Patriot King'. Joseph Warton was quick to detect that Brutus would have been a 'bloodless' hero in more ways than one, an exemplar of piety, reason, enlightenment, and 'benevolence'; this composition would have shown, he thought, 'more of the PHILOSOPHER than of the POET'.[119] Even the skeleton plans of *Brutus* indicate an absence of the deeply emotional sense of British patriotism which Pope had once invested many years back in *Windsor-Forest*. The mental distance one has to travel between *Brutus* and Thomson's 'Rule, Britannia' most surely tells us that, even had Pope lived to complete the plans, his philosophical epic could never have been Lyttelton's long-hoped-for Patriot epic.

[118] See Leranbaum, *Pope's 'Opus Magnum', passim*. One of the best accounts of the primitivist and religious elements in the *Brutus* plans is Valerie Rumbold, 'Pope and the Gothic Past' (Cambridge Ph.D. thesis, 1983), 216–51, which also supplies an accurate transcription of both Ruffhead and BL Egerton MS 1950.

[119] Joseph Warton, *An Essay on the Writings and Genius of Pope*, 2 vols. (1756–62), i. 279. Pope's outline shows that he has eschewed Geoffrey of Monmouth's praise of Brutus's martial prowess.

Part II

Mythologizing History

Prologue

THE FIRST part of this study has traced the dominant political and cultural features of the Patriot campaign as well as its personalities and principles. The second part will focus more closely on the poetry itself, exploring different aspects of perhaps *the* distinctive hallmark of the Patriot literary programme—its imaginative engagement with British myth and legend. The only poet whose work I have examined in detail so far is Pope. Pope shared with the Patriots a Bolingbrokean language of virtue and corruption, but the satiric impulse which, in general terms, distinguishes his verse from theirs symptomizes a more profound difference. Pope, comments Isabel Rivers, shows 'small interest in the appeal to history essential to patriotism'.[1] By the 1730s, there were to be no more *Windsor-Forest*s for Pope, not even a Jacobite one. In the place of *Windsor-Forest*'s richly mythological English landscapes, resonant with a sense of historical significance, Pope fabricated his own personal mythology—a mythology woven from the 'seamless' fabric of the Horatian retirement tradition in its classical and English forms.[2] From the carefully controlled seclusion of his Twickenham 'seat', Pope engaged in a series of sallies with prominent political figures. Determined to show that there was at least 'one who held it [villainy] in disdain', Pope set the record straight for posterity with his roll-call of the worthy and corrupt.[3] The very titles of poems such as *One Thousand Seven Hundred and Thirty Eight* and *One Thousand Seven Hundred and Forty* proclaim Pope's struggle with the contemporary, the here and now. By this stage Pope saw himself as the unofficial historian of his time, a critical and oppositional version of Dryden the Royal Historiographer.

Patriot poetry, by contrast, rarely identifies in detail contemporary names, places, or events. Unlike Pope's, it does not list despairingly 'The Sins of Thirty-nine'.[4] Its optimism derives from a more positive and expansive sense of the relationship between historical past, present, and future than the pessimistic closure symbolized by *The Dunciad*'s apocalyptic ending. Pope's own observation that the Patriots 'Look rather to the past age than the present, and therefore the future may have some hopes of them' applies as much to their poetic vision as it does to their personal promise.[5] Although the Patriots' 'past age' is sometimes located in ancient Greece or republican Rome, it is more often explicitly *British*.

[1] Isabel Rivers, *The Poetry of Conservatism* (Cambridge, 1973), 206.
[2] Maynard Mack, *The Garden and the City: Retirement and Politics in the later Poetry of Pope, 1731–1743* (Toronto, 1969), 11.   [3] *Ep. Satires*, i. 172 (*TE* iv. 309).
[4] *Ep. Satires*, ii. 5 (ibid. 313).   [5] Pope, *Corr.* iv. 51.

Scepticism and Myth

It has often been claimed that enlightened rationalism had gained a stronghold
in English thought by the 1730s. Ernest Jones blames the age's 'general anticlericalism and prevailing rationalism' for the declining reputation of Geoffrey
of Monmouth's *Historia Regum Britanniae*.[6] James Merriman asserts that
Arthur and Merlin vanished from view after the 1720s because the age was
'officially opposed to the supernatural, to mythology and legend . . . such attitudes combined with the essentially anti-historical, critical and satirical spirit
of the times'.[7] Bolingbroke's *Letters on the Study and Use of History* are sometimes read as a Pyrrhonist manifesto for the age, an anticipation of Hegel's
assertion that 'observed and observable reality is a more solid foundation for
history than the transience of myths and epic'.[8] Here Bolingbroke, scorning
those antiquarian scholars who 'have dealt and do deal in fable at least as
much as our poets', drew a firm line below the sixteenth century, dismissing
anything earlier as 'fanciful preludes' and 'broken, perplexed scraps of information'.[9]

D. C. Douglas claimed that this scepticism, epitomized by the writings of
Pierre Bayle, extended to a radical questioning of the value of history itself:
'by the middle of the eighteenth century the leaders of English taste had come
to profess a hatred of the past and a disdain for those who explored it'.[10] One
might speculate just how pervasive, even amongst the intelligentsia, such
French-inspired intellectual scepticism was. Bolingbroke's *Letters on History*,
though written in 1735, were not published until 1752. Even then, they were
better received in France than they were in England.[11] Bolingbroke's attacks
on scriptural authority and divine revelation offended many, including former
Patriot supporters of the 1730s, such as Johnson, and Gilbert West, who
revised his opinions about him.[12] But the English hostility to the *Letters* may

---

[6] Ernest Jones, *Geoffrey of Monmouth, 1640–1800* (Berkeley, Calif., 1944).

[7] James Merriman, *The Flower of Kings: A Study of the Arthurian Legend in England between
1485 and 1835* (Lawrence, Kan., 1973), 80.

[8] Hegel, *Reason in History*, trans. R. S. Hartman (Indianapolis, 1953), 3. Cf. Hegel, 'Myths,
folk songs and traditions are not part of original history; they are still obscure modes and peculiar
to obscure peoples', and Bolingbroke, 'it is impossible that the first ages of any new nation that
forms itself, should afford authentic materials for history. We have none such concerning the originals of any of those nations that actually subsist.'

[9] Bolingbroke, *Works*, ii. 196, 199.

[10] D. C. Douglas, *English Scholars* (1939), 356. For the rise of historical scepticism, see J. G. A.
Pocock, *The Ancient Constitution and the Feudal Law: A Study of English Historical Thought in the
Seventeenth Century. A Reissue with a Retrospect* (Cambridge, 1987), esp. 1–20; *Lord Bolingbroke:
Historical Writings*, ed. Isaac Kramnick (Chicago, 1972), pp. xxviii–xxxviii.

[11] For the reception of the *Letters* see H. T. Dickinson, *Bolingbroke* (1970), 296–301.

[12] In 1753 the pious West described Bolingbroke as a 'Vain & Ostentatious Writer' condemning
his 'Malevolence and Weakness, his Ignorance & Inconsistancy' (Bodleian MS Montague d.16 fo.
199).

also have stemmed from an awareness that Bolingbroke's historical method entailed a dismissal of some of the most deep-rooted sources of British national identity. Bolingbroke's earlier *Remarks on the History of England*, for all their anti-Walpole partisanship, were far closer in temper and outlook to the kind of history familiar to most readers: an interpretation of the recent and the remote past based on a sense of continuity and pride in what it meant to be a Briton. This was the spirit which informed Lyttelton's *History of Henry II*: 'It shows them the birthright they have in their privileges and raises in their minds a generous pride, and makes them ashamed to degenerate from the spirit of their ancestors.'[13] When Lyttelton mentioned this project to Pope in 1741 as a 'disagreable Task' which involved delving in the 'Rubbish of Monkish Annals', his remark smacked of an intellectual *de rigueur* attitudinizing. It did not stop him from devoting many years to the task, or indeed from urging Pope to raise out of the same 'Gothick Ruins' a historical poem of his own, 'a new Edifice that wou'd be fitt to Enshrine the Greatest of our English Kings, and Last to Eternity'.[14] Pope's reticence, symbolized by the unfulfilled promise of the *Brutus* plans and the cynicism which he later lavished on Geoffrey of Monmouth, may have said less about his 'enlightenment scepticism' than about his disillusionment with the Hanoverian monarchy and the partisan sullying of such legends by the Williamite Whig Richard Blackmore. Much of Pope's later political poetry subverts for satirical purposes some of the national myths he himself had woven around Queen Anne in *Windsor-Forest*.

Recovering the Past

Ordinary people still absorbed much of their history from popular almanacs, sermons, and standard family works such as Foxe's *Book of Martyrs*, with their unremittingly Protestant record of English destiny.[15] But the growth of a print culture had given more widespread access to popular histories such as John Oldmixon's *Critical History of England* (1724–6) and the enormously successful Whig Huguenot Rapin de Thoyras's *Histoire d'Angleterre*, immediately translated into a 15-volume English edition by Nicholas Tindal and frequently reprinted in whole or in parts.[16] The political conflicts of the Walpole period,

---

[13] Lyttelton, *The History of the Life of King Henry the Second*, 4 vols. (1767–71), ii, p. ii.

[14] Lyttelton–Pope, 13 June 1741 (*Corr.* iv. 348–9).

[15] See Linda Colley, *Britons: Forging the Nation, 1707–1837* (New Haven, Conn., 1992), 20–9, 41–3.

[16] Rapin's *History* was published in Paris in 1723. It was translated and abridged by Stephen Whateley in 1726–7, and translated by Nicholas Tindal between 1725 and 1731. Tindal's translation with his own notes and those added by the deist republican John Toland made this a very Whig performance, as noted by John, Lord Hervey, *Ancient and Modern Liberty Stated and Compared* (1734), 50–1: Rapin was 'the *Craftsman*'s own political evangelist'.

which pressed English history into partisan service with a vengeance, stimulated an interest in the past which led to a new level of historical awareness. Few days passed when readers of the *Craftsman* were not privileged with an account of some previous age or reign which could provide exemplary or admonitory lessons for Walpolian Britain. Bolingbroke's *Remarks on the History of England*, the twenty-four essays serialized at weekly intervals in its pages between 1730 and 1731, supplied a highly partisan account of English history from its earliest origins to the present day.[17] Bolingbroke depicted English history as a dynamic struggle between the spirit of liberty, embodied in the mixed constitution of Crown, Lords, and Commons, and the spirit of faction, reflecting individual and partisan interest. Only in Elizabeth's reign had England achieved that precarious balance between liberty and prerogative. Other journals followed the *Craftsman*'s lead in using history as a yardstick to measure the shortcomings of the present. When it came to the retrieval and publication of original historical documents, the borderline between objective historiography and the partisan manipulation of the past became blurred. Andrew Millar, Thomson's bookseller, was a fervent disseminator of the Old Whig canon: his enterprise, coupled with the editorial labours of Thomas Birch and others, lay behind the publication in the 1730s of state papers and other documentation from the Interregnum.[18] The last four years of Walpole's office witnessed a flood of historical material in direct response to public demand for reminders of former British naval glories. The market for lives of Blake, Drake, and Ralegh was keen enough to sustain rival publications of new or old hagiographies—and to supply young Samuel Johnson with some of his daily bread.[19]

Drake and Ralegh were as much a part of the patriotic pantheon as Britannia herself. Those staple icons of British national identity—Alfred, Edward III at Crécy, Henry V at Agincourt, Elizabeth I—made a frequent appearance in prints and poems. Perhaps more surprisingly, the old racial foundation myths still flourished in modern, 'enlightened' Hanoverian Britain. Both Court Whigs and their opponents still drew upon accounts of Britain's Saxon or Trojan 'originals' for political purposes. Dynastic self-justification was not significantly less intense after 1714 than it had been in either the sixteenth or the seventeenth century. It prompted the staunch Hanoverian apologist Edmund Gibson to dedicate his 1722 edition of Camden's *Britannia* to

[17] For a discussion of the debates initiated by the *Remarks* and the 1734 *Dissertation on Parties*, see Isaac Kramnick, *Bolingbroke and His Circle: The Politics of Nostalgia in the Age of Walpole* (Cambridge, Mass., 1968), 177–81, and *Bolingbroke: Historical Writings*, ed. Kramnick, pp. xxxix–xlvii.

[18] See above, Ch. 1. For Millar's publications, see Guido Abbattista, 'The Business of Paternoster Row: Towards a Publishing History of the *Universal History* (1736–65)', *Publishing History*, 17 (1985), 29–38.

[19] For the lives of Drake and Blake Johnson produced for Cave's *Gentleman's Magazine*, see Thomas Kaminski, *The Early Career of Samuel Johnson* (New York, 1987), 110–15.

George I, extolling him as a Germanic restorer of his British subjects' Saxon liberties.

History offered enormous satirical potential. Opposition writers, especially dramatists, ransacked past periods (classical and European as well as British) for their typology of weak kings, wicked ministers, and dominant queens.[20] Walpole saw himself refracted in the distorted glass of oppositional history as Gaveston, Wolsey, Buckingham, Stafford, Burghley, and Clarendon. These bold, over-simplified figures entered into the rich satirical mythopoeia which the opposition wove around the figure of Robert Walpole over a twenty-year period. An essay entitled 'Of Mythology' in the *Gentleman's Magazine* smugly claimed that 'in this allegorizing Age, when all the real persons of ancient and modern history are exhausted, it is happy we can have recourse to known fables . . . the pictures of tyrannical Princes and bad ministers have been drawn very early'.[21] Party writers on both sides turned political events into a vast morality play more medieval than modern: the fire-breathing dragon Excise burns the protesting pamphlets of the patriotic few in a new version of George and the dragon of Spenser's Red Crosse attempting to confute the monster Error.[22] Walpole and Bolingbroke were the contending forces of light and darkness, Bolingbroke a 'haughty, ambitious and revengeful spirit, like *Satan* driven from power', Walpole (from an opposition view) a Satan throwing golden apples to an Adamic nation from his Tree of Corruption, or a spell-binding evil wizard enchanting an unwary populace.[23] The very stability and longevity of Hanoverian rule and 'Robin's reign' fostered the opposition's cultivation of both the affirmative and the subversive forms of mythology.

The next three chapters will investigate three separate but interrelated myths which dominate both the overtly polemical and the more imaginative forms of political writing in this period. Each chapter attempts to recover a pattern of thought and argument which more recent interpretations have either obscured or not fully addressed. The first, 'Patriot Gothic', deals with the controversy over Saxon liberty, one of the great 'set pieces' of Walpolian political debate. Bolingbroke's *Remarks on the History of England* opened with a glowing account (cited at the start of Chapter 5) of the early Britons, part of the liberty-loving Gothic cousinage of northern races who established that first

[20] See John Loftis, *The Politics of Drama in Augustan England* (Oxford, 1963), 105–8, 118–22, 150–1; Mack, *Garden and the City*, 116–62; Herbert Atherton, *Political Prints in the Age of Hogarth: A Study of the Ideographic Representation of Politics* (Oxford, 1974), 191–208, esp. 192–3.

[21] *GM* 2 (1732), 945, 1072. The essay was published in two instalments.

[22] See 'Britannia Excisa', Atherton, *Political Prints*, plate 16. Richard Savage's satiric poem, *On False Historians* (written *c.*1735) captures the superstitious and diabolic slant to partisan history. See Savage, *Poetical Works*, ed. Clarence Tracy (Cambridge, 1962), 238–43.

[23] *Plain Matter of Fact; Or Whiggism the Bulwark of the Kingdoms* (1742); *Craftsman*, 25 Mar. 1732. There are several excellent studies of the mythopoeic dimension of opposition satire. See e.g. Ronald Paulson, *The Fictions of Satire* (Baltimore, Md., 1967), esp. 120–8; Mack, *Garden and the City*, 116–62; Atherton, *Political Prints*, *passim*; Brean Hammond, *Pope and Bolingbroke: A Study of Friendship and Influence* (Columbia, Mo., 1984), 142, 146–9.

model of Parliament, the Saxon witenagemot. The traditional Old Whig plea—pristine Saxon virtue under threat—supplied the opposition with a powerful tool to attack the 'spurious' Whiggery of a corrupt government. The ministry countered opposition claims to Whig 'liberty' by appropriating the arguments of the royalist historian Brady, who had asserted that medieval England had been a feudal tyranny in which parliamentary liberty had been impossible. Writing from a modernist perspective, Court Whigs dated English liberties from no earlier than 1688. Hanoverian Britain was infinitely 'freer' than the Saxon past.

The debate and its accompanying ironies of Tory–Whig historiographical role reversal have been thoroughly analysed and documented by several notable historians.[24] But it is very much 'The Case of Bolingbroke versus Walpole'. Some have depicted the re-emergence of Whig Saxonism in the 1730s as little more than a cynical political point-scoring oppositional manœuvre. 'How better to attack Walpole than with traditional Whig conceptions of the past!', notes Kramnick.[25] But these 'traditional Whig conceptions', if odd coming from that former arch-Tory and secret sceptic Bolingbroke, were part of the political heritage of the Patriot Whigs, whose political writings of the 1730s gave them a newly emotive oppositional cast. The invocation of Gothic or Saxon liberty is invariably related to larger myths of national identity. In pursuing the source of ancient laws and liberties back to the primitive and Germanic, seventeenth-century historians, notes Pocock, 'made many contributions to the legend of primitive Teutonic freedom and virtue'.[26] This was equally true of the 1730s, but a striking feature of the Gothic debate conducted by the Patriots in the 1730s was its ready translation into poetic and cultural terms.[27] Patriot poets turned their attention to the widespread notion

---

[24] Discussion of this subject has been very extensive. See among others, Kramnick, *Bolingbroke and His Circle*, 127–36, 177–81; Kramnick, 'Augustan Politics and English Historiography: The Debate on the English Past, 1730–35', *History and Theory*, 6 (1967), 33–56; Pocock, *The Ancient Constitution*, 369–70; Quentin Skinner, 'The Principles and Practice of Opposition: The Case of Bolingbroke versus Walpole', in Neil McKendrick (ed.), *Historical Perspectives: Studies in English Thought and Society in Honour of J. H. Plumb* (1974), 93–128; Robert Zaller, 'The Continuity of British Radicalism in the Seventeenth and Eighteenth Centuries', *Eighteenth-Century Life*, 6 (1981), 17–38, esp. 31–2; R. J. Smith, *The Gothic Bequest: Medieval Institutions in British Political Thought, 1688–1832* (Cambridge, 1986), 43–70.

[25] Kramnick, *Bolingbroke and His Circle*, 129.   [26] Pocock, *The Ancient Constitution*, 20.

[27] For the Gothic as a source of national identity, see S. J. Kliger, *The Goths in England: A Study in Seventeenth- and Eighteenth-Century Thought* (Cambridge, Mass., 1952), and Hugh A. MacDougall, *Racial Myth in English History: Trojans, Teutons and Anglo-Saxons* (Montreal, 1982). See Colley, 'Radical Patriotism in Eighteenth-Century England', in Raphael Samuels (ed.), *Patriotism: The Making and Unmaking of British National Identity*, 3 vols. (1989), i. 168–88, 173, for the later links between radical movements and Saxonist ideology. Gerald Newman, *The Rise of English Nationalism: A Cultural History, 1740–1830* (1987), esp. 114–18, 83–191, discusses this subject and also suggests (p. 116) that 'the Teutonising and Saxonising—in its largest sense, the Gothic—revival of this period was the creation of literary men'. Newman's account begins in the post-Walpole period and he does not make the connection between party-political writing and Gothic literature.

of a Gothic 'cousinage' of early peoples who inhabited Britain, including not only the Saxons but the ancient Britons and Celts. Could rugged British liberty become a source of literary as well as political inspiration? Patriot poetry of the 1730s gave a powerful impetus to the strain of literary nationalism which accompanied the romantic antiquarianism of the second half of the eighteenth-century. Mid-century 'pre-romanticism', so often defined as a rejection of the political concerns which preoccupied poets during the Walpole era, might in fact be better explained in terms of continuity and assimilation rather than simple repudiation.

Chapter 6 examines the Elizabethan revival of the Walpole era. Here the problems are rather different. Surprisingly little scholarship exists on one of the most inescapable features of this period: the widespread cult of Elizabeth I.[28] Elizabeth's reign supplies the focal point for Bolingbroke's major political writings of the 1730s—including, of course, the *Remarks on the History of England* and *The Idea of a Patriot King*—and historians have duly examined its significance. But most readings are confined to equating Bolingbroke's Elizabethan 'nostalgia' with his reactionary conservatism.[29] When most opposition writers wrote about Elizabeth, their bias was far from conservative or nostalgic. If they were nostalgic, it was not for E. M. Tillyard's stable, socially hierarchical Elizabethan world-picture, but for the aggressive, expansionist Protestant mercantilism associated with the victories of Cadiz and the Armada, an Elizabethanism shaped above all by pressure for war with Spain. But war with Spain was only one source of the complex patriotic manipulations of Elizabeth's golden age. Both Patriot Whigs and Court Whigs, operating from within a shared Protestant Hanoverian idiom which stressed the continuity of Protestant freedoms, competed over rival claims to represent 'Elizabethan' values.

In literary terms the 'Elizabethan Revival' has always been depicted as a feature of the *post*-Walpole period. 'In one respect the period 1740–80 is engaged on a quest for a lost literary culture, which was found in the Elizabethan age.'[30] The mid-century romantic enthusiasm for Gothic manners and imagination unleashed a flood of new works on Shakespeare and his plot sources, on Elizabethan beliefs and customs, and especially on Spenser. By the early nineteenth century, it was a critical commonplace to attack the 'strange and ungrateful forgetfulness' which writers and readers before 1740 supposedly

---

[28] For a discussion of Elizabethan material, see the standard 'literary' work, Earl Wasserman, *Elizabethan Poetry in the Eighteenth Century* (Urbana, Ill., 1947). Wasserman deals with the 'Elizabethan Revival' and mentions some of the plays and histories, pp. 192–252, but does not locate them in a political or historical context.

[29] See primarily Kramnick, *Bolingbroke and His Circle*, esp. 'Lord Lyttelton's *Persian Letters* and the Elizabethan Model', 230–5; Jeffrey Hart, *Viscount Bolingbroke, Tory Humanist* (Toronto, 1965).

[30] Arthur Johnston, 'Poetry and Criticism after 1740', in Roger Lonsdale (ed.), *Sphere History of Literature 4: Dryden to Johnson* (1971), 325.

accorded Elizabeth's most famous literary sons.[31] But like many common-places, this view was based on a certain ignorance. The interest in both Spenser and Shakespeare had never really died out in the early eighteenth century: in 1706 the Tory statesman and poet Matthew Prior claimed that all his friends now had 'the Fairy Queen . . . on their Toilette table'.[32] It was put there by his own, very political, Spenserian imitation of that year. And in the Walpole period it was the political climate which once again prompted the most active forms of Elizabethan literary appropriation. Michael Dobson, charting the public row over Shakespeare's monument at Westminster Abbey in the late 1730s, shows that the Patriots emphasized Shakespeare's proud and patriotic independence, claiming him as an outspoken critic of 'bad ministers'. Court writers, conversely, saw within this 'national poet' the dominant cultural values of an age in which court and nation had been united behind the monarch.[33] Spenser was an even richer source for controversy owing to the ambiguities already inherent in both his writings and his legend. Spenser's reputation as a critic of court corruption and advocate of a more extreme foreign policy than Elizabeth herself made him a highly suitable literary figure for a political opposition which was both anti-Spanish and anti-court. Writers on both sides drew either affirmative or satirical parallels between Spenser's enemy—the prosperous peace-loving Burghley—and Walpole. When Caroline attempted to appropriate Spenser in his 'other' role as a creator of royal and dynastic myths through her much-publicized Merlin's Cave, oppositional writers subverted Hanoverian stratagems for self-glorification by 'rewriting' her iconography to quite different ends—those which revealed an uncanny likeness between Spenser's malign Archimago and the 'great wizard' Walpole.

The question of Elizabeth's reputation overlaps with the subject of Chapter 7, 'Ideas of a Patriot King'. The plural form of the title of Bolingbroke's well-known political tract is deliberate. Bolingbroke's *Idea of a Patriot King*, with its exalted account of royal conduct and influence, looks outmoded and bizarre only from the perspective of a political history of the Hanoverian period from which kingship has been abstracted. Jeremy Black has written that there 'was a period when scholars could write about eighteenth-century British politics as though Britain was not a monarchy'.[34] This is no longer possible, even if one rejects some of the more extreme arguments concerning the prevalence of divine-right theory. Court Whig defences of the Hanoverians did not present 'a secularised monarchy in a materialist universe'.[35] Plenty of evidence for this

[31] Francis Jeffrey, *Edinburgh Review*, Mar. 1819, cited in Johnston, 'Poetry and Criticism', 324.

[32] Matthew Prior, *Literary Works*, ed. M. B. Wright and M. K. Spears, 2 vols. (Oxford, 1959), ii. 896.

[33] Michael Dobson, *The Making of the National Poet: Shakespeare, Adaptation and Authorship 1660–1789* (Oxford, 1992), 135–46.

[34] Jeremy Black, *British Foreign Policy in the Age of Walpole* (Edinburgh, 1985), 36.

[35] J. C. D. Clark, *English Society 1688–1832: Ideology, Social Structure and Political Practice during the Ancien Regime* (Cambridge, 1985), 178.

has been drawn from the places where one might most expect it—coronation sermons. But as yet we still await a proper full-length study of Court Whig literary propaganda, especially its symbolic forms of royal myth-making.[36] It will be argued that Bolingbroke's treatise shared many features in common with certain Whig works on kingship in the 1720s and 1730s, not least its idealizing language.

The Hanoverian context is vital for an understanding of how Patriot poets, working from within a shared dynastic idiom, celebrated their oppositional royal figurehead Prince Frederick, converting a German prince through his role as Prince of Wales into an identifiably British Protestant prince. The messianic language of Patriot kingship focusing on a revival or 'redemption' in the person of a prince can also be seen to parallel certain forms of Jacobite rhetoric. It is not surprising that many of the 'Patriot King' writings described in detail at the end of Chapter 7 exploit royalist myths formerly associated with the Stuart monarchy. The revival of Arthurian chivalry in a Hanoverian context did not await the Garter splendours of George III and his Windsor festivals. It was there in the 1730s in the court of his father Frederick.

[36] But see Judith M. Colton, 'Merlin's Cave and Queen Caroline: Garden Art as Political Propaganda', *ECS* 10 (1976), 1–20. Some of the best accounts emerge from scholarship devoted to Pope's satiric attacks on the Hanoverians, e.g. Pat Rogers, *Literature and Popular Culture in Eighteenth-Century England* (Brighton, 1985), 120–50; and esp. Manuel Schonhorn, 'Pope's *Epistle to Augustus*: Notes towards a Mythology', in Maynard Mack and James Winn (eds.), *Pope: Recent Essays by Several Hands* (Brighton, 1985), 546–64.

5

Patriot Gothic

READERS of the *Craftsman* in 1730 encountered an unusually fervent declaration of patriotism embedded in the fourth instalment of the weekly *Remarks on the History of England*.

I feel a secret pride in thinking that I was born a Briton; when I consider that the Romans, those masters of the world, maintained their liberty little more than seven centuries; and that Britain, which was a free nation above seventeen hundred years ago, is so at this hour.

However savage our British ancestors may be represented by the Romans, whom the luxury of Greece, and the effeminacy of Asia had already corrupted, they certainly were a people of spirit and of sense, who knew the ends of government, and obliged their governors to pursue those ends.[1]

Nationalism may be a more suitable term than patriotism, if we can define one strand of nationalism as a return to those indigenous qualities which define a nation's original character or 'genius'.[2] Bolingbroke, the author, may subsequently have professed contempt for the usefulness of any nation's earliest history in affording instructive lessons. But the *Remarks on the History of England* began with those very 'uncertain preludes' he later derided, and ran all the way through to the present day. This was an unremittingly partisan interpretation of the British past, dramatizing the Manichaean struggle between the forces of faction and the spirit of liberty—a liberty which was held to originate in Britain's earliest peoples.

Letter 4 began with a spirited discussion of the 'original freedom of the British and Saxon constitutions'. 'The principles of the Saxon commonwealth were very democratical, and these principles prevailed through all subsequent changes.'[3] Bolingbroke was rehearsing a theme dear to all good Whigs to the discomfiture of the Walpole administration. His account of Saxon liberty, a liberty first expressed in political rather than martial form in the witenagemot or Saxon assembly and subsequently confirmed and enshrined in Magna Carta, was an elegant reformulation of what was by this time effectively a political commonplace. As early as the 1610s, Saxon scholars had defended the antiquity and unbroken continuity of the Saxon constitution against James I's rigorous application of royal prerogative. Saxon theory continued as a staple of Commonwealth polemic throughout the seventeenth century, emerging most strongly at periods when parliamentary rights were threatened: notably in the

---

[1] Bolingbroke, *Works*, i. 316–17.
[2] See Gerald Newman, *The Rise of English Nationalism: A Cultural History, 1740–1830* (1987), 52–6.   [3] Bolingbroke, *Works*, i. 317.

period leading up to the Exclusion Crisis. Atwood, Petyt, Hare, Molesworth, Tyrell, and numerous others contributed to the argument that successive waves of Saxon, Danish, or Norman invasions had not interrupted ancient parliamentary rights. They challenged the feudal interpretation supplied by Filmerian royalist scholars such as William Brady, who argued that William I had conquered absolutely and had granted parliaments the right to meet as an act of royal favour. Tyrell, one of the most assiduous Saxonist Common-wealthmen, was still beavering away on a massive anti-Filmerian history of England on his death in 1718.[4]

'Gothic' (which still retained many of its pejorative cultural associations) came into use as the term explaining the ethnic cousinage of liberty-loving northern races who had emerged from ancient Scandinavia. The *translatio*, or transmigration theory, derived in large measure from the sixth-century Swedish historian Jordanes, found popular transmission in England initially through Richard Verstegen's 1605 *Restitution of Decayed Intelligence*. Ancient 'Scandza', the hive or womb of nations, had sent forth Huns, Vandals, Lombards, Saxons—all those of Germanic or broadly 'Gothic' origin. They were fierce lovers of liberty who established their own system of mixed government, the origins of Britain's mixed constitution.[5] The Norman 'conquest' was a myth if William I and his invaders shared the same racial characteristics and forms of government as the Britons. By the 1730s, the Gothic origin of Britain's constitution was taken as read by historians of a Whittish cast, even by the rather more sceptical Swift, and forms the prefatory material to both Rapin and Oldmixon's popular histories of England. Molesworth defines a 'real Whig' as one who is for 'exactly keeping up to the Strictness of our old Gothick Constitution'.[6]

But by the eighteenth century what that 'Strictness' entailed had become somewhat submerged. After 1688 the debate over institutional origins became less heated. Discussion shifted from the origins to the balance of the constitution, from the foundations of political authority to its use. Country oppositions to successive Whig administrations marshalled 'the myths, shibboleths and

---

[4] See Christopher Hill, 'The Norman Yoke', in his *Puritanism and Revolution* (1958), 50–122; S. J. Kliger, *The Goths in England; A Study in Seventeenth- and Eighteenth-Century Thought* (Cambridge, Mass., 1952); J. G. A. Pocock, *The Ancient Constitution and the Feudal Law: A Study of English Historical Thought in the Seventeenth Century. A Reissue with a Retrospect* (Cambridge, 1987). Pocock discriminates between those who upheld the antiquity of the English Common Law and those who based their defence on the Gothic institutions common to the cousinage of nations in western Europe. But see also William Klein, 'The Ancient Constitution Revisited', in N. Phillipson and Q. Skinner (eds.), *Political Discourse in Early Modern Britain* (Cambridge 1993), 23–44.

[5] See Kliger, *The Goths in England*, esp. 189–209, and his 'The "Goths" in England: An Introduction to the Gothic Vogue in Eighteenth-Century Aesthetic Discussion', *Modern Philology*, 43 (1945), 107–17.

[6] Cited in John Ker, *The Memoirs*, 3 vols. (1726), ii. 192. For Swift's praise of Gothic 'balance' but scepticism about superior Gothic racial genius, see Swift, *Prose Works*, ed. Herbert Davis et al., 16 vols. (Oxford, 1939–74), v. 36–7, and Kliger, *The Goths in England*, 205–7.

arguments of the seventeenth century' and called for a return to 'original principles' from which government had departed through corruption: original principles which were never clearly defined and were subject to ambiguous
interpretation.[7] Even though Bolingbroke modelled his own account of the
'original sketch of the British parliament' on the stridently republican seventeenth-century controversialist Nathaniel Bacon, he was far less concerned
with the unbroken continuity of the institution of Parliament than with 'that
uniformity of *spirit* which created, and has constantly preserved or retrieved
the original freedom of the British and Saxon constitutions'.[8] As R. J. Smith
has shown, Bolingbroke's most striking contribution to Gothic debate was his
addition of a powerful vein of Machiavellian corruption theory.[9] All institutions are naturally subject to change and decay: without a periodical revival
and maintenance of the spirit of liberty, not even the British Parliament could
endure. All that was needed was for the people to become corrupt and to allow
some king or minister to control the Commons. The growing influence of the
Crown on the Commons and the proliferation of Walpole's parliamentary
placemen posed a threat more insidious and therefore more dangerous than the
Stuarts' former open display of proud prerogative. Lyttelton's *Persian Letters*
show even more clearly the shift from institutional origins to moral impera-
tives. In his account of the Gothic constitution, he dismisses the old and
'mighty Controversy' over 'the ancient Power of the Crown, and that of the
Parliament' as 'rather matter of Speculation, than of Use'. Far more important
is the erosion and dilution of the Gothic spirit of our forefathers.[10]

Historians have perhaps focused too much attention on the apparent reversal
of ideologies which led the former High Tory Bolingbroke to out-Whig the
Whigs and the Court Whigs to resort to the Tory Brady for their defence of
modern liberties. Robert Zaller claims that 'the radical and conservative traditions had abruptly switched poles like reverse magnets'.[11] Kramnick notes the
anomaly of the sceptical historian Bolingbroke who four years later wrote a
dismissive account of the value of early historical enquiry.[12] Skinner 'out-
Namiers' Namier in his account of Bolingbroke's carefully constructed ideological platform to 'legitimize' opposition, a set of ideas which apparently neither

---

[7] Pocock, *The Ancient Constitution*, 367. For the 18th-cent. modification of Gothic theory, see
pp. 362–7; and R. J. Smith, *The Gothic Bequest: Medieval Institutions in British Political Thought,
1688–1832* (Cambridge, 1986), 43–70.

[8] Bolingbroke, *Works*, i. 316. Italics mine.

[9] Smith, *The Gothic Bequest*, 67–9.

[10] Lyttelton, *Persian Letters*, 179–80.

[11] Robert Zaller, 'The Continuity of British Radicalism in the Seventeenth and Eighteenth
Centuries', *Eighteenth-Century Life*, 6 (1981), 31.

[12] See *Lord Bolingbroke: Historical Writings*, ed. Isaac Kramnick (Chicago, 1972), p. xxxix;
Kramnick, *Bolingbroke and His Circle: The Politics of Nostalgia in the Age of Walpole* (Cambridge,
Mass., 1968), 177. But see Smith, *The Gothic Bequest*, for the counter-argument showing a mea-
sure of consistency between Bolingbroke's *Letters on History* and his political use of history.

he nor his followers believed.[13] Questions of Bolingbroke's moral sincerity and even of his High Tory pedigree seem curiously irrelevant. Bolingbroke may have been the opposition's foremost ideologue, but he was neither its 'leader' nor its sole representative. There were many Whigs in the opposition to Walpole for whom notions of Gothic liberty were part of their mental and, in one case, literal furniture. When Richard Temple, Lord Cobham, embarked on his gardening schemes at Stowe he was still a staunch Court Whig, and his shrine to the Saxon gods originally a monument to Whig Gothic ideals.[14] Only after his move into opposition did the statues acquire an oppositional, Patriot Whig meaning. Cobham's near neighbour and fellow colonel in Marlborough's wars, James Tyrell, was the son of the famous Saxon Commonwealth scholar James Tyrell the Elder. The influence of Sir William Temple's spirited essays on northern virtue and Gothic liberty on the circle surrounding his distant relative Cobham was not insignificant. Many of the books that filled James Thomson's library were staple Whiggish reading that might have inspired him to quite independent reflection on Gothic liberty and the northern races: works such as Temple's essays, the works of Tacitus, Rapin's *History of England*, Nathaniel Bacon's *Historical and Political Dicourse on the Laws and Government of England*, Carl von Blomberg's *Account of Livonia*, Olaus Magnus's *Compendious History of the Goths, Swedes and Vandals*, and Molesworth's highly influential *Account of Denmark as it was in the Year 1692*.[15] Thomson did not need to resort to Bolingbroke for warnings of the rapid descent of a free nation into self-induced political slavery. Molesworth's history of Denmark's transition from a freely elective to an absolutist monarchy in 1660 supplied a Machiavellian model of decline and fall closer than that of republican Rome.[16]

This is not to minimize the impact of Bolingbroke's Gothic writings either on a wider audience or on the Patriot poets. Bolingbroke's prose was nothing if not poetic. His invocation both in the *Remarks* and in the *Dissertation on Parties* of the spirit of Saxon liberty under threat, a spirit which must be kept 'alive and warm', deployed highly figurative and emotive language.

Whilst her sacred fires have been extinguished in so many countries, here they have been religiously kept alive. Here she hath her saints, her confessors, and a whole army of martyrs, and the gates of hell have not hitherto prevailed against her: so that if a fatal reverse is to happen; if servility and servitude are to overrun the whole world, like

[13] Quentin Skinner, 'The Principles and Practice of Opposition: The Case of Bolingbroke versus Walpole', in Neil McKendrick (ed.), *Historical Perspectives: Studies in English Thought and Society in Honour of J. H. Plumb* (1974), 93–128, esp. p. 127. Skinner (95 n.) describes the parliamentary opposition to Walpole as 'Bolingbroke's campaign' which gives a misleading impression of its political composition.

[14] The Saxon circle with 7 stone deities sculpted by Rysbrack belonged to the first phase of Cobham's gardening programme in the 1720s.

[15] See A. N. L. Munby (ed.), *Sale Catalogues of Libraries of Eminent Persons*, i (1971), 45–66.

[16] Thomson drew heavily on Rapin, Temple, and Molesworth for *Liberty*. See Caroline Robbins, *The Eighteenth-Century Commonwealthmen* (Cambridge, Mass., 1959), 98–104.

injustice, and liberty is to retire from it, like Astrea, our portion of the abandoned globe will have, at last, the mournful honor, whenever it happens, of showing her last, her parting steps.[17]

Bolingbroke's characteristically heady mixture of nationalistic pride and impending doom invited, and certainly inspired, poets to follow suit. Gilbert West's account in his descriptive poem *Stowe* of his uncle Cobham's Saxon shrine contains an overtly oppositional thrust. Written just as the *Remarks* were first making an appearance in the *Craftsman*, it resonates with a Boling-brokean fervour. Pausing in reverence before Woden, Sunna, Thor, Freya, and company, he exclaims

> Hail! Gods of our renown'd Fore-Fathers, hail!
> Ador'd Protectors once of *England*'s Weal.
> Gods, of a Nation, valiant, wise and free,
> Who conquer'd to establish *Liberty*!
> To whose auspicious Care *Britannia* owes
> Those laws, on which she stands, by which she rose
> Still may your Sons that noble Plan pursue
> Of equal Government prescrib'd by you.
> Nor e'er indignant may you blush to see
> The Shame of your corrupted Progeny![18]

One of the features which first strikes the modern reader about Boling-broke's account of Saxon liberty is his extremely flexible application of ethnic labels. All those who had invaded Britain, he asserts, 'were originally of Celtic, or Gothic extraction, call it which you please, as well as the people they sub-dued. They came out of the same northern hive; and therefore they naturally resumed the spirit of their ancestors when they came into a country where it prevailed.' In a footnote he adds that 'we have thought fit to explain the expression in this place, though we know the word Celtic, as well as the term Scythian, hath been used in the same large and general sense'.[19] Celts, Goths, Saxons, and their accompanying mythologies could all find shelter under the same Gothic roof. Pope's reading of William Temple's 'Of Heroic Virtue' led him to fill his Gothic northern wall in the *Temple of Fame* (1715) with Goths, Scythians, the Norse god Odin, and Celtic Druids with their bards. But the spirit in which Pope fashioned his poetic wall was very different from Boling-broke's enthusiastic account of Gothic liberty. Pope's interpretation of Tem-ple's essays was characterized by ignorance and distaste. He was far less

---

[17] Bolingbroke, *Works*, i. 320; ii. 108.

[18] Gilbert West, *Stowe, the Gardens of the Right Honourable Richard Lord Viscount Cobham* (1732), repr. in G. B. Clarke (ed.), *Descriptions of Lord Cobham's Gardens at Stowe, 1700–1750* (Buckingham, 1990), 37–51, p. 48. It was written in 1731 and submitted for Pope's approval that November. It is not otherwise a poem with an oppositional cast.

[19] Bolingbroke, *Works*, i. 318. Cf. Lyttelton, *Persian Letters*, 186, and Thomson's *Liberty*, iv. 736–45, for similar accounts of the 'mix'd Genius' of the 'Gothic Nations'.

interested in the Goths as law-givers than in the *frisson* of romantic barbarism epitomized by their 'horrid Forms' perched on 'rude Iron columns smear'd with Blood'.[20] Despite a life-long and ambivalent fascination with the Gothic in its aesthetic, historical, and cultural manifestations, Pope was never engaged with the political myths of Gothic liberty and Britain's constitutional forefathers. He was not a Whig.[21]

Tacitus on the Stage

'Gothic' is as highly charged a term as 'Augustan' and equally malleable in both political and cultural terms. Even in the most avowedly pro-Gothic works of the 1730s, such as Thomson's *Liberty*, the negative and positive implications of the term and concept sit side by side. But before addressing this most complex of subjects it is appropriate first to consider the more narrowly partisan uses of Gothic liberty made by Patriot writers and dramatists in this period. A. D. McKillop has detected two distinct strands in the political representation of the northern theme.[22] Both come from different stages in the Polybian or Machiavellian historical cycle of the foundation, origins, and development of nations from the first 'seeds of freedom' to the skills of government and civilization. Thus we have the 'primitive' Goth as 'fierce lover of liberty', the hardy individual who never submits to tyranny; and the 'civil' Goth as law-giver and culture hero. The first version—that of Gothic primitivism—had considerable poetic appeal. It also had pointed political applications in the 1730s, stimulated by the publication of Thomas Gordon's translations of Tacitus's *Annals* in 1728. Gordon, former co-author of the radical Whig *Cato's Letters*, had sold out, as we have seen, to become supervisor of Walpole's press: the volume was dedicated to Walpole. Tacitus was the most stringent critic of Augustan tyranny and corruption. His praise, especially in the *Germania*, of the simple virtues of the liberty-loving Germans, contrasting with their over-civilized Roman oppressors, also had a barely disguised political import. In 1728 the *Craftsman* took up the challenge not only by ridiculing Gordon, but by quoting sections of Tacitus back at the ministry, especially those passages dealing with corruption, standing armies, and the debasement of the Roman senate under tyrants. How appropriate, it argued, that this work should have been subsidized by the (by implication) equally corrupt Walpole

---

[20] *TE* ii. 263–4.

[21] See Valerie Rumbold, 'Pope and the Gothic Past' (Cambridge Ph.D. thesis, 1983). Disagreements about the nature of Pope's Whiggishness abound. But Pope never subscribed to the Whig notion of Saxon liberty.

[22] A. D. McKillop, *The Background of Thomson's 'Liberty'*, Rice Institute Pamphlet 38, no. 2 (July 1951), 75–85.

administration under George Augustus.[23] Bolingbroke based his account of the Gothic races in the *Remarks* and the *Dissertation on Parties* in part on Tacitus. In 1738 a three-volume translation of the *Annals, Agricola,* and *Germania* also appeared. This recent revival of Tacitus provided the context for West's poetic defence of the Goths and Britons in his 1742 *Order of the Garter*. Edward III soundly reprimands two foreign potentates, thinly veiled representatives of Walpolian luxury and political corruption, by asserting the superiority of the 'valiant Sons of Poverty, the *Goths,* | The *Huns* and *Vandals*' who descended on the luxurious Romans from their 'barren hills' and 'rugged woods'. Like their German cousins, Edward would rather 'see my *Britons* roam | Untutor'd Savages, among their Woods, | As once they did, in naked Innocence, | Than polish'd like the vile degenerate Race | Of modern *Italy*'s corrupted Sons'.[24]

But a far more flagrantly political version of anti-Augustan Gothic liberty came in the shape of two of the Patriot plays banned by the Stage Licensing Act: Henry Brooke's *Gustavus Vasa* (1739) and William Paterson's *Arminius* (1740). The controversy they created came less, I would suggest, from their stock-in-trade allegorical parallelism of 'types' for Walpole, George, Caroline, and Frederick than from their very Gothicism. Brooke's play was all about a 'Deliverer of his Country' from foreign oppression (notionally Frederick, but, as we have seen, thought by some to be the Pretender).[25] The setting is six-teenth-century Sweden, 'Queen of the North!', home of 'A Race of hardy, northern Sons', 'Whose Hands scorn'd Bondage, for their Hearts were free'. Gustavus leads his brave mountain peasants in a revolt against domestic cor-ruption and foreign oppression. The Prologue proves that this is a play as much about Britons as Swedes.

> Ask ye what Law their conq'ring Cause confess'd?
> Great Nature's Law, the Law within the Breast,
> Form'd by no Art, and to no Sect confin'd,
> But stamp'd by Heav'n upon th'unletter'd Mind:
> Such, such, of old the first born Natives were,
> Who breath'd the Vertues of *Britannia*'s Air,
> Their Realm, when mighty *Ceasar* vainly sought;
> For mightier Freedom against *Ceasar* fought,
> And rudely drove the fam'd Invader Home,
> To tyrannise o'er polish'd—venal *Rome*.

[23] For the opposition responses to Gordon, see Bertrand A. Goldgar, *Walpole and the Wits: The Relation of Politics to Literature, 1722–1742* (Lincoln, Nebr., 1976), 65–6. See also Howard Erskine-Hill, *The Augustan Idea in English Literature* (1983), 249–66, and Howard Weinbrot, *Augustus Caesar in 'Augustan' England: The Decline of a Classical Norm* (Princeton, NJ, 1978), 45–8, 109–15.

[24] Gilbert West, *The Institution of the Order of the Garter* (1742), 29, 36.

[25] For Jacobite interpretations, see M. J. W. Scott, *James Thomson, Anglo-Scot* (Athens, Ga., 1988), 288; James Sambrook, *James Thomson, 1700–1748: A Life* (Oxford, 1991), 191; John Loftis, *The Politics of Drama in Augustan England* (Oxford, 1963), 150.

And dare they, dare the vanquish'd sons of Spain
Enslave a Briton?

1. *The Voice of Liberty* (1738). Engraved frontispiece to Mark Akenside's poem. British sailors imprisoned and tortured by 'insulting' Spaniards while the spirits of Elizabethan naval heroes look down aghast from the clouds.

2. *Admiral Hosier's Ghost* (1740). Engraved illustration to Richard Glover's ballad. The deaths of Hosier and his crew in 1727 became an opposition *cause célèbre*.

G. Vandergucht inv^t. et sculp:

3. Van der Gucht's engraved frontispiece to Aaron Hill's *Progress of Wit:*
A Caveat (1730). Alexander Pope turning away from the epic slopes of
Parnassus and refusing to heed divine advice.

4. The Gothic Temple at Shotover Park, Oxon. (c.1718).

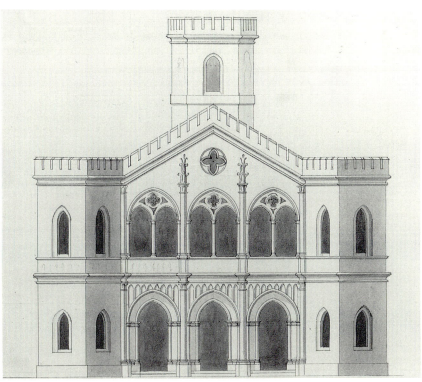

5. James Gibbs, Design for the Temple of Liberty, Stowe, Bucks (c.1741), front elevation.

Such was the glassy globe, that Merlin made,
And gave unto King Ryence for his guard,
That never foes his kingdom might invade,
But he it knew at home, and them debarr'd.
    Spen: Fai: Queen.

Fair Britomartis, to strange Love a Slave,
Glauce her Nurse conveys to Merlins Cave,
The Martial Bradamant, a prisoner made,
Was thence releas'd by sage Melissa's aid.

6. Engraved frontispiece to Jane Brereton's *Merlin: A Poem Humbly Inscrib'd to Her Majesty* (1735). Interior of Queen Caroline's Merlin's Cave at Richmond, with waxwork figures including Elizabeth I, Britomart, and Merlin with his globe. The verses below draw on Spenser and Ariosto.

7. George Vertue's engraved frontispiece to William Oldys's edition of Sir Walter Ralegh's *A History of the World* (1736).

The following text appears within the engraving:

THE TREACHEROUS PATRIOT UNMASK'D.

A Man may be known by his look. Eccles: 19. 29.

This is the Mask he wore all the memorable 12th. of March.

You are all Bit, Ha ha ha!   price 6ᵈ

Unmask'd, with bare-fac'd Insolence and Sneer,
Behold your Patriot;—who from year t' year
Flatter'd your hopes with promised relief;
Now laughs with Scorn at your too fond belief!
The face he wore e're he beguild your trust,
Bespoke an honest heart, upright and just:

But wonder not; since thus you see his face,
That he's ungrateful, Treacherous and Base,
Let Loyal minds with patience drag their Chain,
Despise his Smiles; his Frowns with scorn disdain;
This Sneering St—tes—n may be cloath'd wᵗʰ shame,
When fetter'd Loyliſts ſhall be Crown'd with fame.

* We know not of your Majesties having among us an open, a secret or suspected enemy. Dissenter's Address.

8. The Treacherous Patriot Unmask'd (1742). The Patriot William
Pulteney shows his true colours after Walpole's fall. The print captures
the widespread mood of cynicism after the opposition's 'betrayal'
of patriotism.

> Our Bard, exalted in a freeborn Flame,
> To ev'ry Nation wou'd transfer this Claim.[26]

After the play was banned, Brooke's preface to his sell-out subscription edition made the connection even more explicit. Innocently proclaiming his allegiance to patriotism rather than to party, Brooke defends his subject on the grounds of the 'similitude of the natural Constitution of *Sweden* and *Britain*'. Sweden is one of those '*Gothic* and *glorious* Nations, from whom our Form of Government is derived, from whom *Britain* has inherited those unextinguishable *Sparks* of Liberty and Patriotism'. These sparks alone can adorn the British Crown: they will remain 'till Corruption grow universal; till Subjects wish to be Slaves, and Kings know not how to be Happy'. Brooke is, of course, hinting that this time has already come.[27]

The dangerous equation of King and Caesar, Augustus and George Augustus, was made even more overt by Thomson's friend William Paterson in *Arminius*. The tale circulated by Thomson's biographer Murdoch—that the Chamberlain banned the play on recognizing the same handwriting that had transcribed Thomson's previously banned *Edward and Eleanora*—seems disingenuous.[28] Paterson modelled his story of Arminius, the German leader who routed Varus's forces in AD 8 and conducted a spirited resistance to Germanicus, directly on Tacitus's *Annals*. Arminius, or 'Herman', was already a nationalist German folk hero.[29] John Loftis's argument that Arminius and his collaborationist future father-in-law Segestes are 'thinly disguised portraits of the Prince of Wales and Walpole' is not entirely convincing.[30] The play's highly inflammatory nature stems less from any satirical 'types' than from its stringent anti-Augustanism. The Prologue comes close to sounding the clarion call to revolt. Liberty has fled 'degenerate *Rome*' for the uncorrupted soul of the 'rugged *North*'. Arminius successfully checks Roman tyranny, and Paterson opens the invitation to his audience.

> Who e'er for Freedom has, unyielding, stood,
> And to be truly Great, was just and good,
> Who'er has wild despotic Power confin'd,
> And scourg'd th'insulting Tyrants of Mankind;
> Each brave Avenger of his Country's Wrongs,
> *Britons*, to you, and to your stage belong.

---

[26] Henry Brooke, *Gustavus Vasa: or, The Deliverer of His Country* (1739), Prologue.

[27] Ibid., Prefatory Dedication, pp. iv–v.

[28] Patrick Murdoch, 'An Account of the Life and Works of Mr. James Thomson', in *The Works of James Thomson*, 2 vols. (1762), i, p. xiii.

[29] For the Arminius cult, see Kliger, *The Goths in England*, 56–7.

[30] Loftis, *Politics of Drama*, 150. See also Sambrook, *James Thomson*, 200.

Who droop the Slaves of arbitrary sway—
And who the Laws of Liberty obey—
Our scene displays—How nobler, kinder far,
Than a false treacherous Peace is open War.[31]

In Act II's famous set piece between Segestes and Arminius, Arminius asserts
Germanic virtues over Roman corruption, 'Deceit, 'Cunning', and 'splendid
Crimes'—and for Rome read modern Britain. If the equation between the two
Augustuses holds good, then *Arminius* borders on the treasonable.

I'll strike the Blow
That shall make CESAR tremble on her Throne,

.   .   .   .

Yes, even for this, the Gods have set me free;
To teach th'unconquer'd Nations of the North
To crush the Tyrant—Lo! they greatly rise![32]

Gothic Monarchs

Tacitus on the stage was one thing; but on the whole, poets such as Thomson,
whose *Liberty* provides the fullest account of the Gothic *translatio*, showed a
political, if not a poetic preference, for the Goth as law-giver rather than as
rugged barbarian. Thomson waxes warm on the heroic martial qualities of the
Scythians, Germans, Swedes, and early Britons and Saxons with a com-
pendium of stirring adjectives—'fierce', 'invigorating', 'hardy', and 'manly'—
but he depicts the proper fulfilment of liberty in the later stages of the
historical cycle. Germania, 'ferocious Nurse | Of hardy Men and Hearts
affronting Death', is soon blessed with cities to give it a 'nobler Brow' (IV.
364–5); the Saxons renounce the 'surly Gifts of War' for 'The calm Grada-
tions of Art-nursing Peace' (IV. 685–8). In Britain the apotheosis of Gothic lib-
erty is 'the full the perfect Plan . . . | Of BRITAIN's matchless *Constitution*,
mixt | Of mutual checking and suporting Powers, | KING, LORDS, and COM-
MONS' (IV. 813–15). Thomson's hero is Alfred the law-giver rather than Odin
the war-god. Historical definitions of the 'Gothic' period extended loosely to
anything up to the Renaissance.[33] Thus Edward III and Edward the Black
Prince as well as Alfred could be 'Gothic' heroes. All three were especially
favoured by the Patriots and enjoyed cults of their own. In Edward III's case
it was very much as the chivalric hero of Crécy and Poitiers and as the

---

[31] William Paterson, *Arminius* (1740), Prologue, p. v. The play was originally dedicated to Frederick's brother William—a curious choice probably prompted by political caution as a way of legit-
imizing it from an oppositional implication. It didn't work.

[32] Ibid. 18–19, 36.

[33] For discussions of the dating of the Gothic Age, see Rumbold, 'Pope and the Gothic Past',
18–27; Earl Wasserman, *Elizabethan Poetry in the Eighteenth Century* (Urbana, Ill., 1947), 192.

founder of the Order of the Garter. But it was Alfred the great Saxon law-giver who enjoyed particular prestige, one close in time to the primitive past but whose reign married pristine Saxon liberty with the wise, benevolent, and spiritual virtues of an educated Christian king. Alfred occupied a niche in Cobham's Temple of British Worthies at Stowe as well as a prominent place in Thomson's poetic pantheon of Whig worthies in *Summer*.[34] The use of Alfred as an educative role model for Prince Frederick had been established as early as 1723 when Sir Richard Blackmore addressed to the 16-year-old Frederick his *Alfred: An Epick Poem in Twelve Books, Dedicated to the Illustrious Prince Frederick of Hanover*. This epic was no better than the others produced by Blackmore's 'indefatigable muse' but an interesting example of the educative programme for English Patriot kingship which many writers other than Bolingbroke were producing for the German-raised Frederick in the 1720s and 1730s. Since a nation's happiness is dependent on its ruler, Blackmore cannot choose a better means to promote it than 'by inspiring into a young Prince such generous Sentiment, such just Idea's of political Prudence, and such an honourable ambition of becoming a publick Blessing, as may form his Mind for Empire, and the steady direction of the Reins of Government'.[35]

By the 1730s Alfred was being invoked by a wide variety of opposition writers, even Pope and Johnson, neither of whom was usually given to valorizing the Saxon past. Frederick capitalized on his earlier identification by commissioning a much-publicized statue of Alfred as the *'Founder of the Liberties and Commonwealth of England'*. The identification between Alfred and Frederick was thus firmly established when Thomson and Mallet came to write the masque of *Alfred* for the Prince in 1740. A newspaper article reported the heartening sight of the heir apparent watching a play in which 'our great King *Alfred* was represented, as rising from the *utmost Distress*, to redeem and establish the *Liberties* of his Country', and saw it as a 'Sort of Pledge' that Frederick would follow suit.[36]

Saxon Brunswick

Gothic liberty and Saxon virtue were very much oppositional property by the mid-1730s. Walpole's journalists undermined opposition Whig Saxonism by defending the far superior liberty enjoyed by Protestant subjects under the blessings of 'modern' Hanoverian rule. But it was impossible to ignore the associations between the German House of Hanover and the Gothic Germanic

---

[34] See Thomson, *Summer*, ll. 1479–83 (OET *Seasons*, 126). For a description of Alfred in Stowe's Temple of British Worthies, see G. B. Clarke, 'Grecian Taste and Gothic Virtue: Lord Cobham's Gardening Programme and Iconography', *Apollo*, 97 (1973), 566–71.

[35] See Blackmore, *Alfred*, Dedication and pp. xxxii–xxxiv.

[36] See *Craftsman*, 6 Sept. 1735. For the newspaper responses to Alfred see *London Magazine*, 9 (1740), 393, and A. D. McKillop, 'The Early History of Alfred', *PQ* 41 (1962), 311–24.

past. In his *Stowe*, West made a genealogical connection between ancient and modern 'German' kings:

> Tiw, ancient Monarch of remotest Fame,
> Who led from Babel's Tow'rs the German Name,
> And warlike Woden, fam'd for martial Deeds,
> From whom great Brunswick's noble line proceeds.[37]

Nine years earlier, Bishop Edmund Gibson had seized on the same connection to demonstrate his unswerving loyalty (and that of all good subjects) to the Hanoverian dynasty. The new dedication to his second edition (1722) of Camden's *Britannia* adopted the Gothic racial cousinage theory to extol George I as the restorer of the ancient ties between the liberty-loving Britons and Germans. Our histories, laws, customs, language, and buildings all show

that the greatest part of your Majesty's Subjects here, are of SAXON Original. And if we enquire from whence our Saxon Ancestors came, we shall find that it was from your Majesty's Dominions in *Germany*, where their Brethren who staid behind, spread themselves through a noble and spacious Country which still retains their Name. So that the main Body of your People in both Nations, are really descended from one and the same common Stock; and now, after a Disunion of so many Ages, they live under the Protection and Influence of the same common Parent.[38]

Most Britons did not care to be reminded so frankly of their modern German cousins. George II's Hanoverianism was more often a source of grievance than of satisfaction to his subjects, especially when his long visits to Germany made him rather a different kind of 'king over the water'. A staple figure of Jacobite innuendo was the British lion bled dry by the white horse of Hanover: particularly pertinent for Britain's potential involvement in a Hanoverian-dictated foreign policy. Like Dutch William and his Arthurian panegyrist Blackmore, the Hanoverians and their apologists preferred to identify themselves with British rather than with German dynastic myths.[39] The message encoded in Caroline's Merlin's Cave (to be discussed more fully in the next chapter) linked the House of Brunswick with the British line by coupling Spenser's Troynovant myth with Ariosto's account in *Orlando Furioso* of the House of Este from which Brunswick supposedly originated.[40]

---

[37] West, *Stowe*, repr. in Clarke (ed.), *Descriptions of Lord Cobham's Gardens*, 48.

[38] William Camden, *Britannia: or a Chorographical Description of Great Britain and Ireland, Together with the Adjacent Islands*, ed. Edmund Gibson, 2 vols. (2nd rev. edn. 1722), i, 'Dedication'. The first edition of 1695 was dedicated to the Whig Lord Sommers.

[39] The Hanoverians claimed their hereditary right through the British line. See *Memoirs of the House of Hanover . . . To which is added, A Genealogical Table of that Illustrious Family* (1713); p. 82 asserts that the Hanoverians have 'a double claim to their Descent from the blood of England'.

[40] See Judith M. Colton, 'Merlin's Cave and Queen Caroline: Garden Art as Political Propaganda', *ECS* 10 (1976), 13–14.

William Giffard's 1735–6 revival of Dryden's *King Arthur*, with its conflict between Saxons and Britons, was turned to Hanoverian use. In 1691 Dryden may have intended his play to be read as a covert Jacobite allegory equating Saxon bellicosity with William's unpopular wars, and Arthur with the exiled Stuart line.[41] But the play did invite a reconciliation between Saxons and Britons in the prophecy that 'Britains and Saxons shall be once one people'. James Sterling's new Prologue of 1735–6, however, made the identification between Arthurian Britons and Hanoverians gloriously obvious.[42] By the 1730s the prevalence of a broadly 'Gothic' label for all non-Romanic early European peoples had tended to blur the former sharp divisions between the Saxon and British 'originals' claimed respectively by Parliamentarians and Royalists. But the revival of Dryden's *King Arthur* (now retitled *Merlin: Or, The British Inchanter. And King Arthur, The British Worthy*) enabled an ingenious partisan manipulation of an older political idiom. The Patriot opposition championed Saxon freedom and political enlightenment, and Dryden's play was anything but flattering to Saxon customs. The Hanoverian *King Arthur* was being staged just as Thomson's Saxonist *Liberty* appeared. Giffard's revival was a runaway success, whereas sales of Thomson's poem were near-disastrous.[43] *King Arthur* contains a Saxon altar scene pertinently similar to Cobham's own circle of Saxon deities at Stowe as Samuel Boyse described it, 'Sacred to Woden and the Saxon Jove | Around the central altar seems to stand, | The Gods ador'd by Hengist's valiant band'.[44] Near the beginning of Act I of Dryden's play we find '*The SCENE represents a Place of Heathen Worship: the three Saxon Gods, Woden, Thor and Freya, placed on Pedestals. An Altar*'. The scene which follows involves some hocus-pocus sacrificial rites and the slaughter of six naïve Saxon victims dressed in white, accompanied by solemn hymns offered up by 'Priests and Singers' to Woden and Thor—including an early version of the death song of Radnar Lodbrog and the legend of Valhalla described so fully by Thomson. Dryden's tone, remarks David Bywater, was one of mockery. The bathetic rhyme of the chant

> Brave Souls to be renown'd in Story
> Honour prizing,
> Death despising,
> Fame acquiring,
> By expiring

[41] See David Bywater, *Dryden in Revolutionary England* (Berkeley, Calif. and Los Angeles, 1990), 81–93.
[42] Dryden, *King Arthur: or, The British Worthy*, in *Dramatic Works*, ed. M. Summers, 6 vols. (1932), vi. 283. In the 1736 printed version of Giffard's production, *Merlin: Or, The British Inchanter. And King Arthur, The British Worthy. A Dramatic Opera*, 32, these lines were altered to read 'Britons and Saxons shall become the people'.
[43] See Thomson, *Letters*, 104–6.
[44] Samuel Boyse, *The Triumphs of Nature* (1742), repr. in Clarke, *Descriptions of Lord Cobham's Gardens*, 100. See ibid. 111 for an anonymous attack in the *GM* which Boyse's eulogy prompted. The poem criticized Cobham's 'pretence' of 'patriot virtue' since his heathen statues (and his anticlericalism) were not features of a true Patriot.

sends up Saxon heroism and by implication untempered military aggression.[45]
Yet other, unintended ironies arise from this scene. Dryden may originally
have been implicitly ironizing the Saxon death-cult, but audiences in 1735–6
found the rituals awe-inspiring. Furthermore, although one of the few new
passages added to the play in 1735–6—Merlin's prophecy—deliberately links
the Hanoverian emblem, the 'Stately' white horse, with the 'British Lyon', in
a vision of a renovated Arthurian line, there is a problem. Another white horse
appears in the altar scene—the one sacrificed by the Saxons. 'Woden, first to
thee, | A Milk-white Steed, in Battle won, | We have sacrific'd.'[46]

Few poets rose to the challenge thrown down by Aaron Hill in *Advice to the
Poets* (1731) when he asked 'Why are they slow, to sing the *Saxon* Fame? |
From whose Long Lineage Sovereign *Brunswic* came: | When their WHITE
COURSER, by brave *Hengist* borne, | Did, *first*, in *Albion*, War's wav'd Pomp
adorn'.[47] It was Hill himself who explored the story of Hengist in his detailed
plans for an opera to be called *Hengist and Horsa, or, The Origins of England*.
This is a work which would have fulfilled the reconciliation of Britons and
Saxons, pointed to in the conclusion of Dryden's *King Arthur*, by effectively
marrying the Saxon 'invaders' to the native Britons in a myth of peaceful inte-
gration. Vortigern, King of Britain, loses his enthusiasm for resisting the
Saxon invaders after falling in love with Hengist's daughter Matilda, renounc-
ing his former engagement to Merlin's daughter Godiva. Like Thomson and
Mallet's *Alfred*, the opera would have ended with a prophetic historical vision.
Merlin as 'presenter' traces the British royal line from Ethelred through to
Charles. The last scene would have ended in a baroque Hanoverian royal
tableau:

the back scene breaks away, and discovers, in effigy (as lately done to a great perfection) the whole present Royal Family, surrounded above, with angels, smiling, and
pointing thro' the clouds; from the midst of which a beam of light shoots down, over
the head of the king, in the centre.[48]

It would be hard to think of a more obvious (or tasteless) way of suggesting
the divine anointment of the Hanoverian monarch. These plans were almost
certainly made before Frederick had gone into opposition. When Hill
described Frederick as 'Prince Germanicus' in his 1737 *Tears of the Muses* he
was precariously close to a political double-think. Germanicus, the popular
Roman republican hero (like Frederick) detested by his parents, earned his
sobriquet 'Germanicus' by his martial victories over the German Arminius.

---

[45] *Merlin: Or, The British Inchanter*, 4, 6. Bywater, *Dryden in Revolutionary England*, 83, says
that 'it is impossible to take this seriously'. But the chant sounds like the Saxon death song which
Aylett Sammes, author of *Britannia Antiqua Illustrata* (1676), had just printed. Dryden may have
been showing his antiquarian knowledge. See Ethel Seaton, *Literary Relations of England and Scandinavia in the Seventeenth Century* (Oxford 1935), 257.

[46] *Merlin: Or, The British Inchanter*, 'Alterations', and 5.

[47] Hill, *Advice to the Poets*, 36.

[48] See Roger Fiske, *English Theatre Music in the Eighteenth Century* (Oxford, 1973), 143–4.

One area where praise of the Prince did not entail praise of the parents was Frederick's marriage to Augusta of Saxe Gotha in 1736, seen by many as a double confirmation of Protestant securities and Old Whig liberties.

Her Royal Highness is descended from that ancient SAXON Race whence the Nations of *Britain* and *Germany* were peopled as from common Ancestors and descended as she is, from the *Founder* of the Liberties of *England*. . . . The *Saxon* Virtue is still unextinguished, and that ancient Family which gave so many Heroes to maintain the *Liberties* of *Germany* hath blessed the World with a PRINCESS to protect the *Liberties* of Britain.[49]

THE SECOND part of this chapter will turn to what is a far more complex and tendentious subject: the interplay between political ideas and the formation of cultural and literary taste. Put simply, did the new currency which Whig Patriots of the Walpole period gave to the Gothic play any part in shaping aesthetic debate about the Gothic? The evolution of 'Gothic' in the eighteenth century from a term of cultural censure to one of praise underpins one of the great movements in the history of taste: the transition from 'Augustan to Romantic', from 'reason' to 'imagination', from 'order and decorum' to the 'wilderness of sensations'. It is reflected in the growing mid-eighteenth-century taste for Gothic as opposed to Palladian styles of architecture, the appreciation of Spenser with his 'Gothic' stanzas and world of enchantment and fine fabling, the literary preference for the primitive as opposed to the civilized, the turning back to native British poetic models—Milton, Spenser, Shakespeare, and, even earlier, the inspired Celtic or Nordic bard. This was the age in which the 'forgeries' of Macpherson and Chatterton came to be seen by many as manifestations of the true poetic spirit. This is a huge subject, one which I can touch on only briefly. But there are two areas in particular that will be addressed. The first is concerned with Gothic architecture and will explore the concept of a 'Whig aesthetic' in which (so it has been argued) Gothic ideals of political liberty find expression in architectural form. The second, a contribution to current critical debates about the origins of literary nationalism, will examine the possible literary implications of the political admiration for Gothic ruggedness and integrity. Were the Patriot poets of the 1730s and early 1740s engaged in a process of recovering British cultural as well as constitutional roots? And if so, what influence did they have on their immediate literary successors—poets of the generation of Thomas Gray, William Collins, and the Warton brothers?

* * *

[49] *Old Whig*, 6 May 1736.

Gothic Architecture and the Gothic Constitution

Cobham's Temple of Liberty in the grounds of Stowe is a striking architectural expression of Patriot Gothic. This is political architecture *par excellence*. Designed by William Gibbs, it was erected some time around 1741, but could easily be mistaken for the product of a slightly later period when the Gothic revival had gained full sway in the stately homes and gardens of the English landowner. Its unusual triangular form and dark red-gold ironstone stand out from Stowe's cooler limestone neo-classical Palladian temples and arcades. Over the entrance stood the inscription LIBERTATI MAIORUM—'to the liberty of our ancestors'—a consummate symbol of Gothic political ideals. To the temple I shall shortly return. But there are many other examples of the symbolic symbiosis between political ideals and architectural forms in this period. As in earlier periods, writers frequently employed architectural metaphors to talk about politics. Bolingbroke himself claimed that 'In all these ages, Britain hath been the temple, as it were, of Liberty'.[50] Journals as diverse as the *Old Whig*, the *Craftsman, Common Sense,* and (slightly later) *The World* drew extended comparisons between Gothic architecture and the Gothic constitution. So did poets. By the time William Collins wrote his 'Ode to Liberty' in 1746 the image of an at least partly Gothic Temple of Liberty was almost a commonplace: it appears in poems by Thomson, West, and Akenside among others.[51]

But what were the salient architectural correlatives of the Gothic or Saxon constitution? Samuel Kliger, examining the interplay between political ideology and aesthetics in the eighteenth century, has described in some detail a 'Whig aesthetic': one in which 'Whig' principles of popular government and political liberty were reflected in artistic 'freedom' of form—blank verse, naturalized landscape gardening, 'Gothic poetry' such as Spenser's *The Faerie Queen*.[52] Tory desire for stability and hierarchy was, conversely, reflected in neo-classical symmetry and balance—the constraints of the rhyming couplet, 'rules' of taste and composition. He remarks:

The political bias affecting the critic's taste was especially strong in architecture. Elsewhere I have been able to show that the Gothic taste was a Whig taste. The Gothic edifice came to stand for the entire liberalising tendency of the Whig movement towards parliamentary supremacy unfettered by monarchical control. What is important is the association formed in some eighteenth-century minds between Whig principles of popular government and the freedom from neo-classical restraints displayed in the

[50] Bolingbroke, *Works*, ii. 108.

[51] See e.g. Akenside, *Pleasures of the Imagination* (1744), Book II, ll. 43–4; Collins, 'Ode to Liberty', ll. 116–20; West, *Order of the Garter* (1742), 63–4. The notion of a Temple of Liberty, whether Grecian or Gothic, was by no means exclusively 'Whiggish' property. See the Jacobite William King's *Templum Libertatis*, 2 vols. (1742–3).

[52] Kliger, 'The "Goths" in England'; 'Whig Aesthetics: A Phase of Eighteenth-Century Taste', *English Literary History*, 16 (1949), 135–50; *The Goths in England*.

inexhuastible imaginative energy of the Gothic building; from the opposing Tory point of view, the symmetry and balance of the Grecian building apotheosized the Tory aim of maintaining national stability through a vested aristocratic interest and a strong monarchy.[53]

I would contend, conversely, that prior to at least 1740 there is little evidence of a 'patriotic aesthetic of irregularity' which drew on the Gothic constitution as a defence.[54] If such an aesthetic did emerge, it was in the period of Horace rather than Robert Walpole and drew far more from the new informal taste in landscape gardening than it did from architecture.[55] Whig Patriots throughout the eighteenth century, inspired by the powerful classical tradition of liberty, frequently used Grecian models, both in poetry (the Pindaric ode) and in building, to express not Tory but Whig ideals. Stowe's political garden programme owes far more to the classical than to the Gothic. Nearly all its buildings are based on Roman models. The Temple of Ancient Virtue houses busts of the Greek heroes Epaminondas, Lycurgus, Homer, and Plato.[56] When Patriot Whigs did turn to the Gothic, 'freedom of form' and 'inexhaustible imaginative energy' played no part in their political and architectural vocabulary. This is a misplaced retrospective projection of what 'liberty' meant. Kliger, writing from Harvard in the 1950s, repeatedly uses the terms 'liberal' and 'democratic', but these are terms Whig Patriots would have defined very differently—and, in the case of democracy, virtually shunned.[57] It was later Tory critics of the new fad for decorative 'Gothick' architecture of the Strawberry Hill variety who tried to score political points by suggesting that its stylistic licentiousness mirrored Whig clamours for popular liberty and dangerous democracy. When Whig Patriots praised the 'Gothick' constitution they praised its mixed order of king, Lords, and Commons: constitutional balance under the rule of law. This is what we see in Thomson's (rather symmetrical) version of the Temple of Liberty or 'Palace of the Laws'.

> To the four Heavens
> Four Gates impartial thrown, unceasing Crouds,
> With Kings themselves the hearty Peasant mix'd,

[53] Kliger, 'Whig Aesthetics', 135.

[54] Michael Meehan, *Liberty and Poetics in Eighteenth-Century England* (1985), 76–7. Meehan expresses reservations about Kliger's 'Whig aesthetic' noting the overlay of the classical with the Gothic.

[55] See esp. Richard E. Quaintance, 'Walpole's Whig Interpretation of Landscaping History', *Studies in Eighteenth-Century Culture*, 9 (1979), 285–300.

[56] See Clarke, 'Grecian Taste and Gothic Virtue', 655–81; James Sambrook, *The Eighteenth Century: The Intellectual and Cultural Context of English Literature, 1700–1789* (1986), 175–81; J. Buxton, *The Grecian Taste: Literature in the Age of Neo-Classicism* (1978); T. Webb, *English Romantic Hellenism, 1700–1824* (Manchester, 1982).

[57] Thomson uses 'democracy' in qualified form in *Liberty*, iv. 811 to describe the third part of the balanced constitution—the Commons. But see also ii. 150. 'Democracy' and 'democratic' are equated with republicanism and anti-constitutional anarchistic sentiments: terms used most often by government journalists to attack opposition Whigs.

Pour urgent in. And tho' to different Ranks
Responsive place belongs, yet equal spreads
The sheltering Roof o'er all.[58]

The mixed constitution, which Swift, among others, also saw in ancient Athens and Sparta, often leads in architectural terms to a mingling of the Grecian and the Gothic: notably in Collins's 'Ode to Liberty', where 'Gothic pride' and 'Graecia's graceful orders join | Majestic through the mixed design'. So too in Gilbert West's *Order of the Garter*. The Patriot King must

Complete the noble *Gothick* Pile,
That on the Rock of Justice rear'd shall stand
In Symmetry, and Strength, and Fame,
A Rival of that boasted Frame
Which Virtue rais'd on *Tiber*'s Strand.[59]

'Symmetry' and 'strength' are the vital adjectives. We need to return to what writers of the first three decades of the eighteenth century generally understood by 'Gothic' architecture. There was a fairly widespread confusion about its historical provenance and distinctive features.[60] In 1742 Batty Langley observed that, although the Goths themselves had probably built no edifices in Britain, none the less 'every ancient Building, which is not in the *Grecian Mode* is called a *Gothic Building*'. Langley points to Rapin's account of the Gothic cousinage and the Goth/Getae/Jute etymology. The Goths had united with the Saxons before they came to Britain 'and ever after looked on themselves as one and the same people, and were in general called Saxons'.[61] Thus the Gothic was variously described as the Romanesque, Norman, or Saxon style brought to Britain by the Goths or other northern invaders. Yet 'Gothic' was also used to describe the 'fantastic and licentious manner of buildings' supposedly introduced by the Arabs or Saracens. John Evelyn, writing at the turn of the seventeenth century, attacked both versions: 'Ancient' Gothic was rude, stiff, ponderous, 'Congestions of heavy, dark, melancholy and *Monkish* piles'. 'Saracenic Gothic' was 'sharp *Angles*, *Jettoes*, narrow *Lights*, lame *Statues*, *Lace*, and other *Cut-work* and *Crinkle-Crankle*'—that is, fanciful, over-laden with ornament, confusing the eye with a multiplicity of parts and details.[62] Horace Walpole, who contributed most to the mid-century enthusiasm for Gothic architecture, was seemingly indifferent to its historical origins

---

[58] *Liberty*, iv. 1180–5.

[59] Collins, 'Ode to Liberty', ll. 118–20; West, *Order of the Garter*, 63–4.

[60] See A. O. Lovejoy, 'The First Gothic Revival and the Return to Nature', *Modern Language Notes*, 47 (1932), 419–46; E. D. de Beer, 'Gothic—Origin and Diffusion of the Term', *Journal of the Warburg and Courtauld Institutes*, 2 (1948), 142–62; Michael McCarthy, *The Origins of the Gothic Revival* (New Haven, Conn., 1987); Lawrence Lipking, *The Ordering of the Arts in Eighteenth-Century England* (Princeton, NJ, 1970), 146–55.

[61] Batty Langley, *Ancient Architecture Restored* (1742), 'A Dissertation' (no page).

[62] Cited in Lovejoy, 'The First Gothic Revival', 420–1.

and more interested in developing an aesthetic in which the qualities of the Saracenic derided by Evelyn became the very hallmarks of Gothic sensibility. 'The Gothic of the *Anecdotes* is the Gothic of proliferation, of unrestrained licentiousness, of a thousand graces and ten thousand inspirations.'[63] It is only one step from here to the *frisson*-charged winding staircases, turrets, and towers of the Gothic novel.

All this is a very long way from Patriot Whig Gothic. Although the Patriots probably had no clearer notion than did Batty Langley of the provenance of Gothic architecture, they knew what they wanted their imaginary edifices to symbolize. As Lipking remarks, 'Eighteenth-century Gothic, as architecture and as conception, was created in the image of eighteenth-century men'.[64] It should not be forgotten that some critics attached a quite different set of political associations to Gothic architecture. They connected it not with a 'liberal' or 'free' form of government, but, on the contrary, with the Dark Ages, superstition, priestcraft, and tyranny. In 1746 John Upton imagined an unsightly dark Gothic palace inhabited by a monster 'whose name is TYRANNY, but his flatterers call him KINGLY POWER'.[65] When the Patriots turned to the Gothic, they admired those very qualities that Evelyn condemned in the 'ancient' Gothic style. The 'massive' and 'bold' nature of the Norman arches are frequently praised; but so too are the 'Cathedrals, Collegiate Churches and other monuments of Antiquity', 'Saxon monuments' which testify to the strong devotional and constitutional inheritance of the Saxon past.[66] If there was an architectural correlative to the populist origins of the freely elected Saxon assembly, it lay not in Gothic 'multiplicity of parts' but in Gothic simplicity, rudeness, and ruggedness. This is apparent even in the half-formed image which Bolingbroke supplies in Letter 4 of the *Remarks*. Britain's Gothic constitution is 'a rough building raised out of the demolitions which the Normans had made, and upon the solid foundations laid by the Saxons. The whole fabric was cemented by the blood of our fathers.'[67] This stability was now imperiled by the insidious moral corruptions of the Walpole regime. In prophesying the possible fall of the Palace of the Laws, Thomson infused his architectural similes with Machiavellian corruption theory, 'Nor outward Tempest, nor corrosive Time, | Nought but the felon undermining Hand | Of dark CORRUPTION, can its Frame dissolve, | And lay the Toil of Ages in the Dust.'[68]

This set of equations becomes clearer when we look at some real examples of political Gothic architecture. The Temple of Liberty at Stowe, although

[63] Lipking, *Ordering of the Arts*, 151.   [64] Ibid. 146–7.

[65] John Upton, *Critical Observations on Shakespeare* (1746), 146.

[66] [John Campbell], *The Polite Correspondence; Or, Rational Amusement* (1741), 275. Campbell's popular treatise associates reverence for the Saxon constitution with an admiration for Gothic architecture and early British poetry.

[67] Bolingbroke, *Works*, i. 319.

[68] *Liberty*, iv. 1188–91.

early, was by no means the first example of eighteenth-century Gothic revivalism. In many places, notably Oxford, it was more a case of Gothic survival than of Gothic revival.[69] Well before 1740 both Hawksmoor and Vanbrugh were working in the Gothic style. Vanbrugh's 'Castle Gothic' of turrets and battlements emerged in full sway at his picturesque sham castle built at Greenwich between 1717 and 1726. The Tory Bathurst was equally proud of his crumbling ruin, Alfred's Hall, built at Cirencester between 1721 and 1731, which slowly evolved from a wooden construction to a stone building with rounded towers. The eccentric Thomas Coningsby was busily Gothicizing Hampton Court, his Herefordshire family seat, between 1703 and 1706. Another notable example was James Tyrell's small Gothic Temple erected at Shotover Park between 1716 and 1718. But discriminations need to be made. There is a subtle difference between using Gothic buildings to supply a romantic or antiquarian feature to the landscape and using them to make a statement of political principles. Bathurst's Alfred's Hall, this 'hermitage in the woods', a 'pretty little plain work in the Brodingnag style', was also known indiscriminately as Arthur's Castle, suggesting a relative indifference to any specific political symbolism.[70] Coningsby, though a violent Whig and a close friend of Molesworth, was more intent on buttressing the Coningsby family pride in its antique pedigree; to this end he revived the chivalric tournaments of his Elizabethan ancestors and hired blind Welsh bards to supply suitably romantic background music.[71]

James Tyrell's motives were different. He was one of the leading anti-Filmerian scholars among the 'Grecian tavern set' of Commonwealthmen, and a very close friend of Locke's. He retired to Shotover primarily to be close to Oxford's Bodleian Library. Landscaping Shotover while writing his monumental *History of England*, he was evidently inspired by both his Saxonist researches and the inescapable sight from his library desk of Hawksmoor's new Gothic façade (matching the 1438 chapel end) going up at All Souls. Tyrell's admiration for the Saxon constitution found concrete expression in the temple he erected at the end of the Shotover canal, close in appearance to the All Souls façade and probably constructed by the same master stonemason, William Townesend. This is not simply a picturesque Gothic folly. As Mavis Batey puts it, 'The Shotover Gothic Temple is authentic and self-assured and does not anticipate rococo frivolity or romantic feelings for decay: it is not half-hidden from the hermitage but is on the main axis of the house and seen

[69] See H. M. Colvin, 'Gothic Survival and Gothic Revival', *Architectural Review*, 103 (1948), 91–8.

[70] Pope, *Corr.* iii. 299–300. See Morris Brownell, *Alexander Pope and the Arts of Georgian England* (Oxford, 1978), 272–5.

[71] See Sabin Galleries, *A Country House Portrayed: Hampton Court, Herefordshire, 1699–1840* (1973); John Cornforth, 'Hampton Court, Herefordshire: II', *Country Life*, 1 Mar. 1973, 518–23.

prominently from all the principal rooms.'[72] So in what form did Gothic or Saxon liberty express itself? The turrets and octagonal towers of the Shotover temple with their finial acanthus traces are similar to Hawksmoor's twin towers at All Souls. But most important, this is a relatively simple and symmetrical building: three arches beneath a castellated triangular pediment with a rose window flanked by two towers. Although it stands in a new informal garden, the Temple does not (as Avray Tipping mistakenly thought) symbolize 'wild Gothic irregularity and barbarism'.[73] It has a touch of the Saxon perpendicular; above all, it suggests Gothic enlightenment.

This seems important when we come to think about what 'Gothic' meant not only to the earlier generation of Tyrell and the Commonwealthmen but also to the Patriot Whigs of the 1730s. It may be easy to 'misread' Stowe's Temple of Liberty, especially because in the 1750s that well-known Gothicizer Sanderson Miller, a close friend of the Cobham family, added some of the decorative architectural embellishments (pinnacles, cupolas, battlements) associated with the later 'Gothick' revival; but it is important that we do not. Cobham was friendly with James Tyrell's only son and heir, also called James. They were near neighbours, former Williamite Whig generals, both commanders of the dragoons in Marlborough's wars, both heaped with honours on the accession of the Hanoverians. The pattern of their careers was strikingly similar until Cobham went into opposition in 1733. Tyrell remained a Court Whig and (having remained single) bequeathed Shotover to Augustus Shutz, George II's cousin. Both were soldiers who turned to landscape gardening on their retirement.[74] Cobham's Gothic Temple, if a grander project than James Tyrell the elder's, bears an unmistakable resemblance to it: a nice example of the continuity between Commonwealth thought and Patriot Whig thought.

Cobham's Temple of Liberty was only one part of his very extensive political gardening programme—a programme impressively well-documented and explicated by George Clarke, Michael Gibbon and, recently, Michael Bevington.[75] The Gothic Temple was erected in Hawkwell Fields and overlooked

---

[72] See Mavis Batey, 'Shotover's Continuity with the Past', *Country Life*, 29 Dec. 1977, 1978-9. For an earlier account of Shotover and the Tyrell family, see also Avray Tipping, *English Homes* (1929), 247-56.   [73] Ibid. 248.

[74] For James Tyrell jun. (*c*.1674-1742) see Romney Sedgwick, *The History of Parliament: The House of Commons 1715-1754*, 2 vols. (1970), ii. 489. The Tyrell family lived principally at Oakley, Bucks., close to Cobham's Stowe. James Tyrell sen. m. Mary Hutchinson from Fladbury, Worcs., close to the Lyttelton seat of Hagley. Tipping, *English Homes*, 253, draws a parallel between the two retired soldiers—Cobham and Tyrell the younger—both exponents of the new taste in landscape gardening.

[75] There is a formidable body of scholarship on Stowe, esp. Cobham's phase of landscape gardening. See in particular G. B. Clarke, 'Grecian Taste and Gothic Virtue'; id., 'William Kent: Heresy in Stowe's Elysium', in Peter Willis (ed.), *Furor Hortensis* (Edinburgh, 1974), 48-65; G. B. Clarke and Michael Gibbon, 'The History of Stowe: I to XXVI', *The Stoic*, Mar. 1967-July 1977; Christopher Hussey, *English Gardens and Landscapes, 1700-1750* (1967), 89-106; J. D. Hunt (ed.), *The Gardens at Stowe*, xvi, *The English Landscape Garden* (New York, 1982); John Martin Robinson, *Temples of Delight: Stowe Landscape Gardens* (1990).

Stowe's east side, the Elysian Fields begun in the 1730s, whose neo-classical temples of Ancient Virtue, Modern Virtue (ironic, this), and British Worthies made a powerful allegorical statement of Patriot Whig ideals. Judith Colton supplies intriguing evidence to suggest that, when Queen Caroline turned her hand to garden architecture in the grounds of Richmond between 1730 and 1735, her Kent-designed Hermitage and Merlin's Cave were part of a political rivalry to appropriate similar themes for the court.[76] In the Hermitage stood busts of British Whig intellectual heroes such as Newton and Locke (also in Stowe's Temple of British Worthies); the thatched and wooden-pillared 'Cave' represented Gothic virtue and ancient wisdom. Caroline's Cave will be looked at in more detail in the subsequent chapter since its 'Gothic' depends less on rustic poles than on its reformulations of Elizabethan and Spenserian symbolism.

James Gibbs's preliminary sketch for the Temple of Liberty (housed in the Ashmolean Museum, Oxford) shows a relatively simple structure. Three Romanesque arched porticoes and a quatrefoil window are flanked by two pentangular towers—an almost neo-classical symmetry very like Tyrell's Gothic façade.[77] The strange *mélange* of architectural shapes—a triangular floor plan containing a domed circular room, three towers (one taller than the others, which lends an asymmetry when viewed from the side rather than the front)—shows that this was 'Gothic' in its most purely symbolic rather than historical form.[78] What can we read from the symbolism? The Gothic Temple's domed interior resembles the interior of the Temple church in London, one of the oldest Gothically conceived and executed buildings in England (there are links between the Temple family and the original Knights Templar). The plastered ceiling is painted with the Temple family shields, some of which reveal the family's supposed descent from the Saxon Earls of Mercia. The Saxon theme enlarges on Stowe's earlier tribute to the Saxons, including the nearby Gothic Walk and Thanet Walk—Thanet was the landing-place for the Saxon leader Hengist. Rysbrack's statues of the seven Saxon deities were transferred in 1745 from the west of the gardens to a semicircle close to the Gothic Temple. Stained-glass windows were later added, featuring the arms of the Saxon heptarchy. The motto which stood over the door from a 1738 play by Corneille— 'JE RENDS GRACES AUX DIEUX DE NESTRE PAS ROMAIN'—was added in the 1740s. Walpole had long since fallen from power but Cobham must have thought such a stringently Tacitean statement in keeping with the spirit of the design;

---

[76] See Colton, 'Merlin's Cave and Queen Caroline', 6–9.

[77] The fullest accounts of the Temple of Liberty are Michael Gibbon, 'A Manifesto in Ironstone: The Gothic Temple at Stowe', *Country Life*, 1 June 1972; Michael Bevington, *Templa Quam Dilecta*, vi, *The Gothic Temple* (Stowe, Bucks., 1990) which includes Gibbs's sketch.

[78] See Bevington, *Templa*, 9: 'It is questionable . . . how far Gibbs was actually aiming to produce a "Gothic" temple in 1740 and 1741, as opposed to a Temple of Liberty, the building's original dedication, which subsequently acquired Gothic additions.'

it implicitly praises those liberty-loving Gothic ancestors who rejected Roman tyranny.[79]

None of these features suggest Gothic licentiousness, 'fancy', or medieval gloom of either the barbaric or the romantic variety; they symbolize solidity, stability, and reverence for the Gothic past not as an antiquarian curiosity but as part of a still vital political heritage. The armorial shields deliberately link the past with the present. In one of the first Stowe guidebooks, written in 1750, George Bickham said of the Temple: 'You see not the least Ornament; and yet there is an extraordinary Pleasure in this antique Simplicity. The whole Edifice seems old, and is left unfinished.'[80] Bickham's response has a touch of that 'Constitutional Sort of Reverence' which a 1739 contributor to *Common Sense* (possibly Lyttelton himself) claims to feel on entering 'These old hospitable *Gothic* halls, hung round with the Helmets, Breast-Plates, and Swords of our Ancestors'.

Nay, I even imagin'd that I here saw some of these good Swords, that had procured the Confirmation of *Magna Charta*, and humbled Spensers and Gavestons. And when I see these thrown by to make way for some tawdry Gilding and Carving, I can't help considering such an Alteration as ominous even to our Constitution. Our old *Gothick* Constitution had a noble Strength and Simplicity in it which was well enough represented by the bold Arches, and the solid Pillars of the Edifices of those Days. And I have not observed that the modern Refinements in either have in the least added to their Strength and Solidity.[81]

This is a much-cited passage. Less familiar is the long essay from which it is taken, which resembles Pope's *Epistle to Burlington* in its scorn for the efforts of vulgar *nouveaux-riches* landowners to 'improve' their houses and estates by gimcrack modern 'refinements'. The corruption and luxury of the times are mirrored in the '*Venetian* Windows' and '*Grecian* Porticoes stuck on to an old decaying Mansion seat' and in the newly landscaped gardens where 'the good old profitable Orchards' have been laid out in a 'Waste of Green'. The essay belongs to a long line of country estate symbols of false luxury, culminating in Smollett's wretchedly hollow Baynard's estate in *Humphry Clinker*. The *Common Sense* essay ends with an imaginary landscaped garden laid out as a monument to modern Court Whiggery, the symbolic antithesis to Stowe, with a grotesque temple called the '*Excise Office*' and a new '*Convention Room*' (Walpole was in the throes of the deeply unpopular Pardo Convention) which would 'be the most expensive Thing of all'.

[79] The motto was from a speech of the Alban Curiace in Corneille's *Horace* (II. iii. 481) posthumously published in 1738. It could also reflect Cobham's Protestant abhorrence of 'Romish' Catholicism.

[80] George Bickham, *The Beauties of Stow* (1750), 47.

[81] *Common Sense*, 15 Dec. 1739. Stowe is (by implication) exempted from the censure; landscape gardening is 'a very pardonable Excess in those whose Ranks and Fortunes conspiring enable them to raise, and entitle them to possess such noble and sumptuous monuments'.

'Modern' refinements, the 'tawdry Gilding and Carving' on an older simpler structure, are equated with modern Court Whig corruption. Here the refinements are Italianate, but the modern taste for 'Gothick' ornament was also used in the same metaphorical way. The 'Temple of Justice' in Lyttelton's *Persian Letters* is an 'Old *Gothick* Pile' whose 'Foundations . . . are deep and very lasting; it has stood many Ages, and with good Repairs may stand many more. But the Architecture is loaded with a multiplicity of idle and useless Parts: when you examine it critically, many Faults and Imperfections will appear, yet upon the whole it has a mighty awful Air, and strikes you with Reverence and Respect.'[82] Here, Gothic 'multiplicity' can be read as the undesirable additions, 'Faults and Imperfections' which the constitution has acquired over time since its first foundation—perhaps even the corruptions into which it has degenerated, and which require 'good Repairs', that is, a Machiavellian *ritorno* to first good principles. This is the very reverse of Kliger's 'Whig aesthetic' where Gothic multiplicity supposedly equals political liberty. For Whig Patriots, 'Gothick' intricacy and ornateness were usually equated with Walpolian parliamentary corruption. This notion is fully developed in an unusual essay in the *Old Whig* of 8 May 1736, the journal's sole venture into political allegory. The editor claims to have 'procured the correspondence of a *Political* Architect'. This architect is clearly a modern Court Whig. He despises 'your Greek and Tuscan Orders' and prefers the 'truly Gothic' where he can borrow or invent 'Ornaments' at will. He is much taken with the novel idea propounded by Swift's Lagadan academicians of building from the roof downwards, thereby saving the time and expense of foundations.

I am going to make the Experiment in a Building in a Friend's Garden, which now wants repairing. My Friend calls it the Temple of *Liberty*; 'twas originally composed of two Orders of Columns supporting a lofty Dome, to which some ingenious Architect has added a large Gothick Spire, whose Weight, my friend complains, has shaked the Foundation and almost destroyed the Fabrick; which made him think of taking down the Spire, and reducing the Building to its ancient Form.[83]

The spire is the overnight work of a swarm of locusts who hold it up by golden chains (a jibe at political patronage and financial chicanery). Clearly the temple's owner, who wants to remove the spire and return the building to its 'ancient Form', is an 'Old' Whig. Again, he metaphorically voices the opposition refrain for a return to first constitutional principles before the 'Fabrick' is destroyed for good. The modern Court Whig architect wants to narrow the foundation (the principles of the constitution) yet further but the workmen are afraid that the 'massy Pillars' will fall on them. Here the Temple of Liberty is classical, and 'Gothick' is entirely associated with modern Court Whiggery. So far, the only real evidence I can find of the political association between Gothic freedom of form and constitutional liberty lies in the post-Walpole

---

[82] Lyttelton, *Persian Letters*, 71.   [83] *Old Whig*, 8 May 1736.

period, the much-cited essay by William Whitehead printed in *The World* in 1753. It derides the 'Tricks and conceits' of the new Gothick style in furnishings and architecture which 'modern' taste prefers to the purity of the Grecian. 'There is something they say, in it congenial to our old Gothic constitution; I should rather think, to our modern idea of liberty, which allows everyone the privilege of playing the fool, and of making himself ridiculous in whatever way he pleases.'[84] It is no coincidence that the association should have been made by a staunch Tory.

Patriot expressions of Gothic in some ways stand apart from the more widespread underlying impulses behind the Gothic revival, with its predilection for the picturesque, the romantic, and the ruined. In the 1750s Stowe's Temple of Liberty was 'Gothicized' by Sanderson Miller and 'adored' by Horace Walpole in some 'heretical corner of [his] heart'.[85] Over the years, the original political statement was lost, absorbed in the mainstream of romantic taste which led Lyttelton, a foremost admirer of Gothic revivalism and sublime landscapes, to commission from his friend Miller in 1752 plans for a new Gothic design for Hagley Hall. Reverence for the past could express itself in both romantic and political terms: the two were not entirely antithetical. But it is the intention of this study to recover from the 1730s and early 1740s patterns of political myth-making which have subsequently become submerged in accounts of mid-century antiquarianism and pre-romanticism. As we shall see in the next chapter, the dualities behind the romantic 'Gothick' and the political Gothic were nowhere more apparent than in the mid-century appropriations of Spenser's *Faerie Queene*.

Political Primitivism and Literary Primitivism

In 1746 Joseph Warton added a pithy marginal note to one of his Runic Odes: 'Better uncivilis'd than civilised'—four words which serve to sum up one of the major transformations of eighteenth-century literary taste.[86] Stephen Duck and other rustic poet-swains were tamer versions of the untutored poet whose 'original genius' was unspoilt by the overlay of education and civilization. By the following decade poets, antiquarians, and critics were actively engaged in a quest for the primitive origins of the true poetic spirit—a search that led them into the far-flung reaches of Hebraism and Hellenism, North America and

---

[84] *The World*, 22 Mar. 1753.

[85] Walpole to John Chole, 4 Aug. 1753. Sanderson Miller erected a sham Gothic tower at Hagley for Sir Thomas Lyttelton, in place by 1749. George Lyttelton's friendship with Miller dates from *c.*1748. He rejected the Gothic design for Hagley Hall in favour of a neo-classical design. See *An Eighteenth-Century Correspondence . . . Letters . . . to Sanderson Miller*, ed. L. Dickins and M. Stanton (1910).

[86] Bodleian MS Dep. 671, fo. 22v.

Chile, 'the Erse, Norwegian and Welsh fragments, the Lapland and American Songs'.[87]

Before turning to the forms in which the Patriot poets of the Walpole era expressed their engagement with the literary as opposed to the merely political implications of Gothic primitivism, it is important to perceive some of the problems entailed. Thomson's *Liberty*, written between 1734 and 1736, is a peculiarly tense poem, underscored by cultural and political anxieties. That sense of tension is, of course, also a hallmark of *The Seasons*, where Thomson's ambivalent views about the respective virtues of primitivism and progress lead to a pattern of repeated self-contradictions. Cities are both the epitome of man's civilized achievement and the sink of vice and corruption. Primitive peoples can be both pure and innocent and brutish and depraved. The 'want of method' which Johnson perceived in *The Seasons*, its loosely eclectic structure, enables such contradictions to coexist as no more than a series of juxtapositions mirroring the complexity and even paradoxical nature of life itself. *Liberty*'s more rigorous historical framework raises to the fore problems which only half-surface in the earlier work. Thomson shared many of the cultural assumptions of his age which made Augustan Rome the pinnacle of cultural aspiration. When Thomson thought of a classical (as opposed to Miltonic) epic, it was to Virgil rather than the bardic Homer that he turned for inspiration. Like many of his contemporaries, Thomson also freely applied the 'Gothic' epithet in an almost ahistorical manner to anything that savoured of bad taste or rude manners. Even in *Liberty*, a work which gives the fullest account of the Gothic *translatio* theory—the historic movement of the liberty-loving tribes who swept across the failing Roman empire and brought with them Britain's 'first seeds of freedom'—we can find '*Gothic* Rust', 'GOTHIC WAR', 'the fierce *Demon, Gothic Duel*', even the sins committed against Grecian rules of architecture by '*Goths* of every Age'.[88]

But the real contradictions arise less from this relatively untroubled adjectival application than from Thomson's adherence to a Polybian or Machiavellian perception of the rise, growth, civilization, and fall of nations—a structure which also underpins *The Castle of Indolence*. *Liberty* is not quite the manifesto of an untroubled Whiggish progressivism that many critics seem to assume. Britain may be *Liberty*'s 'favour'd Isle', the sense of national election and imperial destiny later echoed in the Knight of Art and Industry's exclamation, 'Be This my great, my chosen Isle'.[89] But much of *Liberty*'s admonitory

---

[87] Gray, *The Progress of Poesy*, l. 54 n. (*The Poems of Gray, Collins and Goldsmith*, ed. Roger Lonsdale (2nd edn. 1976), 168). All Gray and Collins quotations from this edition.

[88] *Liberty*, iv. 207; iv. 42; v. 479; ii. 377. See also the '*Gothic* Forms' which the Byzantine emperor Constantine erected in place of Trajan's arch (iii. 510). Thomson's admiration is always for classical architecture: see esp. ii. 373–90. See also Lipking, *Ordering of the Arts*, 148, for the (often comically bizarre) use of the 'Gothic' epithet.

[89] *Liberty*, iv. 461; *Castle of Indolence*, II. xvii. For a far more confident sense of national election, see opening lines of 'Rule, Britannia'—'When Britain first at heaven's command | Arose from out the azure main.'

strength lies in the gloomy possibility that Britain may and perhaps must go the same way as Rome: 'But as from Man to Man, Fate's first Decree, | Impartial Death the Tide of Riches rolls, | So States must die and LIBERTY go round' (ii. 418–20). And the cyclical view of history places primitive liberty— whether Grecian, Roman, or Gothic—on the opposite side of the cycle from poetic achievement. In the ascent from virtuous but rugged primitivism through the steps of law, government, agriculture, trade, and commerce, the fine arts emerge when civilization reaches its zenith. From then on things can only go downhill. Poetry itself might even be rendered suspect from its location at the point in the cycle where high civilization imperceptibly degenerates into luxury, where the free man becomes the slave to his sensual appetites. The smooth tongues of poets might even become the tool of tyrants. The Goddess Liberty upbraids both Virgil and Horace for their complicity in a literary propaganda exercise alternately glorifying and disguising Augustus's imperial ambitions. The dismal modern ruins of a once fertile Italy serve as a reprimand to poets: 'First from your flatter'd CAESARS This began' (i. 286).

As J. G. A. Pocock observes, 'culture and liberty were ultimately incompatible; the Goths were both despicable as artists and admirable as freemen; and what raised man above the condition of the savage must ultimately sink him below the level of the citizen'.[90] This is what Aaron Hill also perceived when he read the first draft of *Liberty* in 1734. His commentary, far more than mindless praise, seeks the kind of reconciliation Thomson could not fully make.

We have always been lovers of liberty, in her coarseness, and rugged simplicity; teach us to *taste* her in her politeness; teach us to be *free*, without *insolence*; and *elegant*, without *luxury*; to be *learned*, at once, and *warlike*: to be *traders*, but not *tradesmen*.[91]

The 'polite' Whigs of Addison's age, with their modern vision of the refinement that comes from trade and commerce supporting the arts, thought the synthesis possible: so too did later Scottish Enlightenment Whigs.[92] But Patriot Whigs of the 1730s (and equally of the days of 'Cato' and the South Sea Bubble) who placed liberty and luxury in such fierce antithesis could not reconcile the two so easily. Thomson's account of the political conditions which favour national poetic achievement is deeply troubled. 'Th' *Eternal Patron*, LIBERTY' is supposedly the only true source of artistic inspiration.[93] Thomson advances the familiar theory that Virgil and Horace derived their inspiration from republican rather than imperial Rome. 'That sometimes Arts may flourish for a while under despotic Governments, tho' never the natural and genuine Production of them.'[94] French cultural achievement, as we have

[90] J. G. A. Pocock, *Virtue, Commerce, and History* (Cambridge, 1985), 98.

[91] Hill, *Works*, 4 vols. (1753), i. 215.

[92] See Pocock, *Virtue, Commerce, and History*, 252; David Spadafora, *The Idea of Progress in Eighteenth-Century Britain* (New Haven, Conn., 1990), 253–320.

[93] *Castle of Indolence*, II. xxii.   [94] *Liberty*, iv, 'Contents' (OET *Liberty*, 89).

seen in Chapter 3, posed a greater challenge. Corneille, Racine, and Molière, who flourished under the patronage of the absolutist Louis XIV, would have been 'Superiour still' if they had 'branch'd luxuriant to the Skies | In BRITAIN planted, by the Potent Juice | Of *Freedom* swell'd' (v. 526–9). In envisioning a new British cultural golden age, Part V 'Recommends as ITS last Ornament and Finishing, SCIENCES, FINE ARTS, and PUBLIC WORKS. The Encouragement of These to be urged from the Example of France, tho' under a Despotic Government.'[95] The examples Thomson proffers point to the unspoken conclusion that the arts *only* flourish 'under a Despotic Government' and the protective patronage it affords. Thomson's silence on the great poets and dramatists of the English Renaissance (no mention here of Spenser, Sidney, or Shakespeare) might stem from fear that acknowledging an earlier British cultural golden age would imply that it was gone and past. As Shaftesbury had remarked, ''Twas the fate of Rome to have scarce an intermediate age, or single period of time, between the rise of the arts and the fall of liberty'.[96] In both *Liberty* and *The Castle of Indolence*, aesthetic efflorescence is never past or present but always future, perpetually postponed. 'Yet the fine Arts were what he finish'd least. | For Why? They are Quintessence of All, | The Growth of labouring Time.'[97] In *Liberty* Britain's prevailing genius is mercantile, not yet artistic: that age is located in the final prophetic vision of a future British Augustan era, modelled not on native sources but manifestly vying with despotic France and imperial Rome.

The Goths may have brought liberty: they were also, quite literally, vandals. The political and cultural ambivalence is caught in Thomson's two quite separate accounts of the northern *translatio*, one from a political, the other from a cultural perspective. In Part III Thomson depicts the energetic northern hordes carrying the seeds of political enlightenment:

> Till from almost perpetual Night they broke,
> As if in Search of Day; and o'er the Banks
> Of yielding Empire, only Slave-sustain'd,
> Resistless rag'd.
>
> (iii. 535–8)

But political enlightenment brings cultural destruction.

> Ah poor *Italia*! what a bitter Cup
> Of Vengeance hast thou drain'd? *Goths*, *Vandals*, *Huns*,
> *Lombards*, Barbarians broke from every Land,
> How many a ruffian Form hast thou beheld?
> What horrid Jargons heard . . .

. . . .

---

[95] *Liberty*, v, 'Contents' (ibid. 126). For Thomson's ambivalent views about literary patronage and 'Maecenases' see *Liberty*, v. 538–43. Cf. *Castle of Indolence*, II. xxii and above, Ch. 3.

[96] Anthony Ashley Cooper, 3rd Earl of Shaftesbury, *Characteristicks of Men, Manners, Opinions, Times*, 3 vols. (1711), i. 143.   [97] *Castle of Indolence*, II. xxii.

> These hungry Myriads, that thy Bowels tore,
> Heap'd Sack on Sack, and bury'd in their Rage
> Wonders of Art.

(iv. 108–12; 125–7)

Yet certain Patriot works, transcending the deeply entrenched prejudices that equated the Gothic with the iconoclastic, began to establish the connection later made explicit by Thomas Gray: 'the Extensive influence of poetic Genius over the remotest and most uncivilis'd nations: its connections with liberty, and the virtues that naturally attend on it.'[98] Here Sir William Temple's 'Of Heroic Virtue' and 'Of Poetry' provided a formative influence. His attempt to pursue an unprejudiced enquiry into the religious beliefs and customs of the northern races was far removed from Aylett Sammes's (virtually simultaneous) account of Odin and Valhalla, the Norse hero 'LOTHBROK, in his Fur-Leather Breeches . . . hugging himself with the hope of Full-pots in the world to come'.[99] Temple had also cited Olaus Wormius's Latin translation of the Death Song of Radnar Lodbrog (or Lothbrok) but had thought it written in 'a vein truly Poetical', showing that the Nordic races 'wanted not the true Spirit of Poetry . . . or that natural Inspiration which has been said to arise from some spark of the Poetical Fire'.[100] Thomson gives these myths an imaginative treatment in *Liberty* very different in spirit from the impulses which had led Pope, working from the same source, to fashion his *Temple of Fame*. In *Alfred*, the Danish sisters of 'furious Ivar' weave their 'Reafan Banner' to the accompaniment of a rhythmic song, which, along with the Death Song of Radnar Lodbrog, became one of the leitmotivs of the Scandinavian revival: a passage which strikingly anticipates the grim weaving scenes in Gray's *The Bard* and his 'Gothic' 'The Fatal Sisters'.[101] But the Norse myths still remained extrinsic to Thomson's sense of British literary tradition. In *Alfred* the Danes remain resolutely foreign, even barbaric, defeated by the piously English Patriot King Alfred who receives instruction from a very native *genius loci*, an ancient hermit living in a cave by the Athelney Marshes. Alfred's last

---

[98] Gray, *The Progress of Poesy*, l. 54 n. (*Poems of Gray*, ed. Lonsdale, 168).

[99] Sammes, *Britannia Antiqua Illustrata*, 62.

[100] William Temple, *Works*, ed. Jonathan Swift, 2 vols. (1720), 'Of Heroic Virtue', ii. 216; 'Of Poetry', ii. 243. For a general discussion of the pre-1740 approach to northern mythology, see Seaton, *Literary Relations of England and Scandinavia in the Seventeenth Century*; F. E. Farley, *Scandinavian Influences in the English Romantic Movement* (Cambridge, Mass., 1903). The first full-scale use of Norse myths in the mid-century were two Runic Odes which appeared in the Revd. Thomas Warton's *Poems on Several Occasions* (1748), now thought to have been written by his son Joseph Warton.

[101] For Thomson's account of Valhalla, see *Liberty*, iv. 667–83; he also briefly describes (iv. 709 n.) the Reafan Banner. In *Alfred* this had grown into a full-blown piece of northern romanticism. See McKillop, *Background of Thomson's 'Liberty'*, 82–3. Cf. Devon's speech in Alfred (1740), 37–8 and the weaving scenes in Gray's *The Bard*, ll. 44–55 and 'The Fatal Sisters', ll. 11–16 and Preface. Gray transferred Norse myths into his Celtic *The Bard*. 'The Fatal Sisters' appears in G's commonplace book as a 'Gothic' poem. See *Poems of Gray*, ed. Lonsdale, 210–14.

triumphant song is uttered by a visionary bard, 'venerable and blind', a modest
British version of Homer.

It was, once again, the endlessly curious Aaron Hill who did most to
explore the relationship between northern virtue and poetic liberty. His entre-
preneurial eye for novelty led him in 1731 to formulate plans for staging his
Patriot drama *Athelwold* in original Saxon dress sketched out from suggestions
in Verstegen's *Restitution of Decayed Intelligence*, right down to costing the
expense of imitation furs indistinguishable from real ones at a distance.[102] His
1737 *The Tears of the Muses* concludes with a northern *translatio* in reverse,
with the Muses taking flight from a corrupt and philistine Britain back to
those lands where the 'icy *pole* dissolves'. Here 'no knighthood blazes, on a
miser's back: | No bought emblaz'nings, eminence efface, | No dirty dignity
sublimes disgrace'. In this renewed Gothic enlightenment 'new nations for-
ward draw | And the drain'd wilds of nature crowd to *law*'.[103] Hill's satire on
political corruption, with the transmigration of the Spirit of Liberty followed
by the arts, culminating in a tentative prophecy of British artistic renewal, is
curiously echoed in James Miller's 1741 *Carmen Seculare*, one of Goldgar's
'Patriot satires'.[104] But elsewhere Hill clearly saw the northern bard himself as
a mouthpiece for outspoken moral denunciation of the times and of patriotic
prophecy, not unlike Gray's *The Bard*. In *Cleon to Lycidas: A Time Piece*
(?1738), Hill castigates a Britain where 'seduction's *drowth* has choak'd | With
venal dust, *Castalia*'s dwindled rill' and urges some '*priest Poet*' to write
'Rugged truth, untun'd | To flattry's dulcid lentor':

> Oh! for some hoarse *Teutonic* note, more stern
> Than *Runic* bard, o'er hostile scalp, e'er sung,
> When *Woden's hall* resounded to his *clang*![105]

Restoring the Druids

When the Patriots looked to the Gothic past for idealized versions of the
opposition poet-bard, they identified less with the Nordic than with the Celtic.
The mid-century 'restoration' of the Druids began not in the 1740s, with
Stukeley's *Stonehenge: A Temple Restored to the Druids* (1740), but in the previous decade, the 1730s, when Druidism acquired (or reacquired) a sharply
political edge. It was this oppositional conception of the Druidic and, in
broader terms, of the bardic figure which lay behind a number of Gray's and
Collins's odes. But the mid-century assimiliation of the bard's role and political identity posed irresolvable problems for the Patriots' poetic heirs.

As we have seen, the northern *translatio* theory espoused by Whig Goth-

---

[102] Hill outlined these schemes in two letters of Oct. 1731 to the actor Wilks. See Hill, *Works*,
i. 88, 90.   [103] Ibid. iv. 169, 174.
[104] Goldgar, *Walpole and the Wits*, 211–13.   [105] Hill, *Works*, iv. 292–3.

icists in the eighteenth century depicted all the northern races who invaded Britain's shores as a kind of Gothic 'cousinage'. Bolingbroke was rehearsing a familiar argument when he claimed that Britons, Goths, Celts, and Scythians all 'came out of the same northern hive' and 'were originally of Celtic, or Gothic extraction, call it which you please'.[106] Pope had found nothing anomalous about placing the Norse gods alongside the Celtic Druids and their bards; and when Samuel Boyse paid his poetic respects to Stowe's Saxon shrine in 1742, he quite naturally added a few Druids to the picture.

> But solemn scenes demand th'attentive muse,
> Such as the Druids lov'd of old to chuse.
> For lo conspicuous stands the awful grove
> Sacred to Woden and the Saxon Jove.[107]

Political panegyrists in the previous century would have been less comfortable with the imaginative leap from Saxon altars to Druidic groves. Parliamentarians and Royalists had fought fierce historiographical battles over the respective authenticity of the Saxon and Trojan 'originals'. The immense labours of the Saxon scholars such as Speed and Spelman had originated in a quest to find a Saxon origin for the common law in defence of the Stuarts' claims to Divine Right. Battles were fought over Geoffrey of Monmouth's *Historia* recounting the settlement of England by Brutus and his descendants: it was from this foundation myth that the Stuarts traced their royal lineage. Throughout the seventeenth century the Druids were implicitly identified with Cambro-British, not Saxon mythology, and invariably appear in poems or masques celebrating the Stuart monarchy.[108] Thomas Carew's elaborate Caroline masque *Coelum Britannicum* (1634) depicts the Druids as part of a heroic line incorporating Arthur and St George and culminating in Charles I. Selden's scholarly footnotes to that very Druidic poem, Drayton's *Polyolbion* (1622), identifies the Druids with the descendants of Brutus, who 'by the incroachment of *Saxons, Jutes, Angles, Danes* [were] driven into these westerne parts of the now *Wales* and *Cornwales*'. Mona, governed by 'the last Prince of *Wales* of the *British* bloud', linked Henry Prince of Wales and subsequently King James with Druidic wisdom and priesthood.[109] The oak groves in which the Druids worshipped came to be associated with the symbol of the royal Stuart oak.[110]

[106] Bolingbroke, *Works*, i. 318.

[107] Samuel Boyse, *The Triumphs of Nature*, repr. in Clarke, *Descriptions of Lord Cobham's Gardens*, 100. First printed in instalments in *GM* June–Aug. 1742. Boyse added the Druids himself. George Clarke assures me there are no Druids at Stowe.

[108] See Roberta F. Brinkley, *Arthurian Legend in the Seventeenth Century* (Baltimore, Md., 1932), *passim*. For a fascinating but slightly wayward account of Druids in 17th-cent. political poetry, see Douglas Brooks-Davies, *The Mercurian Monarch: Magical Politics from Spenser to Pope* (Manchester, 1983). See also A. L. Owen, *The Famous Druids: A Survey of Three Centuries of English Literature on the Druids* (Oxford, 1962); T. D. Kendrick, *The Druids: A Study in Keltic History* (1927); Stuart Piggott, *The Druids* (1983).

[109] Michael Drayton, *Works*, ed. J. W. Hebel et al. (2nd edn., Oxford, 1961), iv. 28.

[110] See Brooks-Davies, *Mercurian Monarch*, 158–9.

Douglas Brooks-Davies's claims notwithstanding, there is (as far as I can detect) little firm evidence in the late seventeenth century for republican Druids representing 'the strengths of an ancient British philosophy and religion, an imagined return to which signified the ultimate overthrowing of the Norman yoke and affirmation of British liberty'.[111] Milton's attitude towards the Druids after *Lycidas* (1637) and *Mansus* (1638) seemed to become increasingly hostile; the Druids, like the Arthurian legend and Geoffrey of Monmouth, were by implication associated with Stuart tyranny. Milton's *History of Britain* (1670) depicted the Britons struggling with Suetonius's Roman forces as barbarous and superstitious, 'Progenitors not to be glori'd in'.[112] The 'republican' image of heroic Britons inspired by their patriotic Druid priests in a resistance movement against Roman (and by implication more modern) tyranny awaited the Patriot poetry of the Walpole period.

By the end of the seventeenth century the Druids had all but vanished from political poetry. When Dryden linked Stonehenge with the restored Stuart monarchy in 1662, he drew on Walter Charleton's new theories—that Stonehenge was a Danish rather than a Druidic temple—to construct a complex symbolic statement about constitutional monarchy.[113] The growth of the antiquarian movement in both France and England prompted a steady stream of scholarship on Stonehenge and the Druids. But it was not, on the whole, conducive to the propagation of idealizing myths, especially about Druidic religion. Stuart Piggott notes that 'The general attitude of scholars and the educated public they addressed on Celts and Druids was, by the early eighteenth century, objective and unromantic'.[114] William Stukeley was busy between 1719 and 1724 carrying out the fieldwork which would eventually translate itself into his eulogistic accounts of Druidism in *Stonehenge* and *Abury*, but his findings were not broadcast for another twenty years.[115] Both William Temple and Rapin touch on the subject of the Druids in their histories of England; but the most extensive accounts are those by Aylett Sammes (1676), Henry Rowlands (1723), and John Toland (1726). None of these three writers minimized Druidic heathenism, barbaric human sacrifices, and pagan superstition: a climate of feeling which informed the mood of Pope's blood-smeared iron columns.[116]

---

[111] See Brooks-Davies, *Mercurian Monarch*, 151.

[112] See Brinkley, *Arthurian Legend*, 129–33.

[113] See Earl Wasserman, *The Subtler Language: Critical Readings of Neoclassic and Romantic Poems* (Baltimore, Md., 1959), 15–33.

[114] Piggott, *The Druids*, 121. There is nothing noble about the Druids George Granville added to his opera, *The British Enchanters*, some time after 1708. They are 'infernal' and barbaric, and may function as a negative, not benign, political force. See his *Genuine Works in Verse and Prose*, 3 vols. (1732), i. 175.

[115] By 1723 Stukeley had finished two sections of a draft for a book on stone circles, but even here the Druids appear on only a single page.

[116] See Temple, *Works*, ii, 531; Paul Rapin de Thoyras, *A History of England*, trans. Nicholas Tindal, 15 vols. (1725–31), i, pp. xvii–xviii; Sammes, *Britannia Antiqua Illustrata*; Henry Rowlands, *Mona Antiqua Restaurata* (Dublin, 1723); John Toland, *A Critical History of the Celtic*

But the 1730s witnessed a striking reversal of attitudes towards primitive Britons and Celts—a reversal for which the Patriot campaign was almost entirely responsible. As late as the mid-1720s, both John Toland and Henry Rowlands were unsparingly sceptical about Druidic 'priestcraft' and the gullibility of the Britons, though from different perspectives—Toland as a republican free-thinker who disliked priestcraft in any shape, Rowlands as a devout Anglican vicar from Anglesey (ancient Mona) who struggled between patriotic respect for ancient Welsh learning and an orthodox Christian hostility to paganism. Rowlands produced a very biased version, similar in temper to Milton's, of Tacitus's account of the battle which had taken place on Mona between Suetonius Paulinus and the Britons. The 'fearful slippery *Druids*', finding their incantations useless, run off into the wood leaving their people stranded. The 'fierce', 'undaunted', and 'fearless' Romans win an easy victory over the exhausted Britons; and in a new version of the fortunate fall, the defeated Britons are liberated from the 'ancient *Shades* of Heathenism' by Romans bearing with them the '*Light* of the Gospel'.[117]

Less than a decade later, Bolingbroke was loudly proclaiming the myth of British resistance in the pages of the *Craftsman*. 'Caesar himself acknowledges that they fought boldly for their liberties, when he invaded them; and there is good reason to believe, from his manner of writing, and abrupt way of leaving this island, that they gave him a warmer reception than he is willing to own.'[118] Both here and in *A Dissertation on Parties* (1734) he turned to Tacitus, Dio Cassius, and Caesar for evidence of the unbroken legacy of British freedoms. Even if the Britons themselves could not supply an authoritative account of their origins, the Romans could.

The ancient Britons are to us the Aborigines of our island. We discover little of them through the gloom of antiquity, and we see nothing beyond them. This, however, we know, they were freemen. Caesar, who visited them in a hostile manner, but did not conquer them, perhaps was beaten by them. . . . a lawless power, a government by will, never prevailed in Britain.[119]

In Book IV of *Liberty* Thomson gave full emotional colouring to Bolingbroke's assertion.

> Witness, *Rome*,
> Who saw'st thy *Caesar* from the naked Land,
> Whose only Fort was *British* Hearts, repell'd,

Religion and Learning, printed posthumously in *A Collection of Several Pieces by Mr. John Toland* (1726), repr. in *A New Edition of Toland's 'History of the Druids'*, ed. R. Huddlestone (Montrose, 1814). For a summary of available literature on Druids in the 18th century see J. M. S. Tompkins, 'In Yonder Grave a Druid Lies', *RES* 22 (1946), 1–16. But Tompkins does not mention Rowlands and dismisses Toland and (surprisingly) Stukeley as 'eccentrics'.

[117] Rowlands, *Mona Antiqua Restaurata*, 97–106.

[118] Bolingbroke, *Works*, i. 317.

[119] Ibid. ii. 108–9. Bolingbroke's use of more trustworthy Roman sources seems in keeping with the sceptical approach to national myths outlined in the *Letters on History*.

> To seek *Pharsalian* Wreaths. Witness, the Toil,
> The Blood of Ages, bootless to secure,
> Beneath an *Empire*'s Yoke, a stubborn *Isle*,
> Disputed hard, and never quite subdued.
>
> (iv. 640–6)

In a near reversal of Rowlands's descriptive epithets for Britons and Romans, Thomson claims that the Celts certainly never conceded defeat to a Roman army 'yielding' and 'weary' in its efforts to 'support | The last Remains of Empire' (iv. 657–8). The myth of the patriotic British resistance is reworked in simple allegorical form in *The Castle of Indolence*. Like the hero of Pope's *Brutus* (whose Druids will shortly be discussed), Thomson's Knight of Arts and Industry makes a westerly Hesperidean progress from an exhausted Italy to the 'clement skies' of Britain. The native Britons, in an idealized description (derived from William Temple), combine the virtues of hard and soft primitivism.

> Their Wealth the Wild-Deer bouncing through the Glade;
> They log'd at large, and liv'd at Nature's Cost;
> Save Spear, and Bow, withouten other Aid,
> Yet not the *Roman* Steel their naked Breast dismay'd.
>
> (II. xvii)

The Tacitean view appropriated by the opposition in the 1730s confirmed the Britons as well as their Germanic cousins as the well-spring of rugged integrity. Brooke's inflammatory Prologue to *Gustavus Vasa* links the 'first-born natives' who 'breathed the virtues of *Britannia*'s air' with their Swedish cousins. Just as Gustavus defied the corrupt tyrant Trollio, so the ancient Britons defended their native liberties against Roman encroachments: 'For mightier Freedom against *Ceasar* fought, | And rudely drove the fam'd Invader Home, | To tyrannize o'er polished—venal *Rome*.'[120]

Where were the Druids in all this? They are not named in Bolingbroke's glowing account of British liberties but start to appear in Patriot verse both as ancient British philosophers and as figures for the opposition poet himself. Both Pope and Thomson perceived a connection between the Druidic religion and the Norse myths of Valhalla: immortal glory for those who die in battle. But Thomson's account of the Druidic doctrine of metempsychosis is far more elevated: British souls do not die but return in different form, ascending upwards through a long process of purification. Belief in an afterlife prompts them to fight on to the end.

> For by the *Druid* taught, that Death but shifts
> The vital Scene, they that prime fear despis'd;
> And, prone to rush on Steel, disdain'd to spare
> An ill-sav'd Life that must again return.

[120] Brooke, *Gustavus Vasa*, Prologue.

> Erect from *Nature*'s Hand, by *tyrant Force*,
> And still more *tyrant Custom*, unsubdu'd,
> Man knows no Master save creating HEAVEN.
> Or such as Choice and common Good ordain.
> This general Sense, with which the Nations I
> Promiscuous fire, in BRITONS burn'd intense.
>
> (*Liberty*, iv. 630–9)

Antiquarian research had discovered that the Druids shared the doctrine of metempsychosis with Pythagoras; Rowlands and, later, Stukeley believed that Pythagoras had first derived it from the Druids, rather than vice versa. Thomson's own personal lifelong interest in metempsychosis and notions of spiritual ascent might have attracted him to the Druids quite independently. But *The Seasons*, the poem in which Thomson first expounds the doctrine of the transmigration of souls, is, in fact, the least explicitly 'Druidical' of any of his longer poems.[121] In *Summer* (1727), Thomson had depicted himself as poet-philosopher, wandering in gloomy groves: these are the 'Haunts of Meditation' where 'antient Bards th'inspiring Breath, | Extatic, felt'.[122] When Thomas Rundle read *The Seasons* he descanted fulsomely on the early origins of 'sacred verse' and found its roots in biblical prophecy and 'the chronicles of the Bards and the instruction of the Druids'.[123] But there is no evidence that at this stage Thomson's conception of the bardic had extended beyond the Old Testament prophetic poets Moses and Job, named as his inspiration in the 1726 preface to *Winter*. The passage in *Summer* is heavily indebted to the rhapsodic groves of Shaftesbury's *The Moralists*.[124] Thomson's failure to mention the Druids in *The Seasons*, a poem not sparing in its accounts of primitive peoples, suggests that they first entered his imaginative vocabulary not through romantic musings on contemplation, woods, and poetry, but through the more rigorous avenues of Patriot Gothicism.

Although both Milton and Pope had equated Druids with bards, some antiquarians thought they constituted two separate orders in the Druidic hierarchy: the superior order, the Druids, were 'vates' or philosophers, the bards were singers and poets. It is the first kind who inspire the Britons to battle in *Liberty*. But by the time Thomson reached Canto II of the *The Castle of Indolence*, a poem begun in 1733–4, he conflated the Druid with the bard in an idealized amalgam of the patriotic oppositional philosopher-poet. Philomel accompanies the Knight of Arts and Industry in his quest to liberate the Castle dwellers. Joseph Warton was almost certainly correct to surmise that Philomel was a fictional portrait of Pope: 'a Bard | A little Druid-Wight, | Of

---

[121] Thomson's doctrine of the ascent of souls is stated in *Spring*, ll. 336–78; *Castle of Indolence*, ii. xlviii, lxiii. See Owen, *The Famous Druids*, 175–7; Tompkins, 'In Yonder Grave', esp. p. 13. I argue the opposite case to Tompkins, who sees *The Seasons* as the most 'Druidical' of all T's poems.   [122] *Summer*, ll. 522–4.
[123] Rundle, *Letters*, i. 127.   [124] See Shaftesbury, *Characteristicks*, ii. 390–1.

wither'd Aspect; but his Eye was keen'. His dress of 'Russet brown . . . , | As is his sister of the Copses green' seems more appropriate to the younger Pope, whom Charles Gildon described as 'this little *Aesopic* sort of animal in his own cropt Hair, and dress very agreeable to the Forest he came from'.[125] But it is Pope the opposition poet of the 1730s Thomson is thinking of. Philomel accompanies his song with a patriotically '*British* Harp'. This modern Druid, like his forebears, will stir the Britons to rise against corruption and enslavement; but this time the threat lies within rather than without. A 1741 popular treatise on early British, Norse, and Celtic poetry—*The Polite Correspondence: Or, Rational Amusement*, attributed to John Campbell, saw Pope as the true heir to the ancient British bards. 'Surely if ever Poetry was useful in any State, we may affirm it to have been of public Benefit among the *Britons*', it remarked. The bards' songs (unlike those of most modern poets) were as powerful as 'the short Sword of the bold *Briton* in the Time of Caesar'. But Pope is different from other modern poets. 'While others admire the Energy and Sweetness of *Pope*, my Eyes are fix'd on his Candour and Courage: in him revives the true Spirit of Verse.'[126] Yet Thomson was also using Philomel to project some of his own aspirations about the power of the poet to sway public opinion and to change national affairs. If (as I argue in the next chapter) *The Castle of Indolence* can on one level be read as an opposition allegory for the present state of Britain, then it is the bardic Philomel rather than the sensual Archimago who comes closest (at least in conscious terms) to Thomson's own poetic ideal.

The Druids and ancient Britons, like liberty, patriotism, and the image of Elizabeth, were not exclusively oppositional property. As in the rival Gothic edifices of Stowe's Temple of British Worthies and Caroline's Hermitage and Cave, Court and opposition Whigs were competing to appropriate British mythology. When Richard Powney celebrated Frederick in his *The Stag Chace in Windsor Forest* (1739) it was as a Cambro-British Prince of Wales, with '*Celtick* Trophies crown'd', the 'Pride of *Cambria*', crowned by some rather Stuart-like Windsor royal oak invested with the antiquity of mystic Druids: 'Ye sacred Oaks, that hoary Temples crown'd, | When the Steer bled, and Altars blaz'd around; | When Priests with measur'd Dance, with mystick Lay | And rising Incense hail'd the God of Day.'[127] The royalist implications of Druidic wisdom and lore, associating the Hanoverian monarchy with ancient British learning and priestly authority, make a strange reappearance in some of

---

[125] Thomson, *Castle of Indolence*, ii. xxxiii; Joseph Warton, *An Essay on the Writings and Genius of Pope*, 2 vols. (1756–62), ii. 325–6; Charles Gildon, *Memoirs of William Wycherley* (1718), 16.

[126] *The Polite Correspondence: Or, Rational Amusement*, 252–3. The Druids are discussed on pp. 249–53; Campbell claims they wrote satirical moral songs denouncing corrupt governments and tyrannical leaders. Cf. the Druid's poetry as sword and Pope's 'sacred Weapon', in *Ep. Satires*, ii. 212–19. See also A. D. McKillop, 'A Critic of 1741 on Early Poetry', *SP* 30 (1933), 504–21.

[127] [Richard Powney], *The Stag Chace in Windsor Forest* (1739), 2, 4, 16.

the poetry celebrating Queen Caroline's championship of science and philosophy. In 1735 Jane Brereton as 'Melissa' linked the old popular myth of Merlin's magical spiriting to England from Ireland of the stones of Stonehenge with (strange bedfellow!) the astronomical discoveries of Locke, recently enshrined in Caroline's Hermitage. The Merlin who glorifies George and Caroline's dynastic pedigree is indubitably a Druid.

> Then, lo! beneath a venerable *Oak*,
> Which oft repell'd the Tempest's furious stroke;
> Whose spreading Arms, a wide Circumf'rence show
> And from whose Trunk, springs sacred *Misseltoe*:
> Methought, I saw an awful *Shade* arise;
> (Fit object only, for Poetick Eyes.)
> The Form Majestick, and the Front serene;
> *Angles*, and *Circles*, on his Robe were seen.
> The *Northern Crown*, around his Temples shone,
> And the *Celestial Signs* adorn'd his Zone.
> The *British Harp*, seem'd to support one Hand;
> While t'other, gently wav'd the sacred *Wand*.[128]

Oaks, mistletoe, northern crowns, and British harps: a Hanoverian appropriation of some very native (and formerly Tudor-Stuart) properties.

When Pope returned to the subject of the Druids after a gap of some twenty-eight years, it was no longer in the mood of romantic barbarism with which he had inscribed the northern wall of the Temple of Fame. *Brutus* reflects his new interests in primitive religions and peoples and his acquaintance with Stukeley.[129] That Pope had at least some of the tenets of opposition thought at the back of his mind is apparent in the prophetic vision to be spoken by an old Druid, one of the company of Druid priests who first welcome Brutus to the west coast with offerings of fruit and flowers and who preach a doctrine 'tending to a nobler Religion'.[130] The Druid foresees that 'the Britons should Degenerate in an Age or Two' but 'be Redeemd again'—a rehearsal of Bolingbroke's Machiavellian *ritorno* theory clarified by Pope's note: 'With observations upon the Impossibility of any Institution being Perpetual without some Changes.' Yet the *Brutus* plans allude to another set of 'bad' Druids: this time on Mona, which is 'under *Superstition* governed by *Priests*'—the footnote shows a source in Tacitus's *Annals*. Pope's hero needed a real enemy to overcome in his civilizing mission to 'extend good government' and banish political and priestly tyranny in Britain. And of course Brutus is essentially a Roman hero; it is his successor Julius Caesar, rather than the Britons themselves, who will 'redeem' Britain

---

[128] [Jane Brereton], *Merlin: A Poem Humbly Inscrib'd to Her Majesty* (1735), 4–5.

[129] Pope and Stukeley both belonged to the Gentlemen's Society at Spalding.

[130] Quotations from Frederick Brie's transcription of BL Egerton MS 1950 in his 'Pope's *Brutus*', *Anglia*, 63 (1939), 148–52, and from Owen Ruffhead's paraphrase of a now lost source for the Brutus plans in his *Life of Pope* (1769), 410–23.

once again from barbarism. This is not Patriot Gothicism. Even the 'good' Druids, for all their Stukeleyite apparel as heirs of the Patriarchs, lack martial backbone. It is the Roman Brutus who first introduces to their 'good and gentle dispositions' those very qualities the Patriots themselves thought indigenous to the Britons: 'Love of Liberty . . . the Martial Spirit, & other Moral Virtues'.

During the period Pope was sketching out the *Brutus* plans, Stukeley had published *Stonehenge* (1740) and *Abury* (1743). In the intervening year came the fall of Walpole, and the last and fullest literary expression of Patriot King ideals, Gilbert West's *Institution of the Order of the Garter*, whose exuberant patriotic myth-making will be more fully explored in Chapter 7. When West wrote this masque he was thinking both of Milton's *Comus* but more specifically of Carew's royalist *Coelum Britannicum*, with its choruses of Druids and bards. In West's own masque, the bards and Druids are given a central rather than simply choric role. His account of their dress is both colourful and precise: British bards wearing 'sky-colour'd Robes spangled with Stars, with Garlands of oaken Boughs upon their Heads, and golden Harps in their Hands, made like the *Welsh* or old *British Harp*', Druids carrying oaken branches and wearing full-length 'dark-colour'd coarse stuff Gowns'.[131] West noted that he was describing the Druid as he appeared in an illustration to Henry Rowlands's *Mona Antiqua Restaurata* of 1723. Stukeley had recently adapted Rowlands's sketch of the Druid for his own *Stonehenge*, trimming short his beard and removing his oak branch.[132] The fact that West's account retains Rowlands's 'beards . . . very large and long, reaching below their Waist' and the 'Oaken Branch' suggests that Stukeley's influence on his own ideas may not have been predominant. But West's Druids bear no resemblance other than the physical to Rowlands's wily prelates; his imaginative conception of them may have been inspired as much by Patriot myth-making as by Stukeley. West's Druids are ardent patriots, sages, and '*Britain*'s old Philosophers'. Driven out but not defeated by Suetonius Paulinus's forces, their spirits still hover over their ancient haunts,

> Nor . . . wont they to forget
> Their Native Country and the Public Weal
> To which on Earth, their Labours and their Lives
> They once devoted.

They play an active role in the testing of the monarch, proving his worth to be a Patriot King. They are not contemplative mystics but public spokesmen who perform 'patriot Lays', both inspiring and recording the deeds of their

---

[131] West, *Order of the Garter*, 8. Cf. Collins, *Ode on the Popular Superstitions of the Highlands of Scotland (c.1748–9)*, ll. 41–3: 'Old Runic bards' with 'uncouth lyres, in many-coloured vest | Their matted hair with boughs fantastic crowned' (*Poems of Gray*, ed. Londsale, 505).

[132] See Stuart Piggott, *William Stukeley: An Eighteenth-Century Antiquary* (2nd edn. 1985), plates 21, 22, 23.

countrymen. But the Stukeleyite mood of romantic mysticism has infused what in the 1730s was a more stridently military context for patriotic Druidism. Sacred groves and mist-shrouded stone circles replace Thomson's 'woodland Wars'.

> they hover round
> Their ruin'd Altars, consecrated Hills,
> Once girt with spreading Oaks, mysterious Rows
> Of rude enormous Obelisks, that rise
> Orb within Orb, stupendous Monuments
> Of artless Architecture, such as now
> Oft times amaze the wandr'ing Traveller,
> By the pale Moon discern'd on Sarum's Plain.[133]

Mid-Century Assimilations

By this stage it should be apparent that I am claiming a far closer relationship than is often held to exist between the political poetry of the Walpole years and the poetry of a period variously described as 'mid-century' or 'pre-romantic'—the age of Collins, Gray, and the Warton brothers. The chronological division between 'Augustan' and 'pre-romantic' is often predicated on a series of events which signal the end of one literary era and the start of another—the fall of Walpole in 1742, the deaths of Pope in 1744 and Swift in 1745. With the fall of Walpole, suggests John Sitter, ended the 'Opposition literary contract' whereby all good poets concurred in their opposition to Walpole. Poetry would no longer be opposed to a particular politics (i.e. Walpolian Whiggery) but to all politics. The widespread refusal to engage in public affairs signalled a new 'apolitical' literary politics.[134] These are slightly misleading generalizations. Joseph Warton may have distanced himself from Pope's classicism, preferring Spenser's shadowy Una to Pope's bright Belinda, Nature and Passion to Wit and Satire. But not all political poetry in the preceding decades had been witty and satiric. Nor was all poetry after 1742 quite as devoid of an active political preoccupation as Sitter seems to suggest.

Considered purely in terms of theme, style, and subject-matter, it would be hard to deny a kinship between the Patriot poetry of the Walpole era and the literary and scholarly movements gaining sway in the 1750s and beyond. The Patriot poets' valorization of the northern and the Gothic, even if it originated in the oppositional quest to revive the native spirit of British liberty in the

---

[133] West, *Order of the Garter*, 10, 50, 11.

[134] John Sitter, *Literary Loneliness in Mid-Eighteenth Century England* (Ithaca, NY, 1982), 108. Sitter's argument is based on the theory that all opposition is typified by Pope's satiric procedures; 'Not only specific allegiance but an allegiance to the specific, i.e. an assumption of direct and usually combative referentiality' (p. 108 n. 7). As I have argued, this allegiance to the specific is not a feature of Patriot poetry.

face of Walpolian corruption, undoubtedly involved a revival and validation of British cultural as well as constitutional origins. Gerald Newman even goes so far as to see in Thomson the 'stirrings' of literary nationalism: Thomson is one of those 'restive and socially sensitive bourgeois intellectuals' engaged in recovering native cultural roots against a dominant aristocratic Gallophile neo-classicism.[135] There is something strange about Newman's account which places the Patriot Whig Thomson and the Patriot Whig Chesterfield on opposing sides in a cultural class warfare. When Thomson praised Chesterfield's 'Patriot-Virtues' he was quite sure that Chesterfield embodied British cultural strength and a healthy '*British Scorn*' in the face of 'presumptuous *France*'.[136] But Newman's observations suggest a sense of cultural continuity that makes Patriot poetry more significant than mere propaganda. A 'blind' reading of the passage cited from West's description of Stonehenge would probably inspire the guess that it was written by one of the Wartons. And in 1756 we find Joseph Warton singling out for special praise 'two or three lyric pieces superior to any he [Pope] has left us . . . I mean a Chorus of British Bards by Mr. Gilbert West, at the end of the Institution of the Order of the Garter'.

Both these [a lyric by Akenside and West's chorus] are written with the regular returns of the Strophe, Antistrophe and Epode, which gives a truly Pindaric variety to the numbers . . . In the pieces here commended, the figures are strong, and the transitions bold, and there is a just mixture of sentiment and imagery: and particularly, they are animated with a noble spirit of liberty.[137]

Joseph Warton so admired West's 1749 translation of Pindar with its important prefatory account of the freedom of the Pindaric ode that he immediately wrote an ode 'On Reading Mr. West's Translation of Pindar'. Collins's platonic Druidic Temple in the 1746 'Ode to Liberty' was clearly modelled in large part on West's own very similar account, published only four years earlier, of the hallowed fane in the celestial blessed isles housing Albion's heroes and Druidic bards.[138] When in 1753 *Alfred* was adapted for the stage it was thought appropriate to interpolate within Act II Collins's ode 'How Sleep the Brave' as 'A New Funeral Dirge in Honour of the Heroes who die in the Service of their Country'.[139] The Patriot poets overlapped with the literary generation of Collins, Gray, and the Wartons. Thomson's Druidic *Castle of Indolence* may have begun life in the 1730s, but by the time it was (finally) published in 1748 shortly before Thomson's death it came after Thomas

[135] Newman, *The Rise of English Nationalism*, 58–60, 111.

[136] For Thomson's praise of Chesterfield, see *Winter*, 656–90.

[137] Joseph Warton, *Essay on Pope*, i. 69–70.

[138] A source not noted by Lonsdale, or by Tompkins (pp. 4–5) who claims that Collins's Temple is 'an unsupported sally of his imagination, stimulated . . . by a hint in Thomson's poem'. Collins's synthesis of classical and Gothic form in his Temple can be traced to *Order of the Garter*, 63–4. For very close verbal parallels, see 'Ode to Liberty', ll. 109–12; cf. *Order of the Garter*, 50.

[139] See A. S. P. Woodhouse, 'Collins in the Eighteenth Century', *TLS* 16 Oct. 1930, 383.

Warton's dreamy *The Pleasures of Melancholy* of 1747, where a Druid nurtures the poetic babe Contemplation in his oaken bower to the sound of 'The rapid roar | Of wood-hung Meinai, stream of Druids old'.[140] The following year, Collins published his well-known elegy to Thomson, his close Richmond friend, with the enigmatic lament 'In yonder Grave a DRUID lies'.

The meaning behind Collins's descriptive epithet for Thomson continues to provoke conjecture and dispute.[141] Was Collins thinking of Thomson the poet-philosopher of *The Seasons* who had haunted the groves of meditation where 'antient Bards th'inspiring Breath, | Extatic, felt', or was Thomson's claim to the title of Druid informed in Collins's eyes by the political sense it had recently acquired? Probably both. Up to this point I have suggested that much of the original political import of the Patriots' use of Gothic forms and ideas—especially in terms of architecture and Spenserianism—was lost upon the poets and antiquarians of the subsequent decades. They either aestheticized the political dimension of Patriot Gothic or, in a post-Walpole context where it was no longer relevant, simply failed to recognize it. But this argument requires some important qualification.

The Patriot poets were deeply committed to the notion that the poet should and must play an active public role. In Thomson's case (as critics are fond of observing) this almost certainly led him into forms of writing for which his own natural genius was not best fitted. John Lucas has recently pointed out that Gray and Collins's own preoccupation with the bard figure was not unconnected with the role which Thomson and other writers of his kind had mapped out for themselves.[142] But the politicized 'bardic' role that Gray and Collins later 'discovered' for themselves was, he argues, a quite separate matter: it had nothing to do with Thomson and his peers, who represented nasty values such as capitalism and imperialism. Lucas defines political opposition only in terms of the political left, whereas of course Thomson and the Patriots had other notions of what opposition entailed. These are notions which would have been familiar to Gray and Collins who also lived through the period of fervent opposition to Walpolian Whig policies. Gray and Collins's sense of the 'Gothic, the bardic, the druidic' had never been purely 'literary-historical' or free of political implications.

---

[140] *Poetical Works of the Late Thomas Warton B.D.*, 2 vols. (Oxford, 1802), i. 95.

[141] See Tompkins, 'In Yonder Grave a Druid Lies', *passim*; Owen, *The Famous Druids*, 172–8. Owen usefully notes that Collins's original edition included a footnote mentioning *The Castle of Indolence*—the model in mind for Thomson as Druid. The Druid in the *Ode Occasion'd by the Death of Mr. Thomson* is a 'Woodland Pilgrim' but his grave is also revered by 'musing Britons' suggesting an emphatically patriotic sense of the epithet. But see John Lucas, *England and Englishness* (1990), 46–7. Lucas claims that Thomson's Scottishness may be 'the only good reason for calling Thomson a Druid'. None of these writers thought of the Druids as being Scottish. West places them in Anglesey, then in Hibernia; Thomson's Deva's Vale in *The Castle of Indolence* is on the Welsh borders (cf. *Lycidas*, l. 55); Thomas Warton locates them by the Welsh Menai; Collins in Anglesey (and possibly the Isle of Man).

[142] Lucas, *England and Englishness*, 39–48.

It is, however, indisputable that many mid-century poets were suffering the kind of identity crisis that Lucas, echoing John Sitter, explores.[143] The 'anxiety of influence' was as much political as it was literary, expressing itself most painfully in doubts about the poet's social function and the identity of his audience. When Gray and Collins tried to imagine themselves in the role of inspired bards and spokesmen for the people, they were writing in a period where 'opposition' could not be so clearly or comfortably defined as it had been for the Patriot poets of the Walpole period. Pope and Thomson may have complained about Walpole's contempt for the place of poets in society; but both of them played a far more central role in shaping public opinion than any poets in the two subsequent decades. The political context in which Gray and Collins were living and writing had changed, had become less clear-cut. 'Public service' might demand the endorsement of values over which they felt profound ambivalence. In the late 1730s Britain had been at peace for twenty years, the realities of war a long-distant memory; patriotic values could be asserted and glamorized against a context of Walpolian stagnation, corruption, and ignominy. By 1746 Collins cannot confidently proclaim the values of patriotic liberty in a Britain torn by the recent brutal retributions against the Scots after the '45 rebellion: an ambivalence which underlines even those odes ostensibly in praise of the English forces under Cumberland.[144] The Druidic Temple of British Liberty in Collins's 1746 'Ode to Liberty' remains hidden and remote, curiously absent from the heart of Britain's 'ravaged shore'; it only 'seems' to rise, no longer (as in West's 1742 poem) a sure source of inspiration.[145] The suicidal plunge taken by Gray's Bard—in a poem written on the eve of the Seven Years War and Pitt's imperial victories—suggests both the poet's frustrated inability to communicate to a wider audience (he may not even speak the same language as Edward's forces) as well as an implicit identification with the oppressed victims of English victories. By 1770, when Gray discussed with Beattie the role which his poet-bard Edwin should play in *The Minstrel*, he still believed that the poet *ought* to have a public role: Should Edwin be made to perform

some great and singular service to his country? (what service I must leave to your invention) such as no general, no statesman, no moralist could do without the aid of music, inspiration and poetry. This will not appear an improbability in those early times, and in a character then held sacred, and respected by all nations.[146]

---

[143] The view of Thomson as a representative of capitalist and imperialist tendencies rejected by the mid-century poets is advanced in Sitter, *Literary Loneliness*, 75–124.

[144] See e.g. Collins's 'Ode to Peace' (1746) where the desire for peace may be focused as much on Culloden as on the war with France. See also 'Ode on the Death of Colonel Ross' (*c.*1745) with its added patriotic praise of Cumberland's victories juxtaposed with Britain's 'bleeding' feet and 'sated sword' (ll. 47–8).

[145] See Lucas, *England and Englishness*, 43.

[146] Cited in Irvin Ehrenpreis, *Literary Meaning and Augustan Values* (Charlottesville, Va., 1974), 92.

Thomson and the Patriot poets of the 1730s were able to make that leap: but Gray's inability to name that 'service' shows, in the words of Irvin Ehrenpreis, 'just how remote Gray thought a true poet must be, in the middle of the eighteenth century, from any deep influence on his fellow countrymen'.[147]

[147] Ibid.

6

Political Elizabethanism and the Spenser Revival

PATRIOTIC GENUFLECTIONS at Elizabeth's shrine pervade the political writings of the 1730s. Thales, the disillusioned spokesman of Johnson's *London*, captures the mood of the nation in 1738.

> On *Thames*'s Banks in silent Thought we stood,
> Where GREENWICH smiles upon the silver Flood:
> Struck with the Seat that gave ELIZA birth,
> We kneel, and kiss the consecrated Earth;
> In pleasing Dreams the blissful Age renew,
> And call BRITANNIA's Glories back to view;
> Behold her Cross triumphant on the Main,
> The Guard of Commerce, and the Dread of Spain,
> Ere Masquerades debauch'd, Excise oppress'd,
> Or *English* Honour grew a standing Jest.[1]

The Elizabethan cult of the 1730s found expression in a wide variety of media, from the plethora of pamphlets generated by popular pressure for war with Spain, through to drama, painting, poetry, and statuary. Elizabeth's 'Reign and Character' inspired the 24-year-old Lyttelton's first exercise in historical essay-writing. More colourful representations appeared on the stage in plays such as *The Fall of the Earl of Essex* and *The Albion Queens*. Elizabeth's spirit dominates the historical prophecy in Thomson and Mallet's masque *Alfred*, emerging in less ethereal form as a bust in Stowe's Temple of British Worthies and (more surprisingly) as a life-sized farthingaled waxwork figure in Queen Caroline's iconographic garden building at Richmond, Merlin's Cave.[2] Elizabeth could be Court as well as opposition property. When the 'unspeakable' Curll produced a guidebook to Caroline's gardens, *The Rarities of Richmond* (1735), he filled its pages with a Hanoverian-orientated reworking of John Partridge's popular Protestant historical prophecies, *Merlinus Liberatus*. At its heart stood a vision of Elizabeth-as-Astrea:

> Her bright and glorious Sun-beams shall expell
> The vain Clouds of the Candle, Booke, and Bell,
> Domestic Plots and Stratagems Abroad
> Machines from France, th'Italianated God,

---

[1] *Poems of Samuel Johnson*, ed. D. Nichol Smith and E. L. McAdam, rev. J. D. Fleeman (3rd edn., Oxford, 1974), 68–9.

[2] Before 1732 the Stowe bust of Elizabeth had sat in the Belvedere or Gibbs's building, not far from statues of George, Caroline, and William. Caroline copied the bust for Richmond. See Katherine Eustace, *Michael Rysbrack* (Bristol, 1982), 135–7 and plate 51.

The Spanish Engine, Portuguezed Jew,
The Jesuitick Mine, and Politick Crew
Of Home-bred Vipers, let their Threat'ning come
By Private Pistoll, or by Hostile Drum,
Tho' all these Dogs chace her with open Cry
She shall live lov'd, and fear'd, then Sainted Dye.[3]

This cheerful xenophobic Protestant bigotry is as vital to an understanding of the 'cult of Elizabeth' as the more rarefied language of Bolingbroke's essays. The Elizabethan 'nostalgia' of the 1730s cannot be reduced to the longing of a dispossessed gentry for a traditional social hierarchy under assault from the innovations of the eighteenth-century financial revolution. Even the former high Tory Bolingbroke's various uses of Elizabeth, the figure who dominates much of his political writing of this period, cannot be easily accommodated within a neo-Harringtonian framework.[4] If we explain nostalgia for the Elizabethan age purely from a socio-economic perspective, we ignore what lay at its centre—the figure of the queen herself. The cult of Elizabeth was, first and foremost, a monarchical cult: one which had major implications for the way in which the Hanoverians—George, Caroline, and Frederick—both presented themselves and were perceived by their political critics and supporters.

The Elizabethan vogue of the 1730s was complex and multifaceted, rooted in a number of political and historical traditions which had remained active throughout the seventeenth and early eighteenth centuries. Elizabeth's image had never disappeared from view after Fulke Greville and (less tendentiously) William Camden had created the myth of the perfect ruler in the mood of disillusionment following the accession of James I.[5] For the next two centuries the politically disaffected belaboured royal and ministerial shortcomings by holding up the model of Elizabeth. Her virtuous 'marriage' to England and her devotion to her people were contrasted with the corruptions and debauchery of a series of courts, not least Charles II's.[6] Her admirable 'frugality' was juxtaposed with the alarming growth of the Civil List, especially under George I and George II. Above all,

---

[3] Edmund Curll, *The Rarities of Richmond: Being Exact Descriptions of the Royal Hermitage and Merlin's Cave, With his Life and Prophecies* (1736), 172–3. The first part of the work appeared in Nov. 1735, but it was published in 5 complete parts in 1736. All citations are from the 5-part complete work.

[4] *Lord Bolingbroke: Historical Writings*, ed. Isaac Kramnick (Chicago, 1972), p. xliv, notes that Bolingbroke's unqualified admiration for the perfect Elizabethan balance was not derived from Harrington. For the retention of the 'Elizabethan' world-picture, see esp. J. A. Downie, '1688: Pope and the Rhetoric of Jacobitism', in David Fairer (ed.), *Pope: New Contexts* (Hemel Hempstead, 1990), 9–24, pp. 20–1. There is little overt sense of a specifically *Elizabethan* past anywhere in the country-house visions of Pope, who tended to equate the Elizabethan age with the 'Gothic' past. One exception is the (morally) threadbare Elizabethan suit Pope added to his *Fourth Satire of Donne* (*TE* iv. 29) to show how much the present age has degenerated since then.

[5] See Christopher Haig, *Elizabeth I* (1988), 164–9. For the literary aspects, see David Norbrook, *Poetry and Politics in the English Renaissance* (1984), esp. 195–204.

[6] See esp. 'Britannia and Rawleigh' (*c.*1674), sometimes ascribed to Marvell, in *Poems and Letters of Marvell*, ed. P. Legouis and E. Duncan-Jones, 2 vols. (1971), i. 194–9.

Elizabeth was (however inaccurately) celebrated as the ardent defender of Protestant liberties and defier of European Catholic despotism. The Protestant Elizabeth was invoked whenever the security of a Protestant succession was imperilled. The Exclusion Crisis of the 1670s and the Popish plot scare unleashed a wave of Elizabethan sentiment. In 1681 the Pope's effigy was burnt in front of a laurel-decked statue of Elizabeth and celebrated with fairground plays such as *The Coronation of Queen Elizabeth, with the Restauration of the Protestant Religion.* Elizabeth's inauguration day, 17 November, was still being celebrated well into the eighteenth century in cities such as Bristol.[7]

Both William III and Queen Anne invited and cultivated comparisons with Elizabeth. Gilbert Burnet had hoped that the Revolution of 1688 would restore England to the unity it had enjoyed under the Protestant Elizabeth, 'One Church and One Body, as it has One Head'.[8] As Gerald Straka notes, 'the reference to the glories of Elizabeth's time was more than a nostalgic yearning for a past period of greatness; it was a striving for a fulfilment of the Elizabethan ideal of the Reformation'.[9] Like the Protestant Elizabeth, William had vanquished a popish prince, and, like her, had gained the nation's financial confidence. He too was an excommunicant, his lands declared forfeit to the King of France. Just as Elizabeth united the nation against a Spanish threat, William united it against a French threat. Sermons had enjoined William's subjects to remember 1588 while celebrating the '88 of this Age'.[10] Queen Anne, for obvious reasons, was even more closely identified with Elizabeth. She adopted Elizabeth's '*Semper Eadem*' motto and made her first formal parliamentary appearance in 1702 in robes modelled on a portrait of her female predecessor.[11] Blackmore's *Eliza* (1705) was not the only poem inviting the comparison. Poets celebrating the victories of Ramillies and Blenheim made much of the Britomart side of Elizabeth's personal mythology to eulogize Anne. During the last months of her life, Anne's poets, like Elizabeth's, adopted the 'mutability' images of the 1590s to express their anxieties about the security of the succession following the death of a similarly childless queen. The very Whiggish *Protestant Memorial: For the Seventeenth of November Being the Inauguration-Day of Queen Elizabeth* added to its anti-Papist observations 'we have now a *new Motive* to this Zeal; the *Preservation* of our most gracious *Queen* ANN being to be added to the *Vindication* of the most *gracious Queen Elizabeth*'.[12]

---

[7] For the survival of the 17 Nov. processions, see Tim Harris, *The London Crowd in the Reign of Charles II* (Cambridge, 1981), 120–8, and Nicholas Rogers, *Whigs and Cities: Popular Politics in the Age of Walpole and Pitt* (Oxford, 1989), 356. For the popular drama, see Michael Dobson, *The Making of the National Poet: Shakespeare, Adaptation and Authorship, 1660–1789* (Oxford, 1992), 64–72.   [8] Gilbert Burnet, *Sermon . . . 19th Day of October 1690*, 34–6.

[9] Gerald M. Straka, *Anglican Reaction to the Revolution of 1688* (Madison, Wis., 1962), 100.

[10] William Stephens, *A Thanksgiving Sermon . . . April 16 1696*, pp. i–ii.

[11] See Edward Gregg, *Queen Anne* (1970), 96, 152. The motto is recorded by Abel Boyer, *The History of the Reign of Queen Anne, Digested into Annals*, 11 vols. (1703–13), i. 162.

[12] *A Protestant Memorial: For the Seventeenth of November Being the Inauguration-Day of Queen Elizabeth* (1713), 8–9.

Elizabethan sentiment was undeniably more vigorous in the Walpole period than it had been in the reigns of either William or Anne. Much of it was generated by the opposition's demands for war. But one of the reasons for its very pervasiveness lay in the fact that the ministerial press actively responded to oppositional Elizabethanism by staking its own claims to represent Elizabethan values. Historians have sometimes assumed that the Court Whigs were emphatic modernists, repudiating and ridiculing the Patriots' resurrection of past English golden ages, that 'Walpole's regime acted on current necessity, the patriot opposition on bygone identity . . . the Court whigs' resistance to the past, and the patriots' espousal of it'.[13] This may have been true of the debate over Saxon liberty, when ministerial critics read the Gothic past as one long period of feudal tyranny compared with which post-1688 England was infinitely 'freer'. But denigration of the perennially popular Elizabeth was not a position which afforded much mileage to either ministerial apologists or Hanoverian literary propagandists. In the case of Elizabeth, the Court Whigs proved anything but 'resistant to the past'. Although they sometimes took issue with the opposition's exaltation of the rise of the Commons under Elizabeth, and occasionally argued in the face of the opposition's endless invocations of the Armada spirit that the sinking of the Spanish fleet had been simply a lucky accident, they usually took every opportunity to appropriate Elizabethan precedent to defend their own position. Walpole could be both praised as well as attacked as a latter-day William Cecil; George II could be exalted (if inappropriately) as the monarch who presided over Vernon's Porto Bello victories, 'The Master of the Main' emulating 'Eliza's Glorious reign'.[14]

In his *Patriot King* Bolingbroke invoked the unifying figure of Elizabeth as an argument for a burial of the opposition's party-differences. In a harmonious nation state 'All Factions and Parties will be sunk and forgotten; there will be no Whig nor Tory, no Jacobite, no Church-party, Court-party, nor Country-party; for the Interest of Court and Country will be one and the same, which has not been known since the Death of Queen Elizabeth'.[15] But this quotation, which comes in fact not from Bolingbroke, but from a sermon written in 1696 by one of William III's clerics, shows that images of the Elizabethan commonwealth in some respects served better to sanction a ministerial than an oppositional position. Government writers were in the habit of citing Elizabeth's firm handling of 'factious' and seditious pamphleteeers who threatened the order and stability of the body politic. 'Let the Craftsman thank God he did not live in the reign of Elizabeth, of whom he was so fond: she would have hung him as he wrote.'[16] The opposition's very obvious disarray undermined their own

[13] David Armitage, 'The Cromwellian Protectorate and the Languages of Empire', *Historical Journal*, 35 (1992), 531–55, p. 554.

[14] *London Evening Post*, 29–31 Oct. 1741.

[15] Nicholas Brady, *A Sermon Preached . . . March 1, 1696*, 24.

[16] *London Journal*, 16 Jan. 1730.

appeals to Elizabethan unity. The following pages will show just how far the rivalry over Elizabeth could be taken, extending even into the realms of her greatest poetic mythologizer, Edmund Spenser.

Elizabethanism and the War with Spain

The campaign for war with Spain generated by far the most potent forms of Elizabethan sentiment in the Walpole period. Elizabeth herself may have been a reluctant combatant, pressurized against her will into war. But critics of Walpole's ignominious peace-at-any-price policy were not, of course, interested in recovering the objective truth. Historical myths were the essence of their propaganda campaign. The myth of the Virgin Queen as the Armada heroine using English sea power to humble Catholic Spain, first created by Fulke Greville and subsequently expanded by Camden in the fourth volume of his *Annales* (1625), had long since gained unassailable popular currency. The illustrated frontispiece of that work, showing Elizabeth's naval glories—Drake's attack on Cadiz in 1587, the Armada victory of 1588, Cumberland's burning of San Juan de Puerto Rico in 1591, and the Cadiz expedition of 1596—might have served as a prototype for the engraved frontispiece to Edmund Cave's two-volume *History of the Life and Reign of Elizabeth*, a lavish reprinting of Rapin de Thoyras, published by subscription between 1738 and 1739.[17] The shrewd businessman Cave's readiness to embark on such a large speculative venture says much about the vogue for Elizabethan material at this time.

The most violent outbreaks of anti-Spanish zeal occurred with an almost fortuitous ten-year regularity: 1718–19, 1728–9, and 1738–9. In 1718 Britain had entered the Quadruple Alliance to put a stop to Philip V of Spain's imperial ambitions. Admiral Byng's famous victory at Cape Passaro on 11 August, sinking most of the Spanish fleet, increased British confidence in her naval capacities. The following March a Spanish-backed invasion fleet organized by James III and the Duke of Ormonde, loaded with supplies for Scottish Jacobites, was scattered off the Scottish coast by huge storms which recalled the shattering of the Armada. In August British amphibious forces led successful surprise assaults on the Gallician coastal ports of Pontevedra and Vigo. In 1719 Lewis Theobald produced a timely *Memoir of Sir Walter Raleigh*. George Sewell's *The Tragedy of Sir Walter Raleigh*, a hit on the London stage when it first appeared in January 1719, contained a thinly-veiled portrait of Philip of Spain's machinating minister Alberoni in the figure of Gundamar, the Spanish ambassador at King James's court.

The Tragedy of Sir Walter Raleigh was revived for two later winter seasons— 1729 and 1739. James Quin, who originally played the part of Sir Walter, grew

---

[17] See A. D. Barker, 'Edmund Cave, Samuel Johnson and the *Gentleman's Magazine*' (Oxford D.Phil. thesis, 1982), 329.

into the role over a twenty-year period—he starred in the play on all three occasions.[18] Each turn of the decade witnessed a new outburst of Elizabethan sentiment and a revival of previous Elizabethan works, not only from the eighteenth century but from previous periods which had also used Elizabethan precedent to support a more assertively Protestant foreign policy.[19] Opposition discontent with Walpole's conciliatory policy towards Spanish depredations had been rising since 1726 and the fate of Admiral Hosier and his gallant crew. In 1727 Spain declared war on England and threatened Gibraltar. Popular feeling exploded in the first parliamentary session of 1729. Pulteney moved an opposition motion invoking Hosier's ghost; the government won, but with a majority which dropped from over 200 to only 35. In November 1729 Walpole signed the unpopular Peace Treaty of Seville, but the war fever and its accompanying Elizabethanism only temporarily abated. 1729 was the year of pamphlets such as *The Conduct of Queen Elizabeth, Towards the Neighbouring Nations*. 'Paleophilus Anglicanus', the disinterested lover of his country, raises a monument to her naval heroes and a paean to Elizabeth, 'ever Victorious, the *Scourge* of *Tyrants*, the *Patroness* of *Liberty*, the *Sanctuary of the Oppressed*, and the *Deliverer of Nations*'.[20] James Thomson's first opposition sally, *Britannia*, printed on 21 January 1729, was similarly timed to coincide with the opening of the new parliamentary session. The government tried to appropriate for pro-Walpole purposes its qualified lines in praise of peace, 'What would not, *Peace*, the Patriot bear for thee?', but subsequently attacked Thomson for his disloyalty to a minister whom he had panegyrized only two years earlier.[21] Thomson's Spanish Armada, 'Tall, gorgeous and elate; drunk with the dream | Of easy conquest', is shattered by Britannia's winds,

> snatch'd by the vengeful blast
> The scatter'd remnants drove: on the blind shelve,
> And pointed rock, that marks the indented shore,
> Relentless dash'd, where loud the Northern main
> Howls thro' the fractur'd *Caledonian* isles.[22]

Thomson's heroic seascapes may have been inspired by the tapestries in the House of Lords depicting the defeat of the Spanish Armada. These had already appeared in the Court Whig Edward Young's *Imperium Pelagi* of 1730, used to defend the peaceful imperialism heralded by the Treaty of Seville. But the tapestries themselves were scarcely irenic. In 1739 John Pine produced a

---

[18] The play was originally dedicated to James Craggs, Secretary of State for War, and was a pro-ministerial piece of anti-Spanish triumphalism. It also had an anti-Jacobite edge. See John Loftis, *The Politics of Drama in Augustan England* (Oxford, 1963), 81.

[19] e.g. *The Merchant's Complaint Against Spain* (1738) reprinted passages from *Vox Coeli* (1623).

[20] *The Conduct of Queen Elizabeth, Towards the Neighbouring Nations; And particularly Spain; Compar'd with that of James I* (1729), 39.

[21] See Bertrand A. Goldgar, *Walpole and the Wits: The Relation of Politics to Literature, 1722–1742* (Lincoln, Nebr., 1976), 85–6.

[22] OET *Liberty*, 23.

timely series of engravings of the Armada tapestries to rouse anti-Spanish zeal. In 1742 William King used them to furnish the imaginary walls of his *Templum Libertatis*.[23]

The 'pathetic, moving Strains' of *Britannia*'s account of Hosier's death were revived after a decade as the opposition stepped up its propaganda campaign.[24] These two years, 1738 and 1739, leading up to the declaration of war in October, witnessed a flood of pamphlets, poems, prints, and plays drawing on the Elizabethan example, citing the Tilbury speech and Armada victories.[25] Johnson's *London* is firmly a product of its year of publication, as is Glover's *London; or The Progress of Commerce* (also 1738), with its far more optimistic evocation of the spirit of Elizabeth, who actively promoted English trade. In the background of the famous 1739 print, *The Stature of a Great Man or the English Colossus*—depicting a giant Walpole, legs bestriding the ocean—stood an old English castle decorated with an outsize medallion of Elizabeth and a flag inscribed 'In hoc signo Vincet'.[26] At Frederick and Augusta's command performance of Sewell's *Sir Walter Raleigh* on 29 September 1739, Egmont recorded the tense and excited mood of the house. 'When any severe things were said which bore a resemblance to our ministry's transactions, or our backwardness to resent the insults of Spain, the audience clapp'd all over the house.'[27] In the parish of St Martin's, the Reverend Joseph Trapp delivered a controversial sermon, *The Ministerial Virtue: Or, Long-Suffering Extolled in a Great Man*. Trapp, deploying similar stratagems to Pope's ironic praise of the 'peaceful' George II in the *Epistle to Augustus*, praised Walpole's 'forbearance'—'Was ever *Patience* like to this *Patience*?' He shed crocodile tears for 'Poor *Spain*'. 'How I bewail thy Past Sufferings!' Elizabeth, compared with the peace-loving James I, was (by a neat inversion) a deeply flawed monarch: 'she still retained those *carnal* Notions of *Honour* and *Resentment*, and was the Cause of the effusion of so much *Christian Spanish Blood*; which she might have avoided, could she have but sat quietly and peaceably down, and suffered their *Armada* to have shelterd in *her Harbours*.'[28]

---

[23] John Pine, *The Tapestry Hangings* (1739). For an account of their poetic representation, see Jean Hagstrum, *The Sister Arts* (Chicago, 1958), 258.

[24] See *Common Sense*, 9 Sept. 1738.

[25] See e.g. Lyttelton's *Considerations upon the Present State of our Affairs* (1739); *Reasons for a War Against Spain* (1737, repr. 1738); *The British Sailor's Discovery* (1739); *Reasons for Giving Encouragement to the Sea-Faring People of Great Britain in Times of Peace or War* (1739).

[26] Herbert Atherton, *Political Prints in the Age of Hogarth: A Study of the Ideographic Representation of Politics* (Oxford, 1974), plate 32. The tower and medal of Elizabeth feature in other opposition prints of the late 1730s. See *The Europe Race* Heat IId, *BMC* no. 2415. The medallion is inscribed 'ELIZABETH REG. 1588' and looks down over the English Fleet lying inactive.

[27] *Egmont Diary*, iii. 83.

[28] [Joseph Trapp], *The Ministerial Virtue: Or, Long-Suffering Extolled in a Great Man* (1738), dedicated to John Barnard. Sometimes ascribed to Samuel Croxall.

Imperial Expansion and the Ralegh Cult

The oppositional invocation of Elizabethan naval victories was not mere anti-Spanish warmongering. As we have seen in Chapter 1, those pressing for war with Spain viewed it not as a limited trade war but as an opportunity for Britain's greater imperial expansion. David Armitage has shown how Cromwell's Western Design was invoked in this period to support the pressure for war.[29] But Cromwell could, as we have seen, prove a double-edged tool, playing into the hands of ministerial critics all too ready to identify Patriot Whigs as factious radicals. One opposition pamphleteer turned to the reign of Elizabeth instead to find the origins of Britain's imperial greatness, claiming that 'it was owing, in a great Measure, to that Great and Glorious Princess Queen *Elizabeth* . . . that *Great-Britain*, at present, is not only so Rich a Kingdom, but so powerful at Sea, and Master of so considerable a Number of Islands and such vast Tracts of Land in *America*'.[30] This claim was not easy to support in the face of Elizabeth's personal reluctance to initiate colonial expansion. Far more often those oppositional writers who invoked images of Elizabethan empire did so through the figure of Ralegh, even suggesting that his enterprising spirit had been fettered not only by James but by Elizabeth, who listened too much to the prudential policies of the Cecils.

The Elizabethan naval cult might in one sense more properly be called a Ralegh cult. Bolingbroke adopted the pseudonym 'Raleigh' as early as November 1728 for a series of essays in the *Craftsman* attacking Walpole's foreign policy and predicting his fall within a year.[31] Ralegh's uneven relationship with Elizabeth and his martyrdom at the hands of James made him a perfect vehicle for opposition sentiment. As a naval hero, poet, historian, and Renaissance man of letters who incurred the disfavour of the monarchy, he became a potent symbol for patriotic values held in contempt by the administration. Ralegh's close friendship with Prince Henry in his final years in the Tower enabled the Patriots, capitalizing on the identification between the two princes of Wales, to associate Frederick with Ralegh's dreams of imperial expansion. In 1738 Joseph Morgan reprinted Sir Charles Cornwallis's *Life of Prince Henry* with a fulsome dedication to Prince Frederick. Much is made of Ralegh's friendship with Henry, for whom he wrote Part I of *The History of the World* and to whom he sent his *Of the Invention of Ships*, 'proving that no War could be so necessary, or advantageous for England as one with Spain'.[32]

[29] Armitage, 'The Cromwellian Protectorate', 553–4.
[30] *Reasons for Giving Encouragement to the Sea-Faring People of Great Britain*, 14.
[31] See esp. *Craftsman*, 23 Nov. 1728, 8 Feb. 1729.
[32] Sir Charles Cornwallis, *The Life and Character of Henry-Frederic, Prince of Wales*, ed. J. M. [Joseph Morgan] (1738).

In the beautifully engraved frontispiece to John Oldys's 1736 edition of
Ralegh's *History of the World*—a far more lavish affair than Lewis Theobald's
1719 *Memoir of Sir Walter Raleigh*—Ralegh is standing lost in thought over
maps of the world spread out before him—a reminder of Britain's imperial
destiny. Oldys prefaced his edition—the first since 1687—with a scholarly
'Life of Sir Walter Raleigh', followed by an account of his execution. For all
its 'classic' appearance, even this work supplied a covert contribution to opposition polemic. Oldys concludes his 'Life' with a citation of Major Richardson
Pack's Prologue to Sewell's *Tragedy of Sir Walter Raleigh* 'containing a most
notable admonition to succeeding times'.

> Jealous of *Virtue* that was so *sublime*
> His *country* damned his *merit* as a crime.
> The *traytor*'s doom did on the *patriot* wait:
> He sav'd—and then he *perish'd* by the state.

The conclusion asserts 'BRITONS, by His EXAMPLE taught, *unite*.' 'Safely WE
may defy MADRID or ROME | If no sly GONDOMAR prevails at HOME'.[33]

Sewell's famous tragedy played a major role in promoting Ralegh's image.
Ralegh's 'Spirit quicken'd o'er our adventurous Youth | To chace ambition to
her last-flown Length | And hunt her in a new untravell'd World'—a spirit of
youthful enterprise hampered by Elizabeth's caution. The Earl of Howard's
criticisms suggest that Elizabeth was blinded to the possibility of greater glories by a 'home-bred Faction' in court:

> Else, great *Eliza*! strange remoter Lands,
> Than that distinguish'd by thy Virgin Name,
> Had wore the Title of the Maiden Queen.[34]

The play's setting in the reign of James I proved influential. Sewell's
tragedy unfolds in deepening shadows; most of Act II takes place inside the
Tower. The opening of Act V, scene ii, shortly before Ralegh's execution,
shows 'Sir Walter discover'd, with the HISTORY of the WORLD before him'.
The poignant image of lost potential and geographical expansiveness trapped
in a tiny room may have inspired Oldys's choice of engraving in 1736. Many
of the Elizabethan works of the 1730s follow Sewell's model by being set not
in Elizabeth's reign but in its immediate aftermath. This is hall-of-mirrors
nostalgia—the Elizabethan golden age seen through the corruptions of James
I's reign, a reign which was by the mid-1730s commonly identified in opposition polemic with the reign of George II. Ralegh in Stowe's Temple of British
Worthies was 'a valiant soldier and an able statesman, who, endeavouring to

---

[33] Sir Walter Ralegh, *A History of the World in Five Books*, ed. John Oldys, 2 vols. (1736), 'The
Life of the Author', i, p. ccxxxi. The 'Life' was reprinted separately in 1740.
[34] George Sewell, *The Tragedy of Sir Walter Raleigh* (1719), 27. For other timely pieces of
Ralegh propaganda exploiting a similar theme, see *The Tryal of Sir Walter Raleigh Kt. With his
Speech on the Scaffold* (1719); *The Life of Sir Walter Raleigh* (1740).

rouse the spirit of his Master for the Honour of his Country against the ambition of *Spain*, fell a sacrifice to that Court, whose arms he had vanquished, and whose Designs he had opposed'.[35] Thomson's account of Ralegh in the 'Worthies of the MAIDEN REIGN' passage added to *The Seasons* in 1730 is more poignant reflection than aggressive jingoism.

> Nor sunk his Vigour, when a Coward-Reign
> The Warrior fetter'd, and at last resign'd,
> To glut the Vengeance of a vanquish'd Foe.
> Then, active still and unrestrain'd, his Mind
> Explor'd the vast Extent of Ages past,
> And with his Prison-Hours enrich'd the World;
> Yet found no Times, in all the long Research,
> So glorious, or so base, as Those he prov'd,
> In which he conquer'd, and in which he bled.[36]

George Lyttelton's 'Observations on the Reign and Character of Queen Elizabeth' of 1733, like Sewell's play, is set not in Elizabeth's but in James's reign. It takes the form of a private conversation between Ralegh, Sir Henry Wootton, and Sir Francis Bacon in a house where Ralegh has found refuge after being temporarily released from imprisonment. Even before we reach the discussion of Elizabeth, a tone of cynicism and disillusionment with the ministerial cabals and 'servile flatteries' which these men are forced into hangs over the work.[37] They meet on a secret visit, and the mere fact of their praising Elizabeth in the reign of James I courts charges of sedition.

The same mood is evoked by George Lillo's *The Fatal Curiosity* of 1736, a play which bears some examination. Lillo, as we have seen, was one of Prince Frederick's supporters. Thomas Davies records the 'great veneration' in which Lillo held the Prince, even leaving his last tragedy *Elmerick* to be dedicated to Frederick, who, after Lillo's death in 1739, attended a performance in his honour in 1740.[38] Lillo is more famous for his pioneering middle-class tragedy, the popular *The London Merchant: or, The History of George Barnwell* of 1731. *Marina*, his 1738 adaptation of Shakespeare's *Pericles*, contributed to a Shakespeare revival, especially among the middle classes, which thrived on anti-Spanish sentiment.[39] A strong strain of Elizabethanism runs through Lillo's work. *The London Merchant* is set in 1588, just before the attempted

---

[35] G. B. Clarke (ed.), *Descriptions of Lord Cobham's Gardens at Stowe, 1700–1750* (Buckingham, 1990), 139.

[36] *Summer*, ll. 1502–10 (OET *Seasons*, 128).

[37] George Lyttelton, 'Observations on the Reign and Character of Queen Elizabeth. Written in the Year 1733', Hagley MSS, Hagley Hall, Stourbridge, 1. This is a 60-folio MS, carefully copied and corrected in Lyttelton's handwriting, foliated and bound in hard covers. The text is on the rectos, but with corrections and additions on the versos. It carries the inscription 'Not to be published unless any false copy of it should be printed'. All subsequent citations incorporated in the text.

[38] *The Works of Mr. George Lillo*, ed. Thomas Davies, 2 vols. (1775), i, p. xxxix.

[39] See Dobson, *The Making of the National Poet*, 154–6.

Spanish invasion of England. Here the anti-Spanish sentiment in Trueman and Thorowgood's opening discussion of Elizabeth's manœuvres to prevent the funding of the Spanish Armada (a palpable hit at Walpole) sounds like obligatory opposition sentiment: 'Excellent queen! Oh, how unlike to former princes who made the danger of foreign enemies a pretence to oppress their subjects by taxes great and grievous to be born.'[40] But *The Fatal Curiosity* adopts a post-Elizabethan framework to make some rather more interesting political statements. Set in 1618, shortly after Ralegh's return from his unsuccessful voyage for gold in Guiana, it concerns the return home to Cornwall of Young Wilmot, who accompanied Sir Walter on his last fatal mission. Ralegh has been arrested and awaits imminent execution.

> His martial genius does not suit the times.
> There's now no insolence that Spain can offer
> But, to the shame of this pacific reign,
> Poor England must submit to. Gallant man!
> Posterity perhaps may do thee justice
> And praise thy courage, learning and integrity,
> When thou'rt past hearing.[41]

The Raleghan sentiment and historical setting are closely bound up with the domestic tragedy at the heart of the play. The fate of Ralegh, sacrificed in his quest for gold and betrayed on his return by his near-kinsman Sir Lewis 'Judas' Stukeley, vice-admiral of Devonshire, is mirrored in Young Wilmot's similar 'betrayal' and death at a kinsman's hands. Shipwrecked off the Cornish coast, Wilmot returns to the family home disguised in Indian clothes. His sunburnt hue makes him unrecognizable to his ageing parents, the impoverished Old Wilmot and his wife Agnes. Prompted by a perverse desire to witness how his parents might react to his death, he poses as his own friend come to report the tragic news. This is Young Wilmot's 'fatal curiosity': that of his parents, their irresistible urge to peek inside the sleeping stranger's trunk. Old Wilmot is tempted beyond endurance to murder the boy and appropriate the gold which he finds inside. This play says some powerful things about the decayed gentry class of which Old Wilmot and Agnes are so clearly the representatives. The declining relics of their fortune painfully eked out in the play's opening scenes symbolize (so it seems) an impoverished gentry reduced to penury with the rise of the 'money men' under James I. Old Wilmot, lamenting the times, exclaims, 'How men of fortune fall, and beggars rise' (I. i. 49). Lillo invokes audience sympathy for their reduced estate only to undercut it as the play proceeds. Old Wilmot turns out to be a hypocritical old reprobate. He pontificates high-mindedly on Seneca and Stoic fortitude but his adversity turns out to be the consequence not of some inexorable economic change but

---

[40] Lillo, *The London Merchant*, ed. W. M. McBurney (1965), I. ii. 44–8.
[41] Lillo, *The Fatal Curiosity*, ed. W. M. McBurney (1967), I. i. 38–44. All citations incorporated in text.

of his own 'wasteful riots'—a life spent gambling and drinking. His wife maintains a social hauteur quite inappropriate to her circumstances: 'her faded dress, unfashionably fine', her 'haughty swelling heart'. The son, cast out of the family nest to repair their fortunes by his youthful exploits, serves to symbolize the free-wheeling expansionist spirit which accompanied Ralegh's voyages. Here the merchant class is identified with the younger generation, unfettered by the older generation's obsession with social rituals and class hierarchies. Young Wilmot speaks directly to his audience.

> Turn thy eyes then to the prolific ocean
> Whose spacious bosom opens to thy view.
> There deathless honour and unenvied wealth
> Have often crowned the brave adventurer's toils.
> This is the native uncontested right,
> The fair inheritance of ev'ry Briton
> That dares put in his claim.

(II. ii. 8–14)

The Fatal Curiosity was never as popular as *The London Merchant*—the shocking scene in which Old Wilmot stabs his only son for a trunk of gold makes Lillo's domestic context painfully real. Henry Fielding's own championship of the play in 1736 may have been inspired by its political message. Fielding took over its production at the Haymarket after a poorly attended run of seven nights in the spring of 1736. Refurbished with a new preface and some new actors, it returned to the stage in March 1737. The play was performed with his own 'afterpiece', the highly provocative *Historical Register for the Year 1736*. Both plays ran together for eleven nights—the last performed in the season before the passage of the Stage Licensing Act which effectively ended Fielding's theatrical career. Fielding was a great admirer of Lillo and had puffed *The Fatal Curiosity* shortly before it was first staged.[42] But his choice of this play as a preface to his own witty *Historical Register*, with its satire on ministerial corruption and election bribery, seems significant. The minister's foreign policy was not one of that play's targets; Lillo's melodrama supplied a stylistically different but thematically appropriate adjunct to the political thrust of the *Historical Register*.

Queen and Commons

If Elizabeth's foreign policy dominated the political uses of the past in the 1730s, the debate over the Elizabethan constitution did not lag far behind. Opposition writers asserted that Elizabeth's reign had witnessed an ideal balance

---

[42] For the relations between Lillo and Fielding, see Robert D. Hume, *Henry Fielding and the London Theatre 1728–1737* (Oxford, 1988), 208, 267–8.

between Crown, Lords, and Commons, a balance now threatened by Crown power improperly influencing the election of the Commons. In his *Persian Letters* of 1735, Selim the Persian tells his friend Mirzah that 'Thou wilt be surpriz'd to hear that the Period when the *English* Nation enjoy'd the greatest Happiness was under the influence of a *Woman* . . . it was not till the Reign of Queen *Elizabeth* that this Government came to an equall Ballance, which is the true perfection of it'.[43] It was this, and perhaps only this, form of Elizabethan 'nostalgia' which led Court Whigs to repudiate the idealizations of the past, asserting that under the modern Hanoverian regime British subjects enjoyed a far greater degree of liberty than in any period prior to 1688. Lord Hervey asserted that before the Revolution all monarchs, not least Elizabeth, had been tyrants to some degree: 'Never were the reins of prerogative held with a stricter hand or the yoke of slavery faster bound upon the people's neck than at this period of time.'[44] In 1731 the ministerial *London Journal* had claimed that 'The Government of this Kingdom, since the Revolution, and under the present royal family, excels hers [Elizabeth's], almost as much as a government by laws does a government by arbitrary power'.[45] But this was not so much a repudiation of Elizabeth as an endorsement of modern constitutional principles which had enabled 'lawful' government to replace 'arbitrary' government. What Kramnick defines as the government's 'simple device of brightening the present by dimming the past' was not so simple in the case of Elizabeth.[46] Court Whig defences rested on the concept of sovereignty and hereditary right—and the Hanoverians' propagandists, as we shall see, drew heavily on Elizabethan precedent for their own myths of monarchy.

I have argued at the start of this chapter that the Elizabeth cult was above all a monarchical cult. This is true even in oppositional invocations of the 'ideal' Elizabethan polity. Opposition writers were less obsessed with the 'gentry utopia', the 'perfect Elizabethan balance of property and power', than they were with the image of a strong and charismatic monarch uniting the nation under his or her leadership. When he wrote the *Patriot King* in 1738 Bolingbroke had not, as Kramnick suggests, suddenly 'befuddled his institutional insights' with a 'humanist obsession with morality, example and the just ruler'.[47] Bolingbroke may previously have traced the shift in power and its consequent corruption to the unforeseen changes which followed the Revolution of 1688, yet the Machiavellian strain which pervades nearly all his political writing located the source of Britain's decline in the loss of her virtue. Even as early as the *Remarks* of 1730–1, Bolingbroke had invoked the image of the just and, above all, popular ruler infusing a spirit of moral regeneration

---

[43] Lyttelton, *Persian Letters*, 188.
[44] Hervey, *Ancient and Modern Liberty Stated and Compared* (1734), 23–4.
[45] *London Journal*, 30 Jan. 1731.
[46] Isaac Kramnick, *Bolingbroke and His Circle: The Politics of Nostalgia in the Age of Walpole* (Cambridge, Mass., 1968), 136.   [47] Ibid. 168.

into a fallen nation. Elizabeth 'made herself very soon the most popular person in the kingdom. In her reign, the sense of the court, the sense of the parliament and the sense of the people were the same. . . . She threw herself entirely on the affections of her subjects . . . This heroical princess . . . knew that . . . nothing but her own conduct could give her the hearts of her people.'[48]

Even Lyttelton's *Persian Letters* contain more than a hint of regret that the Revolution Settlement necessitated a separation of legislative and executive, of king and state, not evident in the more paternalistic model of Elizabethan government when '*Elizabeth* chose to rule by Parliaments from the Goodness of her Understanding: but Princes are now forc'd to do so *from Necessity*'.[49] The Elizabeth of his earlier 'Observations on the Reign and Character of Elizabeth' functions in far more mystical ways. Prior to her accession

The very last spark of English Virtue seemed to go out. Yet into this People thus sunk and depraved Elizabeth did infuse . . . A National Spirit as high, and a love of the Publick as strong and Heroical as that which animated the people of ancient Rome. To have accomplished this, after such long and inveterate habits of Vice and Corruption is perhaps one of the greatest and hardest efforts of human wisdom. (pp. 17–19^v)

When Aaron Hill took Walpole to task in 1740 he lamented George II's inability to act as a source of royal inspiration.

What would I not give, for that reason, to see, in the *King's speeches* at the opening of a *session*, some of those *spirited* short *flashes* of *majesty* whereby QUEEN ELIZABETH inflamed *parliament* and *people*! Something, properly and peculiarly, *English*! An *open warmth* of attested *affection* for the *subject* that *attracts* the respect it *professes*, and something too, that, asserting a *consciousness* of the *courage*, *fame* and *power* of the *nation*, might imply a *delight*, in its *glory*. Would to God, the *fatigues* you are engrossed by, left room in your *memory* at leisure to *reflect* on the *force* of those *little arts* of condescention, in princes! how they have *dwelt* upon men's *tongues* and *affections*, and, by tempering ideas of *awe*, with a mixture of the more *kind* and *endearing*, shewn a KING, in the mild light of a father, at once the *guide* and the *friend* of his people.[50]

The next chapter will show that this was a model Prince Frederick rather than his father took to heart. Some of the most enthusiastic displays of Elizabethan panegyric focused on Frederick-as-Elizabeth, 'the guide and the friend of his people'.

Royal Favourites

The reign of Elizabeth and her successor James supplied opposition critics with a rich source of precedents for their assaults on Walpole as overweening

---

[48] Bolingbroke, *Works*, i. 368.   [49] Lyttelton, *Persian Letters*, 200.
[50] Aaron Hill, *Works*, 4 vols. (1753), ii. 41.

'royal favourite'. The Elizabethan plays which flourished on the London stage in the 1730s often focused on the personal dramas of Elizabeth's court. Some, like the Exclusion Crisis dramatist John Banks's *The Albion Queens*, had little to do with politics, catering for the sentimental tastes of a predominantly female audience.[51] But when James Ralph adapted Banks's *The Unhappy Favourite* in 1731 under the new title *The Fall of the Earl of Essex*, more salient political points were being made. This is not a 'Fall of a Great Man' play on a par with the opposition's revival of Mountfort's *The Fall of Mortimer*. Essex, 'The darling Hero of the British Stage | Still let his Virtue merit your applause, | Still let your Sorrows flow in Virtue's cause', is not to be identified with Walpole, as some critics have averred.[52] The impetuous Essex is, like Ralegh, a symbol of the brave spirit of enterprise betrayed by Burghleian conspiracy.

> His Fault is to discern a Statesman's Guile,
> And scorn the Arts his Soul could never practise.
> His utmost Pride to serve his native Land,
> And plume eternal Conquest on her Arms.
> Already he has humbled in the Dust
> The Pride of *Spain*, and seiz'd upon their Fleets
> When fraught with half the Riches of its Mines.
> —But all this is forgot.[53]

Burghley, 'who builds his Rule | Upon the Vices of a venal World', is, of course, Walpole. Walpole's critics found other sources for 'royal favourite' parallels—especially Cecil's son Robert, and another 'Robin', Robert Dudley, Earl of Leicester, who was the source of a pseudo-historical prophecy, proffered by *Common Sense* in 1738, predicting the downfall of 'Great ROBIN', since 'all do fall who do aspire'.[54] But the most sustained parallels were drawn between William Cecil, Lord Burghley, and his similarly low-born and long-serving counterpart Robert Walpole. Here ministerial apologists made sustained use of the parallel to defend Walpole. What was wrong with being a second Burghley, they asked? Both ministers were praised as 'a faithful servant of his gracious majesty', 'the chief who is his country's friend'.[55] In 1731 the pro-Walpole *An Appeal to the Nation; Or, the Case of the Present Prime Minister of Great Britain truly stated* cited a eulogy to Burghley taken from Francis

[51] See John, Lord Hervey, *Lord Hervey and his Friends 1726–38*, ed. Lord Ilchester (1950), 61. The play was often staged 'At the particular Desire of several Ladies of Quality'. See Arthur H. Scouten (ed.), *The London Stage, 1660–1800. Part 3, 1729–1747*, 2 vols. (Carbondale, Ill., 1961), i, p. clxxii.

[52] James Ralph, *The Fall of the Earl of Essex, Alter'd from the Unhappy Favourite of Mr. Banks* (1731), Prologue. The play continued to be staged in its original as well as in its revived form throughout the 1730s. Loftis, *Politics of Drama*, 107, reads Essex as Walpole.

[53] *Fall of the Earl of Essex*, 10.

[54] *Common Sense*, 16 Sept. 1738.

[55] Discussed in Reed Browning, *The Political and Constitutional Ideas of the Court Whigs* (Baton Rouge, La., 1982), 191–2.

Bacon's posthumous *Resuscitatio* (1657) which had defended Burghley as '*Pater Patriae*' against the charges of a seditious libeller. It concluded: 'Such, the just *Parallel*, we here Behold; | *Walpole* is now, what *Burleigh* was of old.'[56] The debate over Walpole-as-Burghley, played out in the *Daily Gazetteer* and the *Craftsman*, provoked the opposition satirist Paul Whitehead to include the typology in his 1739 *Manners*—'Down, down, ye hungry Garretteers, descend, | Call W — *Burleigh*, call him *Britain*'s Friend'—and to add a note referring us to the 'correct' reading, 'the two Characters distinguish'd in the *Craftsman*'.[57] The seriousness of the government's defence of Walpole as Burghley clearly centred on the need to assert an honourable predecessor for Walpole's prime ministerial role, which the opposition continually attacked as unconstitutional. The *Appeal to the Nation* invokes a long list of suitable models culminating in Burghley. The most interesting case is a popular print of 1740, *The Patriot-Statesman*, whose blurred edges suggest a much-used letter press. Burghley is depicted conducting Walpole to the Temple of Fame: Minerva hovers above, brandishing her spear and directing the rays from her aegis against personifications of Envy, War, Anarchy, and the Vices. Age and Youth look on in admiration and awe. The accompanying verse, 'See virtuous WALPOLE to FAME's *Temple* goes, | Where the known Entrance mighty BURLEIGH shows', clearly enshrines Walpole among the great and loyal servants of the nation. The engraver even tucked in a reference to the 'establishment' Elizabeth by including Elizabeth's stern speech 'to a Nobleman at the Head of a Faction which opposed her Ministry'.[58]

Lyttelton's 'Observations on Elizabeth' argues the Burghley case from both sides. Ralegh indicts the minister for lining his pockets at the nation's expense. Bacon asserts that Burghley's loyal service over long years merited public rewards. But there is a satirical implication to Lyttelton's diplomatic, Camden-like conclusion that Elizabeth had no favourites: how unlike the present age! Lyttelton warns of the dangers which ensue when one 'imperious Favourite' (i.e. Walpole) takes charge of a nation's affairs, leading to 'an infinity of Frauds, corruptions and abuses' (fo. 33). For 'an absolute King may have many Wise and able Counsellors, but an absolute Minister will have none. He communicates nothing; He hears nothing . . . His infallible judgment must determine; His omnipotent hands must Execute' (fo. 34).

But for Lyttelton the focal point of concern in the Walpole–Burghley comparison is the patronage of the arts. Here Lyttelton, although young, was displaying areas of interest in the Elizabethan age not investigated by the Bolingbroke of whom he is sometimes depicted as a mere slavish imitator. The parallel between the 'dry solidity' and supposed philistinism of Walpole and Burghley was later the subject of an essay in *The Prompter* of 1735; it also

---

[56] *An Appeal to the Nation* (1731), 50.
[57] Paul Whitehead, *Manners: A Satire* (1739), 14.
[58] *BMC* no. 2459. See Atherton, *Political Prints*, plate 33 (without written material).

underscored Hill's refashioning of Spenser's *Tears of the Muses* as an attack on the decline of the arts under Walpole.[59] Spenser's own poem of that title had also pointed to the decline of the arts under Burghley. Lyttelton's Ralegh and Bacon engage in a spirited debate on the role of poets in the state. Shakespeare does not come under review, but Sidney and Spenser do. Only eight years earlier Mrs Stanley had 'modernized' Sidney's *Arcadia*, catering to a taste for sentimental romance. Lyttelton is far more interested in Sidney as a Renaissance statesman and in the *Arcadia* as a political work, a 'feign'd Commonwealth', mentioned in the same category as Plato's *Republic* and Bacon's *New Atlantis*. Here the *Arcadia* is clearly recognized as a vehicle for proffering lessons about good kingship. It is for the *Arcadia* alone that Sidney deserves the title of '*One of the Ripest, and Greatest Counsellors of State in Europe*' (fo. 39ᵛ) Ralegh and Bacon concede that Sidney might have earned a higher office under Elizabeth, but that his advancement was barred by youth, not by his potential as a political threat. But Burghley's treatment of Spenser provokes a far more heated discussion. Ralegh wished that 'his Bounties to men of Wit and Learning had been proportionably Great, or at least that his frugality had not been carry'd so far as to Deprive poor Spenser of the just, and moderate Bounties of the Queen'.

Such Men are entitled to the protection of a Minister: He shou'd make it his pleasure to draw them out of Obscurity, and place them under the warm beams of Royal Favour, but to stand between modest merit, and that sunshine, to intercept the Grace design'd them by their prince, is not only an injury to them, but to the publick. (fo. 28)

This has a familiar ring to it—the very argument currently being deployed by poets pressing their right to patronage from George and Walpole. But (more surprisingly) at this early stage Lyttelton permits Bacon to articulate Walpole's own position concerning 'men of wit'. A minister has no obligation to poets, and poets have no place in politics. Burghley's maltreatment of Spenser was a negligible fault.

The World is sometimes the Dupe of the protection given by a Minister to Men of Wit and Genius: the Returns of Flattery are so Great and Imposing . . . All I have said of his Lordship as a judge, a Counsellor, a Minister of State, is not affected by his having a good, or bad taste in poetry. (fos. 28–9)

Political Spenserianism

Lyttelton's careful reconstruction of the Burghley–Spenser antagonism shows that Spenser's 'martyrdom' at ministerial hands could be as relevant to the discontented writers of the Walpole period as it was to those of the early 1600s, when Phineas Fletcher had first turned Spenser 'into a proud symbol of poetic

[59] For the Burghley–Walpole comparison, see *Prompter*, 21 Feb. and 26 Aug. 1735.

and political independence'.[60] Spenser's double-sided political profile—both Elizabeth's royal panegyrist and yet a critic of court corruption and advocate of a more extreme form of Protestant mission than Elizabeth herself—made him infinitely malleable to political manipulation in the century to follow. While the Spenserian poets under James kept alive the Spenserian spirit of Protestantism as an oppositional tool with which to wage war on James's European Catholic interests, those poets who subsequently imitated Spenser in the conflicts leading to the civil wars looked back nostalgically to a lost Spenserian world where a wise monarch presided over social stability, order, and degree. Both Ralph Knevet in his 1633 *Supplement to the Faery Queene* and the anonymous author of the 1648 *Faerie Leveller* identified Spenser's allegorical knights with the Stuart monarchs; the latter work, a key to Book V, identified Cromwell with Spenser's vanquished social egalitarian Gyant Leveller.[61]

Spenserianism enjoyed a powerful political revival in the early years of the eighteenth century, quickened into life by the intense Whig–Tory conflicts of Anne's reign. Both Whigs and Tories appropriated Spenser for their own political agendas in ways which underline the dynastic tensions of the period, particularly in the last two years of Anne's Tory ministry. It was a Tory poet, the Secretary of State Matthew Prior, who, almost single-handedly, initiated the eighteenth-century Spenserian revival with his influential *An Ode, Humbly Inscrib'd to the Queen* (1706). Prior used Marlborough's recent victories at Ramillies as an excuse for producing this barely disguised piece of Stuart dynastic glorification celebrating Anne-as-Elizabeth through a fulsome revival of Spenser's Brutus-Troynovant-Arthur myth, whence 'TUDOR's hence, and STUART's Off-Spring flow'.[62] The Whigs were quick to detect Prior's designs. William Atwood's counterblast revealed that matters deeper than the inappropriateness of Spenser's archaism to a modern subject such as Marlborough's Wars were at stake. The Ode, complained Atwood, is 'a designed *Banter*, to turn the greatest of Actions [Marlborough's victories] into Ridicule. To address her *Majesty* in the Stile of Queen *Elizabeth*'s Reign may be thought as much a Complement, as a *Jacobite Lady*'s coming to court on an Inauguration Day, in a *Ruff* and a *Farthingal*.'[63]

---

[60] Norbrook, *Poetry and Politics in the English Renaissance*, 199.

[61] See Paul Klemp, 'Imitations and Adaptations, Renaissance (1509–1660)', in A. C. Hamilton et al. (eds.), *The Spenser Encyclopedia* (Toronto, 1990), 396. For the Spenserians, see Norbrook, *Poetry and Politics*, 195–214. An indispensable aid for Spenser studies is W. Wells, 'Spenser Allusions in the Sixteenth and Seventeenth Centuries', *SP*, Special Supplements, 68 (1971) and 69 (1972). For the later period see Richard C. Frushell, 'Imitations and Adaptations, 1660–1800', in *Spenser Encyclopedia*, 396–403.

[62] Matthew Prior, *Literary Works*, ed. M. B. Wright and M. K. Spears, 2 vols. (Oxford, 1959), i. 231. Before Prior there were only a handful of 18th-cent. Spenser imitations. After 1706 the number multiplied rapidly. The poem was cited in the ·motto to the anti-Walpole *Grub-Street Journal*, 30 Nov. 1732.

[63] [William Atwood], *A Modern Inscription to the Duke of Marlborough's Fame, Occasion'd by an Antique, In Imitation of Spenser* (1706), repr. in F. H. Ellis (ed.), *Poems on Affairs of State*, vii, *1704–14* (New Haven, Conn., 1975), 201–7.

The Jacobite allusion was not unjust given Prior's later role in negotiating with the French court as Anne's reign drew to a close. His *Ode* had set poets and audiences reading Spenser after years of neglect. As Prior himself put it, 'the Wits have sent for the Book, the Fairy Queen is on their Toilette table'. Everyone now is 'deep in that Mythologico-Poetical way of thinking'.[64] Other poets such as Ambrose Philips, secretary of the Whig Hanover Club, turned their Spenserian pastorals into vehicles for their Hanoverian loyalism. Philips and his supporters engaged in heated 'pastoral wars' with the Tory Pope, ostensibly over Spenserian 'rusticity' and the appropriate pastoral style, but covertly over dynastic allegiance.[65] Gay's Spenserian *Shepherd's Week* was heavily Tory, politicized by its Prologue praising Bolingbroke, Harley, and Arbuthnot, whose medical ministrations had just saved Anne from 'being snatch'd to *Elzabeth*'.[66] Whig Spenserian imitators responded in turn with more ambitious reworkings of *The Faerie Queene*, including Samuel Croxall's two notable *Original Cantos of Spencer* (1713–14), written on the eve of the Utrecht Treaty. Croxall depicted Britain's Protestant warlike spirit as Spenser's Britomart, bound by a wily Archimago (Harley). Harley/Archimago, the Tory minister who negotiated the peace treaty, is in league with Romania and Sans Foy (Catholic Spain and the Stuart Pretender). They devilishly scheme to stop Britomart's marriage to Sir Artegall (Hanover). In a new twist to Spenser's legend, Artegall comes to Britomart's rescue.[67] When the Tory *Examiner* took Croxall's poetic allegory to task in December 1713, it exhibited at full length its own version of the 'real' establishment Spenser—by citing the portrait of Elizabeth-as-Mercilla in the hierarchical Palace of Mercy, and adding for good measure Spenser's account of Bonfont/Malfont, the seditious poet whose tongue was nailed to a post, to show what could happen to factious critics such as Croxall.[68] In 1714 Croxall, conforming to his Protestant Whig loyalties, became an ardent Spenserian panegyrist of George I when he used the Tory Prior's *Ode to the Queen* as a model for his Hanoverian-orientated *Ode to the King*. Croxall resurfaced in the 1730s as an opposition Whig and proved to be one of Walpole's most outspoken critics.[69] Croxall's work was known to Thomson and certainly to Pope, whose prying ministerial critic Esdras Barnivelt in the cryptic *Key to the Lock* of 1715

---

[64] Prior, letter to Lord Cholmondeley 1 Aug. 1706, cited *Works*, ii. 896.

[65] For Philips see Annabel Patterson, *Pastoral and Ideology: Virgil to Valéry* (Oxford, 1988), 212. The Anne/Elizabeth figures are explored by Douglas Brooks-Davies, *Pope's 'Dunciad' and the Queen of the Night: A Study in Emotional Jacobitism* (Manchester, 1985), 1–11, 33–45. See also John M. Aden, *Pope's Once and Future Kings: Satire and Politics in the Early Career* (Knoxville, La., 1978), 62–3.

[66] John Gay, *Poetry and Prose*, ed. V. A. Dearing and C. Beckwith, 2 vols. (Oxford, 1974), i. 93.

[67] *An Original Canto of Spencer, Designed as Part of His Fairy Queen, but Never Printed* (1 Dec. 1713) and *Another Original Canto of Spencer* (1714). Both appeared under the pseudonym 'Nestor Ironside'.

[68] *Examiner*, 14–16 Dec. 1713.

[69] For Croxall's controversial sermons, see Goldgar, *Walpole and the Wits*, 88–9.

exclaimed 'who could imagine that an *Original Canto of Spencer* should contain a Satyr upon one Administration'.[70]

Merlin's Cave and its Progeny

The political Spenserianism of the Walpole period was no less intense than it had been in Anne's reign. Spenserian iconography was deployed by both court and opposition in a series of manœuvres which were almost certainly initiated in the mid-1730s by the controversies over Queen Caroline's famous (or infamous) Merlin's Cave. That a queen should have taken it upon herself to commission a shrine which advertised her dynastic pedigree and her descent from British antiquity suggests both the pressure on the Hanoverians to mythologize themselves, however, crudely, and the absence of either a Spenser or a Prior capable of doing it for them. Merlin's Cave was the second large-scale building the Queen commissioned in Richmond Gardens.[71] The first, the Hermitage, with its pantheon of British intellectuals, had prompted a far less tendentious response from oppositional critics than that which greeted the Cave. The Cave may have started life as a subterranean grotto but it ended up with three beehive-shaped thatched towers topping a building with touches of both Palladian and rococo in its wings and traceried doorway. Its domed room supported by wooden pillars housed six full-size waxwork figures, some modelled from the life from characters in the royal household. One was Merlin with his staff, consulting his globe and conjuring-books, another in a farthingale was Elizabeth I. Henry VII's queen and Merlin's secretary followed suit, then two ambiguous female figures: one described variously as Minerva, Britannia, or Britomart from Spenser's *Faerie Queene*; and the other as Glauce, Britomart's nurse, or Melissa, the prophetess who accompanied Bradamante in Ariosto's *Orlando Furioso*, or (more bathetically) Mother Shipton, a famous popular British prophetess.

Caroline's 'very Gothique' Cave may have been a royal rival to Stowe's recent politicized garden buildings, especially its British and Gothic pantheons.[72] It was certainly caught in the middle of a political crossfire, some of

[70] *The Prose Works of Alexander Pope*, i, ed. Norman Ault (Oxford, 1936), 182. See Douglas Grant, *James Thomson, Poet of 'The Seasons'* (1951), 102, for Croxall and Thomson.

[71] For invaluable accounts of Merlin's Cave, see Manuel Schonhorn, 'Pope's *Epistle to Augustus*: Notes towards a Mythology', in Maynard Mack and James Winn (eds.), *Pope: Recent Essays by Several Hands* (Brighton, 1985), 546–64; Judith M. Colton, 'Merlin's Cave and Queen Caroline: Garden Art as Political Propaganda', *ECS* 10 (1976), 1–20; Michael Wilson, *William Kent: Architect, Designer, Painter, Gardener, 1685–1748* (1984), 143–7. For the Cave's popular offspring, see esp. B. Sprague Allen, *Tides in English Taste, 1619–1800*, 2 vols. (2nd edn., New York, 1958), ii. 135–9; Richard D. Altick, *The Shows of London* (Cambridge, Mass., 1978), 75.

[72] Curll, *Rarities of Richmond*, 7. For this argument, see Colton, 'Merlin's Cave and Queen Caroline', 8; for the comparisons between Stowe and Richmond, see *Fog's*, 6 Dec. 1735, and *GM* 5 (1735), 716. Caroline probably arrived at a taste for the Gothic quite independently. See Michael Wilson, *William Kent*, 148. Summer 1735 witnessed a flurry of historical commissions from both Frederick and Caroline for commemorative busts and statues. See *GM* 5 (1735), 532–3, for rival accounts of his and her 'work-in-progress' on facing pages.

which was stimulated by Caroline's efforts at this late stage to woo her discontented son and heir Frederick back from the hands of the opposition. In *The Faerie Queene* Merlin the prophet, upon looking into his glassy globe, had predicted Britomart's marriage, just as Caroline had recently (so she claimed) secured her son's betrothal to Augusta of Saxe-Gotha. But Merlin served purposes other than the matrimonial. In *The Faerie Queene* he had been the vehicle for Spenser's prophecies of a renovated Arthurian dynasty under Elizabeth, and his new home in a Hanoverian royal tableau made Caroline's intentions all too apparent. The Melissa figure had a special dynastic function in this Hanoverian enclave. The episode in Spenser where Britomart and Glauce visit Merlin in his cave parallels an episode in *Orlando Furioso* where Bradamante and the prophetess Melissa also visit a Merlin figure. Spenser's Merlin envisions the Arthurian line culminating in the Tudors, Ariosto's Merlin foretells the rise of the House of Este. Leibniz, among others, had recently established that it was from the House of Este that the lines of Brunswick and Hanover were descended. Caroline was thus implicitly associating her own royal pedigree with the British Arthurian myth—a double confirmation of the antiquity of the House of Hanover.

Numerous commentators supplied 'readings' of Caroline's waxwork icons in the weeks and months after the Cave was opened to the public. The *Gentleman's Magazine* and the *London Magazine* reported the debates and inserted full-page engravings of the interior.[73] The Cave opened up a new chapter in the history of the Troynovant myth. It also initiated a renewed wave of interest in Spenser. Both *The Faerie Queene* and *Orlando Furioso* were quoted, glossed, and discussed by informed writers contributing to the popular press.[74] The Cave also invited widespread popular curiosity. Opposition journalists, anxious to downplay anything that advertised the merits of George and Caroline, exercised their wit on its grotesqueries. It may have been 'silly childish stuff', to cite George's impatient comments on his more enterprising wife's pastimes, but the Cave occupied an interesting place in the popular imagination. One side of its symbolism derived from highbrow culture—Spenser and Ariosto—but the other derived from lowbrow culture—the widespread common currency given to the Merlin figure by superstitious popular prophecies.

[73] The engraving of the Cave's interior and its figures was reproduced in *GM* 5 (1735), 714. The Cave was first announced as a subterranean grotto ibid. 331; a written description of the figures appeared ibid. 498. For party-political essays and attacks and reproduction in *GM* 5 (1735), see *Craftsman*, 13 Sept. 1735 (*GM* 532–5); *Daily Gazetteer*, 18 Sept. 1735 (*GM* 533); *Prompter*, 12 Sept. 1735; *Craftsman*, 15 Nov. 1735 (*GM* 660–2); essay by 'D.S.' in *GM* 671; *Fog's*, 6 Dec. 1735 (*GM* 715–16).

[74] See the *Craftsman* essay on 15 Nov. (*GM* 660–2) with detailed explication of *FQ* III and a gloss at the bottom of the page, 'The Old Words explained'. After 1735 there was a sudden rise of Hanoverian Spenserian works, including Samuel Boyse's loyalist *The Olive: An Ode, Occasion'd by the Auspicious Success of His Majesty's Counsels, and His Majesty's Most Happy Return* (1736); a number of poems on Frederick's marriage modelled on Spenser in the 1736 *Gratulatio Academiae Oxoniensis*; and Aaron Hill's *Tears of the Muses* (1737).

Since the seventeenth century, Merlin had been the vehicle for penny-pamphlet historical prophecies such as those by the famous astrologist John Partridge, printed annually between 1660 and 1707.[75] Swift's attempts to 'kill' Partridge through his famous Bickerstaff hoax had not succeeded: Partridge spoke from beyond the grave well into the 1720s. His Merlinic prophecies were filled with dire reflections on Papist uprisings and Protestant martyrs. Merlin as necromancer and fortune-teller still frequented the fairground booths and puppet-shows of the early eighteenth century. He appeared in pantomime farces and popular pasquinades well into the 1730s.[76]

Edmund Curll claimed that it was the popular astrologist Partridge, rather than Spenser, who lay behind Caroline's Cave: Partridge's *Merlinus Liberatus* 'is generally thought was the chief Motive for christening this structure— MERLIN'S CAVE'.[77] The highbrow and the lowbrow converged at Richmond Gardens. The Cave itself was a form of public entertainment, a royal version of Madame Tussaud's to which hundreds of people paid visits. Sarah Big— humble wife of the Richmond Gardens' keeper, the former farm-labourer Stephen Duck—supplied guided tours round the Cave's interior. The more ordinary visitors would have recognized the familiar figure of Mother Shipton. They would also have known about the book over which Merlin sat musing— the *Life and Predictions of the Late Celebrated Duncan Campbell*. Campbell was a deaf and dumb rustic who had made his fortunes in London as popular seer, prophesying marriage partners for young girls (and here, presumably, for Frederick too!). Inn-keepers and puppet-booth owners in the Richmond vicinity capitalized on the Cave's popularity. A number of taverns changed their name to Merlin's Cave, and coffee houses supplied 'Merlin in Miniature', scaled-down versions of Caroline's figures.[78]

These popular entertainments did not ridicule the royal family. The linkage in the popular mind between Caroline's Cave, the Hanoverian dynasty, and the Protestant identity of the British nation is suggested by Curll's *The Rarities of Richmond*. Curll's guidebook to the Richmond Gardens also traced the history of England through the visions of popular prophets and seers such as Robert Nixon and John Partridge. It supplied a very Protestant version of the past and the present (as we saw in the Elizabeth 'Astrea' prophecy at the start of this chapter), one which placed the Hanoverians squarely in the tradition of the two great Protestant monarchs, Henry VIII and Elizabeth.

Nixon foretold great Glory and Prosperity to those who stood up in Defence of the Laws and Liberties of their Country, and threatened with Ruin and misery those who

[75] See James Merriman, *The Flower of Kings: A Study of the Arthurian Legend in England between 1485 and 1835* (Lawrence, Kan., 1973), notes to pp. 220–1; Swift's *A Famous Prediction of Merlin, the British Wizard* (1709) and his black-letter *Windsor Prophecy* (1711).

[76] See Altick, *The Shows of London*, 75; Allen, *Tides in English Taste*, ii. 136–8.

[77] Curll, *Rarities of Richmond*, 2–3.

[78] Allen, *Tides in English Taste*, 136–8.

should betray them . . . But that GEORGE, the Son of GEORGE, should put an End to All. That then the Church should flourish, and England be the most flourishing Nation upon Earth. We hope this Aera is now come![79]

More literary tributes to the Cave incorporated allusions to Spenser and Ariosto with allusions to popular superstitions and Merlinic Hanoverian prophecy. 'Melissa' (the Ariostan pseudonym adopted by the poetess Jane Hughes Brereton) prefaced her *Merlin: A Poem* with a frontispiece engraving of the Cave's interior.[80] Underneath was a passage from Book III, Canto ii of *The Faerie Queene* coupled with a rhyming-couplet summary uniting Spenser's Britomart and Merlin with Ariosto's Bradamante and his own Merlin. The work praises Caroline's erudition, linking Merlin and the popular story of his magical transferral of Stonehenge from Ireland to England with the superior scientific achievements of Locke.[81] It goes on to praise Caroline as an Elizabethan Astrea figure: '*Astrea* and Minerva, joyn | To form one finish'd CAROLINE.' Its final Merlinic prophecy, addressed to Frederick, who is enjoined to 'Follow *George*, and *Caroline*', predicts the perpetuation until eternity of '*Brunswick*'s Race'.

> Successive rising to Renown!
> Decree'd *Britannia*'s Throne to grace;
> And give new Lustre to a Crown.
> Ordain'd, to wield the Sceptre Royal,
> With righteous Pow'r, and gentle Sway;
> And rule o'er *Britons*, Brave and Loyal,
> Till Heavn, and Earth, shall melt away.[82]

The lines reappeared in the March 1736 issue of the *Gentleman's Magazine*. Their heady combination of Merlin's prophecy, Hanoverian legitimacy, British patriotism, and the due obedience of loyal subjects emerges in full sway in William Giffard's sumptuous revival on 17 December 1735 of Dryden's *King Arthur*. A new edition of the play, rushed into print by Curll, was renamed *Merlin: Or, The British Inchanter. And King Arthur, The British Worthy* in honour of Merlin's Cave. This edition contains a pull-out engraving of the Cave. On the title-page opposite stands the inscription 'Our Prophet's Fame, great CAROLINE, by Thee, | Is now made Famous to Eternity'. Whatever Dryden's original intention for this play, during the winter season 1735–6 Giffard, theatre-manager of Goodman's Fields, turned it into a massive piece of Hanoverian hype. Giffard's loyalty to the Hanoverian court had previously displayed itself in his celebrations of the Princess Anne's marriage in 1734 and his popular beery

---

[79] Curll, *Rarities of Richmond*, Prologue to Part III, pp. vii–viii.

[80] 'Melissa' [Jane Hughes Brereton], *Merlin: A Poem Humbly Inscrib'd to Her Majesty* (1735). See also John Nixon, *Merlin: A Poem* (1736), a far less elaborate work.

[81] Inspired by Lewis Theobald and John Galliard's preface to their popular pasquinade, *Merlin; Or, the Devil of Stonehenge* (1734). This was an old legend about Stonehenge.

[82] 'Melissa', *Merlin*, 12. For associations of Caroline and Minerva (both serious and ironic) see Schonhorn, 'Pope's *Epistle to Augustus*', 561–4.

street-parties for George II's birthday in 1731 and 1732.[83] *King Arthur* enjoyed an unprecedented run of thirty-five nights. On the twenty-eighth night Giffard had the personal honour of presenting a copy of the play to the Queen.

The subtle alterations of Dryden's original text affirm the Hanoverians as the true successors to the British throne, 'a long Ilustrious Race | Whose future Glory rises to my View'. The golden age will come after 'A reign of many Tyrants' and an 'Abdicated King' (a strictly Whig-worded interpretation of James II's flight).[84]

> Lo a little forward
> Where from the German Shore a Stately Horse
> Advances joining to our British Lyon
> England date thence the whitest Hour of State,
> Thence in a Gay Successive Order Shine
> Peace and her Golden Train—nor can the Eye
> Of long Futurity foresee a Change
> But happiness must last till time Decay.

It is in the new Prologue that the glorification of the Hanoverians reaches its full height—a long Augustan prophecy, full of allusions to the return of Astrea to Albion's sons. It concludes with lines in praise of peace and the 'Glories of a Milder reign'.

> Guardian, as Arbiter, of Peace restor'd,
> Save bleeding Europe from the ruthless Sword!
> Of Sacred Liberty great Patron Shine;
> And prove by Godlike Worth the Right Divine.

As we shall see in Chapter 7, this poetic refashioning of Divine Right language was by no means unprecedented in Hanoverian apologetics, even though the 'Right Divine' may need to be proved by personal worth. Curll's *Rarities of Richmond* cited verses written for Caroline in 1732 by the former Jacobite turned Hanoverian, George Granville, Lord Lansdowne. In her person, Caroline has ended dynastic strife: her smile 'Commands *Obedience*':

> Contending *Parties* and *Plebeian* Rage,
> Had puzzled *Loyalty* for half an Age;
> *Conque'ring our Hearts*, SHE ends the long Dispute,
> All that have eyes confess HER *Absolute*.
> To *Tory Doctrines* now, the *Whigs* resign
> And, *in her Person*, own the *Right Divine*.[85]

---

[83] Giffard apparently leaked the obscene farce *The Golden Rump*, derived from the allegorical vision in *Common Sense*, to Walpole, leading indirectly to the Licensing Act. See *An Apology for the Life of Mr. T[heophilus] C[ibber] Comedian* (1740), 93–4. For Giffard's Hanoverian shows, see Scouten, *The London Stage 3, 1729–1747*, i, pp. lxxx–lxxxvi.

[84] These three 'Alterations Upon the Revival of the Opera' are to be found on the reverse side of the Epilogue.

[85] Curll, *Rarities of Richmond*, pp. i–ii. These lines give an added insight into Pope's attacks on the '"RIGHT DIVINE of Kings to govern Wrong"' (*Dunciad*, iv. 188; *TE* v. 360).

Audiences may have flocked to *King Arthur* more for its marvellous scenic effects than to listen to the Hanoverians being extolled for their lineage and majesty.[86] But the play was irresistibly patriotic, its music stirringly grand. The closing scenes feature figures from British mythology surrounded by choruses of British subjects. Aeolus summons up the spirit of Britannia: the island rises up on the stage, the goddess Britannia surrounded by fishermen. Fishermen and peasants unite in a country dance singing 'hoigh for the Honour of Old England'. Finally, Honour '*attended by Heroes*', celebrates in song 'St. George, the Patron of our Isle, | A Soldier, and a Saint'.

> Our Natives not alone appear
> To court this Martial Prize;
> But Foreign Kings, adopted here,
> Their Crowns at Home despise.
>
> Our Sov'raign High, in awful State,
> His Honours shall bestow;
> And see his scepter'd Subjects wait
> On his Commands below.

These lines were even more apposite for George II than they had been for William III when Dryden's play was first staged. George, after all, shared the same name as St George of Cappadocia, patron saint of England. He too was a soldier, if by no means a saint. The play reaches a swelling climax with a chorus to the sovereign. Purcell's music, with its touch of martial pomp, may have been the model for Arne's tune to 'Rule, Britannia'.[87] Manuel Schonhorn is right to assert that Merlin's prophecies and visions of imperial grandeur

constituted not only a convention that was still current in the eighteenth century but one steadily popularised by poets, playwrights and historians, acknowledged by Church and State, and, in the time of Hanoverian rule, reasserting itself, sustaining its character of a national legend which, true or false, was wholly sympathetic to the popular mind imbued with the spirit of British culture and in perfect harmony with British poetic feeling.[88]

Walpolian Wizardry

The opposition press supplied its own sardonic version of the royal tableau housed in Caroline's Cave. The ridicule was directed far less at Caroline, however, than at Walpole. Writers for the *Craftsman* and other opposition journals

---

[86] Gray was particularly impressed by the Frost scene and the Saxon altar scene, 'a British temple enough to make one go back a thousand years, & really be in ancient Britain'. See *Correspondence of Thomas Gray*, ed. Paget Toynbee and Leonard Whibley, 3 vols. (Oxford, 1935), i. 36.

[87] See Robert E. Moore, *Henry Purcell and the Restoration Theatre* (1961), 73.

[88] Schonhorn, 'Pope's *Epistle to Augustus*', 559.

had long been accustomed to clothing their assaults on the minister in cryptic allegory and mock-prophecy, and the Cave's Elizabethan and necromantic iconography played right into their hands. In the first place, they claimed, the Elizabeth label attached to the farthingaled wax figure was a '*Mistake*' since, added *Fog's*, it was impossible that 'in the present nice and critical Conjuncture of Affairs a Person so obnoxious to *Spain* should be so openly avow'd and distinguished in that Place'.[89] The Merlin figure inspired more ingenious readings. The *Craftsman* reapplied itself to *The Faerie Queene*. On 15 November 1735 it devoted an entire essay to Book III, citing several stanzas including Spenser's description of Merlin's globe. It pointedly remarked how useful such a prophetic looking-glass might have proved to the current genera-tion: all the miseries of Walpole's administration might have been avoided.[90] Spenser's description of the 'Brazen Wall' built by Merlin around Cairmardan offered an apt analogy for a later 'Brazen Wall'—Robert Walpole. Walpole's reputation for covering up or 'screening' corruption had prompted his popular nickname—the 'wall' or 'screen' of brass. The opposition supplied its own ver-sion of Merlin's prophecies, one, as we shall see in Chapter 8, of a distinctly seditious Jacobite kind. The opposition 'Merlin' predicts not a glorious Hanoverian dynasty but a time of shame when the British lion cowers, and the white horse (Hanover) bends to the Spanish mule. He is led through the nose by an 'ass with gaudy trappings'—the low-born Walpole.[91]

But more often Walpole himself was identified with the figure of Merlin and transformed by a sleight of hand into his malign Spenserian counterpart Archimago. Caroline's magician was not really Spenser's benign Merlin, sug-gested opposition writers, but one whose art 'was of the black malignant Kind, and employ'd only in wicked purposes'. The parallels with Croxall's anti-Harley *Original Cantos* of 1713–14, with their sinister Archimago-minister who bewitches Britomart, are close. Britomart, 'The Martial Spirit of Britain', 'seems to be in a very declining Condition, and (being no Conjurer herself) comes in the most anxious and submissive manner to enquire her Fate from the Mouth of that Inchanter, who by his skill in the Black Art had brought it to depend on him'.[92] The typology identifying powerful ministers with wiz-ardry and evil spells went back well into the seventeenth century, later supply-ing both Swift and, as we have seen, Croxall, with analogies between the chancellor's rod of office and the wizard's magic wand.[93] Walpole's critics had

[89] *Craftsman*, 15 Nov. 1735 (*GM* 5 (1735), 662); *Fog's*, 6 Dec. 1735 (*GM* 716).

[90] *Craftsman*, 15 Nov. 1735 (*GM* 5 (1735), v. 660–2).

[91] *Craftsman*, 13 Sept. 1735 (*GM* 533).   [92] *Fog's*, 6 Dec. 1735 (*GM* 716).

[93] The satirical iconography linking evil enchanters and prominent political figures seems to have flourished in the Whig–Tory disputes of Anne's reign. One important source for the later period is the Tory George Granville's dramatic opera *The British Enchanters* (1706), whose Arcalus, 'a wicked Enchanter', may be a figure for the Whig Godolphin. Swift's 'Sid Hamet', descendant of Samuel Butler's Sir Sidrophel, is meant for Godolphin. See Swift, *Poetical Works*, ed. Herbert Davis (Oxford, 1967), 89–91. For Walpole's many wizard costumes, see the engraving of 1737, *The Festival of The Golden Rump*, *BMC* no. 2327, explicated in *Common Sense*, 19 Mar.

long since identified his political chicanery with necromancy: the first extended version seems to have appeared in the story of the magician Lucitario and his magic well in Eliza Haywood's *Memoirs of Utopia* (1724), a brilliant analogy between the South Sea Bubble fraud and ministerial alchemy.[94] Both Milton's Satan and Spenser's Archimago illustrated the larger patterns of deception, enticement, and moral metamorphosis which Walpole's critics perceived underlying people's changed moral behaviour in Walpolian Britain. Pope and Fielding supplied two of the most famous visions of Walpole-as-wizard: *The Dunciad*'s 'WIZARD OLD' proferring his cup of 'Self-Love' and Fielding's *Vernoniad* (1741), tracing Vernon's failure at Cartagena to the effects of the spells wrought by the great magician 'Hishonour'. In 1737 *Common Sense* published a print called *The Festival of the Golden Rump*, and an accompanying explanatory 'Vision' which became notorious. The naked satyr-figure on a pedestal, his large rump turned towards us, is intended for George II. Even more unmistakable is the heavy-bellied wizard standing close by, one 'Gaster Argos' wearing a cloak and carrying a wand. It is Walpole, the 'CHIEF MAGICIAN' who, with his magic spells, officiates at the pseudo-religious ceremony for the round-buttocked deity. *Common Sense* uses the (mock) reverential tones more appropriate for the elaborate Garter ceremony which Walpole had contrived for himself some years earlier. When someone converted the scene into plans for a stage farce, Walpole (so rumour had it) decided that satire had become too bold, and initiated the Stage Licensing Act.

Caroline's Cave gave an added charge to the satirical myth-making process. Pope started to think hard at this time about the political implications of 'old Bards, or Merlin's Prophecy'.[95] The satirical print of 1741 bearing a title like Giffard's version of the Dryden play, *Merlin, or the British Enchanter*, depicting 'His Honour's Pack Ass' laden with the revenue from customs and land tax and sprouting a tree of government corruption, contains no apparent mention of Walpole as enchanter. In an earlier version, *The State Pack Horse*, the engraver had included a small wizard with a magic circle and a large bottle called 'The Cordial Julep', but by 1741 the identification had become so well known that no visual reference was necessary.[96] A cryptic prophetic poem of

1737 (reproduced in Maynard Mack, *The Garden and City: Retirement and Politics in the later Poetry of Pope, 1731–1743* (Toronto, 1969), 143–7); *The State Pack-Horse*, BMC no. 2420; *Merlin: Or the British Enchanter*, repr. in Atherton, *Political Prints*, plate 37; *Craftsman*, 21 Feb. 1736 (*GM* 6 (1736), 88); Fielding, *The Vernoniad* (1741), in *Complete Works*, ed. W. E. Henley, 16 vols. (1903), xv. 43; and the *Champion*, 13 Dec. 1739, in *Complete Works*, xv. 97–10. See Martin M. Battestin, 'Pope's "Magus" in Fielding's *Vernoniad*: The Satire of Walpole', *PQ* 46 (1967), 137–41. For the wizard figure in Pope, see *Dunciad* iv. 515–26, *Epistle to Augustus*, ll. 131–3, *Epistle to Bathurst*, l. 36.

[94] Eliza Haywood, *Memoirs of a Certain Island Adjacent to the Kingom of Utopia* (1724), 5–8. Caroline Lewis drew my attention to the passage. The earliest example cited by Mack, *Garden and City*, 131 n., is *Craftsman*, 2 Dec. 1727.

[95] *TE* v. 201. Discussed in detail by Schonhorn, 'Pope's *Epistle to Augustus*'.

[96] See Atherton, *Political Prints*, 12, 129–30, 162. Repr. in Colton, 'Merlin's Cave', fig. 7.

1737, *Of Legacy Hunting*, subtitled 'A Dialogue between Sir Walter Raleigh, and Merlin the Prophet', makes sense only in the context of Merlin's Cave and the Ralegh cult. Here, the sturdily independent Ralegh is 'Wont to oppose the Great, and check the Brave! | I, that bold Truths at Risque of Life maintain'd, | With *Cecil, Essex*, when *Eliza* reign'd'. He confronts a diabolical Walpolian Merlin who has just sprung up from Hell.[97]

Spenserian Allegory: West, Pope, and Thomson

Opposition poets took this Spenserian typology to heart in a more serious and thoroughgoing fashion. They were less interested in using Spenser's allegory for local satiric effects (Walpole-as-Archimago) than they were in the patterns of moral metamorphosis and corruption of which Spenser was the great poet. Moral and civic decline had pervaded the atmosphere of both *The Faerie Queene* and his lament, the poignant *Ruines of Time*. Spenser's emphasis on moral vigilance, the ever-open eye required by the wary knight for the deceptions and seductions of ease and luxury, accorded with the opposition's Machiavellian prescription of the vigilant maintenance of *virtù* for the avoidance of national ruin.

Gilbert West, James Thomson, and Pope all turned to Spenser in the 1730s and early 1740s; in the case of West and Pope, certainly more for political than for 'romantic' purposes. West's anonymous 1739 satire, *A Canto of the Fairy Queen*, began where the Whig Croxall's similar poems had ended in 1714. It is the kind of poem Croxall might himself have written to attack Walpole. The work's indebtedness to Croxall's *Original Cantos* is unmistakable. West's prose 'Advertisement' to his canto parallels Croxall's own fictitious claims for the authenticity of *his* first Spenserian canto. Claiming to have been sent one of Spenser's 'original' cantos by an Irish friend, West's anonymous editor notes that this undiscovered Spenser item seems to address a subject 'a little more modern, especially in the Characters of the two Foreign Nations therein delineated'. Both in Elizabeth's day and our own, young men were infected with the itch of travelling abroad, especially to Italy. The editor cites the maxims of Elizabeth's tutor, the patriotic and xenophobic Roger Ascham, who 'declares very strongly against the Custom of sending young Gentlemen to travel'. This poem thus promises to be a satire on the Grand Tour, one of the favourite targets of opposition writers inveighing against the 'luxury' of Hanoverian Britain, especially its importation of Italian manners and Italian opera. Yet the 'Advertisement' has a more overt political thrust. West reinterprets Spenser's famous letter to Ralegh on the purpose of *The Faerie Queene* and adds a line which links it explicitly with the language of the Patriot oppo-

---

[97] *Of Legacy Hunting. The 5th Satire of the Second Book of Horace Imitated. A Dialogue between Sir Walter Raleigh, and Merlin the Prophet* (1737).

sition. Spenser's epic, 'as the Author himself tells us, [was] written with a
Design to *fashion a Gentleman, or noble Person in virtuous and gentle Discipline*,
the Perfection of which is a generous and disinterested Love of one's
Country'. And why do the 'two Foreign Nations' depicted in the canto look
more 'modern'?[98]

West's satire on the Grand Tour turns into a satire on Walpolian Britain.
His Red-Cross Knight, who combines the strengths of both Spenser's Red-
Crosse and Guyon, crosses an 'idle' lake to visit two foreign lands which, after
a while, look uncannily similar to different manifestations of the Hanoverian
court. They are, in fact, two separate 'courts'—George II's and Queen
Caroline's. The 'swoln Form of Royal Surquedry' who presides over the first,
a ritualized Pagod-figure found everywhere in opposition prints, is clearly
George II.[99] The Archimago who manipulates him 'behind scenes' is none
other than that arch-puppet-master Walpole.[100] Red-Cross is soon disgusted
and tries to reform a people too ensnared in luxury to realize their enchantment. He finds himself in trouble after raising a Whiggish defence of the
people's rights and holding up an anti-magic mirror revealing the slavery
behind the court's luxury. He departs in haste, leaving the throne trembling, if
not falling. His second visit is no more inspiring. The queen he encounters
presiding over the ruins of a 'once-goodly city'—a sure pointer to civic
decline—is evidently Caroline. She is accompanied by an insidious pale
eunuch (the epicene Lord Hervey), 'unseemly Paramour for Royal Maid!'.
Like Caroline, with her penchant for antiquarians, she courts the homage of
the coin-collectors and pseudo-historians who have reduced the spirit of true
learning to trivial pursuits. Perched on a nest of 'Urns, broken Freezes,
Statues half defac'd', the queen claims the 'Praise and Title of Vertu'. Yet this
'vertu' is not Machiavelli's civic virtue, but the spurious virtuosity of the vir-
tuosi, those 'Mimes, Fidlers, Pipers, Eunuchs squeaking fine, | Painters and
Builders, Sons of Masonry'. The genuine 'Sons of Learning' have meanwhile
vanished to other shores. West evidently modelled his account on a passage in
his cousin Lyttelton's *Persian Letters* which had similarly played on the ironies
of etymology. Selim the Persian writes:

They talk'd much of certain Men call'd *Virtuosi*, whom, by the near Relation their
Title bore to *Virtue*, I took at first to be *a Sect of rigid Moralists*: But, upon Enquiry, I

[98] [Gilbert West], *A Canto of the Fairy Queen. Written by Spenser. Never before Published* (1739), 'Advertisement', p. 1. All subsequent citations from this edn. West may have been inspired by Kent's illustrations to *The Faerie Queene*. Kent's illustration for Book II, Guyon's visit to the Bowre of Blisse, shows a lake and a distant landscape very like the one West's Red-Cross first vis-its. Kent's vista also contains a temple architecturally identical to the Temple of Venus at Stowe, designed by Kent, which housed erotic ceiling paintings depicting Spenser's legend of Paridel and Hellenore. See Wilson, *William Kent*, 150–1.

[99] For images of the Pagod in opposition prints and satires, see Mack, *Garden and the City*, 141–50.

[100] For Walpole as screen-master and puppet-master see ibid. 129, 131 n., 132. For similar prints entitled *The Screen*, see Atherton, *Political Prints*, plates 45 and 46.

discover'd that they were a Company of *Fidlers, Eunuchs, Painters, Builders, Gardners,* and above all, Gentlemen *that had travell'd into Italy,* who immediately came home perfect Virtuosi, tho' they went out the dullest Fellows in the World.[101]

West's satire extends to the *ciceroni,* guides paid to show people round the ruins of Rome. Here the gap between the origins of the name and the thing it has come to represent is even more painful. Red-Cross, recalling the Roman republican legacy, appeals for a restoration of the spirit of the 'genuine Cicero'. The queen's surreal court of antiquarian artefacts now looks just like the ruins of Rome, which (like Hanoverian Britain) was first assailed by 'luxury and pride, | Those fell diseases whereof Rome erst dyd'. Red-Cross sheds a manly tear and proclaims that 'Fairy-lond' (Britain) must not be allowed to go the same way. Like Spenser's original knights, he too must fight an unending battle.

Later critics did not detect West's original satirical design—his Spenserian style is so convincing that it invited praise on its own terms. Pope, who knew West well, almost certainly responded to the poem, possibly soon after it had appeared in 1739, when he was designing his *New Dunciad* (1742).[102] That poem—Book IV of *The Dunciad*—contains a familiar scene very similar to West's: Pope's account of the virtuosi trooping up to Dulness's/Caroline's court to receive their just rewards. Pope even described his plans to Hugh Bethel in the words of the alternative title given to West's poem, 'The Abuse of Travelling'.[103] He claimed he was working on a poem 'part of which is to abuse *Travelling* . . . an Army of Virtuosi, Medalists, Ciceronis . . . will encompass me with fury'.[104] Pope was rereading Spenser at around this time; he may also have been inspired by the political airing Spenser's reputation had recently received. Book IV of *The Dunciad* is not only the most political, but also the most Spenserian.[105] Pope's description of the Grand Tour, not unlike West's description of the Grand Tour taken by Red-Cross, transforms the Italian islands, the 'lands of singing, or of dancing slaves', into a Spenserian Bowre of Blisse.[106] Second cousin to the *The Dunciad's* young tourist is the 'Paridel' whom he joins on his return to Dulness's court. We hear Paridel's 'everlasting yawn confess | The pains and penalties of Idleness'. Who was

---

[101] See Lyttelton, *Persian Letters,* 199.

[102] Pope left West a ring and a reversion in his will, and had previously edited his *Stowe.* See Pope, *Corr.* iii. 480.

[103] West's *Canto* was renamed 'On the Abuse of Travelling: A Canto in Imitation of Spenser' in vol. ii of Dodsley's *Collection* of 1748. But Frushell, 'Imitations and Adaptations', in *Spenser Encyclopedia,* 403, claims that it also appeared in London in 1739 under the title *The Abuse of Travelling; a New Canto of Spenser's Fairy Queen.*

[104] Pope, *Corr.* iv. 377.

[105] For a clear account of Pope and Spenser, see Howard Erskine-Hill, 'Pope', in *Spenser Encyclopedia,* 555–6. There was very little Spenser in Books I–III of *The Dunciad.*

[106] See Howard Erskine-Hill, *The Social Milieu of Alexander Pope: Lives, Examples and the Poetic Response* (New Haven, Conn. and London, 1975), 277, and his *Pope: The Dunciad* (1972), 63.

Pope's model for 'Paridel'? The mystery has never been solved.[107] But Pope notes that 'The name is taken from Spenser, who gives it to a *wandering Courtly 'Squire*, that travell'd about for the same reason, for which many young Squires are now fond of travelling, and especially to *Paris*'.[108] The linkage of such strange elements as Spenserian knights and the Grand Tour had been anticipated by West's 1739 *Canto*.

Pope's disenchantment with the Hanoverian court and especially with its royal shortcomings manifests itself a little later in Book IV in the '*Great Yawn*' of Queen Dulness. This is an ironic parody of the '*Roar of a Lion*' with which the 'incomparable Spenser' had ended his *Mother Hubberds Tale*, inviting Elizabeth/Leicester to rise up and punish the upstart usurpers of Crown power. The 1715 Jacobite version of Spenser's beast fable had called for a restoration of the Stuart lion, and this dynastic element may have lurked behind Pope's use of the same image.[109] However, by using Spenser's appeal to regal authority at this point, Pope may also have been appealing, albeit uncertainly, for a Patriot king's authoritative voice. But a far less ambiguous Spenserian symbol is Pope's 'WIZARD OLD' who seduces and transforms all-comers to Dulness's court with his magic cup of self-love. This Spenserian moment forms the focal point of Book IV. Those who taste the liquid—a mixture of liquid gold and Homer's Nepenthe—become morally, if not literally, transformed into hogs, retaining their outward appearance but losing their souls. Fielding's Walpolian magician 'Hishonour' preferred the same *aurum potabile* 'by which he could turn Men into Swine or Asses'.[110]

Revisiting the Castle

Thomson's well-known Spenserian allegory, *The Castle of Indolence*, may well have been inspired in part, if not in entirety, by the wave of oppositional Spenserianism I have described. Thomson's tale of a wizard, who lures passers-by into his enchanted castle where they enjoy a life of hedonistic but increasingly degenerate pleasure until rescued by the Knight of Arts and Industry with his Druid bard, has always inspired widely differing interpretations.[111] A narrowly political reading would destroy the magic which so many

---

[107] For suggestions for the 'real-life' model, see *TE* v. 376 (l. 341 n.). Pope probably saw the murals of Paridel and Hellenore inside the Temple of Venus at Stowe.

[108] See note to *Dunciad*, iv. 341–4.

[109] *Mother Hubbards Tale of the Ape and the Fox, Abbreviated from Spencer* (1715).

[110] Fielding, *Works*, xv. 43.

[111] For the 'moral' reading see Donald Greene, 'From Accidie to Neurosis: *The Castle of Indolence* Revisited', in M. E. Novak (ed.), *English Literature in the Age of Disguise* (Los Angeles, 1978), 131–56. For the 'artistic conflict' reading, see Morris Golden, 'The Imagining Self in the Eighteenth Century', *ECS* 3 (1969), 4–27. For social and class conflicts, see John Barrell, *English Literature in History, 1730–80: An Equal, Wide Survey* (1983), 79–90, and John Sitter, *Literary Loneliness in Mid-Eighteenth Century England* (Ithaca, NY, 1982), 93–6. For anti-Jacobite allegory,

readers have found in Thomson's delicious Spenserian stanzas. Yet the political-literary context does add an extra dimension to our understanding of the poem, since Thomson wrote it at a time when all his other major poems and plays were an active contribution to the Patriot campaign. We do not know much about the stages by which Thomson proceeded through the work from its inception as a handful of burlesque stanzas some time in 1733–4 to its transformation into the two-canto allegory finally published in 1748. No critic in 1748 read the work politically, but this is not surprising. By this stage critics were admiring other things in Spenserian verse such as Gothic fine fabling, chivalry, and romance; and the fall of Walpole in 1742 had put an abrupt end to the rich vein of satirical myth-making enjoyed by a receptive audience during the twenty years of his office.

Indolence had already acquired a political meaning by the time Thomson came to write his poem. Pope's 'Dulness' can be defined in several ways. Torpor is one. Pope included in his poem a reference to '*Indolent Persons* abandoning all business and duty'—another version of the 'POLITICAL LETHARGY' which the *Craftsman* in 1727 had warned was creeping over Britain. When the people 'give themselves up entirely to the pursuits of private pleasure' it does not even take a Walpole (though it helps) to destroy our civic virtue, to 'blind the eyes of the people or lay us asleep in *luxury* and *indolence*'.[112]

Thomson's early scenes where his enchanting Archimago lures passers-by into his magic kingdom bear a certain similarity to Fielding's 1739 satire on Walpole, printed in the *Champion* of 13 December 1739, in which a 'great magician' in a beautiful landscape magnetizes and ensnares wayfarers. Both wizards share the same morally strength-sapping dexterity, Fielding's magician with a 'gentle squeeze by the hand' reducing the passers-by to acquiescence, Thomson's Wizard melting his travellers into pliant wax by taking them 'by the Hand'.[113] Thomson's subsequent courtyard scene in which the pilgrims drink magic waters from the Wizard's fountain bears an uncanny resemblance to Eliza Haywood's account of Lucitario's (Walpole's) magic well in her 1724 *Memoirs of Utopia*. This well can be reached by the pilgrims' passage through a narrow gateway (again like Thomson's). Among Haywood's travellers who enter the courtyard, waiting to partake of the waters, are, interestingly, 'Knights of Industry'—the title carried by Thomson's own Knight of Arts and Industry. Where Haywood's, Thomson's, and Pope's accounts of the wizard and his initiands all correspond closely is in the language of mystical ritual with which each dresses up his seduction. The same language had also been

see M. J. W. Scott, *James Thomson, Anglo-Scot* (Athens, Ga., 1988), 278–9; for a 'Scottish Enlightenment' reading, see John MacQueen, *The Enlightenment and Scottish Literature*, i, *Progress and Poetry* (Edinburgh, 1987), 64–5. The present discussion is based on my previous account, 'The *Castle of Indolence* and the Opposition to Walpole', *RES* NS 41 (1990), 45–64.

[112] *Craftsman*, 10 Mar. 1727.
[113] Fielding, *Works*, xv. 102.

the characteristic feature of *Common Sense*'s famous account in the *Golden Rump* of the rituals presided over by the great 'Tapanta', the wizard Walpole, dressed up in his magic cloak. Haywood's Lucitario and his helpers are also tricked out in those 'Vestments which Priests are wont to wear when they officiate at the sacred Altars'.[114] Pope's lengthy gloss to *The Dunciad*, iv. 517— the Wizard's proffering of his cup—could equally be applied to Thomson's initiation ceremonies. As in *The Dunciad*, each aspirant takes his '*Libation*' and 'putteth on a *new Nature*', subsequently guided by a 'Conductor' (Thomson's porter) into the magical realms of '*Self-interest, Pleasure, Epicurism* &c.'.[115]

These three principles—self-interest, pleasure, and epicureanism (as we now call it)—dominate Thomson's Castle. The Castle-dwellers' refined pleasures soon become submerged in opiate trances and epicureanism, until, by the end of Canto I, they are (like Pope's Paridel) literally 'dying with laziness'. Self-love is what Pope's wizard was really offering in his magic cup, and so was Thomson's Wizard; his proclamation ' "Ye Sons of INDOLENCE, do what you will; . . . | "Be no Man's Pleasure for another's staid" ' (I. xxviii) simply dresses up self-love in palatable fashion for the eager inhabitants.

The relationship between Thomson's poem and oppositional tenets becomes more manifest in the second canto, which abruptly shifts the scene to recount the history of the Knight of Arts and Industry and his foundation of Britain's 'matchless' constitution. This is the prehistory of Canto I, not a departure from the story of the Castle. For in one sense Walpolian Britain *is* the Castle, its inhabitants fallen into civic decline. The Machiavellian civic cycle is suggested by the Knight's similarity to Thomson's earlier goddess Liberty in his long poem of that title. Both allegorical or symbolic figures make a westwardly progress through Egypt, Greece, and Rome. Thomson's Knight is on one level an embodiment of the same spirit of civic liberty; it is he who establishes (as well as embodying in his childhood and adolescence) all the stages through which a nation passes in its ascent on the upward slope of the historical cycle—from rugged primitivism through to the first seeds of government, followed by commerce, learning, and the arts, only then to hover on the brink of decline. It is at the point of decline that the inhabitants of the Castle summon the (now-retired) Knight to the rescue: ' "Come, come, Sir Knight! thy Children on thee call; | Come, save us yet, ere Ruin round us close" ' (II. xxxi). The Knight may on one level represent either Bolingbroke or Cobham (both, like the Knight, living a life of virtuous retirement on a country estate) but he is far closer to an allegorical embodiment of British virtue; for this request is nothing less than the opposition's cry for a Machiavellian *ritorno*, a revival of Britain's pristine spirit. Echoing Machiavelli, Thomson asks, 'But in prime Vigour what can last for ay'.

---

[114] Haywood, *Memoirs of Utopia*, 7. Thomson would have known Haywood indirectly through her friendship with Hill and Savage. She had also been a member of the Hillarian circle.

[115] *TE* v. 393.

> That soul-enfeebling Wizard INDOLENCE,
> I whilom sung, wrought in his Works decay:
> Spred far and wide was his curs'd Influence;
> Of Public Virtue much he dull'd the Sense,
> Even much of Private; eat our Spirit out,
> And fed our rank luxurious Vices; whence
> The Land was overlaid with many a Lout;
> Not, as old Fame reports, wise, generous, bold, and stout.
>
> (II. xxix)

As Bolingbroke asserted, 'corruption *alone* could not destroy us. We must want *spirit*, as well as *virtue*, to perish.'[116] Canto II, stanzas xxix–xxx adopt the very idiom and language of 1730s opposition polemic. The self-indulgence enjoyed by the Castle-dwellers of Canto I has hardened into selfish rapacity.

> A Rage of Pleasure madden'd every Breast,
> Down to the lowest Lees the Ferment ran:
> To his licentious Wish Each must be blest,
> With Joy be fever'd; snatch it as he can.
> Thus *Vice* the Standard rear'd; her Arrier-Ban
> *Corruption* call'd, and loud she gave the Word.
> 'Mind, mind yourselves! Why should the vulgar Man,
> 'The Lacquey be more virtuous than his Lord?
> 'Enjoy this Span of Life! 'tis all the Gods afford.'
>
> (II. xxx)

There is more than an echo here of the climax to Pope's *Epilogue to the Satires*, Dia. II, ll. 141–70. Pope's triumphal car of Vice, inspired in part by Spenser's description of Lucifera, leads the thronging millions: 'Hear her black Trumpet thro' the Land proclaim, | That "Not to be corrupted is the Shame"'.

Like Bolingbroke's *Idea of a Patriot King*, Thomson's poem ends with an optimistic vision of moral renewal. The Knight and his bard manage to rout the enchanter and liberate the Castle by their powerful speeches and songs. The Druid's song—highly reminiscent of Thomson's *Britannia* in its call to arts, industry, and arms and its attack on the 'soft, penetrating plague' of 'waste Luxury'—counterbalances the Wizard's song.[117] It inspires its audience to public service rather than self-indulgent quietism. Castle-dwellers who need further persuasion soon see, after a wave of the Knight's 'anti-magic' wand, that they have been living in an illusion. Britain is a barren and enslaved land. We have seen a similar exposure take place in West's *Canto*: Red-Cross holds up Una's mirror of truth, exposing the ugly reality of Hanoverian Britain. In both cases, Archimago is put to flight. False and true reflections in a magic

---

[116] Bolingbroke, *Works*, ii. 363.
[117] Cf. *Britannia*, ll. 248–55 and *Castle of Indolence*, II. lv.

mirror also appeared in the *Craftsman*'s satirical interpretation of Merlin's glassy Globe in Caroline's Cave. Thomson's Archimago, with his 'Mirror of Vanity' which had cunningly reflected the activities of *all* men—whether noble or not—as futile, was deliberately engaging in acts of moral confusion to serve his ends.

Thomson's own presence as one of the characters living inside the Castle makes the allegory seem even more powerful. On one level, the artistic, the enhancing dreams and visions he enjoys there belong to the poet's creative imagination; they have real power. Yet on another, moral level, the indolence to which Thomson himself fell victim in real life was a product of too much 'ease'. Thomson's original burlesque portraits of his friends, which he retained and even expanded, now seem to contain a rather more serious implication: Lyttelton, the active Patriot and public figure, refuses to become an inmate of the Castle, but Paterson, author of only one Patriot drama, *Arminius*, becomes the archetypal romantic dreamer, unable to convert his 'noblest morals' into words (I. lvii). Gilbert West's virtuous few in his 1739 *Canto*'s corrupt Hanoverian islands had been similarly found wanting when it came to speaking out against the prevailing national apathy and servile court-worship. And Thomson himself, shown laughing 'careless in his easy Seat' (I. lxviii), sounds a bit like Pope's indolent Paridel, 'stretch'd on the rack of a too easy chair'. For all our own later critical preference for the enchanting music of Canto I over the moral invigoration of Canto II, in which the Druid bard stirs the nation to action, Thomson actively if not subconsciously sided with the latter—perhaps a response to the frequent oppositional warnings about national decline. Thomson's Muse will not lie on the 'Bed of Sloth' but raise a 'bolder Song' celebrating the 'bold Sons of Britain' (II. iv, I. xxxii)—a pointer to the programme of Patriot poetry and drama he produced during the 1730s.

Thomson's own indolence may have delayed the progress of *The Castle of Indolence*. It seems to have simmered on his creative back-burner while he was engaged in more public forms of political writing for the theatre. After 1742 political circumstances had changed: a poem which recalled oppositional politics would scarcely have been welcome to Thomson's now ministerial patron Lyttelton. The Spenserian vogue of the late 1740s was not the same as the active party-political Spenserianism of the 1730s. By 1748 the Elizabethan age, including its two most famous literary sons Shakespeare and Spenser, was beginning to yield new romantic and 'Gothick' glories to receptive readers and poets, who found things other than political lessons to admire in both West's and Thomson's Spenserianism.

7

Mythologizing the Monarch: Ideas of a Patriot King

BOLINGBROKE'S *The Idea of a Patriot King* has been described as an eloquent epitaph to the Patriot campaign, the 'great testament of Bolingbroke's opposition, which explains and bears witness to the movement's failure'.[1] In 1738 Bolingbroke wrote this slim treatise on monarchy for the private use of Frederick and his followers, describing in idealized, even visionary terms the policies and conduct of a Patriot King waiting in the wings, whose accession would end party-political conflicts and bring healing at a touch: a sure sign, say some critics, that by 1738 Bolingbroke had lost his grasp of politics as the art of the possible. If the *Patriot King* is indeed a failure (a debatable point), it is a failure which continues to exert a peculiar fascination for both literary critics and political historians.[2]

The fascination derives in part from the work's mysterious nature. As a text, the *Patriot King* raises a number of unresolved questions, questions which the present chapter will attempt to address. The first, and most obvious, derives from its complex publication history.[3] The *Patriot King* was not published for sale until 1749, when Bolingbroke was forced into printing his 'authorized' edition after a newspaper started to leak extracts of an earlier clandestine edition, secretly printed by Pope probably in 1740–1. Bolingbroke had discovered this edition of 1,500 copies only on Pope's death in 1744 and destroyed (or so he thought) all remaining copies. The 1749 phase of the *Patriot King*'s life is well known, not least for the unsavoury charges both Bolingbroke and Mallet levelled at the memory of their former friend Pope. The 1749 publication also fortuitously (and perhaps deliberately) coincided

---

[1] Isaac Kramnick, *Bolingbroke and His Circle: The Politics of Nostalgia in the Age of Walpole* (Cambridge, Mass., 1968), 168.

[2] For recent discussions see Herbert Atherton, *Political Prints in the Age of Hogarth: A Study of the Ideographic Representation of Politics* (Oxford, 1974), 141–6; Brean Hammond, *Pope and Bolingbroke: A Study of Friendship and Influence* (Columbia, Mo., 1984), 137–43; Erskine-Hill, 'Alexander Pope: The Political Poet in His Time', *ECS* 15 (1981–2), 123–48, esp. p. 15; id., 'Literature and the Jacobite Cause: Was There a Rhetoric of Jacobitism?', in Eveline Cruickshanks (ed.), *Ideology and Conspiracy: Aspects of Jacobitism, 1689–1759* (Edinburgh, 1982), 49–69, esp. p. 56; Simon Varey, 'Hanover, Stuart and the *Patriot King*', *BJECS* 6 (1983), 163–72; id., *Henry St. John, Viscount Bolingbroke* (Boston, Mass., 1985); J. C. D. Clark, *English Society 1688–1832: Ideology, Social Structure and Political Practice during the Ancien Regime* (Cambridge, 1985); Chester Chapin, 'Pope and the Jacobites', *Eighteenth-Century Life*, 10 (1986), 59–73.

[3] The fullest account of the textual history is in Giles Barber, 'Bolingbroke, Pope and the Patriot King', *Library*, 5th ser. 19 (1964), 67–89. See also Fannie E. Ratchford, 'Pope and the Patriot King', *University of Texas Bulletin: Studies in English*, 6 (1926), 157–77.

with Frederick's new Leicester House campaign which, like the Patriot campaign of the late 1730s, rested on broad-bottom tenets promising a new age
purged of Whig oligarchy. Since the reversionary implications of Patriot kingship looked a lot closer in 1749 than they had done ten years earlier, Frederick
publicly capitalized on his identification with Bolingbroke's model, asking Lord
Lichfield, one of his Tory followers, if he had read the work and telling him
'Well, my lord, I shall be that patriot King'.[4]

We know far less about the *Patriot King* in the period which concerns us
here—the late 1730s. Bolingbroke probably wrote, or completed the work
while he was staying with Pope on his extended visit to England between July
1738 and April 1739. As a manuscript, it was (one surmises) circulated among
and discussed by Frederick's close followers. Pope was also given permission
to print a small run of approximately ten copies. His 'secret' larger edition was
kept hidden in a safe place for the use of posterity, and not circulated or read.
Thus we have a coterie text with a deliberately limited circulation.
Bolingbroke's manuscript is lost and only a small part of the tiny first printed
run survives, so we have no definite evidence of exactly what the *Patriot King*
first looked like in 1738. Nor do we have any real idea of who read the work
either in the manuscript or in one of the very small original set of printed
copies. The *Patriot King* is often credited with inspiring the cult of Patriot
kingship which appears everywhere in the Patriot plays and poems of the late
1730s. If this was the case, then their authors remained curiously silent on the
subject of their inspiration. There are no direct references to the *Patriot King*
in any of the private correspondence of this period.

Further problems ensue from trying to divine Bolingbroke's intentions in
writing the *Patriot King*. What was he trying to achieve by it? As a political
manifesto, it seems long on promises and notably short on policies—a characteristic, perhaps, of most political manifestos, but the *Patriot King* seems to
function on an altogether different level. The platonic nature of its title—the
'idea' of a Patriot King—suggests that Bolingbroke was deliberately aiming at
abstraction. Added to this is the work's deployment of a wide range of rhetorical tropes and metaphors—the Augustan panegyric of its closing lines, its
echoes of the 'advice to princes' tradition, its messianic language—which suggests a provenance not in party politics but in literary tradition. If the work is
indeed 'utopian', it is utopian in a quite specific sense, carrying strong traces
of the ideal commonwealth tradition evolved from Plato's *Republic* to More's
Utopia and a variety of fictional commonwealths from Harrington's *Oceana* to
Fénelon's *Aventures de Télémaque*.[5]

Such works often contained an implicitly satirical dimension—their ideal
polities contrasting with the current and unideal state of political affairs which
prompted their writer to imagine an alternative. More's satire on the corrup-

---

[4] Cited in Clark, *English Society*, 182.
[5] For some of the utopian aspects, see Hammond, *Pope and Bolingbroke*, 139–41.

tions of Henry VIII's court is not far from the surface of *Utopia*—nor is Bolingbroke's satire on George II and Walpole far from the surface of the *Patriot King*.[6] The *Patriot King* shares something of the *Craftsman*'s earlier manipulation of the contrasts between the reigns of good and bad monarchs, history functioning here as an endorsement of the superior merits of a reign distinguished not by factionalism and favouritism but by unity and a paternalistic concern for the common good. Here, as earlier, Bolingbroke passes from Elizabeth to James I to show the effects of both. But who was the 'ideal king' who would restore the nation to political health? Bolingbroke's 'panegyric without the prince', to use Howard Erskine-Hill's suggestive phrase, supplies a mirror image of the 'preceding bad reign'.[7] But could Charles Edward Stuart rather than Frederick Louis also be reflected in that mirror? Bolingbroke's very lack of specificity, as recent critics have surmised, might deliberately have been designed to leave the role open to either Hanoverian or Stuart, as the occasion might arise. If the crown fits, the prince should wear it.

A further question posed by the *Patriot King*, one closely related to the question of Stuart monarchy, lies in the constitutional and political nature of Bolingbroke's account of kingship. The work is not simply a paean to a good prince. In its earlier stages it grapples (or seems to grapple) with the problems of hereditary and elective origins of monarchy. It repudiates the divine right of kings, asserting that the only divine right British kings can claim is 'a divine right to govern *well* and conformably to the constitution at the head of which they are placed'.[8] Bolingbroke, as many critics have noted, was trying to appeal to all-comers, both Whigs and Tories, by synthesizing seemingly incompatible monarchical languages, tapping both elements of Whiggish legalism and contractualism as well as an unmistakable element of divine monarchical presence and power. Herbert Atherton writes that the *Patriot King* is an 'ingenious conjunction' of the 'majesty and assertiveness of Stuart Kingship with the constitutionalism of the Revolution Settlement . . . Tory romance and Whig ideals'.[9]

A PATRIOT KING is the most powerful of all reformers; for he himself is a sort of standing miracle, so rarely seen and so little understood, that the sure effects of his appearance will be admiration and love in every honest breast, confusion and terror to every guilty conscience, but submission and resignation in all. A new people will seem to arise with a new king. (pp. 84–5)

---

[6] See Varey, 'Hanover, Stuart and the *Patriot King*', 168–9.

[7] Erskine-Hill, 'Pope: The Political Poet', 39.

[8] Bolingbroke, *Letters on the Spirit of Patriotism and on The Idea of a Patriot King*, ed. A. Hassall (Oxford 1917), 54. All future quotations are taken from this edn. and incorporated in the text. The only modern edn. of the *Patriot King* (not readily available in the UK) is edited by Sydney K. Jackman (Indianapolis, 1965).

[9] Atherton, *Political Prints*, 141.

The appeal to a messianic, charismatic monarch, the 'Deliverer of His Country', is a familiar strain in Jacobite rhetoric.[10] This may well have attracted Frederick's Tory supporters in the late 1740s, especially after the failure of the '45 when the Prince was inviting a 'legitimist transferral' of Tory Jacobite support to his cause.[11] But it must be remembered that in the late 1730s, the majority of Frederick's supporters were Hanoverian Whigs. Those poets and playwrights who wrote Patriot King poems and plays, many of them quite independently of Bolingbroke and his ideas, were writing not from within a Tory-Stuart idiom but from within a Whig-Hanoverian idiom.

Whigs and Hanoverians

In recent years historians have been engaging in a searching reappraisal of seventeenth- and eighteenth-century conceptions of kingship. It is now widely asserted that contract theory, especially of a Lockian kind, played little part in the debate over the legality of the Revolution of 1688.[12] Monarchy was neither secularized nor demystified by the Glorious Revolution nor by the 1702 Act of Settlement. William III and later George I and George II claimed their entitlement primarily by providential right to the throne, but, as Straka notes, in William's case the 'divine right of providence' functioned as a form of theological endorsement for his legal position as *de facto* monarch.[13] George I and George II also stressed in addition their hereditary right to the throne. In 1714 George I attempted to scotch Whig claims that he had been granted his title by the 'free consent of the people' through Parliament by asserting that he came to Britain as a ruler by hereditary right, that right having been made extinct 'only for Catholic members of the House of Stuart'.[14] The Hanoverians certainly repudiated the 'slavish' Stuart doctrines of divine indefeasible hereditary right and passive obedience, but their apologists, most notably (of course)

---

[10] See Paul Monod, *Jacobitism and the English People, 1688–1788* (Cambridge, 1989), 70–92. See esp. p. 72; 'Seeing the king's picture, in other words, would result in an instant recognition, and a sudden conversion'; and p. 36: 'The Restoration . . . brought with it a general revival of morality; it was a cosmic event, modelled on Christ's resurrection.' Bolingbroke's passage echoes the messianic prophecy of the book of Isaiah, frequently used by Stuart panegyrists.

[11] Linda Colley, *In Defiance of Oligarchy: The Tory Party 1714–60* (Cambridge, 1982), 257–60.

[12] See John Locke, *Two Treatises of Government*, ed. Peter Laslett (1960); Gerald M. Straka, *Anglican Reaction to the Revolution of 1688* (Madison, Wis., 1962); J. P. Kenyon, 'The Revolution of 1688: Resistance and Contract', in Neil McKendrick (ed.), *Historical Perspectives: Studies in English Thought and Society* (1974), 43–69; id., *Revolution Principles: The Politics of Party, 1689–1720* (Cambridge, 1977). The argument has been most fully stated and extended into the Hanoverian period by Clark, *English Society*, esp. ch. 3. For recent work on Whig ideals of kingship in the Protestant tradition, see Mark Goldie, 'Priestcraft and the Birth of Whiggism', in Nicholas Phillipson and Quentin Skinner (eds.), *Political Discourse in Early Modern Britain*, (Cambridge, 1993), 201–31.

[13] Straka, *Anglican Reaction*, 65–79.

[14] Ragnild Hatton, *George I, Elector and King* (1978), 119.

in the form of coronation sermons, stressed the age-old sanctity of the monarchy and the due obedience of all loyal subjects to the throne, whose occupant was 'a prince lineally descended from a long race of great progenitors, who for many ages have happily swayed the same august sceptre, which, through the gracious disposal of providence, is now delivered into his sacred hands'.[15] The Hanoverians' literary propagandists engaged in a similarly sacrosanct-sounding form of panegyric to George and Caroline which translates the 'divinity of kings' into poetical terms. George II was the 'great Patron' of 'Sacred Liberty' who will prove 'by Godlike Worth the Right Divine!' Queen Caroline 'Commands OBEDIENCE': 'To *Tory* Doctrines now, the Whigs resign | And, *in her Person*, own the *Right Divine*.'[16]

This idiom, especially its emphasis on the monarch's personal character, conduct, and bearing, his 'divine right to govern *well*', was also shared by Patriot Whigs. If, as Reed Browning suggests, in one sense the Court Whigs were all Hanoverian royalists, then Patriot Whigs were oppositional Hanoverian royalists, whose campaign after 1737 and even before Frederick broke with his father was focused on the legitimate heir to the throne.[17] A paradox emerges from the fact that Patriot Whigs, certainly before 1735, voiced in both Parliament and the press an assertive defence of contract theory in their attempts to curb the influence of Crown power on the Commons. Kings were accountable to and appointed by the nation. In 1734 Bolingbroke's *Dissertation on Parties* had described the king as nothing more than a 'supreme magistrate instituted for the service of the community'.[18] In his *Persian Letters* of 1735 Lyttelton clearly stated that the Act of Settlement was 'A Covenant between the People and their Sovereign. . . . As the Parliament plainly disposed of the Crown in altering the Succession, the Princes who have reigned since that Time, could pretend to none but a *Parliamentary Title*.'[19] The *Craftsman* asserted that the Hanoverians 'have too lately received their Crown from the Hands of the Nation, to forget that it is to them only they owe it'.[20] Such assertions prompted Court writers to defend the Hanoverians' hereditary right to the throne as well as to brand all opposition Whig Patriots as dangerous radicals bent on 'lessening the power of the King and increasing the power of the people' who, if they had their way, would 'reduce this *Monarchy* to a meer *Republick*'.[21]

---

[15] John Potter, *A Sermon Preach'd at the Coronation of King George and Queen Caroline, October 11 1727*, cited in Clark, *English Society*, 177.

[16] John Dryden, *Merlin: Or, The British Inchanter. And King Arthur, The British Worthy. A Dramatic Opera* [rev. William Giffard] (1736), Prologue; Curll, *The Rarities of Richmond* (1736), pp. i–ii.

[17] Reed Browning, *The Political and Constitutional Ideas of the Court Whigs* (Baton Rouge, La., 1982), 199.   [18] Bolingbroke, *Works*, ii. 126.

[19] Lyttelton, *Persian Letters*, 143–4, 138–9.   [20] *Craftsman*, 11 Aug. 1733.

[21] *London Journal*, 29 Sept. 1733; *The Persian Strip'd of His Disguise* (1735), 9. Much of the latter is concerned with defending Hanoverian hereditary right.

However, when it came to a prince to whom the Patriots looked as a royal figurehead for an oppositional campaign designed to rally all supporters under a monarchy above faction or party, they emphasized not the limitations on the prince's role but precisely the opposite. The Machiavellian strain within opposition thought which called for a national *ritorno* after a purging of faction and corruption went with a powerful moral appeal to a redemptive 'great man'.[22]

This was not a new strain in either Whig Williamite or Whig Hanoverian writing. Mark Goldie points out that 'early Whiggery was as capable of deep respect for sound Protestant Kingship, as of denigrating monarchs who failed in this role . . . early Whiggism remained profoundly reverential to monarchy'.[23] In 1720 the radical Whig John Trenchard wrote a eulogistic account of George I asking him to

. . . call up all our antient Virtue, and to restore so great a People to themselves. Almighty God cannot open a larger or nobler Scene to a truly Great Man for the exercise of his Virtues, than to set him at the Head of a corrupted People, that he may have the honour of restoring and reforming them, which is a Glory beyond all the gaudy Triumphs of fabulous and imaginary heroes.[24]

Trenchard claimed that he 'seemed to hear a voice from heaven which promised us a second Redemption'; George has been sent 'by Heaven'—a divine sanction absent from Machiavelli's *The Prince*, which might have otherwise supplied his model. The Machiavellian strong prince operating through his grasp of *fortuna* might have seemed more suitable by this stage as a justification for a Stuart restoration.[25] When the republican deist John Toland listed those 'glorious qualities' which made the Whigs 'admire King George almost to adoration', he listed 'true piety, fortitude, temperance, prudence, justice, knowledge, industry, frugality, and every other virtue'.[26]

Opposition Whig Patriots in the Walpole period condemned the Stuarts' 'monstrous and till then unheard-of Doctrines of Divine Indefeasible Hereditary Right, Passive Obedience & c.'.[27] Yet they credited their Hanoverian prince with personal powers to lead, guide, and transform, which transcended the notion of the king-as-servant. In 1733 Thomson fulsomely

---

[22] See Kramnick, *Bolingbroke and His Circle*, 165–8.

[23] Goldie, 'Priestcraft and the Birth of Whiggism', 215. Goldie's comment, 224, that 'we are accustomed to assume that Whigs identified the autocratic inclinations of the crown as the chief enemy of English liberties', whereas they may have looked to a strong prince committed to Protestant liberty, seems relevant to a later period than the Restoration. Whig Patriots in the 1730s attacked the perverse symbiosis of High-Church episcopal tyranny and Hanoverian monarchy, and many expressed strong anticlerical views.

[24] John Trenchard, *Some Considerations upon the State of Our Publick Debts in General and of the Civil List in Particular* (1720), 31, 11.

[25] See J. G. A. Pocock, *The Machiavellian Moment* (Princeton, NJ, 1975); for the Jacobite argument of a 'restoration to virtue', see Monod, *Jacobitism and the English People*, 36.

[26] John Toland, *Memorial to a Minister of State on the Accession of George I*, cited in C. J. Abbey and J. H. Overton, *The English Church in the Eighteenth Century*, 2 vols. (1878), i. 98.

[27] Thomson, *Liberty*, iv. 970 n.

described Frederick as 'a Prince of his so noble equal humane and generous dispositions . . . Oh happy as a God he, who has it both in his hand and in his heart to make a people happy!'[28] On 20 March 1735 the *Old Whig* defined the monarchical principles of 'true and genuine Whiggism'. While true Whiggism bears 'an irreconcilable and mortal Enmity to Tyrants and Oppressors', none the less

it places benevolent wise and righteous Princes amongst the most exalted Characters of human Life, honours them as the true Vicegerents of Almighty GOD, the best as well as the greatest of beings, and pays them an obedience that is the effect of natural Inclination, and flows equally from a sense of Duty, Gratitude and Interest.[29]

Even the former Filmerian Tory-turned-republican-Whig Robert Craggs Nugent found his ardent Lockianism required readjustment in his role as Frederick's follower. His 1741 *Ode to Mankind* addressed to Prince Frederick, for all its invocation of Locke, Sidney, and Hampden, is a panegyric dedicated to a redemptive Prince.[30] Equally interesting is Henry Brooke's banned Patriot drama *Gustavus Vasa*. Historians of radical thought have detected a Paine-like language of the rights of man: 'Great Nature's Law—the Law within the Breast, | . . . stamp'd by Heav'n upon th'unletter'd Mind'.[31] The play claims the rights of the common man to be equal to the 'sweeping of the proudest Train | That shades a Monarch's Heel'. The young Samuel Johnson, as we shall see, made much radical mileage out of it. Yet Brooke's 'Gothic' Prologue finally rests not on a defence of Gothic parliaments originating in elective kingship but on a thoroughly patriarchal image of monarchy:

The Monarch or Head of such a Constitution, is as the Father of a large and well regulated Family, his Subjects are not Servants, but Sons; their Care, their Affections, their Attachments are reciprocal, and their interest is one, is not to be divided.

Such a monarch partakes of the 'DIVINE INCLINATION'.[32] Brooke's Patriot prince Gustavus, at work in the tin-mines of Dalecarlia, radiates an ineffable mystique:

> Six moons have chang'd upon the Face of Night,
> Since here he first arriv'd, in servile Weeds,
> But yet of Mein majestic. I observ'd him,
> And ever as I gaz'd, some nameless Charm,
> A wond'rous Greatness not to be conceal'd
> Broke thro' his Form, and aw'd my Soul before him.[33]

---

[28] Thomson, *Letters*, 83. [29] *Old Whig*, 20 Mar. 1735.
[30] Nugent, *An Ode to Mankind: Address'd to the Prince of Wales* (1741). For Nugent's political views, see Romney Sedgwick, *The History of Parliament: The House of Commons 1715–1754*, 2 vols. (1970), ii. 302.
[31] Brooke, *Gustavus Vasa: or, The Deliverer of His Country* (1739), Prologue. For radical readings, see *Yale Johnson*, x. 52.
[32] *Gustavus Vasa*, 9; Prefatory Dedication, p. vii. [33] Ibid. 3–4.

One critic wryly commented that Gustavus and other kings in Patriot drama such as Thomson's Alfred, emanate an unmistakable royal aura. Their 'je ne scai quoi heroical fashion, in taking a walk, or sitting down on a bank, betray[s] an air of majesty that you know may be a compliment to our countrymen . . . that, like lions, they can smell the blood royal'.[34] Brooke was an assertively Whig dramatist who held no truck with Jacobites, but it is easy to see why hostile critics chose to interpret this play as a covert Jacobite drama.[35]

We know a good deal about satirical representations of George II in popular prints and satires—far less about more positive appraisals of his kingship.[36] But if the prints and poems tell us anything, it is about the qualities of kingship which were widely regarded as missing from his reign. Linda Colley has argued that the Hanoverians were respected not for who they were but for what they stood for—Protestantism, stability, reason, and caution.[37] Neither George I nor George II could claim to be 'Patriot' monarchs in either the political or the national sense of the term. Both were party-political kings, identified with Whig oligarchy rather than with a Patriot programme of government above faction or party. George II's reliance on Walpole prompted either the more charitable representation of him as a 'King in Toils' or less flattering images of puppet-kings and puppet-masters. More deep-seated were the doubts about both George I and George II's divided national loyalties, with Hanoverian interests too frequently gaining the upper hand. George II's heavily accented English was a common source of ridicule; even more so his frequent extended visits to Hanover, known to be dictated at least in part by his unpatriotic amours with German mistresses such as Madame Walmoden. He plumbed the depths of his unpopularity during his six-month extended stay in Hanover between the summer of 1736 and the start of January 1737. His return crossing in the January gales seemed to show a singular indifference to British anxiety about the safety of their monarch. It was at this time that rumours began to circulate about a move to establish Frederick on the throne.

Were George and Caroline unable or unwilling to cultivate a popular image? Linda Colley presses the case too far in claiming the complete absence of 'a popular cult of the monarchy' and 'of royal ceremonial, public display and propaganda' under the first two Georges.[38] George I's triumphal entry into the city in 1714 took three hours so that due respects to the new sovereign could be paid.[39] George II's coronation in 1727 was a spectacular affair, the opportu-

---

[34] *Letters of Mrs. Elizabeth Montagu*, ed. Matthew Montagu, cited in A. D. McKillop, 'The Early History of *Alfred*', *PQ* 41 (1962), 311–24, p. 315.

[35] For Brooke's anti-Jacobitism, see below, Ch. 8.

[36] See Atherton, *Political Prints*, 142–6, plates 19, 28, 45, 46. There is no political biography of George II. But see J. B. Owen, 'George II Reconsidered', in A. Whiteman, J. Bromley, and P. G. M. Dickson (eds.), *Statesmen, Scholars and Merchants* (Oxford, 1973), 113–34.

[37] Linda Colley, *Britons: Forging the Nation, 1707–1837* (New Haven, Conn., 1992), 202.

[38] Ibid. 201, 203.

[39] See Rogers, *Whigs and Cities*, 357–8.

nity for the City to demonstrate its loyalty to the new regime by expensive civic festivities and theatrical performances: a lavishly mounted event energetically promoted to bolster a still fragile dynasty.[40] The Princess Royal married the Prince of Orange in 1734 in an impressive candlelit ceremony, prints of which were widely on sale. Lord Hervey observed that George II 'loved a show better than his daughter' or he would have saved the expense and given her a larger dowry.[41] Caroline's eagerness to popularize the House of Hanover is at least hinted at by her publicity exercises in Merlin's Cave and the widespread attention given to the pro-Hanoverian production of Dryden's *King Arthur* in 1735–6. But the harmonious relations between King and 'cits' rapidly evaporated after the coronation honeymoon. George's high-handed dealings with the Mayor and Aldermen on the occasion of Anne's marriage in 1734 (he refused them permission to kiss his hand) led to widespread resentment and alienation.[42] Neither George nor Caroline were prepared to appear to the London crowds. Their notion of popular contact seems epitomized by the exercise of admitting ticket-holders to watch the royal Sunday lunch being consumed from behind the safety of a roped-off walkway.[43] Neither George I nor George II ever made royal progresses to the provinces as had their Stuart predecessors. The 'nostalgia' for Elizabeth's reign was at one level nostalgia for a popular patriotic monarch, the Elizabeth of the Tilbury Docks speech offering her hand and heart to her people. Royal dignity, grace, and bearing were conspicuously absent from the domestic wrangles of St James's. The petulant kicking king who turned his ample royal posterior on those who incurred his displeasure was, of course, the central figure of the famous 1737 print *The Festival of the Golden Rump*. Caroline may have been more popular and her death genuinely lamented. A print which carried the date of her death, 20 November 1737, and which undoubtedly referred in some way to the event, was called *The Glory of Old England*. But it was an odd kind of compliment. 'Old England's Glory' was represented here not by Caroline but by an engraving of Queen Anne, to whom the oppositional Sarah Duchess of Marlborough had recently erected a statue at Blenheim.[44] The memory of Anne, last reigning Stuart, the last monarch to exercise the practice of touching for the King's Evil, remained strong. In 1731 Swift, no Jacobite, looked back to Anne's reign and noted that 'Things are strangely changed since then, | And *Kings* are now no more than *Men*; | From whence 'tis plain, they quite

[40] See Pat Rogers, *Literature and Popular Culture in Eighteenth-Century England* (Brighton, 1985), 120–50.

[41] Hervey, *Memoirs*, i. 263–72, quotation p. 271. See also Michael Wilson, *William Kent: Architect, Designer, Painter, Gardener, 1685–1748* (1984), 133–4.

[42] *Egmont Diary*, ii. 67; Hervey, *Memoirs*, i. 280–1.

[43] See Averyl Edwards, *Frederick Louis, Prince of Wales, 1707–1751* (1947), 16.

[44] *BMC* no. 2331. The statue inspired a poem advertised in the *Daily Post*, 1 June 1737, *On the much lamented Death of the most pious and illustrious Princess, her late Majesty Queen Anne*. For the oppositional uses of the statue, see *Common Sense*, 18 Mar. 1738.

have lost | God's *Image*, which was once their Boast'.[45] *The Glory of Old England*, like the Blenheim statue, carried the legend:

Queen Anne was very graceful & Majestic in her Person. Religious without *Affectation*, she always meant well. She had no *false Ambition* . . . Upon her Accession to the Throne the Civil list was not increased . . . She was extremely well bred . . . Her behaviour to all that approach'd Her was decent & full of Dignity, and shew'd *Condescention* without *Art* or *Meanness*.[46]

'Extremely well bred', 'decent & full of Dignity', '*Condescention* without *Art* or *Meanness*'—we are not far from the idiom of Bolingbroke's *Patriot King*.

Rival Princes

When Bolingbroke wrote the *Patriot King* he contributed to an existing cult of Hanoverian princely myth-making, one which Frederick himself had done much to foster. Colley speculates that residual Jacobite sentiment in Britain might have been 'at base a far more neutral hunger for a sentimental, highly-coloured royalism that the early Hanoverians left unsatisfied'.[47] This may not fully explain the persistence of Jacobitism, but it does supply a context for one element in Frederick's own self-constructed princely identity: his association with Stuartism. The history of the rival 'Princes of Wales' deserves further exploration, not least the mutually interchangeable set of political languages and princely images both deployed. Both James and his son Charles appropriated the language of the Patriot opposition, holding out tempting inducements of a new era of constitutional government free from corruption and party division. In the '45 Charles sounded more Whiggish than Whig Patriots, proclaiming 'Would you have your Constitution restor'd? Would you have your Liberties secured against all future encroachments?'[48] The millennial image of the Patriot King was a staple feature of the political platform constructed by both Frederick's and Charles Edward Stuart's supporters: as Monod remarks, 'it is debatable as to who was copying whom'.[49]

Frederick's fascination with the Stuarts achieved some notoriety after the

---

[45] Swift, 'A Panegyric on the Reverend Dean Swift', in *Poetical Works*, ed. Herbert Davis (Oxford, 1967), 435.

[46] *BMC* no. 2331.   [47] Colley, *Britons*, 202.

[48] See W. A. Speck, *The Butcher: The Duke of Cumberland and the Suppression of the '45* (Oxford, 1981), 23–4. For the 'Whiggish' Jacobites, see Monod, *Jacobitism and the English People*, 23–7.

[49] Ibid. 85. For an interesting argument about Frederick's instatement into the Freemasons in 1737 and its overlap with Jacobitism and Freemasonry, see P. Jenkins, 'Jacobites and Freemasons in 18th-century Wales', *Welsh History Review*, 9 (1979), 391–406, esp. 401–2. For the opposing Jacobite and Patriot Whig arguments for a 'revolution' in 1739 based on the rival focuses of Frederick and the Pretender, see Eveline Cruickshanks, *Political Untouchables: The Tories and the '45* (1979), 17.

'45 when he intervened on behalf of the rebel Jacobite lords and employed the sister of the Pretender's mistress Catharine Walkinshaw as Augusta's maid of honour.[50] Frederick was reputedly seen walking round in plaid at the Middlesex election of 1750.[51] By this stage Frederick was angling for the support of disappointed Jacobite Tories and signalling his separation from the atrocities of his brother William's military campaign, a campaign from which he had been excluded. But Frederick's interest in the Stuarts and particularly what he considered to be the Stuart style of monarchy had begun well before. Frederick conspicuously modelled his artistic tastes and his royal collection on those of his famous art-loving predecessor Charles I.[52] This was a far cry from his mother's hostile reaction on catching sight of a bust of James I during a 1735 visit to Rysbrack's studio: 'she turnd about & said—fi il me semble a une Boureau I wont have that done, she said'. Frederick's friend the pro-Stuart engraver Vertue (the pair met, appropriately, when Vertue was copying Van Dyck's portrait of Charles I at Hampton Court) noted wryly that 'one may guess, she forgot from whence her succession came'.[53] When Frederick saw himself as a prince, it was as a flamboyant crowd-drawing quasi-Stuart rather than as a dull Hanoverian Elector. He was trying to re-create himself as a British prince, one marrying the emotional appeal of the Stuarts to the solid merits of Hanoverian Protestantism. In 1728, shortly after Frederick's arrival in Britain, Thomas Rundle noted that

He is one universally beloved in the town . . . He . . . knows how to familiarise his greatness, and make it more amiable, without making it less awful. He is sprightly beyond all things; and is above the mean-spirited sullenness that often hath been mistaken for majesty; and he seems to think the way to be beloved is to shew in reality good qualities, instead of requiring people to believe he hath them. . . . PLATO rightly says, that beauty is only the soul and temper made visible, and if that is true, how delightful is the grace which flows from the social and sweet virtues.[54]

The most visible example of Frederick's princely image-making was the royal barge he commissioned from William Kent in 1732. Elaborately carved, gilded, and adorned with dolphins, scallop shells, and the Prince of Wales's feathers, it took up a large part of his expendable income that year.[55] Accompanied by boatmen in gold-filigree rococo costumes and sometimes by an entire string-ensemble following in another boat, Frederick made his progresses up and down the Thames, waving his hat at the cheering crowds. He used it to carry Augusta up the Thames in 1736; 'the ships saluted their

---

[50] Colley, *In Defiance of Oligarchy*, 257. [51] *Walpole Correspondence*, xx. 131.

[52] Stephen Jones, *Frederick, Prince of Wales and His Circle* (Sudbury, Suffolk, 1981), 15–18.

[53] *The Notebooks of George Vertue*, 7 vols., Walpole Society Annual Volumes 18, 20, 22, 24, 26, 29, 30 (numbered *Vertue Notebooks* i–vi; Vol. 29—the index vol.—is unnumbered) (Oxford and London, 1930–55), iii. 75. [54] Rundle, *Letters*, ii. 47–8.

[55] There are numerous contemporary accounts of the barge, now housed in the National Maritime Museum at Greenwich. For an extravagant Cleopatran simile by Lady Irwin, see *Carlisle MSS*, 174. See also Wilson, *William Kent*, 130–3, plates 49, 50, 51.

Highnesses all the way they pass'd, and hung out their Streamers and Colours, and the River was cover'd with Boats'. The same report tells of the pair dining at Greenwich, 'the Windows being thrown open, to oblige the Curiosity of the People'.[56] Lord Hervey contemptuously noted Frederick's 'vulgar' habit of holding late-night musical concerts at Kensington with all the windows thrown open for the gathering crowds to watch 'this royal object of theatrical attention'.[57] As we have seen, Frederick was busy creating his own 'court culture' even before he set up a separate establishment, hosting a full-dress rehearsal for the Opera of Nobility's *Arianna* in his royal apartments at St James's in 1735. He and his supporters were trying to capture the popularity which George and Caroline never fully attracted. In 1735 Lady Irwin wrote from the court to her husband in Yorkshire:

I delivered your message to the Prince . . . he should one day be able to make you a visit at Castle Howard. He has a great inclination to make a progress, but I believe that will never be allowed till he is king, his popularity having already given offence; so nothing will be suffered to increase that.[58]

This rivalry peaked between 1736 and 1738 after Frederick's popular marriage and George's subsequent disappearance to Hanover. At the very time that George was reported missing in the briny waves, a fire broke out on 6 January 1737 in the Temple in London. Frederick stepped in to help, staying up all night to wield buckets and encourage workmen. It was Charles II, the Great Fire of London, and Dryden's *Annus Mirabilis* all over again in miniature, celebrated this time by a painter rather than a poet.[59] Lady Irwin noted the 'mad multitude's caress': the contrast between absent father and omnipresent son 'makes the unreasonable populace so extravagantly angry that 'tis not to be imagined the outrageous things that is every day spoken against the King and on the other hand how exceeding the Prince is caressed by all ranks'.[60] On the day that George was hissed and booed as he walked through the London streets after his safe return, Frederick capitalized on his popularity by bestowing bankbills worth £500 on needy debtors in London jails; he had, as Egmont noted, some 'wise heads about him'.[61]

In hard political terms probably the most important aspect of this cultivation of a princely personality cult lay in Frederick's courtship of the 'cits' in both London and other trading cities such as Bristol. He won for himself a special place in the merchants' hearts by his public declarations of his concern

---

[56] *GM* 6 (1736), 231.   [56] *GM* 6 (1736), 231.   [57] Hervey, *Memoirs*, i. 310.
[58] *Carlisle MSS*, 158.

[59] The picture was by Richard Wilson whose cousin Charles Pratt, a lawyer, knew Lyttelton. The scene is of the Temple the morning after the fire: Frederick wearing the ribbon of the Garter stands in the middle of the scene surrounded by spectators. The painting is not very accomplished but it is hard to agree with Kimerly Rorschach, 'Frederick, Prince of Wales (1707–51) as a Patron of the Visual Arts: Princely Patriotism and Political Propaganda' (Yale Ph.D. thesis, 1985), 109, that it 'trivialises' Frederick.

[60] *Carlisle MSS*, 175–6.   [61] *Egmont Diary*, ii. 330.

for trade and commerce. Frederick's role as a Patriot Prince protective of British trade and a future 'father of his people' was played out to the full in the royal progress he and Augusta made in their tour to Bath and Bristol in October–November 1738. The people of both cities greeted them with a wild adulation which smacked of the royal 'entries' made by previous Stuart monarchs. After accepting the Freedom of Bath and the post of Lord High Steward, Frederick moved on to Bristol where he was 'received with all the Joy and Solemnity imaginable'. Triumphal arches, scaffolds, and pageants marked the route taken by the royal couple, who witnessed an extraordinary display of civic pride from various guildsmen bearing crowns, swords, and sceptres made of glass. Their progress was marked by 121 gun salutes, and the whole occasion was rounded off by an extravagant civic banquet in which 'the Princess talked freely with the Ladies in good *English*, which entirely won their Hearts'. Frederick made a speech stressing his particular wishes for the advancement of trade 'which is so valuable an Effect of Liberty, and so strong a Support of the Honour and Happiness of this Nation'.[62] The event invited many newspaper tributes, including the poetical. Most striking is this contribution by one 'R. N.' from Bath, published in the December issue of the *Gentleman's Magazine*—a Tudor-style 'gratulatorie' poem celebrating 'the Prince's entry to the City':

> With secret Joy I saw the ROYAL YOUTH,
> A friend to Britain, Liberty and Truth,
> Enter our Gates; but not a Guard appear'd,
> Lest it should seem the God-like *Frederick* fear'd.
> So great *Elizabeth*, whose glorious Name
> Shall live forever in the Voice of Fame,
> Spoke with Contempt on Guards (those useless Things)
> The fit Concomitant of fearful Kings.
> Thus she: That Prince the best Protection finds,
> Who reigns the Monarch of his People's Minds.[63]

Frederick's Elizabethan Bristol 'entry' poem of 1738 should be juxtaposed with Isaac Kramnick's critical account of Bolingbroke's *Patriot King*.

Bolingbroke devoted the last pages of his essay to a minute description of the desirable private and public character of this King. He outlined his proper education, upbringing, social dealings, all of which were designed to make him a 'great and good man'. Bolingbroke's retreat into humanism is completed when he offers 'a mirror for princes', an 'education for a Christian Prince', a 'book for governors'. With this minute description of princely deportment, the *Patriot King* also becomes the most ludicrous example of Bolingbroke's insistence on the theatrical image of politics over the administrative image. How appropriate, then, that the essay ends by invoking that greatest and most dazzling of all political actors—Elizabeth.[64]

---

[62] The account is in *GM* 8 (1738), 602–4.   [63] Ibid. 655.
[64] Kramnick, *Bolingbroke and His Circle*, 168.

Bolingbroke's emphasis on royal image-making of the Elizabethan variety should not be dismissed so lightly. Recent historical scholarship on the Hanoverian period has paid far more attention than it did in the 1960s (when this passage was written) to royal rituals of power, the mythologizing of the monarch through public appearances, ceremony, and display. As Pat Rogers reminds us, 'politics is drama as well as ideology, and the public awareness of major issues is rarely as minutely attentive as their observation of impressive spectacle'.[65] By 1738 Frederick was already well-versed in the art of presenting himself to the public as Elizabeth's spiritual heir. Read in the context of the widespread cult of Elizabethan sentiment which reached a peak in 1738–9 as pressure mounted for war with Spain, the *Patriot King*'s invocation of that great royal actress, Elizabeth, might seem timely rather than absurdly anachronistic.

Of Royal Education

The *Patriot King* is indeed, as Kramnick observes, an educative manual for the guidance of a Christian prince. Its most famous predecessors were Renaissance works such as Petrarch's *De republicae optime administranda*, Erasmus's *Institutio* and, of course, Machiavelli's *The Prince*. Bolingbroke's debt to Machiavelli is apparent in the *Patriot King*'s frequent references to Machiavelli's famous treatise; and the two works look even closer when one compares the chapter headings inserted in the rare *c.*1740 edition of the *Patriot King* with those of *The Prince*.[66] The *Patriot King*, like much of Bolingbroke's political writing (and indeed like much earlier oppositional writing) draws heavily on Machiavellian corruption theory for its diagnosis of Britain's decline. The body politic, like the natural body, is prone to decay. The nation must be regularly refounded, brought back to first principles if it is not to perish. Machiavelli's prescription for regeneration lay in a strong prince, whose *virtù* was not necessarily always virtuous. Bolingbroke follows Machiavelli in appealing to the prince as a powerful source of leadership, although the *Patriot King* is anti-Machiavelli in so far as it takes issue with Machiavellian morality. Bolingbroke 'would have the virtue real: he [Machiavelli] requires no more than the appearance of it' (*Patriot King*, 71).

Jeffrey Hart has explored the parallels between the *Patriot King* and not only *The Prince* but a whole tradition of classical, medieval, and Renaissance advice-to-princes texts.[67] This merely reaffirms the widely held view that by 1738 Bolingbroke, the 'Tory Humanist' poring over the contents of his library,

---

[65] Rogers, *Literature and Popular Culure*, 145.

[66] Printed and compared in Jeffrey Hart, *Viscount Bolingbroke, Tory Humanist* (Toronto, 1965), 86–7.

[67] See ibid., esp. pp. 83–163.

had become entirely detached from political reality. Hanoverian Britain was not sixteenth-century Florence, nor was Bolingbroke an Erasmus, a Petrarch, or a Castiglione, tempering advice with flattery to guide a potential tyrant ruler. But there was a more immediate context for princely education which makes the concerns of the *Patriot King* seem far less outmoded. The education of Hanoverian princes during the reign of the first three Georges was a subject of considerable public interest and not a small amount of political controversy. The row which erupted over Lord Bute's suspected indoctrination of the young George III in 'Jacobite principles' prompted a royal enquiry and the resignation of his preceptors. Horace Walpole, who played a major part in stirring up the rumours, asserted that 'the education of a Prince of Wales is an object of the utmost importance for the whole nation' which 'should be entrusted to noblemen of the most unblemished honour'.[68] Princely education had also been a debating-point in the preceding decades. The row between George I and his son in 1717 was in large measure over the education of the royal grandchildren. The question was even put to the legal test when ten out of twelve English judges opined that George I had rights of supervision—which he subsequently took. Furthermore, George II and Frederick, the heirs to the British throne, were left behind to be raised in the Hanoverian court when their parents came to England. Jacobites made much of the dangers of autocratic Lutheran German princes accustomed to absolutist forms of rule to minimize, by comparison, the associations between the Stuarts and political despotism. In 1742 the Tory MP John St Aubyn complained that 'we live under a Prince who being used to arbitrary power in his dominions abroad, was minded to establish it here'.[69] Few British subjects would have shared this view in such undiluted form. Of more immediate concern was the fear that the Prince of Wales would come to England trained in 'foreign' ways and with his loyalties already divided. Could a Hanoverian prince be a British, indeed a 'Patriot' prince? Would he care for the liberties, welfare, and loyalty of his subjects? In 1720 'Cato' complained that the government was paying scant regard to Frederick's education abroad. 'They know that it is of great Concernment to any People, that the Heir apparent to the Crown be bred amongst them . . . that he may grow reconciled to their Customs and Laws, and grow in Love with their Liberties.'[70] Richard Blackmore's concerns over the national royal identity crisis prompted him in 1723 to exhibit to the 16-year-old Frederick the exemplary model of Alfred in a very British variety of *de regimine principis* writing, his *Alfred: An Epick Poem*. In his dedication, he asserted that

---

[68] See John Brooke, *King George III* (1972), 28, 35–40.

[69] Cited in Eveline Cruickshanks, 'The Political Management of Sir Robert Walpole, 1720–42', in Jeremy Black (ed.), *Britain in the Age of Walpole* (1984), 23–43, quotation p. 30.

[70] *London Journal*, 25 Mar. 1720; response in the ministerial the *Patriot*, 3 Apr. 1720.

The Welfare and Glory of a People so much depend upon the wise Administration and powerful Example of an excellent King, that he who loves his Country, and wishes well to Mankind, cannot chuse a more effectual Means to promote their Happiness, than by inspiring into a young Prince such generous Sentiment, such just Idea's of political Prudence, and such an honourable Ambition of becoming a publick Blessing, as may form his Mind for Empire, and the steady Direction of the Reins of Government.[71]

Advice-to-princes manuals were still enjoying a vigorous life on the Continent in France and especially Germany. Philosophers such as Leibniz and Fénelon, both of whom shared the Enlightenment faith in the power of education, wrote treatises for the guidance of future monarchs—Leibniz's essay 'Le Projet de l'éducation d'un prince' (1693) and Fénelon's famous *Les Aventures de Télémaque* (1699). The mode became even more popular later in the century. Both these authors were writing in countries where absolutist monarchy still seemed an enduring fact, and where princely qualities such as 'wisdom', 'virtue', and 'moderation' could usefully temper tyrannical tendencies. Character formation was the chief goal, since 'it is necessary that a prince be a man of goodness, a man of heart, a man of judgment, as well as an honest man'.[72] Fénelon's *Télémaque* even reverses the role of subject and tutor by 'sacramentalizing' the prince's guide in the figure of Astrea/ Minerva, leading the prince on a grand educational tour through a fictional landscape. The Tory Hanoverian Delarivier Manley appropriated Fénelon's model for her *New Atalantis* of 1709, written in part to address the moral education of the future George II being raised by his grandmother Sophia, since 'the young Prince descended from her, born indeed with generous Inclinations, is in danger of suffering under the greatest of Misfortunes, the want of Royal Education'. Manley's aim is to 'make him deserving to be Great, as well as to be so, and of the two, rather to be Good than Mighty', to 'render a Hero truly such, fond of the improvement of his People's Good, both in War and Peace, cautious of their Safety, and yet, wisely expensive of his own'.[73]

Bolingbroke, closely in touch with Enlightenment thought, would have been familiar with both Fénelon and Leibniz. So would Frederick, who probably learnt French, like many other Germans, through the help of *Télémaque*, which was standard reading for German noblemen. William Coxe later compared the *Patriot King* with *Télémaque*, since both works 'bribe the imagination' with 'scenes of domestic felicity'.[74] The generic parallels are not close, but the aims of both were not dissimilar. Far closer to the *Patriot King* in its concern with the models of kingship which former English monarchs could offer to Hanoverian princes is Daniel Defoe's *Of Royall Educacion*, written

---

[71] Richard Blackmore, *Alfred: An Epick Poem* (1723), Dedication.

[72] Cited in Gabrielle Bercier, 'The Education of the Prince: Wieland and German Enlightenment at School with Fénelon and Rousseau', *Eighteenth-Century Life*, 10 (1986), 1–13, p. 2.

[73] Delarivier Manley, *Secret Memoirs and Manners of Several Persons of Quality, of Both Sexes, from the New Atalantis, An Island in the Mediterranean* (1709), 7–8. For the history and influence of the work, see Manley, *New Atalantis*, ed. R. Ballaster (1991).

[74] Coxe, *Walpole*, i. 213.

some time in the 1720s. This work was inspired by the controversies over the education of Hanoverian princes.[75] It was aimed at 'such illustrious branches as are by their birth and blood to succeed to kings and to the thrones and governments of their country, whether by apparent or presumptive heirship' (pp. 7–8). Defoe writes for the 'protestant succession from Germany' and its 'numerous royall issue', the 'princes of the Blood now properly call'd such' (pp. 60–1). The Whiggish Defoe's notions of the 'souls of princes, men of nobility in birth and blood' (p. 3) contain some very un-Lockian mystical traits. 'When education does adorn | The minds of children nobly born, | They seem to spring of some angelick race, | Of some, of some angelic race.'

In some ways, *Of Royall Educacion* bears a striking resemblance to the *Patriot King*. Defoe's treatise is not fictional or utopian but historical—a voyage through the reigns of good and bad English monarchs not unlike the format deployed in the *Craftsman*'s historical essays and (in a more modified form) in the *Patriot King*. History affords instructive lessons for future monarchs, explicitly the lessons set by patriotic British monarchs such as Henry V, Henry VII, and the Elizabeth whom Defoe gave hints of planning to eulogize before circumstances forced him to curtail his work. The modernist Defoe refuses to romanticize the feudal past. Before Henry VII, most reigns were 'meerly military', when 'The phylosopher had been discouraged and thrust out of court by the soldier, and our princes, instead of the book in their hands, have put the helmet on their heads' (p. 15). Henry VII is Defoe's real hero, even more than the martial Henry V, because it was he who first supported and encouraged the widespread growth of the wool trade and established England as a modern commercial nation.

Bolingbroke probably did not know Defoe's *Of Royall Educacion*, but it shares some of the *Patriot King*'s salient features, not least its idealization of a body politic united under a benevolent monarch who champions trade and commerce. Commerce and world trade were subjects on which Renaissance advice-to-princes manuals had little to say. Even Machiavelli's *The Prince* did not address the issue; as David Hume noted, 'There is not a word of Trade in all Matchiavel, which is strange considering that Florence rose only by trade'.[76] Defoe ascribes to his Henry VII some of the qualities Bolingbroke saw in Elizabeth. It was he, Defoe argues, who had first 'lay'd the foundation of all the wealth and greatness which England now enjoys by the advantage of commerce' (p. 44).

---

[75] Daniel Defoe, *Of Royall Educacion: A Fragmentary Treatise*, ed. Karl D. Bülbring (1895), pp. x–xv. Bülbring dates the latter section of the work to *c*.1728 and claims that the first part was written not long before. The interruption may have been caused either by George I's quarrel with his father or by the accession of George II in 1727. All further quotations inc. in text. Manuel Schonhorn, *Defoe's Politics: Parliament, Power, Kingship and 'Robinson Crusoe'* (Cambridge, 1991), 8, 96, 20, discusses this work but misrepresents its political context and its dominant concerns. Defoe does not idealize Old Testament martial heroes to the extent he suggests.

[76] Ernest Campbell Mossner (ed.), 'Hume's Early Memoranda, 1729–40: The Complete Text', *Journal of the History of Ideas*, 9 (1948), 508. This section is dated to *c*.1737–40.

Of Royall Educacion's pattern of good and bad reigns lends it a satiric dimension—one which it shares with those early issues of the *Craftsman* which probably appeared around the time Defoe was writing it. He was later charged, as he notes, with writing 'a pointed satyr at our own times and that I am preparing to fall upon the particular conduct of familyes and persons' (p. 60). The seditious implications emerge in his 'pointed' use of historical arche-types such as the contrast between the weak Henry III, manipulated by his favourite Hugo de Bourg, who 'was not onely Lord Chief Justice, but Lord Chief Minister as he might be call'd, for he manag'd not only the realme for the King but the King too . . . Heavens grant we may never see the like reign of favourites' (pp. 23–4).[77] The contrasting and idealized portrait of Henry VII might have been taken directly from Bolingbroke's *Patriot King*. Henry knew that

the wealth of the subjects is the strength of a king, and that therefore a prince, even for his own sake, ought to study what might most conduce to the prosperity of the people who he was to govern, knowing that, while he by such a care for their benefit engag'd their affecions, they would allways make a double return in fidelity and love . . . to make them wealthy would be to make himself strong, a prince's glory being truly inseparable from his people's good. (pp. 43–4)[78]

There are even verbal parallels. Defoe praises the king's increase of the national prosperity 'by the advantages of commerce and by the improvements of trade and manufactures' (p. 42). Bolingbroke observes that 'The wealth and power of all nations depending so much on their trade and commerce . . . the government of a PATRIOT KING, will be directed constantly to make the most of every advantage that nature has given, or art can procure, towards the improvement of trade and commerce' (*Patriot King*, p. 17). Defoe's comment that 'the wealth of the subjects is the strength of the king' (p. 43) anticipates Bolingbroke's statement 'the wealth of the nation he will most justly esteem to be his wealth' (*Patriot King*, p. 120). Just as Defoe's Henry VII was educated as a prince in the 'state of afflicion . . . and afflicion may be esteem'd one of the best schools for the education of a prince' (p. 38) so Bolingbroke's Patriot King would similarly 'be formed in that school out of which the greatest and the best of monarchs have come, the school of affliction' (*Patriot King*, p. 69). Both these works justify at the outset their *raison d'être*—the need for royal education. Defoe asserts that

Those that think the education of princes needless, and that the most early polishing and refining their understandings and genius by instruccion and learning is out of the

---

[77] The *Old Whig*, 8 May 1735, contained an attack on Walpole under the ironic pseudonym 'Hugo de Burgo'. In 1738 Thomson's *Edward and Eleanora* was censored for dramatizing the contrast between Henry III and his superior son Edward.

[78] Cf. Pope's Patriot King poem *1740* (*TE* iv. 337): 'Esteem the public love his best supply, | A [king's] true glory his integrity; | Rich with *his* [Britain] in *his* [Britain] strong.'

way; that they are above what we call teaching and tutoring in their infancy, or instilling principles of vertue and glory into their minds . . . those who think thus think in a manner too grossly almost to mencion. (p. 4)

Bolingbroke argues that

the characters of princes are spoiled many more ways by their *education*. I shall not descend into a detail of such particulars, nor presume so much as to hint what regulations might be made about the *education of princes*, nor what part our *parliaments* might take occasionally in this momentous affair, lest I should appear too refining or too presumptuous in my speculations. But I may assert that the indifference of mankind on this head, especially in a government constituted like ours, is monstrous. (*Patriot King*, p. 64)

Both writers focus not only on the king's moral substance but on his royal decorum, grace, and 'decency of manners', deploying images of polishing, refinement, and works of art as metaphors for the outward displays of kingship.[79] Both Defoe and Bolingbroke emphasize the need for a circle of trustworthy wise men surrounding the king, 'counsellors and advisers of their princes'.

Defoe's work was not published in his own time. Accusations of a satirical intention led him first to lie about the date of its composition (he claimed to have written it for Anne's last surviving son, not for George I or George II), then to abandon the scheme for royal education and adopt a new design—the education of the English gentry. But the theory behind royal educational manuals was clearly not too outmoded for a wider audience. The *Gentleman's Magazine* of 1740 printed two long extracts four months apart from a purportedly French work entitled *The Institution of a Prince: Or, A Treatise on the Qualities, Vertues and Duties of the Sovereign*, coupled with a long disquisition on princely education and on an ideal polity in which the king governs his people 'with a Union like that of his Father and his Children'.[80]

I should like to return to the political circumstances in which the *Patriot King* was first written. Bolingbroke probably composed it when he was staying in England, ostensibly for the sale of Dawley between July 1738 and August 1739. The date at the head of the printed version of 1749 is 1 December 1738. Some critics have suggested that its utopianism reflected Bolingbroke's profound disillusionment with opposition politics, that it was 'born out of battle fatigue' and was a sign that Bolingbroke had 'entirely lost his grasp of politics as the "art of the possible"'.[81] This was not Bolingbroke's mood in the

---

[79] Cf. *Of Royall Educacion*, 1–2, 4; and *Patriot King*, 124.

[80] *GM* 10 (1740), 54–6, 291–3. These extracts were first printed in the oppositional *Common Sense*, 20 Feb. and 7 June 1740

[81] Hammond, *Pope and Bolingbroke*, 138. For a similar view see Kramnick, *Bolingbroke and His Circle*, 166–9; H. T. Dickinson, *Bolingbroke* (1970), 262–4. This interpretation stems from predating Bolingbroke's mood of disillusionment of Apr. 1739 back to the summer and autumn of 1738. In 1737–8 the opposition had begun to recover momentum; but all hopes of union disintegrated after the disastrous secession of Mar. 1739. Barber, 'Bolingbroke, Pope and the *Patriot King*', 70, places the *P.K.* in the more optimistic context of late 1738.

autumn of 1738. Bolingbroke, like Pope at this time, was actively involved in both the behind-scenes politics and the literary side of the Patriot campaign. Walpole was meeting increased resistance to his foreign policy in that autumn's parliamentary session; Frederick was capitalizing on his popularity in the provinces. The London stage was taking on a newly vigorous political life with the Patriot dramas which Pope and Bolingbroke had helped edit that summer. As Goldgar remarks, 'here, for once, there seems to have been a planned, organised literary attack from the circle surrounding Prince Frederick, with the prince himself taking a hand in the complicated negotiations'.[82] Yet at the same time, as the letters rapidly exchanged between Pope, Wyndham, and Lyttelton show, the Cobham circle was also attempting to fend off Pulteney and Carteret's advances on the Prince and to establish contact with the Tories for a 'New' version of the planned Patriot alliance predicated on a tactical recognition of separate political groupings in which 'his R. H. shou'd exert his whole Influence' and become 'the Head of the Party'.[83] Pope's letters reflect their uncertainty as to whether Frederick could really act as a 'centre of union, a superior authority among yourselves, under whose influence men of different characters and different views will be brought to draw better together'.[84]

The Prince's Visit to Lord Bathurst was too quick for a Letter which I intended him on that occasion: it was a Letter of Instruction, in what manner a Great Man should treat a Prince, when Fortune gives him the Leading of one: Especially if the Prince happens to be a little Short sighted: *What* things one should make him see, and *how far*? What kind of Notions to give him, of the Extent, Nature & Situation of the *Land* about him?[85]

When Bolingbroke first circulated the manuscript of the *Patriot King* at around this time he intended it to be a coterie text designed for a small group of the Prince's supporters, not a timeless classic of political thought or even one which could exercise a direct bearing, other than the inspirational, on the world of tactical politics.[86] Much of its language of princely virtue and courtly conduct was aimed at converting the 'outs' of Leicester House into the 'ins'. In March 1738 George II had publicly reconfirmed his edict placing a strict ban from St James's on all of the Prince's followers. Bolingbroke's treatise is designed to make Frederick's court (like the exiled Duke Senior's in *As You Like It*) more courtly than the court. It is for this reason that Bolingbroke

---

[82] Bertrand A. Goldgar, *Walpole and the Wits: The Relation of Politics to Literature, 1722–1742* (Lincoln, Nebr., 1976), 180.

[83] Pope, *Corr.* iv. 143.   [84] Bolingbroke to Wyndham, 3 Feb. 1738 (Coxe, *Walpole*, iii. 506).

[85] Pope, *Corr.* iv. 142.

[86] Dickinson, *Bolingbroke*, 260, claims that Bolingbroke wrote the work 'with an eye to posterity'. But his attempts to make sure it did not get published suggest the reverse. It was Pope who seemed to be more concerned for Bolingbroke's timeless reputation. See Spence, *Anecdotes*, i. 124–5, nos. 283–4: 'he spoke of it as too valuable to the world to be so used, and said he would not suffer it to be lost to it.'

repeatedly stresses the vital role to be played by the Prince's 'advisers', the selfsame courtiers marginalized by St James's. A Patriot prince should 'chuse his *companions* with as great a care as his *ministers*' (p. 137). 'Every man here, who stands forward enough in rank and reputation to be called to the councils of his king, must have given proofs before-hand of his patriotism as well as his capacity' (p. 89).

Hanover and Stuart

If the *Patriot King* was written in a 'private' language, could that private language contain an even more private set of signals, an 'exoteric message to an open readership and at the same time an esoteric message for a closed one'?[87] Both Howard Erskine-Hill and Simon Varey, demonstrating the extent to which Bolingbroke was ready to dabble in Jacobite activities at various points in the 1730s, claim for the *Patriot King* a dynastic dualism. The work is 'a political weapon nicely judged to turn in either direction, as the opportunity offered, Hanover or Stuart'.[88] The text printed in 1749 openly condemns non-juring Jacobites, but this passage may have been an editor's insertion.[89] None of Frederick's supporters were (as Varey claims) 'secret Jacobites', but both the Tory Cornbury and Lord Chesterfield later dabbled with the Jacobite alternative.

The only difficulty in attributing an active Jacobite intention to the *Patriot King* lies in the fact that it was almost certainly written at a time when Bolingbroke was throwing all his political energies into the campaign behind Frederick. Bolingbroke's renewed flirtations with Jacobitism, as Varey points out, were dated *c.*1731–3 and after his return to France in April 1739 at a time when he was depressed by the opposition's failure to make any headway.[90] There is little evidence to support Varey's argument that Bolingbroke's 'idea' of a Patriot King (if not the text itself) somehow came into being as a result of his 1731–2 Jacobite activities when he was trying to get James's two young sons 'educated' as Protestant princes under the Duke of Ormonde's care.[91] John Gay's first series of *Fables*, written (though not published) at around this time, may allude to images of a Patriot King, but there is no reason to suppose that Gay derived them from Bolingbroke. Such images were widespread and more often associated with Hanoverianism than Stuartism. The *Fables* actually bear little direct resemblance to Bolingbroke's text.[92]

---

[87] J. G. A. Pocock, *Virtue, Commerce, and History* (Cambridge, 1985), 26.

[88] Erskine-Hill, 'Alexander Pope: The Political Poet in His time', 139. This argument is extended in his 'Literature and the Jacobite Cause', 56. The fullest statement of the Jacobite argument is in Simon Varey, 'Hanover, Stuart and the *Patriot King*'.

[89] Varey, 'Hanover, Stuart and the *Patriot King*', 167.   [90] Ibid. 164–5.

[91] See Cruickshanks, *Political Untouchables*, 13.

[92] The argument that Bolingbroke influenced Gay's *Fables* was first made by Sven Armens, *John Gay, Social Critic* (New York, 1954), 190–1, and adopted by Dickinson, *Bolingbroke*, 259. But the argument has been discredited by V. Dearing and C. Beckwith in their edn. of Gay's *Poetry and Prose*, 2 vols. (Oxford, 1974), ii. 632.

But if Bolingbroke was alert to other windows of opportunity, the *Patriot King* could be made to support a Jacobite reading. The problems of the education of princes taxed both Jacobites and Hanoverians, though in different ways. Jacobitism and Whig Patriotism, as I have suggested, shared an overlapping set of political idioms and a similar language of redemptive kingship. Jacobite writers like David Morgan used the appeal to 'His Royal Highness the Prince of Wales' as a cloak for his appeal to the 'other' Prince of Wales.[93] The *Patriot King*'s very dynamic of a 'precedent bad reign' to be followed by a renovated Britain under a Patriot King, especially if the prince waiting in the wings remained unnamed, was inherently as applicable to Charles Edward Stuart as to Frederick Louis. The 'school of affliction' in which Bolingbroke's prince will be formed, when the good prince 'may suffer with the people, and in some measure for them' under a bad king (p. 69), recalled the traditional Jacobite language of martyrdom, exile, and suffering—like Dryden's Charles II, 'inured to suffer ere he came to reign, | No rash procedure will his actions stain'.[94] Frederick could, however, claim a more direct experience of persecution and suffering: surely it is only the son of George who could have made himself 'obnoxious' to the king 'in how near a Relation soever he may stand to the other'.[95] The keynote of Frederick's speech to the Aldermen of London after he was turned out of St James's was one of fellow victimization with those persecuted by the administration. But the two resonant notes of Jacobite rhetoric noted by Howard Erskine-Hill, a 'stubborn and resentful nationalism' and the theme of pervasive degeneracy, are certainly the hallmarks of the Introduction to the *Patriot King*.[96] 'Stripped of the rights of a *British* subject, of all except the meanest of them, that of inheriting, I remember I am a Briton still' (p. 47). Here Bolingbroke predicts an apocalyptic moment based on the Machiavellian disposition of 'fortune' which might suggest restoration by the sword rather than a peaceful accession.

to save or redeem a nation under such circumstances from perdition, nothing less is necessary than some great, some extraordinary conjuncture of ill fortune or good, which yet may *purge*, yet *so as by fire*. Distress from abroad, bankruptcy at home, and other circumstances of like nature and tendency, may beget universal confusion. Out of confusion order may arise: but it may be the order of a wicked tyranny, instead of the order of a just monarchy. Either may happen: and such an alternative, at the disposition of fortune, is sufficient to make a stoic tremble! We may be saved indeed by means of a very different kind; but these means will not offer themselves, this way of salvation will not be open to us, without the concurrence, and the influence, of a PATRIOT KING, the most uncommon of all phaenomena in the physical and moral world. (p. 46)

[93] See Erskine-Hill, 'Literature and the Jacobite Cause', 55–9.

[94] Dryden, *Astrea Redux*, ll. 88–9.

[95] This line is from a passage in one of the three surviving versions of Pope's edn. of the *Patriot King*, omitted from Bolingbroke's 1749 edn. Cited by Varey, 'Hanover, Stuart and the *Patriot King*', 170.

[96] Erskine-Hill, 'Literature and the Jacobite Cause', 58.

Which is the wicked tyranny and which the just monarchy? What is the 'means of a very different kind' hinted at? What is the 'alternative, at the dis-position of fortune'? Bolingbroke's typically flexible rhetoric leaves open both a Hanoverian and a Jacobite interpretation. When Pope wrote *One Thousand Seven Hundred and Forty*, clearly inspired by the *Patriot King*, he was certainly alert to the work's dynastic ambiguities. Like Bolingbroke, Pope calls for an anonymous Patriot King whose honesty will 'redeem the land': 'whatever his religion or his blood, | His public virtue makes his title good'—either a call for former Hanoverian patriots to accept a Catholic Stuart prince, or a call for Jacobites to accept a Hanoverian prince.[97]

Bolingbroke's Theory of Kingship

Bolingbroke's account of the origins and political foundations for kingship is characterized by similar ambiguity and equivocation. His discussion of consti-tutional and hereditary monarchy is an elaborate verbal balancing-act between theories designed to appeal to Whigs and Tories of very different political per-suasions, possibly Jacobites and even Whig radicals. Bolingbroke sets out to supply '*the duties of a king to his country*: of those kings particularly who are appointed by the people, for I know of none who are anointed by God to rule in *limited monarchies*' (p. 41). He explicitly refutes the doctrine of indefeasible divine right by asserting that the dignity of kings descends via their offices rather than their persons. Hereditary right is a more convenient form of monarchy than elective, but even when the Crown descends by hereditary suc-cession, the last of the line hold it by the same right as the first. But although Bolingbroke, presumably with a glance at the Hanoverians' propagandists, recalls the 'scribbler' who 'was employed or employed himself, to assert the *hereditary right* of the present family', he is careful not to deny this claim—merely to say that it is a 'task unnecessary to any good purpose' (p. 77). Although he repeatedly reiterates the term 'a free commonwealth' and 'a free monarchical state', the work contains no discussion of the natural rights which a subject might plead against a bad sovereign or any information about the checks which can be applied to a sovereign whose title has been divinely endorsed.[98] 'My aim is to fix this principle, that *limitations* on a crown ought to be carried *as far* as is necessary to secure the liberties of the people; and that all *such limitations* may subsist, without weakening or endangering monar-chy' (p. 60).

Bolingbroke caricatures both extreme royalist and contractarian positions when he asserts: 'I neither *dress up* kings like so many *burlesque Jupiters*, weigh-ing the fortunes of mankind in the scales of fate, and darting thunderbolts at

---

[97] *TE* iv. 337.   [98] See Clark, *English Society*, 181.

the heads of rebellious giants; nor do I strip them naked, as it were, and leave them at most a few *tattered rags* to clothe their *majesty*' (p. 60). But for all his rhetorical tightrope-walking, aided by a sentence structure whose balanced antithetical clauses and litotes make it difficult to gauge just what is being asserted and what is being refuted, Bolingbroke's treatise resonates with the emotional language of the divine nature of kingship even while it is explicitly refuting 'these pretensions to divine right' (p. 49). Kings have a 'right divine to govern *well*': 'the office of kings then is of *right divine*, and their persons are to be reputed *sacred*' (p. 54). The Patriot King has 'a mind so rare, so nearly divine' (p. 140). The model at the centre of this work is not a contract between sovereign and subject but the traditional sentimental Filmerian image of a 'patriarchal family, where the head and all the members are united by one common interest, and animated by one common spirit' (p. 93).

This kind of language may have had the right 'emotional appeal (thought its inventors) to appeal to the Tories', but, as Clark suggests, the *Patriot King* was found wanting by some Tory critics in 1749 when placed side by side with legitimist Tory doctrine.[99] Frederick was trying to widen the basis of his support in both 1738 and 1749 by appealing to the Tories; but many Hanoverian Whigs would not have considered Bolingbroke's invocation of divine monarchical sanction especially 'Tory'. At the heart of the *Patriot King* lies a paean to a powerful national leader who will govern above party or faction, cleanse the Augean stables of government, and set the nation to rights. The entire account stresses the *personal* moral qualities of princely leadership and inspiration that a good king must possess, to 'reinfuse the *spirit* of *liberty*, to reform the *morals* and raise the *sentiments* of a people' (p. 45). This is not far from the radical Whig Trenchard's idealized account of George I, tasked to 'call up all our antient Virtue, and to restore so great a People to themselves'.[100] It is certainly close to the Whig Lyttelton's 1733 account of Elizabeth, who 'into a people thus sunk and depraved . . . did infuse . . . a National spirit as high, and a love of the Publick so strong'.[101] Charismatic monarchs are as much part of the Whig tradition as they are of the Tory.

As a political manifesto, the *Patriot King* is found wanting. But in 1738 it was intended not so much as a political manifesto (as we might understand it) as an imaginative vision designed to inspire and invigorate a political opposition centred on the heir to the throne. Critics have attempted to trace Bolingbroke's pervasive influence on poets and playwrights, but few have noted the influence of playwrights and poets on Bolingbroke.[102] The *Patriot*

[99] See Clark, *English Society*, 183–4.

[100] John Trenchard, *Some Considerations upon the State of Our Publick Debts in General and of the Civil List in Particular* (1720), 31.

[101] George Lyttelton, 'Observations on the Reign and Character of Queen Elizabeth. Written in the Year 1733', Hagley MS, 17ᵛ.

[102] Except Hammond, *Pope and Bolingbroke*, 142, who notes that its language draws on biblical archetypes used by Pope and the *Craftsman*.

King derives much from the language of patriotic kingship which was then currently being expounded in equally high-flown terms in poetry and on the stage. Bolingbroke's swelling closing lines borrow the very language and cadences of Augustan panegyrical prophecy.

Of such a prince, and of such a prince alone, it may be said with strict propriety and truth.

> *Volentes*
> *Per populos dat jura, viamque affectat Olympo.*

Civil fury will have no place in this draught: or, if the monster is seen, he must be seen as *Virgil* describes him,

> *Centum vinctus ahenis*
> *Post tergum nodis, fremit horridus ore cruento.*

He must be seen subdued, bound, chained, and deprived entirely of the power to do hurt. In his place, concord will appear, brooding peace and prosperity on the happy land; joy sitting in every face, content in every heart, a people unoppressed, undisturbed, unalarmed; busy to improve their private property and the public stock; fleets covering the ocean; bringing home wealth by the returns of industry; carrying assistance or terror abroad by the direction of wisdom; and asserting triumphantly the right and the honour of *Great Britain*, as far as waters roll and as winds can waft them. (pp. 140–1)

'*Windsor-Forest* once more', notes Frederick Keener.[103] But a far more recent version of the same Augustan 'banishing of the Vices' topos had appeared not in a Stuart but in a Hanoverian work, the extravagant new Prologue to Giffard's popular production of *Merlin: Or, The British Inchanter* of 1735–6, declaimed to theatre audiences and printed at the front of the 1736 edition of the play.

> Lo! Civil Rage, and Discord light their Brand;
> See! the fell Furies half consume the Land!
>
> .   .   .   .   .   .
>
> — But, now—I see — wrapt into distant Times—
> (He springs to Light) a Prince to purge our Crimes:
> With Regal state to joyn the gen'rous Mind;
> And rise the Benefactor of Mankind!
> See, Strife and Faction grin with hideous Yell!
> See, the chain'd Monsters shrink within their Cell!
> He comes, he comes! — Old Ocean hears the Word;
> Smooths his rough Face, and hails his Sovereign Lord!
> To other Worlds the British Thunder rolls,
> Beholds New Stars, and visits both the Poles!

---

[103] Frederick M. Keener, *An Essay on Pope* (New York, 1974), 153. See *Windsor-Forest*, ll. 413–22. The 'banishing of the Vices' topos is taken from Virgil's *Aeneid*, i. 295–6, but the lines also derive from *Georgics*, iii. 37–9.

Now shall fair Commerce Arts, and wealth explore,
And her Sails whiten Earth's remotest Shore!
While Heav'n-born justice breaks Oppression's Bands
And lifts her Scales with uninclining Hands!
Let Purple Tyrants the scourg'd Globe deface,
And riot in the Blood of Human Race!
War's Ravage; Thou, O warlike Prince, restrain!
Be thine the Glories of a Milder Reign!
Guardian, as Arbiter, of Peace restor'd,
Save bleeding Europe from the ruthless Sword!
Of Sacred Liberty great Patron shine:
And prove by Godlike Worth the Right Divine![104]

When Bolingbroke asserted that 'The office of kings . . . is of *right divine*, and their persons are to be reputed *sacred*' and that a good king has 'a divine right to govern *well*', he was tapping a familiar strain of Hanoverian royalist language.

Patriot King Poetry

The 'Mr. Sterling' who wrote this Prologue was almost certainly the minor Irish Whig writer James Sterling whose *An Ode on the Times. Addressed to —, the Hope of Britain* appeared in the February 1738 issue of the *Gentleman's Magazine*, five months before Bolingbroke arrived in England and became reinvolved in oppositional activities.[105] Sterling would have had no contact with Bolingbroke or his ideas—he moved in very different circles. Yet this ode contains ideas and language which anticipate Bolingbroke's fuller account of patriotic kingship. Sterling denounces a corrupt and failing nation, and calls on 'one man amongst th'untainted few' to heal a nation rent by 'Civil Discord' and 'fell Furies'. He will be a 'patriot of this World', one 'generous in manners as in Blood', refined but not corrupted by the court. He will 'rule the land with righteousness'. The refrain 'Rise, ****, rise' is clearly aimed at Frederick, whose name in elided form fits the scansion. It is Frederick who is '—, the Hope of Britain'. This poem was not initially written for Frederick. It first appeared in 1734, then addressed to 'His Grace the Duke of Dorset Lord Lieutenant of Ireland' in the context of an Ireland divided over the Repeal of the Test Act. The poem was sufficiently unspecific for Sterling to recycle it in 1738. By excising Dorset's name from the text and replacing it with some suggestive blanks he could cash in on what by this stage must clearly have been a recognized mode of writing about Frederick.

[104] Dryden, *Merlin: Or, The British Inchanter*, Prologue [James Sterling].
[105] See Christine Gerrard, '*An Ode on the Times*: The Political Fortunes of James Sterling and Matthew Concanen', *N&Q* NS 231 (1986), 502–4. The poem is printed in *GM* 7 (1738), 97–8.

We therefore need to be cautious about the ideas advanced in an influential essay by Mable Hessler Cable tracing the purported influence of Bolingbroke's treatise on a number of Patriot works in the late 1730s. Mallet's *Mustapha*, Brooke's *Gustavus Vasa*, Thomson's *Edward and Eleanora*, and Glover's *Leonidas* are described as 'a dramatisation of Bolingbroke's ideas', the 'Idea of a Patriot King in verse'. 'Certainly nothing more clearly illustrates the conversion of political propaganda into literary material than does the relation between the *Idea of a Patriot King* and such works as Glover's *Leonidas* and Brooke's *Gustavus Vasa*.'[106] Since we can only guess which writers read the text, this kind of influence-hunting is not very helpful.[107] The only works which directly parallel Bolingbroke's text and where verbal traces can be seen are Pope's *1740*, possibly the Prologue to Brooke's 1739 *Gustavus Vasa* and, most clearly, West's 1742 *Institution of the Order of the Garter*. But other writers far earlier in the 1730s had been using the phrase 'Patriot King' and language not dissimilar to Bolingbroke's. As early as 1730 the *Craftsman* contained an essay asserting that 'A *good King* therefore is only another word for a *Royal Patriot*'.[108] Thomson's Dedication of *Liberty* in 1735 had proclaimed that in Frederick we behold 'the noblest Dispositions of the Prince, and the Patriot, united'.[109] In that year George Lillo's *Christian Hero* announced in its Prologue that 'To Night we sing | A Pious Hero, and a Patriot King'.[110] In that year, too, the thoroughly Whig squire William Somerville produced *The Chace*, dedicated to Frederick, which combines precisely the same synthesis of constitutional monarchy, with a defence of liberty and commerce and a romantic appeal to a charismatic popular prince. It is far more helpful to consider the *Patriot King* along with a series of other Patriot King works as the products of a more widespread cult of Hanoverian princely myth-making. In the last section of this chapter I shall look more fully at some

[106] Mabel Hessler Cable, 'The Idea of a Patriot King in the Propaganda of the Opposition to Walpole, 1735–1739', *PQ* 18 (1939), 119–30. For other discussions of the relationship between Bolingbroke's work and its literary 'progeny', see W. R. Irwin's very negative account in 'Prince Frederick's Mask of Patriotism', *PQ* 37 (1958), 368–84; Goldgar, *Walpole and the Wits*, 138–9, 180–1; Kramnick, *Bolingbroke and His Circle*, 205–35; Dickinson, *Bolingbroke*, 259; Varey, 'Hanover, Stuart and the *Patriot King*', 165–7. All these accounts limit discussion to Brooke, Mallet, Thomson, Glover, Pope, and Gay.

[107] See James Sambrook, *James Thomson, 1700–1748: A Life* (Oxford, 1991), 202–3, for the plausible conjecture that Mallet and Thomson dined with Pope and Bolingbroke between Apr. 1738 and July 1739 and probably saw the manuscript. It is reasonable to suppose that the manuscript was seen by poets close to Lyttelton and Frederick, including Glover and West. But there is no information about other writers such as Henry Brooke, William Paterson, and Paul Whitehead. Whitehead's *Manners*, Jan. 1739, contains a prophecy like Bolingbroke's, but critics accused him of stealing it from Pope's *Messiah*.

[108] *Craftsman*, 28 Nov. 1730. Dramatists were by this stage writing oppositional Patriot King dramas, e.g. Samuel Madden's *Themistocles, the Lover of His Country* (1729) dedicated to Frederick, and Benjamin Martyn's oppositional *Timoleon* (1730).

[109] OET *Liberty*, 40.

[110] John Loftis, *The Politics of Drama in Augustan England* (Oxford, 1963), 121–2. The Epilogue enunciates the ideal of a monarchy above party or faction.

hitherto unacknowledged 'Patriot King' works of the 1730s. It should come as no surprise to see that they often resound with a 'Tory' royalist note and draw much of their iconography from what were traditionally Stuart and even Jacobite literary images of kingship.

Myths of Princehood

In 1751 the funeral elegies on Frederick's sudden death were filled with historic references to princely promise poignantly cut off in its prime, placing him in the heavenly company of Edward the Black Prince, Henry VII's son Arthur and, most frequently, 'STEUART HENRY', the admirable son of James I.[111] The comparisons had been made throughout Frederick's lifetime, undoubtedly prompted by the Prince himself.[112] This was a form of royal myth-making not available to either of his parents. Frederick identified himself with previous notable princes of Wales, particularly with the strain of chivalric patriotism epitomized by the Black Prince's exploits at Crécy and Poitiers and revived by Prince Henry in the 1610s. In 1735 newspapers widely reported Frederick's commissioning of a statue of the Black Prince with an inscription promising that he would make '*that amiable Prince the pattern of his own Conduct*'.[113] Shortly after his arrival in England, Frederick purchased for his collection Robert Peake's famous 1606 portrait *Henry Prince of Wales in the Hunting Field*, depicting Henry in full hunting-dress on the point of killing the stag. It may have inspired him to commission a very similar portrait of himself from John Wootton entitled *The Death of the Stag*.[114] There was a certain appositeness in the fact that Frederick carried Henry's second Christian name. Frederick went on to name one of his sons Henry-Frederic. Prince Henry was a particularly suitable role model. Not only was he distinguished for his patronage of the arts and learning, but, as Roy Strong notes, he publicly presented himself 'as the exponent of a policy diametrically opposed to the royal one. We see the

---

[111] Richard Rolt, *A Monody on the Death of His Royal Highness Frederic-Louis, Prince of Wales* (1751), 5. Rolt was a Jacobite from Shrewsbury who joined the Jacobite army in 1745. He transferred his loyalty to Prince Frederick, here tracing his linkage through the blood line of the Stuarts, praising him as a 'fair Descendant of the STEUART line.' He later dedicated his *Cambria* to Prince George. For the comparisons between Frederick and previous princes of Wales, see *The English Poems collected from the Oxford and Cambridge Verses on the Death of His Royal Highness Frederick Prince of Wales* (Edinburgh, 1751), esp. James Clitherow's poem, p. 39. A striking example is the Revd Hudson of Bywell's *An Ode on the Death of his Royal Highness, Frederick Prince of Wales* (1751), in which Merlin summons the 'much-loved *British* Prince' into the company of Arthur, Henry, and the Black Prince.

[112] See Lady Charlotte Clayton, Viscountess Sundon, *Memoirs of Viscountess Sundon, Mistress of the Robes to Queen Caroline*, 2 vols. (1847), i. 66, for an early comparison between Frederick and the Black Prince; see Pulteney's speech, 22 Feb. 1737, *Carlisle MSS*, 178–9.

[113] *Craftsman*, 6 Sept. 1735.

[114] Oliver Millar, *Tudor, Stuart and Early Georgian Pictures in the Royal Collection*, 2 vols. (1963), no. 100 (i. 79), plate 36; no. 545 (i. 180), plate 203.

young Prince present at the new court of St. James's as the thinly-veiled focus for a revival of the Elizabethan war party.' Like Prince Henry, Frederick also became associated with 'a cult of British history: the mythology of [Elizabeth's] reign'.[115] Frederick revived the earlier pattern of a neo-Elizabethan Prince of Wales opposed to his father's conciliatory European foreign policy. It was this that prompted Joseph Morgan to produce in 1738 (the first time since 1626) a new edition of Sir Charles Cornwallis's *Life of Henry*. The edition was fulsomely dedicated to Frederick.

> If your ROYAL HIGHNESS vouchsafes to honour these few pages with a Perusal, you will find, that they contain some authentic memoirs of HENRY-FREDERIC, one of Your Most Noble Predecessors in Titles, dignities and uncontested Right to the inestimable Diadem of the *British* Empire: which magnanimous Great-Uncle of your late Royal GRANDFATHER was, not much more than a Century since, the same as your Princely Self is now, the Joy, the Delight, the Hope, the Expectation of these Realms.[116]

There is more than an echo here of Michael Drayton's dedicatory poem to Prince Henry in his *Polyolbion*, printed opposite the chivalric frontispiece depicting a martial Henry in breastplate holding a lance: 'BRITAINE *behold here portray'd, to the Sight,* | Henry, *thy best hope, and the world's delight.*'[117] Another *Life of Henry* by Sir Richard Connak appeared in 1747, probably timed to coincide with Frederick's Leicester House campaign. Both were printed again in 1751, the year of Frederick's death. The 1738 Cornwallis *Life of Henry* was, as I have noted, a highly political work, a contribution to oppositional war propaganda in its exploitation of the Prince's friendship with Sir Walter Ralegh and its assertion of British naval greatness, 'All Nations beside being but Sea Pedlars'.[118] The contrast between jealous tyrant kings and their more popular patriotic sons was highlighted by the extra material in the appendices taken from contemporary accounts such as Arthur Wilson's, pointedly showing 'how far the King's Fears, like thick Clouds, might afterwards blind the Eye of his Reason (when he saw him, as he thought, too high mounted in the Peoples Love) . . . to decline his Paternal Affection towards him, and bring him to the low Condition he fell into'.[119]

Like Prince Henry, Frederick was associated with a chivalric revival of the Garter. One of Henry's devices in his *Barriers* of 1610 was 'King Arthurs round table' and '*Priscum instauro decus*' (I revive the ancient glory).[120] Both James I and George II were accused of corrupting the ancient orders of merit—the Garter, Bath, and Thistle—the 'sale' of which both princes were seen to condemn. During the 1730s Frederick and other young members of

---

[115] Roy Strong, *Henry Prince of Wales and England's Lost Renaissance* (1986), 141.

[116] Sir Charles Cornwallis, *The Life and Character of Henry-Frederic, Prince of Wales*, ed. J. M. [Joseph Morgan] (1738), Dedication.

[117] *The Works of Michael Drayton*, ed. J. W. Hebel et al., 5 vols. (2nd edn., Oxford, 1961), iv, p. iv. [118] Cornwallis, *Life of Henry*, 30.

[119] Ibid. 31–2. [120] Strong, *Henry Prince of Wales*, 145.

his household played at, and perhaps more than played at, creating a chivalric cult. Kew House near Richmond seems to have been its centre. In 1730 Frederick commissioned William Kent to refurbish the interior of the house entirely. Kew was demolished in 1802, but a 1732 painting by Philip Mercier, Frederick's Gentleman of the Bedchamber, indicates something of the main room's thematic scheme.[121] Mercier's painting was entitled *Frederick Prince of Wales with the Knights of the Round Table*.[122] Frederick and eighteen companions are seated at a round table in a room decorated with motifs of the chase and hunting trophies. Over the fireplace hangs a portrait of Frederick's sister Anne in hunting costume; a later view of the interior shows a portrait of Frederick in hunting costume in its place. Stephen Jones claims that the Knights of the Round Table was 'a patriotic opposition club'.[123] The drinking glasses suggest informality, yet all members are painted in full hunting dress, all prominently displaying their respective ribbons of merit—the Garter, the Bath, and the Thistle, a reminder perhaps that the Order of the Garter was established by Edward III to revive the chivalric codes of Arthur's original Round Table. One member carries a paper inscribed *'Orders and Constitution'*.[124] Another portrait (probably by Charles Philips) painted some time between 1730 and 1735 shows Frederick playing out another princely role in 'The Henry the Fifth Club' or 'The Gang'.[125] The club is meeting in a room with a bust of Henry V over the fireplace; an 1813 description showed that members were identified as Falstaff, Poins, Bardolph, and company. This was undoubtedly a gesture at Frederick's own similarly high-spirited defiance of his father, yet carrying the symbolic weight of the young Hal's future role as the patriotic Henry V of the Battle of Agincourt. Frederick also purchased from Vertue a limning of Henry V as Prince of Wales. In 1735 Aaron Hill revived for ten performances his own version of *King Henry V* on the London stage, probably designed (like his other works of this period) to attract Frederick's approval.[126]

Frederick went to even greater lengths to present himself as a Renaissance-style Prince of Wales. After 1736 the portraits he commissioned (unlike Mercier's early informal domestic group portraits) frequently depicted him

---

[121] Wilson, *William Kent*, 127–30.

[122] Millar, *Tudor, Stuart and Early Georgian Pictures*, no. 533 (i. 177), plate 207. The identity of all the members of the club has not been fully established. See Rorschach, 'Frederick, Prince of Wales', 45–6.   [123] Jones, *Frederick, Prince of Wales and His Circle*, 20.

[124] Rorschach, 'Frederick, Prince of Wales', 45–6 n. 17, mentions Judith Colton's suggestion that *'Orders and Constitution'* might hint at Freemasonry. Frederick did not become a Mason until 1737. The Round Table still remains a mystery.

[125] Millar, *Tudor, Stuart and Early Georgian Pictures*, no. 535 (i. 177–8).

[126] Hill seems to have 'given' the play, without the usual author's benefit-night, for performance at Goodman's Fields in 1735–6. See Robert D. Hume, *Henry Fielding and the London Theatre 1728–1737* (Oxford, 1988), 23, 203. Queen Caroline also collected images of Henry V and the Black Prince; she may have inspired Frederick's interest. See Wilson, *William Kent*, 148.

wearing a Prince-Henry-type breastplate and the Garter robes.[127] Frederick was the only member of the royal family to commission a masque for private performance at his own court—Thomson and Mallet's *Alfred*.[128] In December 1731 Frederick and his eighteen household companions had appeared at a masked ball wearing elaborate costumes designed by Kent and loosely modelled on the kind of costumes worn by Prince Henry during the *Barriers*.[129] The only surviving description comes from Lord Hervey, who was typically sarcastic about the whole business, especially since he himself should have appeared in the retinue but his nerve failed him at the last minute. Frederick was 'to be dressed like a shepherd, an Adonis, or an Apollo (I have forgot which), and to have eighteen huntsmen in his suite. The huntsmen are to be dressed after a drawing of Kent's, in green waistcoats, leopard-skins, and quivers at their backs, bows and arrows in their hands, tragedy buskins on their legs, breeches trussed up like rope dancers, antique gloves with pikes up to their elbows, and caps and feathers upon their heads like a Harry the 8th Holbein.'[130]

The Royal Stag-Chase

The hunting costumes publicly paraded by Frederick's followers, and the hunting theme to the interior of Kew Lodge, are mirrored in some of the most interesting Patriot King poems written about Frederick—those which revive the theme of the royal stag-chase in Windsor. In a number of works indebted to Sir John Denham's *Coopers-Hill* and Pope's *Windsor-Forest*, Frederick's poets appropriated for the Hanoverian prince a theme which had previously been strongly associated with Stuart royalism. Denham and Pope had used the scenes and prospects around Windsor for a historically charged allegorical landscape to reflect on recent political events and especially on the

[127] See Rorschach, 'Frederick, Prince of Wales', 59–62.

[128] 'Masques' were frequently performed as afterpieces on the London stage in the first half of the century. They were invariably slight mythological or pastoral musical pieces. See Allardyce Nicoll, *A History of Early Eighteenth-Century Drama 1700–1750* (Cambridge, 1925), 258–9, and Dustin Griffin, *Regaining Paradise: Milton and the Eighteenth Century* (Cambridge, 1986), 59–61. Other dramatists supplied masques for royal occasions; e.g. Lillo's *Britannia and Batavia* and Galliard and Phillips's *The Nuptial Masque*. But these bore little resemblance to the traditional Tudor and Stuart court masques—the royal family did not usually bother to grace them with their presence. *Alfred* was performed by professional actors, but performed for Frederick's court. The Hermit acts as traditional 'presenter' for a visionary historical pageant of patriotic English monarchs very similar to the second pageant in Prince Henry's *Barriers* of 1610. See Strong, *Henry Prince of Wales*, 143–4.

[129] See Wilson, *William Kent*, 132. If Frederick was indeed dressed like a shepherd, his costume might have recalled the shepherd-knight symbolism of Henry's costume in the tilts of 5 June 1610 (see Strong, *Henry Prince of Wales*, 159). The contrast between shepherd and forester had been drawn in Sir Philip Sidney's 1578/9 masque *The Lady of May*.

[130] *Lord Hervey and his Friends 1726–38*, ed. Lord Ilchester (1950), 115–16.

nature of kingship and the relationship between subject and sovereign.[131] In *Coopers-Hill*, Windsor Castle, reconstructed by Edward III as a meeting-place for his newly established Order of the Garter and seated high on the crown of the hill, becomes an 'expans'd hieroglyph', a metaphor for monarchy.[132] These associations are also central to *Windsor-Forest*: 'Make *Windsor* Hills in lofty Numbers rise, | And lift her Turrets nearer to the Skies; | To sing those Honours you deserve to wear, | And add new Lustre to her Silver *Star*.'[133] Both poems use the royal stag-chase in the forests and hills of Windsor to panegyrize a Stuart monarch—Charles or Anne—in the role of hunter-king as well as to allegorize turbulent political events. Denham's hunted stag becomes, in the different versions of his poem, at first the persecuted Earl of Strafford, then finally the executed Charles.[134] Pope's *Windsor-Forest* uses the stag-chase in even more complex fashion. In the context of the recent Treaty of Utrecht the stag-chase becomes a metaphor for war, hunting the containment of or harmless outlet for man's warlike energies. Pope celebrates the blessings of a specifically *Stuart* reign and mythologizes Anne as a hunter-queen in a series of images which evoke memories of Ben Jonson's praise of Elizabeth I as a 'Queen and huntress, chaste and fair':

> Let old *Arcadia* boast her ample Plain,
> The'immortal Huntress, and her Virgin Train;
> Nor envy *Windsor!* since thy Shades have seen
> As bright a Goddess, and as chast a Queen;
> Whose Care, like hers, protects the Sylvan Reign,
> The Earth's fair Light, and Empress of the Main.[135]

Not surprisingly, the genre became moribund after the accession of the Hanoverians. In the late 1730s Mrs Caesar met with no success when she tried to persuade Pope to write a Jacobite version of *Windsor-Forest* for James III, 'But for Thy Windsor a New Fabrick Raise | And There Triumphant Sing Thy Soverain's Praise'.[136] Both George I and George II were keen hunters who exercised their privileges over the royal chases with an unprecedented rigour. Draconian penalties were imposed on local people who continued to exercise their traditional perquisites from the forest's environs. E. P. Thompson has charted the ensuing guerrilla warfare and the summary executions imposed on law-breakers by Hanoverian state control. Pope's brother-in-

---

[131] For the iconography of *Windsor-Forest*, see E. Audra and A. Williams (eds.), *TE* i. 125–44; Earl Wasserman, *The Subtler Language: Critical Readings of Neoclassic and Romantic Poems* (Baltimore, Md., 1959), ch. 4. For the complex history of *Coopers-Hill* see *Expans'd Hieroglyphicks: A Critical Edition of Sir John Denham's 'Coopers-Hill'*, ed. Brendan O'Hehir (Berkeley and Los Angeles, 1969). For later imitations of *Coopers-Hill*, see ibid., App. E (294–7). This list does not go beyond 1700.

[132] See ibid. 184–91 for the iconography of Windsor and the identification of Charles I with St George.   [133] *TE* i. 174–5.

[134] See *Expans'd Hieroglyphicks*, ed. O'Hehir, 35, for the case for identifying the hunted stag with Charles I. He discusses stag-chase sequences on pp. 7–8.   [135] *TE* i. 164–5.

[136] See Valerie Rumbold, *Women's Place in Pope's World* (Cambridge, 1989), 247.

law Charles Rackett was forced into exile as a wanted man; Walpole may even
have 'silenced' Pope's satires during the 1720s by holding Rackett as a hostage
to fortune.[137] Hanoverians and hunting did not sit well together in the popular
mind. Certain newspapers reported with relish the undignified accidents both
George II and Walpole's hunting parties met in the mud of Windsor and
Richmond; as Lord Hervey commented, 'I wonder who is to be the sacrifice
for tomorrow's sport; not one chase has yet been gratis, bad as they have
been.' Walpole's son Robert was the Ranger of Richmond but Walpole senior
appropriated in practice the role for himself, prosecuting his territorial rights
with notorious severity. Hervey was not alone in mocking the 20-stone
Walpole swaggering in his Ranger uniform and hosting royal hunting parties.
'Sir Robert received the king at the Park gates, dressed in green and gold and
a cap as Ranger, with the leash cross his shoulders, which gave occasion to a
joke . . . that we all sung the whole day.'[138] Walpole's fondness for hunting
prompted poetic allegories of a satirical rather than sincere kind, deploying the
traditional parallels between the stag or fox hunt and the 'hue and cry' of a
pack of hounds hunting to ground a political enemy.[139]

Frederick hunted with his brothers and sisters at both Windsor and
Richmond. But he did not attract this kind of scorn, possibly because his taste
for far more popular pastimes such as cricket, fishing, and sailing regattas,
often with his future subjects, negated the criticism associated with the more
élitist sport of deer hunting. When William Somervile and Richard Powney
praised Frederick as a royal hunter, they invested him with the majesty and
charisma woven by Spenser and Jonson around Elizabeth as Diana, by
Denham around Charles I, and by Pope around Queen Anne. Somervile, a
Warwickshire squire of Whig Hanoverian loyalty, dedicated his four-book *The
Chace* to Prince Frederick in May 1735. Much of the poem is concerned with
the history and practice of hunting—a classic example of the eighteenth-century blank-verse 'georgic' didactic manual.[140] But *The Chace* is also a highly
political work, one which celebrates the royalist associations of the Windsor
landscape in a distinctly opposition Whig framework. Frederick as Prince of
Wales appears in the lengthy opening dedicatory passage as the 'Great Prince!
| Whom *Cambria*'s towr'ing Hills proclaim their Lord' and, more extensively,
in Book III's 'Description of the Royal Stag-Chace at Windsor Forest'.[141]
Somervile was clearly thinking of Pope when he described 'the Chace, the
Sport of Kings' as 'Image of War, without its Guilt' (i. 14–15). But the praise

[137] E. P. Thompson, *Whigs and Hunters: The Origin of the Black Act* (1975), esp. App. 2
(278–94).

[138] *Lord Hervey and His Friends*, ed. Ilchester, 81, 76–7.

[139] See e.g. *The Hunter Hunted: or Entertainment upon Entertainment* (1728) and *The Hunting of
the Stag* (1731), both satires on Walpole.

[140] This aspect of the poem is described by John Chalker, *The English Georgic* (1969), 180–95,
who also notes its strongly political quality.

[141] William Somervile, *The Chace* (1735), i. 2–3. All further references to book and line nos.
from this edn.

of royal Frederick, invited to relax from the public rituals of royal life, evokes memories of Denham's account of Charles I: 'Here have I seen the King, when great affairs | Give leave to slacken, and unbend his cares, | Attended to the Chace by all the flower | Of youth'.[142] Somervile even adds some Stuart-style pageantry for Frederick: 'While grateful Citizens with pompous Shew, | Rear the triumphal Arch, rich with th' Exploits | Of thy Illustrious house' (i. 5–7). As early as 1735, Somervile was inviting Frederick to play the role of a Patriot King, protector of British commerce and embodiment of monarchical magnificence.

> And if in future Times, some envious Prince,
> Careless of Right and guileful, shou'd invade
> Thy *Britain*'s Commerce, or shou'd strive in vain
> To wrest the Ballance from thy Equal Hand;
> Thy Hunter-Train, in chearful Green array'd,
> (A Band undaunted, and inur'd to Toils,)
> Shall compass thee around, die at they Feet,
> Or hew thy Passage thro' th'embattled Foe,
> And clear thy way to Fame; inspir'd by thee
> The nobler Chace of Glory shall pursue
> Thro' Fire, and Smoke, and Blood, and Fields of Death.
>
>   (i. 21–31)

John Chalker notes that 'This emphasis upon freedom of trade and the maintenance of Britain's commercial rights blends rather unexpectedly with nostalgic recreation of the past—Whig principles and Tory sentiment'. The 'recreation of the past' was, of course, as much an opposition Whig as a Tory theme in this period. The green-clad hunters, 'fighting boldly for Prince and Country in hand-to-hand battle', provide 'a touch of romantic medievalism which colours Somervile's whole treatement of the chase', notes Chalker.[143] Somervile was a good friend of Lady Sundon, one of Caroline's ladies-in-waiting. He might well have heard reports three years beforehand of Frederick's appearance in the 1731 masque surrounded by his eighteen companions dressed as huntsmen in 'chearful Green'. Book III, lines 344–608, contains a spirited account of the royal stag-chase at Windsor rising to a climax in the pursuit and protracted death of the royal stag. In Book I Somervile had paid passing lip-service to 'Mighty GEORGE' (i. 275), but it is Prince Frederick who dominates the poem and occupies the role of royal hunter, much like King Charles in the first version of *Coopers-Hill* and Anne in *Windsor-Forest*. The prophetic hopes centred on the future glories of Frederick's reign, rather than the current blessings of George's, make this an opposition Whig poem written in a Tory-Stuart idiom.

---

[142] Denham, *Coopers-Hill*, 'B' text, 240–4 (*Expans'd Hieroglyphicks*, 154).
[143] Chalker, *English Georgic*, 181–2, 186–7.

The Morning Sun that gilds with trembling Rays
Windsor's high Tow'rs, beholds the courtly Train
Mount for the Chace, nor views in all his Course
A scene so gay; heroick, noble Youths,
In Arts, and Arms renown'd.

      .   .   .   .

                    But who is he
Fresh as a Rose-bud newly blown, and fair
As op'ning Lillies? on whom every Eye
With Joy, and Admiration dwells? See, see,
He reins his docile Barb with manly Grace.
Is it *Adonis* for the Chace array'd?
Or *Britain*'s second Hope? Hail, blooming Youth!
May all your Virtues with your Years improve,
'Till in consummate Worth, you shine the Pride
Of these our Days, and to succeeding Times
A bright Example.
                (iii. 351–5; 383–93)

Chalker detects a sophisticated level of stylistic manipulation at work here. The praise of Frederick is sincere yet carries the idealizing mode beyond the point of hyperbole almost into the burlesque; the passage carries distinct echoes of Pope's mock-heroic *Rape of the Lock*. In a period when Hanoverian royal panegyric was a genre infinitely susceptible to mockery, Somervile confronts and then transcends the mock-panegyric by incorporating it in his poem.

Although Somervile models his account of the death of the stag closely on Denham's, it does not invite a similarly allegorical interpretation. The most political simile is one appropriate to an oppositional poem of the mid-1730s, comparing the wounded stag with a brave British merchant ship boarded by Spanish corsairs. But Somervile had originally intended another of his chase scenes, the rather more bathetic hunt for the hare in Book II, to yield a pointed political application. The 'poor Hare, | A puny dastard Animal, but vers'd | In subtle Wiles, diverts the youthful Train' (ii. 295–7) was first meant for Walpole. When Somervile sent Lady Sundon the manuscript of *The Chace* in 1734, she evidently took objection to this simile which must have been politically tendentious and could have been 'misapplied'. On her advice he substituted the uncontroversial simile of Orpheus—'Thus, Madam, I am equally unmerciful to poets as ministers, when they will suit my purposes or embellish my poem.' Lady Sundon seems to have objected to the political cast of the poem as a whole. Somervile's lavish praise of Prince Frederick (already engaged in opposition politics in 1734) and even his choice of literary models, Pope and Denham, so closely associated with Stuart/Tory politics, could be read as a sign of his disloyalty. Somervile wrote back protesting his allegiance to 'those honest principles upon which the Revolution was founded . . . Could I be so monstrous as to be wanting in my duty to my King, yet my own safety and the good of mankind would oblige me to persevere in those sentiments which support our religion and liberty'.[144] That *The Chace* was recognized as a Whig oppositional poem is clear from the highly favourable notice given it by the usually unliterary *Old Whig* to 'make amends' for mentioning the ministerial attacks on Lyttelton's *Persian Letters*. Frederick's reception of *The Chace* must have been gracious enough to inspire Somervile to dedicate to the Prince his later *Field Sports* (1742), left in Lyttelton's hands after the poet's death and posthumously presented to Frederick.

Somervile's *The Chace* was a popular work which only a few weeks later spawned an imitative rhyming couplet version. His revival of the 'royal chase' genre inspired other imitations, some written by Court Whigs attempting to appropriate the form for praise of George and Caroline. In May 1736 John Mawer published a translation of Oppian's *Cynegeuticks*, accompanied by a poem inscribed to the Queen and a letter addressed to Robert Walpole. Edward Phillips's *The Royal Chace; Or, Merlin's Hermitage and Cave*, a short masque-like work, was added as an afterpiece to performances of Giffard's Hanoverian revival of Dryden's *King Arthur* of 1735–6.[145] *The Royal Chace* is set in Richmond Gardens with Caroline's Cave as scenic 'Gothic' backdrop and residence for the prophetic Merlin who is visited by the huntress Diana. The figures of Diana and Endymion, as is clear from the dramatis personae promising 'A Royal Hunter' and 'A Royal Huntress, in the character of Diana', are meant to represent George and Caroline, who hunted weekly in Richmond Great Park. The whole piece ends with a pastoral celebration mingling mythical figures with choruses of bacchanalian peasants. It was an extraordinarily popular piece—performed with the Dryden play, with other works, and on its own more times during the second half of the 1730s than any other single dramatic work.[146] Here Merlin's visions mythologize Caroline as a mixture of Diana and Athena, 'Till *Pallas*, like a *British* Queen, descend, | And her great Mind from Toils of Empire here unbend'.[147]

In 1737 Frederick commissioned from John Wootton a pair of portraits on a similar theme to Somervile's 1735 *The Chace* to hang on the walls of Kew House: *The Death of the Stag* and *The Return from the Chace*.[148] The first shows the stag brought to bay by hounds in a pond in Windsor Great Park,

[144] Lady Charlotte Clayton, *Memoirs of Viscountess Sundon*, ii. 275–6. Letter to Mrs Clayton (Viscountess Sundon) 30 Sept. 1734. Her own letter to Somervile does not seem to have survived.

[145] *The Royal Chace* is printed on pp. 33–40 of the 1736 *Merlin: Or, The British Inchanter*. Many of its lines are highly imitative of Somervile.

[146] Nicoll, *History of Early Eighteenth-Century Drama*, 135, shows that *The Royal Chace* was performed at least 35 times in the 1738–9 season. Aaron Hill mentions seeing it in the *Prompter*, 27 Jan. 1736.   [147] *The Royal Chace*, 38.

[148] See Millar, *Tudor, Stuart and Early Georgian Pictures*, nos. 545, 546 (i. 180–1), plates 203, 204.

surrounded by huntsmen in royal livery, who have been identified as members of Frederick's household. In the distance is a finely painted view of Windsor Castle. The Prince is prominently displaying the ribbon and star of the Garter; two of the figures wear the full dress uniform of Ranger of the Great Park. The iconography recalls Walpole's well-known portrait (reproduced in Thompson's *Whigs and Hunters*) as Richmond Ranger wearing the Garter sash and star. In 1739 the Hanoverian Tory Richard Powney produced an even more striking reworking of the royal chase theme in his anonymous *The Stag Chace in Windsor Forest*. Powney's *Stag Chace* is probably the most overtly 'Jacobite' poem from this period in existence. It openly shows its sympathy and admiration for the exiled Jacobite Duke of Ormonde and his brother the formerly Jacobite Earl of Arran. But its allegorical reworking of the death of the stag suggests that Powney's aim was a legitimist 'transferral' of Tory and Stuart sentiment to the person of Frederick. There is no ambiguity here about the identity of the 'Prince of Wales', who is clearly named as Brunswick Frederick. Powney was a fellow of All Souls who went on to play a vital role as Frederick's agent negotiating the Leicester House alliance in the 1747–8 period. His correspondence from this period includes a transcript of the draft of Frederick's Carlton House declaration. Richard Powney acted in close consultation with Theophilus Leigh, Master of Balliol. His elder brother Peniston Powney, Tory MP for Berkshire, was the Prince's link-man in London, handling the Westminster side of affairs. Both brothers had grown up in Windsor. In 1736 Peniston had been appointed one of the four Verderers of Windsor (positions not controlled by court patronage but by local elections, hence Tory-dominated). Richard Powney's inspiration for *The Stag Chace* (like Pope's) had personal as well as literary sources.[149]

During the course of his poem, Powney acknowledges his debts to Somervile, Denham, and Pope in turn. *The Stag Chace* is an expanded version of the royal stag-chase sequences in both *Coopers-Hill* and *The Chace*, describing Frederick and his followers pursuing, then finally slaying the stag. This is too literal an account for what is a richly allusive, mythopoeic work. Frederick is a Brunswick by name but 'The Pride of *Cambria*', inspiring the devotions of '*British* Peers' whose sires pay tribute from beyond tombs 'with *Celtick* Trophies crown'd'.[150] Like Anne as Diana, Frederick becomes Orion the hunter:

---

[149] For information about Powney and some transcripts of his letters I am indebted to Dr Paul Langford. See also Colley, *In Defiance of Oligarchy*, 254–60. For Richard's brother Peniston's relationship with Frederick (who borrowed very heavily from him) see A. N. Newman, 'The Political Patronage of Frederick Lewis', 71. We know very little about Richard Powney's relations with Frederick in the 1738–9 period, but it seems from his apparent friendship with William Talbot that he may have been playing a Tory–Whig alliance-building role very similar to his later activities in the renewed Leicester House opposition of the 1747–50 period.

[150] [Richard Powney], *The Stag Chace in Windsor Forest* (1739); repr. 1740 and 1742. All subsequent refs. to pagination in 1739 edn.

High in th'aetherial Vault *Orion* glows,
And oe'er the Heav'ns a radiant Lustre throws;
Refulgent shines amidst the starry Train,
By Men rever'd a Huntsman on the Plain:
See *Frederick* thus thro' Tracks of Glory steer,
And with diurnal Bounties mark the Year;
To gild for ever Fame's immortal Roll
See Rays of Goodness streaming from his Soul.

(p. 2)

As if to confirm his royalist credentials, Prince Frederick is crowned by Dryads and 'Mystick Priests', clearly the famous Druids, with some 'sacred Oaks' which

hoary Temples crown'd,
When the Steer bled, and Altars blaz'd around;
When Priests with measur'd Dance, with mystick Lay,
And rising Incence hail'd the God of Day;
Still shall our Isle those awful Stores revere,
In Peace her Glory, her Defence in War.
When Time shall Fame to *British* Annals bring,
When all the Prince shall brighten in the King.

(p. 16)

The lines seem to recall Pope's riddle of Charles's oak-tree in his Windsor-based *Pastorals*: 'a wondrous *Tree* that Sacred *Monarchs* bears'.[151] Like Pope in *Windsor-Forest*, Powney links the royal oak and the naval role played by Windsor oak-trees. The subsequent lines, as we have seen in Chapter 1, prophesy Frederick's imperial dominion over 'subject Seas' and 'Nations trembling', when 'the Sons of Earth fall prostrate and adore'—a more aggressive version of Pope's description in *Windsor-Forest* of 'suppliant states' bending before a 'British QUEEN'.[152] This was warmongering 1739, not peace-celebrating 1713.

Powney's design to present Frederick as the legitimate 'substitute' for Tory Stuart loyalty is confirmed in the allegory of the stag-chase. Powney knew Somervile's description of Frederick hunting in the company of his sisters and courtiers; he may have seen the two Wootton portraits in Kew House. But he chooses to portray Frederick hunting in the company of not only his wife, 'Silvia' (Frederick's own poetic name for Augusta), but notable political figures, some now dead. He praises Chancellor Talbot, 'now wrap'd in Night's eternal Veil', as well as his son the radical opposition Whig William. William Talbot was MP for Glamorgan and there may be an underlying association in

---

[151] *Spring*, l. 86 (*TE* i. 69). For the riddle, see John M. Aden, *Pope's Once and Future Kings: Satire and Politics in the Early Career* (Knoxville, Tenn., 1978), 62–3.

[152] *TE* i. 188–9.

this very Welsh poem with Frederick's own connections with the Glamorgan gentry.[153] Powney also praises the Jacobite William, Lord Digby (fifth Baron Digby of Geashill), elderly patriarch of Shelborne and friend of Pope.[154] But it is in the death of the stag that Powney's encounters with Jacobitism become most overt.

> Abandon'd thus, the faithless Herd he flies,
> And wounds an alien Land with plaintive Cries,
> Where *Arran* shuns the servile Pomp of State,
> And silent mourns an exil'd Brother's Fate.

(p. 10)

Arran's 'exil'd Brother' is James Butler, Duke of Ormonde, who had fled to France and the Pretender's service after being impeached in 1715: the man probably most admired and idealized by Jacobite Tories.[155] Ormonde had been the political mastermind behind a series of plans for Spanish and French-backed Jacobite invasions of Britain in 1719 and 1722, as well as playing a prominent role in the plans for the '45. His younger brother and successor, the Earl of Arran, also formerly a Jacobite, was Oxford's Chancellor after 1715; as an Oxford Tory, Powney would understandably praise him. Powney was veering close to the treasonable by sympathetically alluding to a leading Jacobite in the same framework as Denham had dramatized the persecution of Charles I. Powney's cornered stag 'Bewails the Wrongs and Insults of the Plain; | Tears, Innocence and Justice plead in vain' (p. 14). But did Powney think the Jacobite cause just, or, perhaps more importantly, still viable? He must have spent time in the company of Oxford Jacobites; his *Templum Harmoniae* was modelled on the Jacobite William King's *Templum Libertatis* and he was later present, like his brother Peniston, at King's famous 'redeat' oration speech at the Radcliffe Camera on 13 April 1749. Yet in 1739 and in 1745 Powney was clearly loyal to Frederick—perhaps, as Colley suggests, one of those Hanoverian Tories present at King's oration who chose to interpret his 'redeat' as 'an invocation not to the Stuarts but rather to the prospect of a renovated Hanoverian regime'.[156] In his handling of the stag's fate Powney shows a Denham-like balance of sympathy and judgement for a cause now lost. It is, after all, the Hanoverian Prince Frederick who chases and finally kills the Jacobite stag.

---

[153] Philip Jenkins, *The Making of a Ruling Class: The Glamorgan Gentry, 1640–1790* (Cambridge, 1983), 166–72.

[154] For Digby and his relations with Pope, see Howard Erskine-Hill, *The Social Milieu of Alexander Pope: Lives, Examples and the Poetic Response* (New Haven, Conn. and London, 1975), 132–65.

[155] Cruickshanks, *Political Untouchables*, 27.

[156] Colley, *In Defiance of Oligarchy*, 257.

The Order of the Garter

Gilbert West's *The Institution of the Order of the Garter* is the last in the series of 'Windsor' poems centred on Prince Frederick. Published in 1742, the year of Walpole's fall, it epitomizes the revival of the spirit of romantic patriotic chivalry fostered by Frederick's circle. In 1725 George I had revived the second oldest order, the Bath, primarily as a cheap alternative to expensive pensions, 'An artful bank of thirty-six ribbons to supply a fund of favours in lieu of places'.[157] The following year Robert Walpole was granted the uncommon honour of the Order of the Garter. César de Saussure, a foreigner visiting the court, described it as a 'wonder' that Walpole, a mere commoner, should have been thus elevated: the first so honoured since 1660.[158] Walpole, as usual, made the most out of the occasion. His installation ceremony featured such expensive and elaborate pageantry that it was compared to a new coronation. The following year his feast at Windsor outmatched in extravagance that of any nobleman who had recently received the Order of the Garter.

Walpole's installation prompted a series of sycophantic poems from Court Whig poets, notably Edward Young. These were the subject of much mirth and mockery from opposition journals such as *Mist's*, which recommended them as a sure sedative for the sleepless.[159] More savage criticism was directed at Walpole, whose habit of commissioning portraits of himself in full Garter regalia and even ordering the blue ribbon to be painted in on earlier portraits earned him the familiar soubriquet 'Sir Robert Blue-String'.[160] Many critics saw the abuse of England's ancient orders of merit as a symbol of the decline of 'Old England', the star and garter now possessing no value or even an inverse value to their former significance: badges of shame, not honour. In March 1734 Hugh Fortescue, Lord Clinton, recently dismissed alongside Cobham for his criticism of Walpole, 'flung off his garter as Knight of the Bath, saying it was not fit for a gentleman to wear'.[161] Swift's Lilliputian courtiers compete in 'leaping and creeping' contests for the red, blue, and green ribbons. Pope's satirical weapon was aimed (in a memorable line) to 'bare the mean Heart that lurks beneath a Star'. The '*Star*' and '*Feather*' of the Garter are the outward tokens of inner corruption in those who drink the Wizard's cup in Book IV of *The Dunciad*; and in the roll-call of the truly brave and worthy in the *Epilogue to the Satires*, Dia. II, Pope bestows his own personal honours on 'the truly Brave' rather than the worthless ones which '*Anstis*

---

[157] Horace Walpole, cited in *Memoirs of Sarah, Duchess of Marlborough*, ed. A. T. Thompson, 2 vols. (1839), ii. 462.

[158] César de Saussure, *A Foreign View of England*, ed. and trans. Madame Van Muyden (1902), 175.

[159] See *Mist's Weekly Journal*, 10 Sept. 1726; Thomson, *Letters*, 41–2.

[160] See esp. Milton Percival, *Political Ballads Illustrating the Administration of Sir Robert Walpole* (Oxford, 1916), 1–3.   [161] *Egmont Diary*, ii. 52.

[chief Herald at Arms] casts into the Grave'.[162] The ironic disparity between St George of Cappadocia, patron saint of England and the Garter order, and his latter-day namesake George II, lies behind Pope's description of the mock-coronation rituals in the *Dunciad*.[163]

Frederick as Prince of Wales was honoured with the Garter, invested in a modest ceremony shortly after his arrival in Britain. Gilbert West as his pensioner would have seen the 1732 portrait, *Frederick Prince of Wales with the Knights of the Round Table*, and may have been familiar with the aims and ethos of the society it depicts. West's poem concerns the careful judgements which the Order's founder Edward III metes out on a series of foreign potentates who come (unsuccessfully) to press their claims to be admitted to the Garter order, and the bestowing of the very first Garter on Edward the Black Prince, who is clearly to be identified here with Prince Frederick. West's poem was directly inspired by Bolingbroke's *Idea of a Patriot King*: its penultimate verse celebrates the Prince of Wales as 'Thee, thou great Miracle of Earth, a PATRIOT KING' (p. 64)—a line which echoes Bolingbroke's assertion that 'A PATRIOT KING is the most powerful of all reformers; for he is himself a sort of standing miracle'.[164] The lengthy dialogues between Edward and his visitors discuss and affirm the duties and role of the Patriot King in terms broadly similar to those outlined by Bolingbroke. But to describe *The Order of the Garter* merely as the conversion of propaganda into poetry would be doing serious injustice to West's fertile mythopoeic imagination.

The Order of the Garter is a strange fusion of historical romance and royal masque. West footnotes his source as Rapin's account of the tournament held at Windsor on 23 April 1357 and attended by King John of France, 'the most Sumptuous and Magnificent that had ever been seen in *England*'.[165] Claiming poetic licence, West fuses this with the foundation seven years earlier of the Order of the Garter in 1350.[166] But all claims to historical authenticity are subservient to the main design of the piece. *The Order of the Garter* is to all intents and purposes a masque. Its complex mythological apparatus includes 'flourish of aerial Music', singing spirits, the Genius of England descending in a chariot, serial choruses (as we have seen) of Druids and bards and all the symbolic iconography adopted by Caroline masques, most notably Carew's

[162] Pope, *Im. Horace*, II i. 108 (*TE* iv. 15); *Dunciad*, iv. 519–24 (*TE* v. 394). *Ep. Satires*, ii. 235–9 (*TE* iv. 326).

[163] See Douglas Brooks-Davies, *Pope's 'Dunciad' and The Queen of the Night: A Study in Emotional Jacobitism* (Manchester, 1985), 153–4. See also Swift, 'On Poetry: A Rapsody', ll. 460–4 (*Poetical Works*, ed. Herbert Davis (Oxford, 1967), 582).

[164] Bolingbroke, *Patriot King*, 84.

[165] Gilbert West, *The Institution of the Order of the Garter* (1742), 3. All future citations incorporated in text.

[166] West's central theme of visiting foreign potentates, including Italians, seeking admission to the Garter from Edward III may have been inspired by his friend William Kent's account of a picture he saw and described in the collection of one of the great Italian families depicting 'King Edward the Third a-making one of them a Knight of St. Giorgio' (Wilson, *William Kent*, 148).

Coelum Britannicum, which had also disclosed 'SCENE: Windsor Park, with a Prospect of the Castle' and choruses of British Druids.[167] Yet unlike Thomson's masque *Alfred* or Lyttelton's planned but fragmentary *Masque for Children, The Order of the Garter* was never intended for performance.[168] Its length and comparative lack of action led David Garrick to make substantial cuts when he adapted it for the stage in the 1770s. It is a highly academic version of the masque, intended to be read and understood rather than seen and forgotten.

West understood the political dynamics behind both the traditional Caroline masque, with its ritual idealization of king and court in relation to a divinely ordered hierarchy, and the challenge posed to that form by Milton's *Comus*, to which *The Order of the Garter* is also indebted.[169] *Comus* had placed the virtuous individual in opposition not to an abstract disorder but to a corrupt society; *Comus* shows that corruption abounds and virtue needs affirmation. West celebrates his Patriot King as the embodiment of divine order yet extends Milton's challenge to the conventional masque tradition of royal praise yet further by making the test one of the king himself. The visiting foreign candidates are not what they seem; they are disguises worn by the spirits of the ancient Druids called upon by the Genius of England to test the king's virtue, judgement, and fitness to rule. By indignantly rejecting the foreigners' false claims, Edward is finally deemed worthy by the Druids and Genius of England of the order he himself has founded.

The testing and reaffirmation of the moral requirements for the award of the Garter is clearly aimed at its corruption under both George I and George II: 'For Dignities and Titles, when misplac'd | Upon the Vicious, the Corrupt and Vile' will 'Shame retort | Ev'n on the Sacred Throne, from whence they sprung. | So may the Lustre of this Order bright, | This Eldest Child of Chivalry be stain'd' (p. 14). West's 'foreign' claimants all embody different facets of the wrong values which the opposition saw flourishing in Hanoverian England. The Spanish grandee is summarily dismissed. So too the mercenary soldier, representative of standing armies, military aggression untempered by patriotism. The 'Usurer and Senator of Genoa' is the walking embodiment of 'paper credit', the infertile and self-serving use of money which Walpole's opponents saw as one of the causes of Britain's social decline. There is a Machiavellian Venetian politician, skilled in 'Craft of State'; his theory of power, which rests on knowledge and manipulation of 'the false corrupted

---

[167] *Poems of Thomas Carew*, ed. Rhodes Dunlap (Oxford, 1957), 183.

[168] See *The Poetical Works of George, Lord Lyttelton* (1801), 146–7. This is the first printing of the *Masque for Children*, for which the MS now seems to be lost. No date is given. The play was to be performed at Hagley; a child in the character of Queen Mab addresses Pitt and urges him to 'Rule and uphold our sinking state'.

[169] See David Norbrook, 'The Reformation of the Masque', in David Lindley (ed.), *The Court Masque* (Manchester, 1984), 94–110 and his *Poetry and Politics in the English Renaissance* (1984), 246–65.

Heart of Man, | His every Weakness, every Vice' (p. 41), sounds like Walpole's much misquoted dictum 'All these men have their price'. Walpolian 'luxury' is also represented by the 'Syren song' of the Neapolitan courtier who argues the case for the royal enjoyment of luxury at the expense of the common people.

Edward exposes and dismisses all these claims in turn, reaffirming as he does so the true nature of just kingship.

> By holding with a firm impartial Hand
> The steady scale of Justice; not alone
> Betwixt my Subjects in their private Rights,
> But in the gen'ral, more important Cause
> Of Freedom and of just Prerogative:
> Transgressing not myself by boundless Pow'r,
> Nor suffering others to transgress those Laws,
> That in their golden Chain together bind
> For common Good, the whole united State.

> (pp. 45–6)

This balance between 'freedom and just prerogative' is central to the *Patriot King*, as well as to the *concors discordia* models of political balance advanced by *Coopers-Hill*, whose influence can also be seen at work in this poem. West goes further than Bolingbroke in explicitly defending the rights of subjects under law; but like Bolingbroke, West incorporates political doctrines of kingship which are Whig-like in explicitly refuting doctrines of indefeasible divine right (the only right is Edward's right to govern well) while at the same time evoking more mystical powers of kingship. The limitations on Crown power imposed by the 'Laws and Charters of Enfranchisement' (p. 43) are balanced by Britain's need for a strong paternal monarch, a time when 'Kings were cloath'd with Majesty, | Encircled with Authority, rever'd | And almost Deify'd' (p. 46). In the final odes sung by the bards and Druids, it is almost as if West has fully translated Bolingbroke's treatise into the mythological language to which the swelling prophetic conclusion of the *Patriot King* itself has gestured. Within one poem we find the synthesis of Whig and Tory-Stuart mythology which the Patriot opposition had used at different points throughout the preceding decade. Edward's eloquent defence of 'The valiant Sons of Poverty, the *Goths*, | The *Huns* and *Vandals*' (p. 29) prefaces the Whiggish glorification of British liberty in the final ode: the 'Law of Freedom' brought by the 'valiant Sons of *Odin*' and renewed by the Saxon law-giver Alfred (p. 62). As in *Coopers-Hill*, the Thames becomes the symbol of *concors discordia*, flowing past the royalist symbol of Windsor Castle, 'whose proud Battlements | Sit like a Regal Crown upon the Brow | Of this high-climbing lawn' (p. 13), down past Runnymede, where the signing of Magna Carta reconfirms British liberties in one of the poem's many epiphanic moments.

West's richly conceived Druids, too, are both Whig-Gothic and Tory royalist; they are defenders of ancient British liberties against Roman and more recent tyrannies, yet also test and crown a British royal line descending from Troynovant through Arthur to the Patriot Prince.

The most memorable feature of *The Order of the Garter* is West's full-scale evocation of the romantic chivalric past. The memory of Arthur and his Round Table gives rise to visions of white-plumed pomp, 'The Triumphs of the listed Field; | Behold along his level Meads | Careering Knights, encountr'ing Steeds, | Heroic games' (pp. 52–3). We see Pendragon 'burst the veiling Shades | And all his blazing Magnitude unfold' (p. 54). Queen Caroline's waxen Merlin pales before West's exuberant mythologizing.

> Then too in feastful Hall or Bow'r,
> Attendant on the genial Hour,
> The *British* Harp sweet Lyrists strung,
> And *Albion*'s generous Victors sung:
> While valiant *Arthur*'s copious Fame
> Incessant fed the bright poetic Flame.
>
> (p. 53)

There had been no medieval chivalry in the 1735–6 revival of Dryden's *King Arthur*; George II may have been implicitly identified with Arthur, but Dryden's Arthur is not the Arthur of the Round Table but an early British king doing battle with the Saxons.

A final note might be added about the afterlife of West's consummate Patriot King poem. In its purely literary dimension—bards, Druids, Arthurian knights, the chivalric past, the Pindaric ode—it corresponded, as we have seen, with all that mid-eighteenth-century poets and critics were beginning to admire; it was for this reason that Joseph Warton singled out for praise West's 'Chorus of bards'. But it was for another, more political reason that David Garrick, a former member of Frederick's literary circle, converted West's poem into an extravagant afterpiece for the stage in 1771.[170] In February 1771 Lord Gower was installed as Knight of the Garter with regal ceremony; in July, the Prince of Wales, the future George IV, was also inducted into the Garter order. In August Garrick wrote to Lyttelton requesting a copy of Dodsley's *Miscellanies* in which West's poem had been reprinted in 1748. He knew that Colman at Covent Garden was planning a production inspired by the Garter ceremonies entitled *The Fairy Prince, with the Installation of the Knights of the Garter*. Both shows ran together for two weeks in November, drawing huge crowds who came to see the splendour of the painted scenes of

---

[170] David Garrick, *The Songs, Chorusses, and Serious Dialogues of the Masque Called the Institution of the Garter, or, Arthur's Round Table Restored* (1771). See G. W. Stone and G. M. Kahrl, *David Garrick: A Critical Biography* (Carbondale, Ill., 1979), 239–40; *Letters of David Garrick*, ed. D. M. Little and G. M. Kahrl, 3 vols. (Oxford, 1963), ii, nos. 648, 651, 654, 656. See also R. G. Noyes, 'Ben Jonson's Masques in the 18th Century', *SP* 33 (1936), 427–36.

Windsor. Garrick cut West's text and added some comic scenes, but these merely counterpoint the serious lines spoken by the Genius to the Knights seated at the Round Table, prophesying the future glories of Edward's line. It was a piece of right royal myth-making for George III and the Prince of Wales.

There was a certain appositeness in all this. It was George III's reign which witnessed a renovated patriotic monarchy in which the administration was formed for the first time from both Whigs and Tories after the long years of Hanoverian proscription—the 'Patriot' administration above party or faction promised by Frederick and his followers in both the late 1730s and the late 1740s. George III also initiated the cult of royal image-making which his own father Frederick had attempted to promote when Prince of Wales.[171] West's celebration of the splendours of the Garter ceremony at Windsor was perfectly attuned to the mood of George III's reign. Unlike George II, who ignored Windsor, George III finally moved into residence there in the late 1780s and altered the interior in ways designed to celebrate Windsor's history as the seat of the Garter order and the Round Table. Recollecting that 'Windsor Castle had in its present form been created by Edward the Third, [he] said that he thought the achievements of his splendid reign were well calculated for pictures, and would prove very suitable ornaments to the halls and chambers of that venerable edifice'.[172] It seems nicely coincidental that another West, the artist Benjamin West, should have supplied the eight enormous paintings celebrating the achievements and events of Edward III's reign.[173] On St George's Day 1805 George III restored the true identification between Hanoverian George and Cappadocian George by holding an unprecedentedly splendid installation of the Garter Knights at Windsor, with invitations sent out to all foreign ambassadors and Ministers of the Crown. This was, as Colley suggests, a royal British riposte to the upstart Napoleon's new civic ceremonies.[174] That King George, the son and heir of Prince Frederick, the 'once and future' Patriot King celebrated by the Patriot poets of the 1730s, should have fulfilled the revival of the Installation of the Garter in a literal translation of West's fictional ceremonies seems almost prophetic.

[171] Linda Colley, 'The Apotheosis of George III: Loyalty, Royalty and the British Nation, 1760–1820', *Past and Present*, 102 (1984), 94–129; *Britons*, 204–36.

[172] John Galt, cited in Christopher Lloyd, *The Queen's Pictures: Royal Collectors through the Centuries* (1991), 178.

[173] See ibid. 178 and fig. 53; Mark Girouard, *The Return to Camelot: Chivalry and the English Gentleman* (1984), 19–20.

[174] Colley, *Britons*, 216–17.

8

Jacobites and Patriots: Johnson and Savage

THE TITLE of Johnson's famous poem, *The Vanity of Human Wishes*, could aptly serve as an epitaph to the Patriot campaign. By 1742 Walpole, the long-loathed minister, had gone, only to be replaced by 'politics as usual', a Whig party reshuffle which in time came to include previous Patriot Whigs who abandoned their commitment to broad-bottom principles in pursuit of government places. The staunch Court Whig Charles Hanbury Williams gleefully noted that 'As the cry of the hounds ceaseth when the entrails of the beast are divided amongst them, so ceased the clamours of the patriots at the distribution of places'.[1] Former Patriot supporters suffered a profound loss of political faith, none more acutely than the young Mark Akenside, who in 1744 penned an embittered invective on Pulteney, the *Epistle to Curio*. In 1745 Thomson's friend Benjamin Victor, sitting in the audience at Thomson's *Tancred and Sigismunda*, was sickened to see Pitt and Lyttelton, 'both very lately most flaming patriots', smugly applauding all the right pro-ministerial lines.

Did not both these gentlemen act quite counter to this very doctrine when they acquired the amiable and distinguish'd character of PATRIOTS? Were not the unanswerable reasons they gave for their vigorous opposition—'That such encroachments were made on the liberties of the people, by a late overgrown, obnoxious *minister*, that to oppose him in almost all his measures, was VIRTUE.' Did not a late celebrated duchess leave a very great legacy to one of those patriots for his *honest opposition*? Well, Sir, this unwearied opposition was at last, crown'd with success; and most of the patriots are in the administration of affairs—and now follows the material question, viz. *What has been done for the people?* HAS ANY ONE GRIEVANCE BEEN REDRESSED? But their turns are served—they are in good places, and therefore all *opposition* is to cease, or to be construed into party, and treated as criminal.[2]

Some of the most scathing definitions of Patriots, patriotism, and Whigs are supplied, of course, by Samuel Johnson: Whiggism as a *'negation of all principle'*, Whig 'the name of a faction', patriotism as 'the last refuge of the scoundrel'.[3] Johnson's 1770s pamphlet attacks on popular patriotism, Wilkes, and liberty, culminating in his excoriating *The Patriot* (1774), were rooted in his experiences of the Walpole period. Johnson had learnt to be wary of those who 'claim a place in the list of Patriots by an acrimonious and unremitting opposition to the Court'.[4]

---

[1] Sir Charles Hanbury Williams, *Works*, 3 vols. (1822), iii. 32.

[2] Benjamin Victor, *Original Letters, Dramatic Pieces and Poems*, 3 vols. (1776), i. 102–3. This letter was originally printed under a pseudonym in the *Daily Post*, 26 Apr. 1745. Victor at this stage was less openly critical of Thomson than in the later version.

[3] Boswell, *Life of Johnson*, i. 431, 294; ii. 438.   [4] *Yale Johnson*, x. 390.

Yet at least the first of these two adjectives could apply to his own 'opposition to the Court' in the late 1730s. After Johnson went to London in 1737 he wrote some very vigorous, even 'acrimonious', attacks on the administration. By 1741 his patriotic ardour had begun to cool, tempered by a suspicion of opposition motives and a respect for Walpole reflected in the balanced judgements of his parliamentary reports for the *Gentleman's Magazine*. By 1743 his report of the debate following Sandys's February 1741 motion to remove Walpole from office was more generous in its portrayal of Walpole than of the Patriots. By 1744, when he wrote the *Life of Savage*, Johnson had backpedalled sufficiently from his former views to adopt an ironic detachment about Savage's mistaken support for the 'late Opposition'. The *Life of Savage* was the first of several 'Lives' in which Johnson exorcized his former ideals by sidesweeps at the political views of those poets who had played a part in the Patriot campaign. Johnson's political prejudices made his accounts of Pope, Mallet, Thomson, and especially Lyttelton anything but impartial.

But Johnson's political career poses problems more complex than those of disillusioned patriotism. In recent years we have seen very different accounts of the 'Politics of Samuel Johnson'. In his 1960 study of that title, Donald Greene refuted the 'Tory reactionary' Johnson of Boswell's *Life*, especially its Jacobite element, arguing the case for a liberal, rather Whiggish Johnson who championed human rights and a wide variety of political freedoms.[5] Howard Erskine-Hill subsequently turned a more rigorous eye to historical evidence and textual detail to argue that Johnson during certain periods of his life harboured Jacobite principles.[6] The evidence for this seems irrefutable, especially in relation to two works of the late 1730s, *London* (1738) and *Marmor Norfolciense* (1739), and possibly the later *Vanity of Human Wishes* (1749). But the picture is complicated by the fact that only two weeks after the publication of the Jacobite *Marmor*, Johnson savaged Walpole in a work of undiluted Patriot Whiggery, his *Compleat Vindication of the Licensers of the Stage*, an attack on the recent Stage Licensing Act and a defence of the Patriot playwright Henry Brooke.[7] Although the two works adopt the similar device of an

[5] Donald Greene, *The Politics of Samuel Johnson* (New Haven, Conn., 1960; 2nd edn. Athens, Ga., 1990). In his polemical preface to the second edition Greene defends his former views and attempts (unsuccessfully) to demolish all recent revisionist readings of Johnson, as well as most post-Namierite accounts of eighteenth-century politics in general.

[6] Howard Erskine-Hill, 'The Political Character of Samuel Johnson', in Isobel Grundy (ed.), *Samuel Johnson: New Critical Essays* (1984), 107–36; and 'The Political Character of Samuel Johnson: The Lives of the Poets and a Further Report on The Vanity of Human Wishes', in Eveline Cruickshanks (ed.), *The Jacobite Challenge* (Edinburgh, 1988), 161–76. Our understanding of Johnson's political alignments tends to be influenced by current historiographical debate. For a less polarized, Court/Country reading of Johnson's early political writing, see Thomas Kaminski, *The Early Career of Samuel Johnson* (New York, 1987). This is based on earlier historical studies than its date would suggest.

[7] *Marmor Norfolciense* was first advertised for sale on 11 May 1739 in *Daily Advertiser*. Greene (*Yale Johnson*, x. 20) notes that it may have appeared the previous month, as it was listed in the *GM* register of books for Apr. 1739. *A Compleat Vindication* was advertised for sale on 25 May.

ironic narrative persona, vehicle and butt of the satire, their attacks on the administration utilize very different kinds of political language. Johnson, as *Marmor*'s self-styled author 'Probus Britannicus', supplies a seditious account of Hanoverian 'intruders'. Old England's degeneration is blamed on foreign usurpers as well as a corrupt administration. The Jacobite thrust is completely missing from the *Compleat Vindication*, whose attacks on sinister ministerial designs on freedom of speech are written from a Patriot Whig, and indeed a radical Patriot Whig position, filled with the language of liberty and public spirit and the exemplary virtue of republican Rome.

I have argued in previous chapters that Patriot Whiggery and Jacobitism deployed overlapping sets of images and metaphors, especially those of redemptive kingship. But Patriot Whigs were rarely Jacobites.[8] The one thing that emerges from a study of Patriot Whigs is a remarkably consistent level of support for the House of Hanover, even if that support focused on the heir to the throne rather than its present occupant. This is not to deny that a few figures involved in Patriot politics later dabbled with Jacobite intrigue—Bolingbroke, Chesterfield, and Cornbury. But the fundamental tenet cherished by most opposition Whigs—defence of the Protestant succession—was ultimately irreconcilable with Jacobitism. The Jacobite innuendo some hostile critics read into Brooke's *Gustavus Vasa* was almost certainly not its Whig author's intention: Brooke's subsequent alarmist *The Farmer's Letter to the Protestants of Ireland* (1745) made his violent antipathy to James III unambiguous. None of the Patriot poets in this book could have written anything as anti-Hanoverian as Johnson's *Marmor Norfolciense*. There is a vast difference between the Whig Patriot Richard Glover's *London: or, the Progress of Commerce* (1738) and the veiled threats which Johnson levelled at George II in his own *London* of the same year.

The Royal Martyr and the Royal Exile

Johnson's unusual oscillation between Whig Patriot idealism and stubborn Jacobite resentment was also characteristic of Richard Savage, perhaps the dominant influence on the young Johnson during his first years in London.[9] We have already encountered Savage's *The Progress of a Divine* (1735), the audacious satire on clerical abuses under Bishop Gibson. Savage's attack on the Gibson regime and his defence of the heterodox Thomas Rundle appeared

---

[8] For the complex permutations of Jacobitism and radical Whiggery see Paul Monod, *Jacobitism and the English People, 1688–1788* (Cambridge, 1989), 23–44. 'Whiggish' Jacobites were primarily a feature of the 1690s, when Jacobitism attracted Whig radicals disillusioned by William's refusal to sponsor more reform. After 1715 Jacobites 'disguised' themselves in Old Whig or 'Country' rhetoric as subterfuge. Only a tiny number of Whigs turned Jacobite after 1720.

[9] For a full account of this friendship, *c.*1737–9, see Richard Holmes, *Dr. Johnson and Mr. Savage* (1993).

at a time when Whig anticlericalism sharply divided Patriot Whigs from Tories in the opposition. Savage was in one sense a Patriot poet *manqué*. His friendship with Aaron Hill, Thomson, and Mallet dated back to the Hillarian circle of the 1720s. Savage was Master of the Richmond Lodge of Freemasons into which he inducted Thomson, Prince Frederick's Gentleman Usher William Hawley, and his other Patriot friends Paterson and Armstrong in September 1737. Frederick himself became a Mason at the Richmond Lodge two months later.[10] Yet although Savage tried hard to enter Frederick's own inner sanctum, he never quite succeeded. His *A Poem on the Birthday of the Prince of Wales* (1736) failed to make its way into Frederick's hands. So did the longer revised version, *Of Public Spirit in Regard to Public Works* (1737), modelled loosely on Thomson's *Liberty*. Savage's chequered personal reputation, not to mention his promiscuous bids for patronage from Walpole and Caroline, cannot have endeared him to the Prince.[11]

Savage always hated Walpole and regarded him as 'an Enemy to Liberty, and an Oppressor of his Country'.[12] His panegyrics on Walpole and most members of the royal family are filled with stale tropes and empty flattery. *Of Public Spirit* is far more convincing, but its emotional strength, as Johnson noted, lies less in its celebration of the Prince or public spirit than in its accounts of suffering, pain, and exile—forced emigration, slavery, colonial exploitation. Richard Holmes has shown how Savage's extraordinary personal history and turbulent, disordered personality expressed itself in images of exile and alienation, fictional self-projections which also shaped Johnson's *An Account of the Life of Mr. Savage* (1744).[13] Savage claimed to be the illegitimate son of the relationship between Earl Rivers and Anne Brett, former Countess of Macclesfield. He spent most of his highly publicized life trying to reclaim his aristocratic patrimony despite his mother's refusal to acknowledge his existence. Savage's obsession with the 'excluded' may explain his readiness to take up cudgels on behalf of his friend Thomas Rundle, 'exiled' to remote Derry after Walpole refused him the English ecclesiastical preferment his merits deserved.[14] The same obsession with martyrdom and exile drew him

---

[10] *Daily Gazetteer*, 13 Sept. 1737. Frederick became a Mason on 5 Nov.

[11] Savage paid scant attention to Hanoverian feuds. He praised George II in 1727 by holding up his hated father as a model; in 1734 he dedicated to Caroline a poem on her daughter's marriage to the Prince of Orange when the pair's popularity eclipsed her own; he acted as Caroline's 'Volunteer Laureate' while praising her hated son Frederick.

[12] Samuel Johnson, *An Account of the Life of Mr. Savage*, ed. Clarence Tracy (Oxford, 1971), 51. All further citations from this edn., hereafter *Life of Savage*.

[13] Holmes, *Dr. Johnson and Mr. Savage*.

[14] Most recent critics assume that *The Progress of a Divine* had little bearing on Rundle, Gibson et al., and was simply an excuse for Savage to attract attention to himself. Yet Johnson (*Life of Savage*, 83) claimed that Savage was 'a warm Advocate for Dr. *Rundle*'. Thomson's wintry landscape showing Rundle wandering in exile, driven from his 'native Sun-shine' into the 'bleak Crescent' mountains encircling 'Waves | From the frozen Pole', may have been inspired by Savage's *The Wanderer*. See *A Poem to the Memory . . . of Talbot* (1737), ll. 239–44 (OET *Liberty*, 156).

irresistibly towards Jacobitism. Savage's conviction that blue blood ran in his veins, his fantasy that he was a 'prince' wandering in disguise, forced to roam abroad until he could come into his own again and reclaim his rights, made him what can genuinely be described as an emotional Jacobite. His most imaginative poem, *The Wanderer* (1729), draws heavily on all the staple features of Jacobite sentiment and iconography for its fictional self-projections—the disguised monarch, the Christ-like mild and suffering hero surrounded by rays of light, the images of transfiguration and apotheosis. Johnson may have turned Savage into a proto-Romantic figure of the Outcast Poet, yet Savage had also perpetuated his own personalized version of the Tory cult of Charles the Martyr. Whether Johnson recognized this in some subliminal sense is hard to tell, yet it may not be irrelevant to his Jacobite phase, which coincided with his intense if brief friendship with Savage.

Savage would have absorbed such images during his youth, when he was an active Jacobite propagandist. At least one of the five Jacobite poems he published between 1715 and 1716 transcends the level of popular doggerel.[15] 'Britannia's Miseries' conveys both the pathos and the romance of the lost Stuart cause. Curses on George I and his 'dirty Glories' are matched by an emotive account of the sufferings of the 'Royal Exile' and his aristocratic supporters. Why should 'The only Relick of the Royal Race; | (Whose Angel's Nature wou'd the Scepter Grace) | Be forc'd to wander through the World forlorne, | And rue the time, He was your Monarch born?' Charles I, the 'Royal Martyr', was followed by those other 'Martyr'd Sons'.[16] Savage's obsession with birth and legitimacy emerges in his repeated rehearsal of the myth that George II was a 'warming-pan' child, and in his attack on the 'Spurious' origins of the 'Whole Mock-Royal Race' of Hanoverians. They should 'Resign to Royal James what is his Right'.[17]

Savage later covered up his part in the 1715 rebellion. He had been arrested that November, and only narrowly escaped prosecution after months of being trailed by government spies.[18] It is hard to believe that Johnson did not know of Savage's Jacobite sympathies. His complete silence on the subject and his rapid dismissal of Savage's early pamphlets in the *Life of Savage* might be as revealing as his feigned ignorance over the Stage Licensing Act. By 1744

[15] Savage, *Poetical Works*, ed. Clarence Tracy (Cambridge, 1962), 26, 23, 17, 22. For their discovery, see editor's notes, pp. 15–16. Howard Erskine-Hill notes the parallel Jacobite allusion to Hannibal in 'Britannia's Miseries' and Johnson's *Vanity of Human Wishes*. See 'The Political Character of Samuel Johnson' (1984), 172–3. It would be interesting to know how Savage responded to his older (legitimate) half-sister Elizabeth's marriage in 1711 to the Jacobite Irish peer Lord Barrymore, subsequently one of the 5 Jacobite peers behind the '45. Earl Rivers formally disinherited his sole legal heir for marrying a Jacobite. The couple got possession of the family seat, Rock Savage, in 1728 but lived there earlier.

[16] 'Britannia's Miseries', ll. 5, 57–60, 94–5 (*Poetical Works*, 19–23).

[17] Ibid., l. 108; 'An Ironical Panegyrick on his pretended Majesty G—', l. 23 (*Poetical Works*, 17, 23).

[18] See Holmes, *Dr. Johnson and Mr. Savage*, 65–6.

Jacobitism was in any case a dangerous issue. In the course of their famous night route-marches round London, 'brimful of patriotism', the two friends must have touched on the Stuarts, especially if they were speculatively 'dethroning princes' and 'establishing new forms of government'.[19] The 'Patriots' of Savage's early poems are loyal supporters of the Stuarts. 'First grieve her King's a Royal Exile made, | Proscrib'd her Patriots and her Church betray'd'; 'See how the Patriots of the Land become | Martyrs, if here, or Exiles from their Home.'[20]

Savage wrote nothing so overtly Jacobite after 1716, yet the sympathies remain consistent. His poem on the Bangorian controversy, *The Convocation* (1717), charts the row between Atterbury and Hoadly over the Whig doctrine of passive resistance. It attacks those who revile

> a King expell'd his Throne,
> Who for his Conscience sacrific'd his Crown.
> Swoln with Preferment thus the Wretch prophanes
> The Sacred Reliques with unhallow'd Strains.
> Cou'd He no other dark Evasions bring,
> But to asperse a poor departed King?[21]

Savage's 1723 *Prologue to King Henry VI* (written for Theophilus Cibber's production in which he himself played York) was no less emotive. Shakespeare adaptations of 1719–23 responded to fears of renewed Jacobite activity by focusing on the dangers of faction and rebellion.[22] Most were Hanoverian: cautious laments for the necessary passing of the Stuart dynasty. The plot of *Henry VI* was itself tendentious. Colley Cibber had previously been banned from using the murder scene of the deposed king from *III Henry VI* to open his *Tragical History of King Richard III* since it 'wou'd put the Audience in mind of the late King James'.[23] Savage's *Prologue* (23 July 1723) was spoken a fortnight after his friend Atterbury was forced into exile for Jacobite treason. It depicts a 'Monarch's Suffrings' and his 'ruin'd Grandeur': he is 'doom'd by his Grandsire's Guilt' and guilty only of 'Meekness'. The play's 'surprisingly plangent' Jacobite emotion might be traced to Savage, who purportedly helped the young Cibber adapt it.[24] It can be found six years later in the figure of

---

[19] Boswell, *Life of Johnson*, i. 164; Arthur Murphy, *An Essay on the Life and Genius of Samuel Johnson* (1792), 32–3. Cf. Johnson's Jacobite prophecy in *Marmor Norfolciense* (*Yale Johnson*, x. 25, 'Kings change their laws, and kingdoms change their kings').

[20] 'Britannia's Miseries', ll. 5–6, 75–6. See ll. 145–6 for the 'Roman soul in British Mould' of the 'Noble, loyal Patriot' Jacobite (*Poetical Works*, 19–24).

[21] *The Convocation*, ll. 220–5 (*Poetical Works*, 35). The poem also attacks Whig anti-Jacobite plays such as John Philips's *The Earl of Earl Marr'd* (1715) and *The Pretender's Flight* (1716).

[22] Printed in *Poetical Works*, 48–9. See John Loftis, *The Politics of Drama in Augustan England* (Oxford, 1963), 81–2.

[23] See Michael Dobson, *The Making of the National Poet: Shakespeare, Adaptation and Authorship, 1660–1789* (Oxford, 1992), 94–6, 99.

[24] Ibid. 95 n. 59. See Clarence Tracy, *The Artificial Bastard: A Biography of Richard Savage* (Toronto, 1953), 53.

Horatio, one of the three imaginary rebels executed in Book V of *The Wanderer*, Savage's extraordinary long poem.[25] The aristocratic Horatio's treason was prompted by patriotism: 'His pitying Eye saw Millions in Distress'. Echoes of the '15 lie behind this passage, the graves which 'to Mind recall | Rebellion's Council, and Rebellion's Fall'.[26] Johnson admired 'the artful Touches, by which he has distinguished the intellectual features of the Rebels', and cited the passage at full length.[27] Horatio goes to the scaffold with the dignity of a Charles I. Another character, the wandering disguised Seraph/Beggar, is likened to a monarch in exile, 'Wandr'ing from Court to Court, a King distrest'.[28] The three main figures in this poem, Bard, Hermit, Beggar (Savage's romantic self-projections) coalesce in a final portrait that could have been a Stuart icon.

> His Raiment lightens, and his Features glow!
> In shady Ringlets falls a length of Hair;
> Embloom'd his Aspect shines, enlarg'd his Air.
> Mild frown his Eyes enliv'ning Glories beam;
> Mild on his Brow sits Majesty supreme.
>
> .   .   .   .   .
>
> He looks, and forward steps with Mien Divine;
> A Grace celestial gives him all to shine.
> He speaks—Nature is ravish'd at the Sound.
> The Forests move, and streams stand list'ning round.[29]

Savage's readiness to 'justify the Conduct, and exalt the Character of Lord *Bolingbroke*' was rooted in the Queen Anne period.[30] So was his defence of Atterbury. Savage may have known more about Atterbury than we can tell. He

---

[25] In *Poetical Works*, 94–159. *The Wanderer* deploys many figures and motifs which are standard in Jacobite iconography. One is the identification between Charles the Martyr as a meek, suffering Christ, and Charles II as the 'risen son/sun' surrounded by rays of light. Cf. *The Wanderer* ii. 45–64, where the chapel altar depicts a 'transfigured Son', his head radiating an 'overwhelming Blaze' of 'Rays' like 'Summer-Suns' (cf. Savage's self-portrait in the Bard, 'Around his Temples Rays refulgent shine!'). Monod, *Jacobitism and the English People*, 62, notes the Jacobite use of 'an even more powerful religious icon, the crucified Christ, so that the sufferings of the sacred monarch parallel those of his God'. Cf. *The Wanderer*, ii. 51–4: 'What scenes of Agony the Garden brings; | The Cup of Gall; the suppliant King of Kings; | The Crown of Thorns, the Cross, that felt him die'.

[26] *The Wanderer*, v. 561, 397–8. Savage had earlier called himself 'Horatius'. Horatio's execution is followed by the same comets and storms which marked the death of the executed Jacobite lords in 1715, tokens of God's displeasure in 'Britannia's Miseries', ll. 125–32. Cf. *Wanderer*, v. 626–30. Horatio's death is followed by a night scene in which a 'master' puts to flight illegal poachers. 'Thus Treason steals, the Patriot thus descries, | Forth-springs the Monarch, and the Mischief flies' (v. 639–40). The identity of the 'Patriot' and the 'Monarch' is highly ambiguous.

[27] *Life of Savage*, 55. The passage Johnson cited ends with the repentance of Horatio, who recognizes the 'rig'rous Justice' of his sentence for treason—a timely epitaph in 1744 on the principled but wrong exercise of Horatio's patriotism. Johnson is careful to repeat Savage's claim that the rebels are purely fictitious.

[28] *The Wanderer*, v. 326. Cf. Dryden, *Astrea Redux*, ll. 75–6: 'Forc'd into exile from his rightful Throne | He made all Countries where he came his own.'

[29] *The Wanderer*, v. 702–11. Both Charles I and Charles II were always praised for their 'mildness'—a Stuart strength and a weakness. The long dark ringlets are revealing, as is the hint of the Messiah/natural regeneration imagery.   [30] Johnson, *Life of Savage*, 89.

supplied Thomas Birch with information about him for the sensation-provoking biography which appeared in a section of the *General Dictionary* in September 1734.[31] In 1735 he began work on some 'Epistles on Authors', probably finished in 1738 or 1739. The only published section, *On False Historians*, printed in the *Gentleman's Magazine* in 1741, ends with a paean to Bolingbroke. Most of the 'false historians' are Whigs such as Abel Boyer and John Oldmixon, the latter (it is hinted) guilty of Jacobite scaremongering—'*Letters* ne'er wrote', '*secret conf'rence*' and '*Treaties* ne'er plan'd'. Savage explicitly attacks the anti-Jacobite fake *Minutes of Monsieur Menager*, probably written by Defoe, a work '*calculated to vilify the Administration in the four last Years of* Q. Ann's reign'. Savage mocks the Whig-circulated rumour that James III was the product of a warming-pan birth: 'Is a prince born? what birth more base believ'd? | Or, what's more strange, his mother ne'er conceiv'd!'[32]

Savage wrote nothing as vehemently Jacobite in the 1730s as Johnson's *Marmor Norfolciense*, yet it may have been the long conversations with Savage which rekindled in Johnson memories of his own father Michael's Stuart sympathies.[33] They emerge in covert form in *London*, printed anonymously on 12 May 1738. This is in one sense an overtly 'Patriot' poem. It attacks Spanish insults and French hubris, opens with the nostalgic lament for Elizabethan lost glories, and valorizes those past 'golden ages' which shaped the historical iconography of patriot verse—Alfred, Edward III, Henry V, Elizabeth. The patriotic pantheon is remarkably similar to the historical vision at the centre of Thomson and Mallet's *Alfred*—bar one important missing monarch, William III. *London* is an attack on the Hanoverians as well as on Walpole and his corruptions. Thales exclaims 'let [George] live here, for [George] has learnt to live'—a Hanoverian at home in a corrupt Britain.[34] The lines 'Lest Ropes be wanting in the tempting Spring, | To rig another Convoy for the K—g' allude both to George II's much-criticized sea trips to Germany to visit his Hanoverian mistresses as well as to another kind of rope—a noose.[35]

Much ink has been spilt on the possible identification between Savage and Thales.[36] Johnson may have written *London* before he met Savage, as he

---

[31] Tracy, *The Artificial Bastard*, 122–3. Savage was anxious that the details should be accurate. He wrote post-haste to Birch after it was published pointing out three errors, one substantial.

[32] Savage praises Bolingbroke as opposition historian. But the thrust is very pro-Stuart. In *Poetical Works*, 238–43.

[33] The strength of the paternal influence suggested by J. C. D. Clark, *English Society 1688–1832: Ideology, Social Structure and Political Practice during the Ancien Regime* (Cambridge, 1985), 186–9.

[34] Johnson, *London*, l. 50. The insertion of 'George' in the blank of this line is suggested by its similarity to Boileau's 'Que George vive ici, puisque George y sait vivre'.

[35] Ibid., ll. 246–7. See Erskine-Hill, 'The Political Character of Samuel Johnson' (1984), 126. He links the rope to Tyburn and Johnson's contempt for harsh Hanoverian penal law. Johnson may also be hinting at the fate George II himself deserves.

[36] See Thomas Kaminski, 'Was Savage "Thales"?: Johnson's *London* and Biographical Speculation', in *Bulletin of Research in the Humanities*, 85 (1982), 322–35 and his *The Early Career of Johnson*, 97–101. The most convincing argument *for* the identification is Holmes, *Dr. Johnson and Mr. Savage*.

always strenuously claimed. Thales, modelled on the Juvenalian figure of Umbricius, rehearses certain commonplaces of urban discontent. Yet, as Richard Holmes has argued so fully, it would be hard to find a fictional portrait which corresponded so closely to the tone of Savage's own poetic voice as well as to his biographical circumstances. Even if Johnson had not met Savage by the time he wrote *London*, he had certainly read his frustrated poetic attack on Walpole for denying him a promised ministerial pension. *A Poet's Dependance on a Statesman* (1736), published in the *Gentleman's Magazine*, resounds with exactly the same note of moral indignation, resentment, and self-pity as *London*, the grievances of the talented but neglected outsider done down by a conspiracy of the governing élite and corrupt patterns of preferment. Like Thales, with his attacks on the 'Laureate Tribe' with their 'servile verse', Savage censures the 'servile herd' of writers who (unlike him) are 'For meanness honour'd and for guilt preferred'.[37] Thales's imminent departure for Wales may be coincidentally the path that Savage himself took in 1739. But the hidden allusion Howard Erskine-Hill has detected in the lines 'To breathe in distant Fields a purer Air, | And, fix'd on CAMBRIA's solitary shore, | Give to St. DAVID one *true Briton* more' (ll. 7–8) seems strikingly apposite to the Jacobite Savage. 'The idea of Jacobite exile . . . lurks within the printing of Johnson's lines.' The *True Briton* was the title of the journal which the Duke of Wharton established in 1723–4 to defend Atterbury at his trial for treason: Atterbury was forced into exile, which is where Warton also went in the last openly Jacobite phase of his political career.[38]

A 'bloody Jacobite' or a 'virulent Republican'?

Johnson's two political pieces of the following year adopt very different personas. Not the angry Juvenalian Umbricius of *London*, but the self-ironizing Swiftian ministerial narrators of *Marmor Norfolciense* and *A Compleat Vindication of the Licensers of the Stage*. Although both these pieces are concerned with the 'love of posterity' and the nature of patriotism, that patriotism takes different forms—as indeed had Savage's in the 1730s, when he was (probably genuinely) praising Prince Frederick in his *Of Public Spirit in Regard to Public Works* while still clutching on to memories of the House of Stuart and attacking Walpole and even (covertly) Caroline from both positions.[39] The trouble which Johnson courted for himself by *Marmor* (he was reputedly forced into hiding) smacks of the brushes with the administration which Savage, 'never celebrated for his Prudence', seems to have gone out of his way

---

[37] Cf. *London*, ll. 198–200 and *A Poet's Dependance on a Statesman*, 51–2.

[38] Erskine-Hill, 'The Political Character of Samuel Johnson' (1984), 126.

[39] Johnson admired *Of Public Spirit*, one of the first poems by Savage he saw. See *Life of Savage*, 93. In ll. 79–86 Savage attacks Caroline's unpublic-spirited fee-earning gardens.

to provoke.[40] *Marmor*'s lines on the blood-sucking White Horse of Hanover supplied, says Johnson's ministerial narrator, 'an insinuation . . . of so fatal and destructive a tendency, that it may prove equally dangerous to the author whether true or false'.[41]

Marmor Norfolciense concerns the pretended discovery of a stone in a Norfolk field engraved with a cryptic Latin prophecy which proves remarkably seditious when translated. That Johnson had Jacobite precedents in mind for this trope seems highly likely. Swift had written the famous spoof *Windsor Prophecy* of 1711 with which Johnson was familiar.[42] But mock-prophecies were also part of the cryptic rhetoric of Jacobitism—one thinks of the 1715 Jacobite *A Prophecy by Merlyn the Famous British Prophet: Found written on a Wall in Old Saxon Characters.* Merlin's prophecies, as we have seen in Chapter 6, had recently been given a powerful oppositional turn by the abundance of satirical Merlinic predictions which Caroline's Cave had inspired from the authors of the *Craftsman* and *Fog's.* Johnson would almost certainly have been familiar with these. Those printed in the opposition press did not, for obvious reasons, contain Jacobite innuendo—their criticism of the Hanoverians took the form of mockery rather than anything more seditious. The closest they came to denigrating the White Horse of Hanover was in the prophecy attacking Walpole:

> *When* Robin, *erst sirnam'd the Red,*
> *His Breast with Azure shall bespread,*
> *And near the Lattice build his Nest,*
> *Then Woe to* Europe, *sore oppress'd!*
> *The Cock shall o'er the Eagle crow;*
> *The Lyon to the Mule shall bow;*
> *The Ass, with gaudy Trappings, lead*
> *Through many a Maze the milk white Steed.*[43]

Far more subversive was a separate piece inspired by Caroline's Cave, printed in March 1737, *The Year of Wonders; Being a Literal and Poetical Translation of an Old Latin Prophecy, Found near Merlin's Cave, by S— D—.*[44] The parallels with *Marmor* are striking. Johnson prefaces his *Marmor* prophecy by recounting how a stone tablet came to be ploughed up by a farmer working in a field near King's Lynn. Its Latin inscription is translated by a figure 'well known to the learned world and distinguish'd by the patronage of the Maecenas of

---

[40] *Life of Savage,* 83. For the rumour that Johnson went into hiding for *Marmor,* see *Yale Johnson,* x. 20.

[41] *Yale Johnson,* x. 42. Further quotations from *Marmor* and *Compleat Vindication,* all from vol. x of *Yale Johnson,* inc. in text.

[42] See Johnson, *Lives of the Poets,* iii. 14.

[43] *GM* 5 (1735), 533. The adaptation of *Marmor* printed in the *London Evening Post,* 29 June–1 July 1762 claiming that it was 'foretold by NIXON, who wrote the Cheshire prophecy', locates it in the same popular tradition as Merlin's Cave and Curll's *Rarities of Richmond.*

[44] Bodleian copy Vet. A. 4. c. 152 has the lacunae filled in.

Norfolk' (i.e. Walpole)—probably Bentley, the Master of Trinity, Cambridge and highly in favour with Caroline and the court. The monkish Latin is of an 'early kind', Leonine Latin 'of a peculiar cast and air, not easy to be understood' (p. 26). Once translated, it turns out to be a political prophecy concerning the present state of Britain, filled with violence and civil discontent, predicting the imminent fall of the House of Hanover. *The Year of Wonders* also opens with a prefatory essay. The fictional S— D— (the farm labourer Stephen Duck, recently 'discovered' for his poetic talents and made keeper of Richmond Gardens) 'chanc'd to stumble upon a small earthern *Urn* thrown up by some Workmen'.[45] Curious about its contents, he finds an inscription in Latin which he is unable to translate, 'a Language, in which I am yet arriv'd but at the *Primer*'. 'Consulting a neighbouring School-master about the Original, he assur'd me it was indeed *Latin*, but so mix'd with Monkish Rhimes, and the Rubbish of an unintelligible Jargon, that it was as distant from the Purity of the *Augustan* Age, as *Richmond* is from *Rome*.' There then follows a political prophecy 'of the greatest consequence to this Nation', so seditious that it is riddled with lacunae, helpfully penned in by an unknown contemporary hand in the Bodleian Library copy. The prophecy is highly topical: 'When from the *North* loud Discontents do blow, | And *Justice* hangs Men up we know not how'—probably a reference to the aftermath of the recent Porteous riots. Like Johnson's *London*, it alludes to harsh Hanoverian 'justice' and the King's unpopular 1736–7 visit to Hanover, 'When wash'd in *Briny Waves*, a *King* is seen, | Whilst adverse Winds divorce him from his *Queen*'. The closing lines are deeply subversive: 'When a *Saint's House* [divided cannot] stand, | But [father against son] distracts the Land':

> Then may the *White-cliff'd Isle* expect its Doom;
> And dread the Projects of the Sons of *Rome*;
> [The] *Cock*[, the] Eagle[, & the] *Dolphin's* Son,
> [Will joyn to drive the] *White Horse* [from the throne.][46]

This compares with *Marmor*'s similar apocalyptic configurations of the heraldic insignia of the royal houses of Europe.

> Then o'er the world shall Discord stretch her wings,
> Kings change their laws, and kingdoms change their kings.
> The bear enrag'd th'affrighted moon shall dread;
> The lilies o'er the vales triumphant spread.
>
> (p. 25)

Marmor also mentions a white horse which is 'borne in the arms of H—'. Both works share the same satirical dynamic: a seditious prophecy which literally undermines the foundations of Hanoverian Court Whig authority—in one

---

[45] *The Year of Wonders*, 3–4. Duck was not, of course, illiterate, but self-taught. He could be a possible prototype for Johnson's own 'unlettered' farmer who discovers the Norfolk Stone.
[46] Ibid. 6.

case unearthed from the grounds of Caroline's iconographic Cave, symbolizing the pedigree and legitimacy of the House of Hanover, in the other from the fields of King's Lynn, Walpole's own safe political seat. The irony is enhanced by the fact that in both cases the prophecy is discovered by two men, Bentley and Duck, who were notable recipients of Court Whig patronage. It is a striking measure of Johnson's audacity that, unlike the anonymous author of *The Year of Wonders*, he does not clothe his sedition in asterisks and lacunae. *The Year of Wonders* does not venture on an interpretation, but Johnson supplies a long explanatory essay to make sure that his meaning cannot remain veiled. Johnson may go even further than *The Year of Wonders*, whose invocation of the Jacobite threat is less an endorsement of the 'Sons of Rome' than a lament on the divided House of Hanover. The anonymous author ultimately predicts that, in time, 'a White Plume [flung o're the young Colt's] Head | Strikes Eagle, Cock, and Son of *Dolphin* dead'—an undoubted reference to Prince Frederick, the young 'colt' from the Hanoverian white horse who carried the white plume or feathers of the Prince of Wales.[47]

Marmor Norfolciense, conversely, explicitly engages with the questionable legitimacy of the House of Hanover. 'Probus Britannicus', who claims that the Latin poem's author must have been 'born a Briton', comments on 'how common it is for intruders of yesterday, to pretend the same title with the ancient proprieters, and having just received an estate by voluntary grant, to erect a claim of "hereditary right"' (p. 28)—clearly an attack on the Hanoverians' defence of their title on hereditary rather than contractual grounds. Elsewhere he comments that 'foreigners have affected to call England their country, even when like the Saxons of old they came only to plunder it' (p. 27). Most of the Jacobite sedition comes in the interpretation of the heraldic prophecy, with the White Horse of Hanover sucking dry the veins of the British Lion, his 'tortur'd sons' (British sailors) dying before his face 'While he lies melting in a lewd embrace' (p. 40): like *The Year of Wonders* an attack on George's Hanoverian interests and mistresses. But the personal attacks extend beyond George to the Hanoverian court, its domestic wrangles and trivial pursuits. The ironic list of the king's 'important' concerns includes the 'births of heirs' (p. 31)—clearly an allusion to Frederick's row with his father. It also includes 'mock-patriots'. Johnson descants on opposition Whig politics in a tone which anticipates his much later acerbic remarks about 'that unnecessary and outrageous zeal for . . . liberty'.[48] Presumably glancing at Patriot Whigs such as Chesterfield and Pulteney, in *Marmor* he claims that 'The frown of a prince, and the loss of a pension have indeed been found of wonderful efficacy, to abstract men's thoughts from the present time, and fill them with zeal for the liberty and welfare of ages to come' (p. 32).

---

[47] The 'Bunch of White Feathers' as a symbol for Frederick's insignia appears in hostile remarks by Charles Caesar. See Valerie Rumbold, *Women's Place in Pope's World* (Cambridge, 1989), 246.

[48] 'Life of Akenside' (*Lives of the Poets*, iii. 411).

This is a far cry from *A Compleat Vindication of the Licensers of the Stage*
published only two weeks later. This essay may be ironic, but it is not cryptic.
Nor is it in the slightest degree ironic about the Whig Patriots' 'zeal for the
liberty and welfare of ages to come'. The irony is directed not at Patriots who
profess such principles, but at those narrow-minded self-serving ministerialists
whose political lexicon has no place for these terms. 'Love for posterity' is for
them but a 'cant phrase' even though the Patriots 'make no scruple of avowing
it in the most publick manner, notwithstanding the contempt and ridicule to
which it every day exposes them, and the loss of honours and places from
which it excludes them' (p. 56). The implication here, unlike in *Marmor*, is
that the Patriots have lost their places for sticking to their principles rather
than discovering their principles after losing their places. The *Compleat
Vindication* is as Patriot Whig as *Marmor* is Jacobite. Henry Brooke's *Gustavus
Vasa* was the first play to be banned by the Stage Licensing Act. The opera-
tions of arbitrary state power over artistic freedom were obviously one of the
motivating forces behind Johnson's attack. But to read *A Compleat Vindication*
as a 'classic' work, a timeless defence of the freedom of the press, would be to
mistake its immediate political sympathies.[49] Henry Brooke was one of the
leading Patriot playwrights. Johnson also names two works by leading Patriots:
Pulteney's *Enquiries into the Conduct of the Administration* and Lyttelton's
Considerations upon the Present State of our Affairs. The two leading Boy
Patriots Lyttelton and William Pitt come in for ministerial censure (and
thereby Johnson's implicit praise) for their outspoken parliamentary speeches.
'I have heard L— and P—, when they have made a vigorous opposition, or
blasted the blossom of some ministerial scheme, cry out, in the height of their
exultations, "This will deserve the thanks of posterity!"' (p. 37).

When Johnson describes Brooke's play, it is from a radical Whig rather than
a Jacobite perspective. If Johnson was a 'bloody Jacobite' in *Marmor*, then in
the *Compleat Vindication* he is (almost) a 'virulent Republican'.[50] Johnson
makes nothing of the potential Jacobite implications of Brooke's plot about a
Danish tyrant usurping the Swedish throne from the hereditary prince
Gustavus. Yet he might easily have done so given the subversive nature of his
comments in *Marmor* on 'intruders of yesterday' and those 'foreigners [who]
have affected to call England their country, even when like the Saxons of old
they came only to plunder it'—Gustavus's very sentiments. In fact Johnson
makes more radical mileage out of *Gustavus Vasa* than perhaps even Brooke
intended, injecting it with a Paine-like vein by no means explicit in the play
itself.[51] Taking as his text Brooke's line, 'Great Nature's law, the law within

[49] For Greene's defence of the 'timeless' nature of these two pieces, see *Yale Johnson*, x. 21, 55.
[50] The epithets *Marmor*'s ministerial narrator applies to the author of the Norfolk prophecy,
Yale Johnson, x. 42.
[51] Brooke later achieved fame for his novel *The Fool of Quality* (1766–70), favoured Methodist
reading matter. Greene (*Yale Johnson*, x. 52) notes that Brooke 'links up with the French
Revolution and the Romantic movement' but this seems a rather false teleology.

the breast, | Stamp'd by Heav'n upon th'unletter'd mind', the narrator accuses Brooke of harbouring notions of natural law, 'that men are naturally fond of liberty till these unborn ideas and desires are effaced by literature' (p. 56), and proceeds to ridicule the absurdity of 'the high prerogatives of human nature, of a sacred unalienable birthright, which no man has conferr'd upon us, and which neither kings can take, nor senates give away' (p. 59). How dare Brooke claim that an ordinary man's freedom is more divine than 'the sumptuous and magnificent robes of regality itself[?] . . . the "heel of a monarch", or even the print of his "heel" is a thing too venerable and sacred to be treated with such levity' (p. 69). Hanoverian claims to divine sanction are under assault here as they were in *Marmor*—but this time from a radical Whig rather than a Jacobite perspective. Johnson also adopts the historical myth favoured by Patriot Whigs (one which he later scorned) of republican Rome, where the 'fondness for posterity' was 'almost epidemical' (p. 58).[52] The *Compleat Vindication* epitomizes high-flown Patriot idealism, extolling without irony the love of posterity, liberty, and youthful integrity opposed to 'modern' ministerial corruption and complacency intent on stamping out for good those 'old prejudices of patriotism and publick spirit' (p. 72).

Johnson's enthusiasm for the Patriots as well as his assaults on Walpole and the House of Hanover began to change during his experiences as a reporter on parliamentary debates for the *Gentleman's Magazine*. The extent of his contributions to the 'Debates in the Senate of Lilliput', begun in May 1738, remains a matter of speculation. Johnson claimed to have assumed sole authorship of the 'Debates' between July 1741 and March 1744, but had been an active contributor from 1738 onwards.[53] There is one piece written in May 1740 which seems to share some characteristic features of *A Compleat Vindication*—the sketch of Lyttelton in the 'Members of the Lilliputian Senate'. Johnson, who probably met Lyttelton while a pupil at school in Stourbridge, close to Lyttelton's Hagley Park, may have had personal reasons for later attacking him so harshly in the *Life of Lyttelton*. But in 1739 he had clearly admired Lyttelton's political principles enough to praise him as the epitome of youthful patriotism. Johnson could have penned the picture of the 'Urg Lettyltno' in May 1740, since he was back in London at this point after his unsuccessful bid to find a schoolmaster's appointment in Leicestershire.[54] The signs are there, not so much in the praise of Lyttelton, but in the ironic twist marked

[52] See Johnson's review of Thomas Blackwell's *Memoirs of the Court of Augustus*. Only a schoolboy would 'whine over the commonwealth of Rome which grew great only on the misery of the rest of mankind' (*Yale Johnson*, ii. 377).

[53] See Benjamin B. Hoover, *Samuel Johnson's Parliamentary Reporting* (Berkeley, Calif. and Los Angeles, 1953), 23–9; Kaminsky, *Early Career of Johnson*, 123–43.

[54] Hoover, *Johnson's Parliamentary Reporting*, 138 suggests that 'Johnson probably did not write the essays—the style is not his'. But here the style is recognizably Johnsonian. The insertion into the character of Lyttelton is one of the passages pointed out by Greene as possibly Johnson's. See Donald Greene, 'Some Notes on Johnson and the *Gentleman's Magazine*', *PMLA* 74 (1959), 75–84. Kaminski, *Early Career of Johnson*, 230 n. 4, agrees with this attribution.

by an asterisk at the bottom of the page which transforms the essay into a political contribution to Patriot journalism. 'The remaining Part of this Paragraph is a digression that we cannot account for: perhaps some other passages of *Mr. Gulliver*'s papers may explain it.' The passage of 'digression' adopts the familiar pompous and complacent voice of the ministerial narrator of the *Compleat Vindication*, who offers here the standard government line on the opposition's complaint that Walpole failed to give political places or patronage to good writers. Lyttelton may be a poet and a scholar, notes the narrator, but it is to be hoped

that the chief Posts in the Government will be filled with Men of Dignity and Experience, and not with Parasites and Poets. These last may be useful in adding the inferior Ornaments to a Court, but when employ'd in Posts, the faithful Discharge of which gives Weight and Strength to a State, they have been found but feeble Supports.

But the mood of the passage changes to nostalgia for a time not known in 'Lilliput' (modern England) when '*Poetry* and *Publick Spirit* were the same; . . . when the People caught the generous Flame from the Poet, when it spread from the People to the Prince, and united the Efforts of all against the common Enemy. But these Times never were known in *Lilliput*.'[55] The language recalls the Patriot idiom—for example Lyttelton's plea to Pope of 1741, 'Some sparks of Publick Virtue are yet Alive, which such a Spirit as Your's might blow into a flame';[56] a language which Johnson had previously used in the *Compleat Vindication*, where Brooke's play had contained 'such scenes as seem designed to kindle in the audience a flame of opposition, patriotism, publick spirit, and independency, that spirit which we have so long endeavoured to suppress' (p. 64).

Last Words on Patriotism

If this passage on Lyttelton was indeed Johnson's, then it was his last good word on the Patriots' behalf. Even before Walpole's resignation, Johnson's early determination that 'the WHIG DOGS [i.e. ministerial Whigs] should not have the best of it' was being replaced by growing admiration for Walpole and contempt for Whig Patriot demagoguery.[57] These sentiments fully emerge in his dramatic account of Sandys's motion in the Commons calling for Walpole's

---

[55] *GM* 10 (1740), 229–30. For close parallels with the ministerial press's pragmatic responses, see Bertrand A. Goldgar, *Walpole and the Wits: The Relation of Politics to Literature, 1722–1742* (Lincoln, Nebr., 1976), 17–19.

[56] Pope, *Corr.* iv. 369.

[57] Murphy, *Essay on Johnson*, 45. Paul Korshin, in 'The Johnson–Chesterfield Relationship: A New Hypothesis', *PMLA* 85 (1970), 247–59, argues that Johnson's hostility to Chesterfield began to show in his ironic handling of his speeches of 1741. Kaminski, *Early Career of Johnson*, 136–9, suggests at best an 'ambiguity' in his treatment of opposition Whigs in the 'Debates' of 1741.

resignation (which took place in February 1741 but was not reported until early 1743). This is a highly fictionalized version of Walpole's speech, according him a simple and noble dignity in the face of the Patriots' 'loud Exultations, by confirming them in their Opinion of their own Strength'. Johnson credits the 'High-heeled Members', the Tories, most of whom refused to vote on Sandys's proposal, with acting according to their old and confirmed principles; the discontented Whigs (as was indeed the case) denounced them as '*Sneakers*'.[58]

The *Lives of the Poets* describing those poets who were writing during the Walpole administration carry Johnson's disdain yet further. The 1744 *Life of Savage* establishes the pattern of innuendo which distinguishes the later lives of Lyttelton, Thomson, Mallet, Pope, Hammond, and Akenside. Johnson's self-distancing from Patriot politics is mirrored in his new detachment about issues which only five years earlier had provoked him to rage—press censorship and the 'scarlet reptile' hordes of standing armies.

[T]he Liberty of the Press is a Blessing when we are inclined to write against others, and a Calamity when we find ourselves overborn by the Multitude of our Assailants; . . . and a Standing Army is generally accounted necessary by those who command, and dangerous and oppressive by those who support it. (*Life of Savage*, 49)

This is remarkably cool from the author of a *A Compleat Vindication* and *Marmor*. Johnson criticizes Savage for praising Walpole since it indicated a falseness behind his professed sympathy with those 'who were always zealous in their Assertions of the Justice of the late Opposition, jealous of the Rights of the People, and alarmed by the long-continued Triumph of the Court' (ibid. 51). Savage's dislike of a minister 'who has been at one Time so popular as to be generally esteemed, and at another so formidable as to be universally detested' (ibid. 65) smacks of not only Savage's, but the nation's fickleness where ministers are concerned. Johnson does not make much out of Walpole's failure to give the promised pension to Savage. Walpole did not claim to be a patron of poets, but gave Savage £20 for *Religion and Liberty*—not a large sum, but far more than Savage 'afterwards obtained from a person of yet higher Rank, and more desirous in Appearance of being distinguished as a patron of Literature' (ibid. 51).

The lives of Thomson, Mallet, Pope, Hammond, and Lyttelton, written in the 1770s, rehearse the same view of that person 'of higher rank'—Frederick—and his 'pretences' to literary patronage. 'When the Prince of Wales was driven from the palace, and, setting himself at the head of the opposition, kept a separate court, he endeavoured to increase his popularity by the patronage of literature';[59] 'the Prince of Wales was at that time struggling for popularity,

---

[58] *GM* 13 (1743), 179–81. See also Robert Giddings, 'The Fall of Orgilio: Samuel Johnson as Parliamentary Reporter', in Grundy (ed.), *Samuel Johnson: New Critical Essays*, 86–106.

[59] Johnson, *Lives of the Poets*, iii. 404. Further quotations from vol. iii inc. in text.

and by the influence of Mr. Lyttelton professed himself the patron of wit'
(p. 291). Lyttelton 'persuaded his master, whose business it was now to be
popular, that he would advance his character by patronage' (p. 448). Johnson's
loathing of patronage gave added edge to his censure of those poets who sold
themselves to Frederick and the Patriot cause. It was, after all, the former
Patriot Chesterfield who had kept Johnson dangling ignominiously in his
antechambers with empty promises of patronage for his *Dictionary*. The fat
and lazy Thomson receives less sympathy than the mercurial indigent Savage.
Thomson 'being now obliged to write . . . produced (1738) the tragedy of
Agamemnon' (p. 291). That word 'obliged' says much. Pope had even less
excuse. Johnson regretted Pope's inability to maintain into the 1730s his earlier
admirable political non-partisanship. 'Entangled' in the opposition, a mere 'follower' of the Prince, Pope's patriotism was never as strong as it was cracked
up to be, tainted by moral self-aggrandizement and swiftly followed by cow-
ardice. Pope 'pleased himself with being important and formidable, and
gratified sometimes his pride, and sometimes his resentment; till at last he
began to think he should be more safe if he were less busy'. Pope never again
tried to join 'the patriot with the poet' (p. 181).

Johnson ascribes few honourable motives to these poets. Patriot zeal was at
best hot-headed youthful error. But he places a more cynical construction on
those rallying cries for a liberty 'of which no man felt the want, and with care
for liberty, which was not in danger' (p. 289). 'At length, after a long struggle,
Walpole gave way, and honour and profit were distributed among his con-
querors' (p. 449): this is the hue and cry of the pack of hounds described by
Charles Hanbury Williams. Johnson was less critical of some Patriots than
others—Akenside and Hammond for their youth, Gilbert West for a piety of
which Johnson could not fail to approve. Mallet comes in for harsh censure,
doubly at fault for being a 'beggarly Scotchman' who tried to conceal his
Scottishness, and a free-thinker who unleashed Bolingbroke's atheistic *Letters
on History* on the world.[60] But Johnson reserves his harshest treatment for
Lyttelton, whose key role in the Patriot campaign prompted a venom which
Johnson would not otherwise have bothered to waste on so minor a writer.
The nasty portrait, noted Horace Walpole, made Lyttelton's friends want 'to
tear Johnson limb from limb' (p. 458). Johnson attacks Lyttelton's politics, of
course: 'His zeal was considered by the courtiers not only as violent, but as
acrimonious and malignant.' Johnson notes that Lyttelton was not even trusted
in the end by those who had caused Walpole to be 'at last hunted from his
places' (p. 447). But Johnson's hostility spills into Lyttelton's relatively blame-
less personal life, and where he cannot find scandal he mocks probity. 'Human
pleasures are short', he remarked tersely on the tragic early death of

---

[60] The *Dictionary* illustration for 'alias' is 'Malloch *alias* Mallet'. For Mallet's name-change, see
Lives, iii. 402–3. For Johnson's attack on Mallet's role as Bolingbroke's literary executor, see
Boswell, *Life of Johnson*, i. 268.

Lyttelton's much-loved first wife Lucy. He undermines the sincerity of Lyttelton's famous monody on her death by noting that he 'solaced his grief by poetry' and remarried quite soon after 'but the experiment was unsuccessful'. Johnson closes with an insouciance bordering on the insulting. 'Of his death a very affecting and instructive account has been given by his physician, which will spare me the task of his moral character' (p. 454).

Johnson's personal animus had fixed on an unworthy target. But Lyttelton's death-bed assertion that 'In politicks and publick life I have made publick good the rule of my conduct, I never gave counsels which I did not at the time think the best. I have seen that I was sometimes in the wrong, but I did not err designedly' (p. 455) must have epitomized to Johnson's critical eye the passage from patriotism to hypocrisy to complacent self-delusion characteristic of so many former Patriots of 1730s vintage. It is a suitable place to end this book: for, as Johnson says in his closing remarks on Lyttelton, 'to politicks and literature there must be an end'. If, like Lyttelton, Johnson had himself once displayed 'something of that indistinct and headstrong ardour for liberty which a man of genius always catches as he enters the world and always suffers to cool as he passes forward' (p. 446), at least his transition from opposition to establishment was distinguished by a more profound degree of self-knowledge.

Bibliography

1. MANUSCRIPT SOURCES

Bodleian Library, Film MS 1740, Diary of Mrs Charles Caesar.
British Library, MS Egerton 1950, Pope's 'Brutus'.
Hagley MSS, Hagley Hall, Stourbridge, Worcs., George Lyttelton, 'Observations on the Reign and Character of Queen Elizabeth' (1733).
Duchy of Cornwall Office, Bound MSS, Household Accounts of Frederick Louis, Prince of Wales, 30 vols. (1728–49).

2. ORIGINAL SOURCES IN PRINT

(Unless otherwise indicated, place of publication is London.)

An Appeal to the Nation; Or, the Case of the Present Prime Minister of Great Britain truly stated (1731).
AKENSIDE, MARK, *The Voice of Liberty; or a British Philippic* (1738).
—— *An Epistle to Curio* (1744).
ARNALL, WILLIAM, *Opposition No Proof of Patriotism* (1735).
BARRON, RICHARD, *The Pillars of Priestcraft Shaken*, 4 vols. (1768).
BICKHAM, GEORGE, *The Beauties of Stow* (1750).
BLACKMORE, SIR RICHARD, *Alfred: An Epick Poem in Twelve Books, Dedicated to the Illustrious Prince Frederick of Hanover* (1723).
BOLINGBROKE, HENRY ST JOHN, VISCOUNT, *The Works of Lord Bolingbroke*, 4 vols. (1844).
—— *Letters on the Spirit of Patriotism and on The Idea of a Patriot King*, ed. A. Hassall (Oxford, 1917).
—— *Lord Bolingbroke: Historical Writings*, ed. Isaac Kramnick (Chicago, 1972).
—— *Lord Bolingbroke: Contributions to the 'Craftsman'*, ed. Simon Varey (Oxford, 1982).
BOSWELL, JAMES, *The Life of Samuel Johnson, LL.D.*, ed. George Birkbeck Hill, rev. L. F. Powell, 6 vols. (Oxford, 1934–50).
BOYSE, SAMUEL, *The Triumphs of Nature* (1742).
[BRERETON, JANE HUGHES] ('MELISSA'), *Merlin: A Poem Humbly Inscrib'd to Her Majesty* (1735).
BROOKE, HENRY, *Gustavus Vasa: or, The Deliverer of His Country* (1739).
CAMDEN, WILLIAM, *Britannia: or a Chorographical Description of Great Britain and Ireland, Together with the Adjacent Islands*, ed. Edmund Gibson, 2 vols. (2nd rev. edn. 1722).
[CAMPBELL, JOHN], *The Polite Correspondence: Or, Rational Amusement* (1741).
CAREW, THOMAS, *The Poems of Thomas Carew*, ed. Rhodes Dunlap (Oxford, 1957).

CARLISLE, EARL OF, *The Manuscripts of the Earl of Carlisle*, HMC 15th Report, Appendix, part vi (1897).

CHESTERFIELD, PHILIP DORMER STANHOPE, EARL OF, *The Letters of Lord Chesterfield*, ed. Bonamy Dobrée, 6 vols. (1932).

CLAYTON, LADY CHARLOTTE, VISCOUNTESS SUNDON, *Memoirs of Viscountess Sundon, Mistress of the Robes to Queen Caroline*, 2 vols. (1847).

COLLINS, WILLIAM, and GRAY, THOMAS, *The Poems of Gray, Collins and Goldsmith*, ed. Roger Lonsdale (2nd edn. 1976).

Common Sense; or, the Englishman's Journal (5 Feb. 1737–16 Nov. 1743).

The Conduct of Queen Elizabeth, Towards the Neighbouring Nations; And particularly Spain; Compar'd with that of James I (1729).

CORNWALLIS, SIR CHARLES, *The Life and Character of Henry-Frederic, Prince of Wales, with an Appendix Containing Several Curious Authentic Testimonies Relating to the Prince*, ed. J. M. [Joseph Morgan] (1738).

COXE, WILLIAM, *Memoirs of the Life and Administration of Sir Robert Walpole, Earl of Orford*, 3 vols. (1798).

Crafts of the Craftsman, The: Or the Detection of the Designs of the Coalition (1735).

Craftsman, 14 vols. (collected edn., 1731 and 1737).

[CROXALL, SAMUEL], *An Original Canto of Spencer, Designed as Part of His Fairy Queen, but Never Printed* (1713).

—— *Another Original Canto of Spencer* (1714).

CURLL, EDMUND, *The Rarities of Richmond: Being Exact Descriptions of the Royal Hermitage and Merlin's Cave, With his Life and Prophecies* (1736).

DEFOE, DANIEL, *Of Royall Educacion: A Fragmentary Treatise*, ed. Karl D. Bülbring (1895).

DENHAM, SIR JOHN, *Expans'd Hieroglyphicks: A Critical Edition of Sir John Denham's 'Coopers-Hill'*, ed. Brendan O'Hehir (Berkeley, Calif. and Los Angeles, 1969).

DODINGTON, GEORGE BUBB, *The Political Journal of George Bubb Dodington*, ed. J. Carswell and L. A. Drake (Oxford, 1965).

DODSLEY, ROBERT (ed.), *A Collection of Poems by Several Hands*, 6 vols. (1748–58).

DRAYTON, MICHAEL, *Works*, ed. J. W. Hebel et al., 5 vols. (2nd edn., Oxford, 1961).

DRYDEN, JOHN, *Merlin: Or, The British Inchanter. And King Arthur, The British Worthy. A Dramatic Opera* [rev. William Giffard] (1736).

—— *Dramatic Works*, ed. Montague Summers, 6 vols. (1932).

—— *The Poems of John Dryden*, ed. James C. Kinsley, 4 vols. (Oxford, 1958).

EGMONT, EARL OF, *Diary of Viscount Perceval, Afterwards First Earl of Egmont*, HMC, 3 vols. (1920–3).

ELLIS, F. H. (ed.), *Poems on Affairs of State*, vii, *1704–1714* (New Haven, Conn., 1975).

English Poems collected from the Oxford and Cambridge Verses on the Death of His Royal Highness Frederick Prince of Wales, The (Edinburgh, 1751).

ETOUGH, HENRY. *See* 'Parson Etoffe'.

FIELDING, HENRY, *The Complete Works of Henry Fielding*, ed. W. E. Henley, 16 vols. (1903).

Fog's Weekly Journal (1728–37).

GARRICK, DAVID, *The Songs, Chorusses, and Serious Dialogues of the Masque Called the Institution of the Garter, or, Arthur's Round Table Restored* (1771).

—— *Letters of David Garrick*, ed. D. M. Little and G. M. Kahrl, 3 vols. (Oxford, 1963).

GAY, JOHN, *Poetry and Prose*, ed. V. A. Dearing and C. Beckwith, 2 vols. (Oxford, 1974).

GILDON, CHARLES, *Memoirs of William Wycherley* (1718).

GLOVER, RICHARD, *Leonidas* (1737).

—— *London; Or, The Progress of Commerce* (1739).

—— *Memoirs of a Celebrated Literary and Political Character from the Resignation of Sir Robert Walpole, in 1742 . . .* (1873).

—— *Poetical Works*, in R. Anderson (ed.), *A Complete Edition of the Poets of Great Britain*, 13 vols. (1795), xi.

GRANVILLE, GEORGE, LORD LANSDOWNE, *The Genuine Works in Verse and Prose of the Right Honourable George, Lord Lansdowne* (3 vols, 1732).

GRAVES, RICHARD, *Recollections of Some Particulars in the Life of the Late William Shenstone Esq.* (1788).

HARRIS, ROBERT (ed.), *A Leicester House Political Diary 1742–3*, Camden Miscellany, 4th ser. 44 (1992), 373–408.

HAYWOOD, ELIZA, *Memoirs of a Certain Island Adjacent to the Kingdom of Utopia* (1724).

HERVEY, JOHN, LORD, *Ancient and Modern Liberty Stated and Compared* (1734).

—— *Some Materials towards the Memoirs of the Reign of King George II*, ed. Romney Sedgwick, 3 vols. (1931).

—— *Lord Hervey and his Friends 1726–38*, ed. Lord Ilchester (1950).

HILL, AARON, *The Creation* (1720).

—— *The Progress of Wit: A Caveat: For the Use of an Eminent Writer* (1730).

—— *Advice to the Poets. A Poem. To which is Prefix'd, An Epistle Dedicatory to the Few Great Spirits of Great Britain* (1731).

—— *The Tears of the Muses: in a Conference between Prince Germanicus and a Male-Content Party* (1737, 2nd edn. 1738).

—— *Works of the Late Aaron Hill*, 4 vols. (1753).

—— *Dramatic Works*, 2 vols. (1760).

Histoire du Prince Titi, A. R. [Themiseul de Saint-Hyacinthe?] (Paris, 1736).

Hyp-Doctor, [ed. John Henley] (Dec. 1730–Jan. 1741).

JOHNSON, SAMUEL, *Lives of the English Poets*, ed. G. B. Hill, 3 vols. (Oxford, 1905).

—— *The Yale Edition of the Works of Samuel Johnson*, 16 vols. (New Haven, Conn., Oxford, and London, 1958–90).

—— *An Account of the Life of Mr. Savage*, ed. Clarence Tracy (Oxford, 1971).

—— *The Poems of Samuel Johnson*, ed. D. Nichol Smith and E. L. McAdam, rev. J. D. Fleeman (3rd edn., Oxford, 1974).

LANGLEY, BATTY, *Ancient Architecture Restored* (1742).

LILLO, GEORGE, *The Works of Mr. George Lillo; with some Account of His Life*, ed. Thomas Davies, 2 vols. (1775).

—— *The London Merchant*, ed. W. M. McBurney (1965).

—— *The Fatal Curiosity*, ed. W. M. McBurney (1967).

LYTTELTON, GEORGE, LORD, *An Epistle to Mr. Pope, from a Young Gentleman at Rome* (1730).

—— *Letters from a Persian in England to His Friend at Ispahan* (1735).

—— *Considerations upon the Present State of our Affairs, at Home and Abroad* (1739).

—— [?] *A Letter to a Member of Parliament Concerning the Present State of Affairs at Home and Abroad* (1740).

—— *The History of the Life of King Henry the Second*, 4 vols. (1767–71).

—— *The Poetical Works of George, Lord Lyttelton* (1801).

—— *Memoirs and Correspondence of George, Lord Lyttelton*, ed. Robert Phillimore, 2 vols. (1845).

MADDEN, SAMUEL, *Themistocles, the Lover of His Country* (1729).

—— *Memoirs of the Twentieth Century, Being Original Letters of State, under George the Sixth: Relating to the most Important Events in Great-Britain and Europe . . . From the Middle of the Eighteenth, to the End of the Twentieth Century, and the World*, 6 vols. (only 1 published) (1733).

MALLET, DAVID, *Eurydice* (1731).

—— *Mustapha* (1739).

MANLEY, DELARIVIER, *Secret Memoirs and Manners of Several Persons of Quality, of Both Sexes, from the New Atalantis, An Island in the Mediterranean* (1709).

MARCHMONT, *A Selection from the Papers of the Earls of Marchmont*, ed. George Henry Rose, 3 vols. (1831).

MARTYN, BENJAMIN, *Timoleon* (1730).

Memoirs of the House of Hanover . . . To which is added, A Genealogical Table of that Illustrious Family, Brought Down to the Present Time (1713).

MILLER, SANDERSON, *An Eighteenth-Century Correspondence . . . Letters . . . to Sanderson Miller*, ed. Lilian Dickins and Mary Stanton (1910).

Mist's Weekly Journal (1725–8).

MOLESWORTH, ROBERT, VISCOUNT, *An Account of Denmark as it was in the Year 1692* (1694).

Mother Hubbards Tale of the Ape and the Fox, Abbreviated from Spencer (1715).

MOUNTFORT, RICHARD, *The Fall of Mortimer: an Historical Play, Reviv'd from Mountford* (1731).

MURPHY, ARTHUR, *An Essay on the Life and Genius of Samuel Johnson*, (1792).

NICHOLS, JOHN, *Literary Anecdotes of the Eighteenth Century*, 9 vols. (1812–15).

NUGENT, ROBERT CRAGGS, *Odes and Epistles* (1739).

—— *An Ode to Mankind: Address'd to the Prince of Wales* (1741).

Observations on the Present Taste for Poetry; with Remarks, in particular, on a Piece lately published by Mr. Whitehead, called, Manners. A Satire: By an English Christian, of no Party (1739).

Of Legacy Hunting. The 5th Satire of the Second Book of Horace Imitated. A Dialogue between Sir Walter Raleigh, and Merlin the Prophet (1737).

Old and Modern Whig Revived in the Present Divisions at Court, The (1717).

Old Whig; or, The Consistent Protestant (13 Mar. 1735–30 Mar. 1738).

'Parson Etoffe' [Revd Henry Etough], *Free and Impartial Reflexions on the Character, Life and Death of Frederick Prince of Wales* (1751), repr. in *Miscellanies of the Philobiblon Society*, vii/9 (1862–3).

PATERSON, WILLIAM, *Arminius* (1740).

Patriot, [ed. John Harris] (22 Mar. 1714–18 Jan. 1715).

PEMBERTON, HENRY, *Observations on Poetry, especially the Epic, Occasioned by the Late Poem upon Leonidas* (1738).

Persian Strip'd of his Disguise; The: Or, Remarks on a late Libel, intitled Letters from a Persian in England to his Friend at Ispahan (1735).

POLWARTH, LORD, *Manuscript of Lord Polwarth*, HMC, 5 vols. (1911–61).

POPE, ALEXANDER, *The Works of Alexander Pope*, ed. W. Elwin and J. W. Courthope, 10 vols. (1871–89).

—— *The Prose Works of Alexander Pope*, i, ed. Norman Ault (Oxford, 1936).

—— *The Twickenham Edition of the Poems of Alexander Pope*, gen. ed. John Butt, 11 vols. (London and New Haven, Conn., 1939–69).

—— *The Correspondence of Alexander Pope*, ed. George Sherburn, 5 vols. (Oxford, 1956).

[POWNEY, RICHARD], *The Stag Chace in Windsor Forest* (1739).

PRIOR, MATTHEW, *Literary Works*, ed. M. B. Wright and M. K. Spears, 2 vols. (Oxford, 1959).

Prompter, ed. Aaron Hill and William Popple (1734–6).

RALEGH, SIR WALTER, *A History of the World in Five Books*, ed. John Oldys, with a 'Life of the Author', 2 vols. (1736).

RALPH, JAMES, *The Fall of the Earl of Essex, Alter'd from the Unhappy Favourite of Mr. Banks* (1731).

RAPIN DE THOYRAS, PAUL, *A History of England*, trans. Nicholas Tindal, 15 vols. (1725–31).

Remembrancer, [ed. James Ralph] (1747–51).

REYNOLDS, JOSHUA, *Letters of Sir Joshua Reynolds*, ed. F. W. Hilles (Cambridge, 1929).

ROLT, RICHARD, *A Monody on the Death of His Royal Highness Frederic-Louis, Prince of Wales* (1751).

ROWLANDS, HENRY, *Mona Antiqua Restaurata* (Dublin, 1723).

RUFFHEAD, OWEN, *The Life of Alexander Pope Esq. compiled from original manuscripts, with a critical essay on his writings and genius* (1769).

RUNDLE, THOMAS, *Letters of the late Thomas Rundle, LLD., Lord Bishop of Derry in Ireland, to Mrs. Barbara Sandys*, 2 vols. (Gloucester, 1789).

SAMMES, AYLETT, *Britannia Antiqua Illustrata* (1676).

SAVAGE, RICHARD, *Poetical Works*, ed. Clarence Tracy (Cambridge, 1962).

SEWELL, GEORGE, *The Tragedy of Sir Walter Raleigh* (1719).

SOMERVILE, WILLIAM, *The Chace* (1735).

SPENCE, JOSEPH, *Observations, Anecdotes, and Characters of Books and Men*, ed. James M. Osborn, 2 vols. (Oxford, 1966).

SWIFT, JONATHAN, *The Prose Works of Jonathan Swift*, ed. Herbert Davis et al., 16 vols. (Oxford, 1939–74).

—— *The Correspondence of Jonathan Swift*, ed. Harold Williams, 5 vols. (1963).

—— *Poetical Works*, ed. Herbert Davis (Oxford, 1967).

TEMPLE, SIR WILLIAM, *The Works of Sir William Temple, Bart.*, ed. Jonathan Swift, 2 vols. (1720).

THOMSON, JAMES, *The Works of James Thomson*, with 'Life' by Patrick Murdoch, 2 vols. (1762).

—— *James Thomson (1700–48): Letters and Documents*, ed. A. D. McKillop (Lawrence, Kan., 1958).

—— *The Castle of Indolence and Other Poems*, ed. A. D. McKillop (Lawrence, Kan., 1961).

—— *The Seasons*, ed. James Sambrook (Oxford, 1981).

—— *Liberty, The Castle of Indolence, and Other Poems*, ed. James Sambrook (Oxford, 1986).

—— and MALLET, DAVID, *Alfred: A Masque* (1740).

TOLAND, JOHN, *A New Edition of Toland's 'History of the Druids'*, ed. R. Huddlestone (Montrose, 1814).

[TRAPP, JOSEPH], *The Ministerial Virtue: Or, Long-Suffering Extolled in a Great Man* (1738).

TRENCHARD, JOHN, *Some Considerations upon the State of Our Publick Debts in General and of the Civil List in Particular* (1720).

UPTON, JOHN, *Critical Observations on Shakespeare* (1746).

VERTUE, GEORGE, *The Notebooks of George Vertue*, 7 vols., Walpole Society Annual Volumes 18, 20, 22, 24, 26, 29, 30 (numbered *Vertue Notebooks* i–vi; vol. 29—the index vol.—is unnumbered) (Oxford and London, 1930–55).

VICTOR, BENJAMIN, *Original Letters, Dramatic Pieces and Poems*, 3 vols. (1776).

WALPOLE, HORACE, *The Yale Edition of Horace Walpole's Correspondence*, ed. W. S. Lewis et al., 48 vols. (London and New Haven, Conn., 1937–83).

WARTON, JOSEPH, *An Essay on the Writings and Genius of Pope*, 2 vols. (1756–62).

WARTON, THOMAS, *Poetical Works of the Late Thomas Warton B.D.*, 2 vols. (Oxford, 1802).

WEST, GILBERT, *Stowe, the Gardens of the Right Honourable Richard Lord Viscount Cobham* (1732).

[——] *A Canto of the Fairy Queen. Written by Spenser. Never before Published* (1739).

[——] *The Institution of the Order of the Garter* (1742).

WHITEHEAD, PAUL, *Manners: A Satire* (1739).

WILLIAMS, CHARLES HANBURY, *Works*, 3 vols. (1822).

Year of Wonders, The; Being a Literal and Poetical Translation of an Old Latin Prophecy, Found near Merlin's Cave, by S— D— (1737).

3. SECONDARY WORKS

ADEN, JOHN M., *Pope's Once and Future Kings: Satire and Politics in the Early Career* (Knoxville, Tenn., 1978).

ALLAN, D. G. C., *William Shipley: Founder of the Royal Society* (1968).

—— 'The Society of Arts and Government, 1754–1800: Public Encouragement of Arts, Manufactures, and Commerce in Eighteenth-Century England', *Eighteenth-Century Studies* 7 (1974), 434–52.

—— and JOHN L. ABBOTT (eds.), *'The Virtuoso Tribe of Arts and Sciences': Studies in the Eighteenth-Century Work and Membership of the London Society of Arts* (Athens, Ga., 1992).

ALLEN, B. SPRAGUE, *Tides in English Taste, 1619–1800*, 2 vols. (2nd edn., New York, 1958).

ALTICK, RICHARD D., *The Shows of London* (Cambridge, Mass., 1978).

ARMITAGE, DAVID, 'The British Empire and the Civic Tradition 1656–1742' (Cambridge Ph.D. thesis, 1991).

—— 'The Cromwellian Protectorate and the Languages of Empire', *Historical Journal*, 35 (1992), 531–55.

ATHERTON, HERBERT, *Political Prints in the Age of Hogarth: A Study of the Ideographic Representation of Politics* (Oxford, 1974).

ATTO, CLAYTON, 'The Society for the Encouragement of Learning', *Library*, 4th ser. 19 (1938–9), 263–88.

AULT, NORMAN, *New Light on Pope* (1949).

BARBER, GILES, 'Bolingbroke, Pope and the *Patriot King*', *Library*, 5th ser. 19 (1964), 67–89.

BARKER, A. D., 'Edmund Cave, Samuel Johnson and the *Gentleman's Magazine*' (Oxford D.Phil. thesis, 1982).

BARRELL, John, *English Literature in History, 1730–80: An Equal, Wide Survey* (1983).

BATTESTIN, MARTIN M., 'Pope's "Magus" in Fielding's *Vernoniad*: The Satire of Walpole', *Philological Quarterly*, 46 (1967), 137–41.

BENNETT, G. V., 'Jacobitism and the Rise of Walpole', in Neil McKendrick (ed.), *Historical Perspectives: Studies in English Thought and Society* (1974), 70–92.

BERCIER, GABRIELLE, 'The Education of the Prince: Wieland and German Enlightenment at School with Fénelon and Rousseau', *Eighteenth-Century Life*, 10 (1986), 1–13.

BEVINGTON, MICHAEL, *Templa Quam Delecta*, vi, *The Gothic Temple* (Stowe, Bucks., 1990).

BLAND, STEPHEN, 'The Affair of Dr. Rundle: An Examination of Ecclesiastical Patronage under Walpole' (Cambridge BA dissertation, 1985).

BREDVOLD, LOUIS M., 'The Gloom of the Tory Satirists', in J. L. Clifford (ed.), *Eighteenth-Century English Literature: Modern Essays in Criticism* (New York, 1959), 3–20.

BREWSTER, DOROTHY, *Aaron Hill: Poet, Dramatist, Projector* (New York, 1913).

BRIE, FREDERICK, 'Pope's *Brutus*', *Anglia*, 63 (1939), 148–52.

BRINKLEY, ROBERTA F., *Arthurian Legend in the Seventeenth Century* (Baltimore, Md., 1932).

BROOKE, JOHN, *King George III* (1972).

BROOKS-DAVIES, DOUGLAS, *The Mercurian Monarch: Magical Politics from Spenser to Pope* (Manchester, 1983).

—— *Pope's 'Dunciad' and the Queen of the Night: A Study in Emotional Jacobitism* (Manchester, 1985).

BROWNING, REED, *The Political and Constitutional Ideas of the Court Whigs* (Baton Rouge, La., 1982).

BYWATER, DAVID, *Dryden in Revolutionary England* (Berkeley, Calif. and Los Angeles, 1990).

CABLE, MABEL HESSLER, 'The Idea of a Patriot King in the Propaganda of the Opposition to Walpole, 1735–1739', *Philological Quarterly*, 18 (1939), 119–30.

CANNON, JOHN (ed.), *The Whig Ascendancy: Colloquies on Hanoverian England* (1981).

CHALKER, JOHN, *The English Georgic* (1969).

CHAMPION, J. A. I., *The Pillars of Priestcraft Shaken: The Church of England and its Enemies 1660–1730* (Cambridge, 1992).

CHAPIN, CHESTER, 'Pope and the Jacobites', *Eighteenth-Century Life*, 10 (1986), 59–73.

CLARK, J. C. D., 'A General Theory of Party, Opposition and Government, 1688–1832', *Historical Journal*, 23 (1980), 295–325.

—— 'The Politics of the Excluded: Tories, Jacobites and Whig Patriots, 1715–1760', *Parliamentary History*, 2 (1983), 209–22.

—— *English Society 1688–1832: Ideology, Social Structure and Political Practice during the Ancien Regime* (Cambridge, 1985).

—— *Revolution and Rebellion: State and Society in England in the Seventeenth and Eighteenth Centuries* (Cambridge, 1986).

—— *The Language of Liberty: Political Discourse and Social Dynamics in the Anglo-American World, 1660–1800* (Cambridge, 1993).

CLARKE, G. B., 'Grecian Taste and Gothic Virtue: Lord Cobham's Gardening Programme and Iconography', *Apollo*, 97 (1973), 566–71.

—— (ed.), *Descriptions of Lord Cobham's Gardens at Stowe, 1700–1750* (Buckingham, 1990).

CLEARY, THOMAS R., *Henry Fielding: Political Writer* (Waterloo, Ont., 1984).

COLLEY, LINDA, 'Eighteenth-Century English Radicalism before Wilkes', *Transactions of the Royal Historical Society*, 5th ser. 31 (1981), 1–19.

—— *In Defiance of Oligarchy: The Tory Party 1714–60* (Cambridge, 1982).

—— 'The Apotheosis of George III: Loyalty, Royalty and the British Nation, 1760–1820', *Past and Present*, 102 (1984), 94–129.

—— 'Radical Patriotism in Eighteenth-Century England', in Raphael Samuels (ed.), *Patriotism: The Making and Unmaking of British National Identity*, 3 vols. (1989), i. 169–87.

—— *Britons: Forging the Nation, 1707–1837* (New Haven, Conn., 1992).

COLTON, JUDITH M., 'Merlin's Cave and Queen Caroline: Garden Art as Political Propaganda', *Eighteenth-Century Studies*, 10 (1976), 1–20.

CRUICKSHANKS, EVELINE, *Political Untouchables: The Tories and the '45* (1979).

—— 'The Political Management of Sir Robert Walpole, 1720–42', in Jeremy Black (ed.), *Britain in the Age of Walpole* (1984), 23–43.

—— (ed.), *Ideology and Conspiracy: Aspects of Jacobitism, 1689–1759* (Edinburgh, 1982).

—— and JEREMY BLACK (eds.), *The Jacobite Challenge* (Edinburgh, 1988).

CUNNINGHAM, HUGH, 'The Language of Patriotism, 1750–1914', *History Workshop*, 12 (1981), 8–33.

DAVIS, ROSE MARY, *The Good Lord Lyttelton* (Bethlehem, Pa., 1939).

DICKINSON, H. T., *Bolingbroke* (1970).

—— *Liberty and Property: Political Ideology in Eighteenth-Century Britain* (1977).

DOBRÉE, BONAMY, 'The Theme of Patriotism in the Poetry of the Early Eighteenth Century', *Proceedings of the British Academy*, 35 (1949), 49–65.

DOBSON, MICHAEL, *The Making of the National Poet: Shakespeare, Adaptation and Authorship, 1660–1789* (Oxford, 1992).

DOODY, MARGARET M., *The Daring Muse: Augustan Poetry Reconsidered* (Cambridge, 1986).

DORRIS, GEORGE, *Paolo Rolli and the Italian Circle in London, 1715–44* (The Hague, 1967).

DOWNIE, J. A., 'Walpole, "The Poet's Foe"', in Jeremy Black (ed.), *Britain in the Age of Walpole* (1984), 171–88.

—— '1688: Pope and the Rhetoric of Jacobitism', in David Fairer (ed.), *Pope: New Contexts* (Hemel Hempstead, 1990), 9–24.

EDWARDS, AVERYL, *Frederick Louis, Prince of Wales, 1707–1751* (1947).

EHRENPREIS, IRVIN, *Literary Meaning and Augustan Values* (Charlottesville, Va., 1974).

ERSKINE-HILL, Howard, *Pope: The Dunciad* (1972).

—— *The Social Milieu of Alexander Pope: Lives, Examples and the Poetic Response* (New Haven, Conn. and London, 1975).

—— 'Alexander Pope: The Political Poet in His Time', *Eighteenth-Century Studies*, 15 (1981–2), 123–48.

—— 'Literature and the Jacobite Cause: Was There a Rhetoric of Jacobitism?', in Eveline Cruickshanks (ed.), *Ideology and Conspiracy: Aspects of Jacobitism, 1689–1759* (Edinburgh, 1982), 49–69.

—— 'Under Which Caesar? Pope in the Journal of Mrs Charles Caesar, 1724–1741', *Review of English Studies*, NS 33 (1982), 436–44.

—— *The Augustan Idea in English Literature* (1983).

—— 'The Political Character of Samuel Johnson', in Isobel Grundy (ed.), *Samuel Johnson: New Critical Essays* (1984), 107–36.

—— 'Life into Letters, Death into Art: Pope's Epitaph on Francis Atterbury', *Yearbook of English Studies*, 18 (1988), 200–20.

—— 'The Political Character of Samuel Johnson: *The Lives of the Poets* and a Further Report on *The Vanity of Human Wishes*', in Eveline Cruickshanks (ed.), *The Jacobite Challenge* (Edinburgh, 1988), 161–76.

FOORD, ARCHIBALD, *His Majesty's Opposition 1714–1830* (1964).

FOXON, DAVID F., *English Verse, 1701–1750. A Catalogue of Separately Printed Poems*, 2 vols. (Cambridge, 1975).

GERRARD, CHRISTINE, '*An Ode on the Times*: The Political Fortunes of James Sterling and Matthew Concanen', *Notes and Queries*, NS 231 (1986), 502–4.

—— 'Pope and the Patriots', in David Fairer (ed.), *Pope: New Contexts* (Hemel Hempstead, 1990), 25–43.

—— '*The Castle of Indolence* and the Opposition to Walpole', *Review of English Studies*, NS 41 (1990), 45–64.

GIDDINGS, ROBERT, 'The Fall of Orgilio: Samuel Johnson as Parliamentary Reporter', in Isobel Grundy (ed.), *Samuel Johnson: New Critical Essays* (1984), 86–106.

GOLDGAR, BERTRAND A., *Walpole and the Wits: The Relation of Politics to Literature, 1722–1742* (Lincoln, Nebr. 1976).

GOLDIE, MARK, 'Priestcraft and the Birth of Whiggism', in Nicholas Phillipson and Quentin Skinner (eds.), *Political Discourse in Early Modern Britain* (Cambridge, 1993), 209–31.

GOLDSTEIN, MALCOLM, *Pope and the Augustan Stage* (Stanford, Calif., 1958).

GOODALE, J. R., 'J. G. A. Pocock's Neo-Harringtonians: A Reconsideration', *History of Political Thought*, 1 (1980), 257–9.

GREENE, DONALD J., 'Some Notes on Johnson and the *Gentleman's Magazine*', PMLA, 74 (1959), 75–84.

—— 'From Accidie to Neurosis: *The Castle of Indolence* Revisited', in M. E. Novak (ed.), *English Literature in the Age of Disguise* (Los Angeles, 1978), 131–56.

—— *The Politics of Samuel Johnson* (New Haven, Conn., 1960; 2nd edn. Athens, Ga., 1990).

GREGG, EDWARD, *Queen Anne* (1970).

GRIFFIN, DUSTIN, 'Milton and the Decline of Epic in the Eighteenth Century', *New Literary History*, 14 (1982), 143–54.

—— *Regaining Paradise: Milton and the Eighteenth Century* (Cambridge, 1986).

HAIG, CHRISTOPHER, *Elizabeth I* (1988).

HAMILTON, A. C. (gen. ed.), *The Spenser Encyclopedia* (Toronto, 1990).

HAMMOND, BREAN, *Pope and Bolingbroke: A Study of Friendship and Influence* (Columbia, Mo., 1984).

HARRIS, GEORGE, *The Life of Lord Chancellor Hardwicke*, 3 vols. (1847).

HARRIS, MICHAEL, *London Newspapers in the Age of Walpole: A Study of the Origins of the Modern English Press* (1987).

HARRIS, ROBERT, *A Patriot Press: National Politics and the London Press in the 1740s* (Oxford, 1993).

HART, JEFFREY, *Viscount Bolingbroke, Tory Humanist* (Toronto, 1965).

HATTON, RAGNILD, *George I, Elector and King* (1978).

HILL, B. W., *The Growth of Parliamentary Parties, 1689–1742* (1976).

HOLMES, RICHARD, *Dr. Johnson and Mr. Savage* (1993).

HOOVER, BENJAMIN B., *Samuel Johnson's Parliamentary Reporting* (Berkeley, Calif. and Los Angeles, 1953).

HUME, ROBERT D., *Henry Fielding and the London Theatre 1728–1737* (Oxford, 1988).

HUNT, N. C., *Two Early Political Associations: The Quakers and Dissenting Deputies in the Age of Sir Robert Walpole* (Oxford, 1961).

HUSSEY, CHRISTOPHER, *English Gardens and Landscapes, 1700–1750* (1967).

IRWIN, W. R., 'Prince Frederick's Mask of Patriotism', *Philological Quarterly*, 37 (1958), 368–84.

JENKINS, PHILIP, *The Making of a Ruling Class: The Glamorgan Gentry, 1640–1790* (Cambridge, 1983).

JESSE, JOHN HENEAGE, *Memoirs of the Court of England from 1688 to the Death of George the Second*, 3 vols. (1843).

JONES, ERNEST, *Geoffrey of Monmouth, 1640–1800* (Berkeley, Calif., 1944).

JONES, STEPHEN, *Frederick, Prince of Wales and His Circle* (Sudbury, Suffolk, 1981).

JORDAN, GERALD, and ROGERS, NICHOLAS, 'Admirals as Heroes: Patriotism and Liberty in Hanoverian England', *Journal of British Studies*, 28 (1989), 201–44.

KAMINSKI, THOMAS, 'Was Savage "Thales"?: Johnson's *London* and Biographical Speculation', *Bulletin of Research in the Humanities*, 85 (1982), 322–35.

—— *The Early Career of Samuel Johnson* (New York, 1987).

KEMP, BETTY, 'Frederick Prince of Wales', in A. Natan (ed.), *The Silver Renaissance* (1961), 38–56.

KENDRICK, T. F. J., 'Sir Robert Walpole, the Old Whigs and the Bishops, 1733–6: A Study in Eighteenth-Century Parliamentary Politics', *Historical Journal*, 11 (1968), 421–5.

KENYON, J. P., *Revolution Principles: The Politics of Party, 1689–1720* (Cambridge, 1977).

KING, RONALD, *Royal Kew* (1985).

KLIGER, S. J., 'The "Goths" in England: An Introduction to the Gothic Vogue in Eighteenth-Century Aesthetic Discussion', *Modern Philology*, 43 (1945), 107–17.

—— 'Whig Aesthetics: A Phase of Eighteenth-Century Taste', *English Literary History*, 16 (1949), 135–50.

—— *The Goths in England: A Study in Seventeenth- and Eighteenth-Century Thought* (Cambridge, Mass., 1952).

KRAMNICK, ISAAC, 'Augustan Politics and English Historiography: The Debate on the English Past, 1730–35', *History and Theory*, 6 (1967), 33–56.

—— *Bolingbroke and His Circle: The Politics of Nostalgia in the Age of Walpole* (Cambridge, Mass., 1968).

LANGFORD, PAUL, *The Excise Crisis* (Oxford, 1975).

—— *A Polite and Commercial People: England 1727–1783* (Oxford, 1989).

LERANBAUM, MIRIAM, *Pope's 'Opus Magnum' 1729–1744* (Oxford, 1977).

LINDLEY, DAVID (ed.), *The Court Masque* (Manchester, 1984).

LIPKING, LAWRENCE, *The Ordering of the Arts in Eighteeth-Century England* (Princeton, NJ, 1970).

LLOYD, CHRISTOPHER, *The Queen's Pictures: Royal Collectors through the Centuries* (1991).

LOFTIS, JOHN, *The Politics of Drama in Augustan England* (Oxford, 1963).

LOVEJOY, ARTHUR O., 'The First Gothic Revival and the Return to Nature', *Modern Language Notes*, 47 (1932), 419–46.

LUCAS, JOHN, *England and Englishness* (1990).

MCCARTHY, MICHAEL, *The Origins of the Gothic Revival* (New Haven, Conn., 1987).

MACDOUGALL, HUGH A., *Racial Myth in English History: Trojans, Teutons and Anglo-Saxons* (Montreal, 1982).

MACK, MAYNARD, *The Garden and the City: Retirement and Politics in the later Poetry of Pope, 1731–1743* (Toronto, 1969).

—— *Alexander Pope: A Life* (New Haven, Conn., 1985).

MCKILLOP, ALAN DOUGALD, 'Thomson and the Jail Committee', *Studies in Philology*, 48 (1950), 62–71.

—— *The Background of Thomson's 'Liberty'*, Rice Institute Pamphlet 38, no. 2 (July 1951).

—— 'The Early History of *Alfred*', *Philological Quarterly*, 41 (1962), 311–24.

MEEHAN, MICHAEL, *Liberty and Poetics in Eighteenth-Century England* (1985).

MERRIMAN, JAMES, *The Flower of Kings: A Study of the Arthurian Legend in England between 1485 and 1835* (Lawrence, Kan., 1973).

MILLAR, OLIVER, *Tudor, Stuart and Early Georgian Pictures in the Royal Collection*, 2 vols. (1963).

MONOD, PAUL, *Jacobitism and the English People, 1688–1788* (Cambridge, 1989).

MOORE, C. A., 'Whig Panegyric Verse, 1700–1760: A Phase of Sentimentalism', *Publications of the Modern Language Association*, 41 (1926), 362–401.

NEWMAN, A. N., 'The Political Patronage of Frederick Lewis, Prince of Wales', *Historical Journal*, 1 (1958), 68–75.

NEWMAN, GERALD, *The Rise of English Nationalism: A Cutural History, 1740–1830* (1987).

NICOLL, ALLARDYCE, *A History of Early Eighteenth-Century Drama 1700–1750* (Cambridge, 1925).

NORBROOK, DAVID, *Poetry and Politics in the English Renaissance* (1984).

OWEN, A. L., *The Famous Druids: A Survey of Three Centuries of English Literature on the Druids* (Oxford, 1962).

PAULSON, RONALD, *The Fictions of Satire* (Baltimore, Md., 1967).

PERCIVAL, MILTON, *Political Ballads Illustrating the Administration of Sir Robert Walpole* (Oxford, 1916).

PETERS, MARIE, *Pitt and Popularity: The Patriot Minister and London Opinion during the Seven Years War* (Oxford, 1980).

PIGGOTT, STUART, *The Druids* (1983).

—— *William Stukeley: An Eighteenth-Century Antiquary* (2nd edn. 1985).

POCOCK, J. G. A., *The Ancient Constitution and the Feudal Law: A Study of English Historical Thought in the Seventeenth Century. A Reissue with a Retrospect* (Cambridge, 1987).

—— 'Machiavelli, Harrington and English Political Ideologies in the Eighteenth Century', in his *Politics, Language, Time* (1972), 104–47.

—— *The Machiavellian Moment* (Princeton, NJ, 1975).

—— *Virtue, Commerce, and History* (Cambridge, 1985).

RIVERS, ISABEL, *The Poetry of Conservatism* (Cambridge, 1973).

ROBBINS, CAROLINE, *The Eighteenth-Century Commonwealthmen* (Cambridge, Mass., 1959).

ROGERS, NICHOLAS, *Whigs and Cities: Popular Politics in the Age of Walpole and Pitt* (Oxford, 1989).

ROGERS, PAT, *Literature and Popular Culture in Eighteenth-Century England* (Brighton, 1985).

RORSCHACH, KIMERLY, 'Frederick, Prince of Wales (1707–51) as a Patron of the Visual Arts: Princely Patriotism and Political Propaganda' (Yale Ph.D. thesis, 1985).

RUMBOLD, VALERIE, 'Pope and the Gothic Past', (Cambridge Ph.D. thesis, 1983).

—— *Women's Place in Pope's World* (Cambridge, 1989).

SAMBROOK, JAMES, *James Thomson, 1700–1748: A Life* (Oxford, 1991).

SCHONHORN, MANUEL, 'Pope's *Epistle to Augustus*: Notes towards a Mythology', in Maynard Mack and James Winn (eds.), *Pope: Recent Essays by Several Hands* (Brighton, 1985), 546–64.

—— *Defoe's Politics: Parliament, Power, Kingship and 'Robinson Crusoe'* (Cambridge, 1991).

SCOUTEN, ARTHUR H. (ed.), *The London Stage, 1660–1800. Part 3, 1729–1747*, 2 vols. (Carbondale, Ill., 1961).

SEDGWICK, ROMNEY (ed.), *The History of Parliament: The House of Commons 1715–1754*, 2 vols. (1970).

SITTER, JOHN, *Literary Loneliness in Mid-Eighteenth Century England* (Ithaca, NY, 1982).

SKINNER, QUENTIN, 'The Principles and Practice of Opposition: The Case of Bolingbroke versus Walpole', in Neil McKendrick (ed.), *Historical Perspectives: Studies in English Thought and Society in Honour of J. H. Plumb* (1974), 93–128.

SMITH, R. J., *The Gothic Bequest: Medieval Institutions in British Political Thought, 1688–1832* (Cambridge, 1986).

SPECK, W. A., *Stability and Strife: England 1714–1769* (1977).

—— *The Butcher: The Duke of Cumberland and the Suppression of the '45* (Oxford, 1981).

—— 'Politicians, Peers, and Publication by Subscription 1700–1750', in Isabel Rivers (ed.), *Books and their Readers in Eighteenth-Century England* (Leicester, 1982), 47–68.

—— *Society and Literature in England 1700–1760* (Dublin, 1983).

STEPHENS, FREDERICK GEORGE, *Catalogue of Prints and Drawings in the British Museum: Division I, Political and Personal Satires*, vol. iii, parts 1 and 2, 2 vols. (1877).

STRAKA, GERALD M., *Anglican Reaction to the Revolution of 1688* (Madison, Wis., 1962).

STRONG, ROY, *Henry Prince of Wales and England's Lost Renaissance* (1986).

SYKES, NORMAN, *Edmund Gibson, Bishop of London, 1689–1748* (1926).

TAYLOR, CAROLE, 'Handel and Frederick, Prince of Wales', *Musical Times*, 125 (1984), 89–92.

TAYLOR, STEPHEN, 'Sir Robert Walpole, the Church of England and the Quaker Tithe Bill of 1736', *Historical Journal*, 28 (1985), 51–78.

THOMPSON, E. P., *Whigs and Hunters: The Origin of the Black Act* (1975).

TOMPKINS, J. M. S., 'In Yonder Grave a Druid Lies', *Review of English Studies*, 22 (1946), 1–16.

TORCHIANA, DONALD T., 'Brutus: Pope's Last Hero', repr. in Maynard Mack (ed.), *Essential Articles for the Study of Alexander Pope* (Hampden, Conn., 1968), 705–23.

TRACY, CLARENCE, *The Artificial Bastard: A Biography of Richard Savage* (Toronto, 1953).

VAREY, SIMON, 'Hanover, Stuart and the *Patriot King*', *British Journal for Eighteenth-Century Studies*, 6 (1983), 163–72.

WASSERMAN, EARL, *Elizabethan Poetry in the Eighteenth Century* (Urbana, Ill., 1947).

—— *The Subtler Language: Critical Readings of Neoclassic and Romantic Poems* (Baltimore, Md., 1959).

WEINBROT, HOWARD, *Augustus Caesar in 'Augustan' England: The Decline of a Classical Norm* (Princeton, NJ, 1978).

WIGGIN, LEWIS M., *The Faction of Cousins: A Political Account of the Grenvilles, 1733–1763* (New Haven, Conn., 1958).

WILLIAMS, AUBREY M., *Pope's 'Dunciad': A Study of its Meaning* (1955).

WILSON, KATHLEEN, 'Empire, Trade and Popular Politics in Mid-Hanoverian Britain: The Case of Admiral Vernon', *Past and Present*, 121 (1988), 74–109.

WILSON, MICHAEL, *William Kent: Architect, Designer, Painter, Gardener, 1685–1748* (1984).

ZALLER, ROBERT, 'The Continuity of British Radicalism in the Seventeenth and Eighteenth Centuries', *Eighteenth-Century Life*, 6 (1981), 17–38.

Index

Abbattista, Guido 102 n.
Abbott, John L. 56 n., 57 n.
Addison, Joseph 9; *Cato* 62, 79
Aden, John 85, 86 n., 168 n., 222 n.
Agincourt, Battle of 102, 214
Akenside, Mark 122, 235, 246; *Voice of Liberty* 9, 73; *Epistle to Curio* 230
Alberoni, Cardinal, minister to Philip V of Spain 154
Alfred the Great 74, 102; opposition cult of 116–17, 227, 237; *see also* Thomson, James, writings: *Alfred*
Alfred's Hall (Cirencester) 126
All Souls College Oxford 221
Allan, D. G. C. 54 n., 56, 57 n.
Allen, B. Sprague 169 n., 171 n.
Altick, Richard D. 169 n., 171 n.
American Revolution 23
Amigoni, Jacopo 60, 83
Anne, Princess Royal 40, 214; marriage to William IV of Orange 172, 193
Anne, Queen of England 5, 8, 84, 101, 221; and Elizabeth I 152, 216; opposition uses of 193–4
Annual Register 33 n.
anticlericalism, and opposition Whigs 24–34 *passim*
anti-Trinitarianism 24, 25
Appeal to the Nation, An (1731) 164–5
Arbuthnot, John 69
Arianism 24, 27–8, 29; *see also* Rundle, Thomas
Ariosto, Ludovico 61; *Orlando Furioso* 118, 169
Armens, Sven 205 n.
Arminius, cult of 114–16, 121
Armitage, David 8 n., 9 n., 10 n., 153 n., 157
Arnall, William, *Opposition No Proof of Patriotism* 3
Arne, Thomas 3, 174
Arran, Charles Butler, 1st Earl of 221, 223
Arthur, legendary king of Britain 100, 137, 228; and Arthurian myth 107, 137, 170
Ascham, Sir Roger 177
Atherton, Herbert M. 8 n., 103 n., 156 n., 165 n., 176 n., 178 n., 184 n., 187, 192 n.
Atterbury, Francis, Bishop of Rochester 19, 71, 85, 235, 236–7, 238
Atto, Clayton 54 n.
Atwood, William 109, 167

Augusta of Saxe Gotha, Princess of Wales: popularity of 15, 196–7; and cultural tastes 57, 60, 61; and Saxon origin 121; mentioned 42, 64, 170
Augustus, Emperor: as patron of arts 48, 53; and opposition anti-Augustanism 113–14, 133
Ault, Norman 69 n., 83 n.
Ayscough, Revd Dr Francis 34; his diary 45, 58, 64–5

Bacon, Sir Francis 159, 164–5
Bacon, Nathaniel 110–11
Bailey, Nathan 5 n.
Bailyn, Bernard 23 n.
Ballaster, R. 200 n.
Balliol College, Oxford 221
Bangorian Controversy (1717) 25, 235
Banks, John, *The Albion Queens* 164
Barber, Giles 185 n., 203 n.
Bards, and the bardic in opposition verse 141–9; *see also* Druids
Bank of England 5
Barnard, Sir John 12, 63
Barker, A. D. 154 n.
Barrell, John 180 n.
Barron, Richard, *Pillars of Priestcraft Shaken* 25
Barrymore, James Barry, 4th Earl of 234 n.
Bartram, John 66
Batey, Mavis 126–7
Bath, Order of 225
Bath, city of, and Prince Frederick 90, 197
Bathurst, Allen, 1st Baron 69, 83, 86, 91, 126
Battestin, Martin M. 176 n.
Bayle, Pierre 100
Beattie, James 148
Beckwith, C. 73 n., 205 n.
Bedford, Emmet G. 88 n.
Beljame, Alexandre 47
Bennett, G. V. 85
Benson, Martin 28
Bentley, Richard 55, 240, 241
Bercier, Gabrielle 200
Bethel, Hugh 179
Bevington, Michael 127, 128 n.
Bickham, George, *Beauties of Stow* 129
Big, Sarah (Mrs Stephen Duck) 171
Birch, Thomas 9, 102, 237
Black, Jeremy 17 n. 44 n., 48 n., 106

Blackmore, Sir Richard 80, 101; *Alfred* 117, 119; *Eliza* 152
Blackwell, Thomas 243 n.
Blake, Robert, Admiral 9, 10, 102
Bland, Stephen 27 n.
blank verse, and Whig ideology 72–4
Blenheim, battle of (1704) 8
Blomberg, Carl von, *Account of Livonia* 111
blue-water naval policy, and Country party 5, 8
Bolingbroke, Henry St John, 1st Viscount: and patriotism 4–5, 7–8, 11, 12, 13, 17, 45, 108, 111–12; role in opposition politics 19, 22, 32–5, 39, 41–2, 70–1, 86–9, 185–229 *passim*; Jacobitism and 13, 70–1, 85–7, 187–8, 205–7; Patriot Whig mistrust of 13, 32, 70–1; ministerial attacks on 32, 36–7, 71, 103; and Pope 68, 69, 70–1, 85–94 *passim*; as opposition historian 101, 103–5; and commerce 7, 201–2; and 'politics of nostalgia' 17, 105, 151; and historical scepticism 100–1; and Machiavellian corruption theory 183, 110, 162; and Saxon or Gothic liberty 103–4, 108–12, 137, 139; and Elizabeth I 105, 151, 153, 157, 162–3; and kingship 185–9, 197–210, 227
WRITINGS: *Dissertation on Parties* 111, 114, 139, 189; *Idea of a Patriot King* 43, 45, 86, 87, 89, 92, 94, 105, 153, 162, 183, 185–229 *passim*, textual history of 185–7, and advice-to-princes manuals 189–200, cf. Defoe's *Royall Educacion* 200–3, political context of 203–4, Jacobitism and 92, 205–7, theory of kingship in 207–8, influence on 'Patriot King' poetry 210–11, 225; *Letters on . . . History* 100; *Of the State of Parties* 14 n.; *Remarks on the History of England* 7, 101, 102, 103, 105, 108, 111, 114, 125, 139, 162–3; see also *Craftsman*
Bolton, Charles Paulet, 3rd Duke of 35
Borromeo, Cardinal 51
Boswell, James, *Life of Johnson* 231, 246 n.
Bourg, Hugo de 202
Bowles, F. H. 91 n.
'Boy Patriots' 22, 33, 35–8, 44, 45, 70; see also 'Cobham's Cubs'
Boyer, Abel 237
Boyse, Samuel, *Triumphs of Nature* 119, 137; *The Olive* 170 n.
Brady, Nicholas 153 n.
Brady, Robert 104, 110
Bredvold, Louis M. 72–3
Brereton, Jane Hughes ('Melissa'), *Merlin: A Poem* 143, 172
Brett, Anne, Countess of Macclesfield 233
Brewster, Dorothy 51 n.

Brie, Frederick 143 n.
Brinkley, Roberta 137 n., 138 n.
Brissenden, R. K. 72 n.
Bristol, city of, and Prince Frederick 196–7
Britannia, in opposition iconography 17, 55; *see also* Thomson, James, writings: *Britannia*
broad-bottom administration, Patriot plans for 42–3, 58, 89
Brooke, John 199 n.
Brooke, Henry 46, 64, 77, 79, 88–9, 231; *Gustavus Vasa* 79, 114–15, 140, 191, 192, 211, 232, 242–3, 244; *Farmer's Letter to the Protestants of Ireland* 232
Brooks-Davies, Douglas 85, 86 n., 137 n., 138, 168 n., 225 n.
Brownell, Morris 126 n.
Browning, Reed vii, 9 n., 11, 12 n., 23 n., 164 n., 189
Brunswick, House of, and dynastic myths 117–21
Brutus, mythical king of Britain 93–5, 101, 137, 143–4, 167
Buckingham, Catherine Sheffield, Duchess of 88 n.
Buckingham 36
Bülbring, Karl 201 n.
Burghley, *see* Cecil, William
Burke, Edmund 78
Burnet, Gilbert 152
Bute, 3rd Earl of 55, 57, 199
Butt, John 91 n., 92 n.
Buxton, J. 123 n.
Byng, George, Admiral 154
Bywater, David 119, 120 n.

Cable, Mable Hessler 211
Cadiz, conquest of 105
Caesar, Charles 83 n.
Caesar, Julius 94, 144, 139
Caesar, Mrs Mary 76, 83 n., 216
Cambridge, University of 53, 57
Camden, William 102, 118, 151, 154
Campbell, Alexander Hume 36
Campbell, Duncan 171
Campbell, John 125 n., 142
Cannon, John 20 n.
Cape Passaro (Sicily) 154
Carew, Thomas, *Coelum Britannicum* 73, 137, 144, 225, 226
Carlton House Declaration (1748) 221; *see also* Leicester House alliance
Carlyle, Thomas 47
Caroline, Queen of England: praised in Court panegyric 143, 171–3, 189; iconography of her Hermitage and Cave 106, 128, 142, 169–77, 193, 228; and cultural tastes 53,

178–9, 214 n.; unpopularity of 14, 193; satirized by opposition 178–80; poor relations with Frederick 61, 170; attitude to Stuarts 195; death of 193

Carretta, Vincent 85 n.

Cartagena, siege of (1741) 7, 176

Carte, Thomas 9 n.

Carteret, John, 2nd Baron, later Earl Granville 10, 12, 41, 43, 44, 88, 89, 91, 93, 204

Caryll, John 88 n.

Catholics, and anti-Catholicism 31–2

Cato, Marcus Porcius 5, 9, 62, 79; *see also* Addison, Joseph

Cato's Letters (*London Journal*) 6, 23, 24, 113, 199; *see also* Gordon, Thomas; Trenchard, John

Cave, Edmund 154

Cecil, Robert, 1st Earl of Salisbury 157, 164

Cecil, William, Lord Burghley 153, 157, 158; compared with Walpole 164–6

Chalker, John 217 n., 218, 219

Chambers, William 57 n.

Champion, J. A. I. 24

Chandler, Samuel 31

Chapin, Chester 85 n., 90 n., 91 n., 92 n., 94, 185 n.

Charles I, King of England 11 n., 60, 137, 195, 216, 218, 236 n.

Charles II, King of England 196, 206, 236 n.

Charleton, Walter 138

Chesterfield, Philip Dormer Stanhope, 4th Earl of: in Patriot opposition 10, 35, 39, 41–4, 68, 91, 93; and arts 55, 62, 63, 146; and Jacobite intrigue 205, 232; Johnson on 47, 241, 246

Cholmondeley, 3rd Earl of 35

Chubb, William 31

Church of England 24–6, 28, 32, 33–4; *see also* anticlericalism

Cibber, Colley viii, 235

Cibber, Theophilus 235

civic–humanist tradition 5, 13, 14, 23, 24; *see also* Country ideology

Civil List (Hanoverian) 40, 41, 48, 64, 151

Clark, J. C. D. 7 n., 11 n., 13, 21 n., 24, 106 n., 185 n., 186 n., 188 n., 207 n., 208, 237 n.

Clarke, G. B. 33 n., 68 n., 117 n., 119 n., 123 n., 126, 137 n., 158 n.

Clarke, Samuel 31

Clayton, Lady Charlotte, Viscountess Sundon 212 n., 218–20

Cleary, Thomas 17 n., 78 n., 93 n.

Clifford, J. L. 73 n.

Clitherow, James 212 n.

Cliveden House 3 n., 60

Cobham circle 42, 43, 86, 204; *see also* Whigs: dissident or 'Patriot'

'Cobham's Cubs' 35–40; *see also* 'Boy Patriots'

Cobham, Sir Richard Temple, Viscount: dismissed and enters opposition 33–6; and Prince Frederick 43; and Pope 68–9, 80, 91; landscape gardening at Stowe 36, 111, 127–9; mentioned 182, 224

'Codex, Dr' 25, 30, 32; *see also* Gibson, Edmund

Colley, Linda vii, 3 n., 6 n., 11 n., 14, 15 n., 18 n., 21, 22 n., 23 n., 26 n., 38 n., 42 n., 56, 58, 84 n., 89 n., 104 n., 188 n., 192, 221, 223, 229

Collins, A. S. 47

Collins, William 121, 122, 144 n., 146–9

Collinson, Peter 66

Colton, Judith M. 107 n., 118 n., 128, 169 n.

Colvin, M. H. 126

Common Sense 6, 42, 81, 122, 129, 164; political character of 39; 'Vision of Golden Rump' 176, 180, 156 n., 193 n., 203 n.

Commonwealth thought 5–6, 13–14, 23; *see also* civic–humanist tradition

Coningsby, Sir Thomas 126

Connak, Sir Richard, *Life of Prince Henry* 213

Cornbury, Henry Hyde, Viscount 36, 70, 91, 205, 232

Corneille, Pierre 50, 128, 134

Cornforth, John 126

Cornwall, Duchy of 40, 54, 61; and stannaries 63, 65

Cornwallis, Sir Charles, *Life of Prince Henry* 157, 213

Corpus Christi College, Oxford 34

Country party 5–6; validity of label for opposition to Walpole 20–2, 32

Country ideology 4–6, 11–12, 20–1; and war 7–8; and trade 4; and religion 24, 26–7, 32; and poetry 17 n., 24

Court party, *see* Whigs: Court

Courthope, J. W. 77 n., 91 n.

Covent Garden 228

Coxe, William 38 n., 42 n., 86 n., 200

Crafts of the Craftsman (1735) 13 n., 73 n., 74 n.

Craftsman (1726–35) and Patriot platform 4–5, 6–7, 10, 13, 20, 23, 24, 29, 74; secularism of 26–7, 32; established 19; demise of 39, 42; satire on Walpole 170 n., 174–6, 184, 239; and Patriot kingship 187, 201, 211; 'Remarks on History of England' (Bolingbroke) 7, 101, 102, 103, 105, 108, 111, 114, 125, 139, 162–3; mentioned 101, 117, 122, 153, 165, 181, 189, 202

Craggs, James 155 n.

Crécy, battle of 74, 116

Croker, J. W. 91 n., 92 n.
Cromwell, Oliver, and opposition debate 8, 9–10, 157
Croxall, Samuel, *Original Cantos of Spencer* 8, 168–9, 175, 177
Cruickshanks, Eveline 13 n., 21 n., 38 n., 44 n., 85 n., 87 n., 194 n., 199 n., 205 n., 223 n., 231 n.
Cumberland, William, Duke of 148
Cunningham, Hugh 3, 10 n.
Curll, Edmund, *Rarities of Richmond* 150–1, 169, 171–3, 189
Curtis, Henry 58 n.
cyclical view of history 75, 113, 132–4, 182–3; *see also* Machiavellian theory

Daily Courant 31
Daily Gazetteer 26, 46 n., 164
Daily Post 193 n.
Davies, Thomas 159
Davis, Rose Mary 33 n., 62, 63, 66 n.
De Beer, E. D. 124 n.
Dearing, V. A. 73 n., 205 n.
Defoe, Daniel 237; *Of Royall Educacion* 201–3
deism 25
democracy, usage of term in Walpole era 123 n.
Denham, Sir John, *Coopers-Hill* 73, 215–16, 217–18, 219, 221, 223, 227
Dennis, John 51 n., 72 n.
Derry, Ireland 28, 29
Desaguliers, J. T. 60
Dickinson, H. T. 20 n., 23 n., 100 n., 203 n., 204 n., 205 n., 211 n.
Digby, William, 5th Baron Digby 223
Dilligan, Robert J. 88 n.
Dissenters 24, 26, 30
Dobson, Michael 106, 152 n., 159 n., 235 n.
Doddington, George Bubb 41, 60 n., 62
Dodsley, Robert 39 n., 228
Doody, Margaret 73 n., 77 n., 80 n.
Dorris, George 53 n., 61 n.
Dorset, Lionel Cranfield Sackville, 1st Duke of 210
Douglas, D. C. 100
Downie, A. J. 16 n., 17 n., 48 n., 73 n., 85 n., 92 n., 151 n.
Drake, Sir Francis 9, 102, 154
Drayton, Michael, *Polyolbion* 137, 213
Druids and Druidism 136–47 *passim*; in Stuart mythology 137–8; used by Patriot opposition 139–42; in Hanoverian panegyric 142–3; and Prince Frederick 222, 225–8; Pope and 94–5, 112; Thomson and 140–2, 147
Drury Lane theatre 3 n.
Dryden, John: defines 'Patriot' 5 n., 11, 73, 74, 196

WRITINGS: *Amphitryon* 11; *Absalom and Achitophel* 11; *Astrea Redux* 206, 236 n.; *Epistle to Charleton* 138; *Annus Mirabilis* 196; 'To My Honor'd Kinsman John Driden' 5 n., 11; *King Arthur* 119–20, 172–4, 189 n., 193, 220, 228
Dublin Society for the Arts 56, 57
Duck, Stephen 53, 131, 171, 240, 241
Dudley, Robert, Earl of Leicester 164
Dunkirk, fortification of 20

Edward III, King of England, in opposition writing 74, 102, 114, 116–17, 216, 225, 226, 229, 237
Edward the Black Prince 212, 225
Edwards, Averyl 58 n., 61 n., 62 n., 193 n.
Egmont, John Perceval, 1st Earl of 15 n., 28 n., 44 n., 58 n., 59, 156, 196
Ehrenpreis, Irvin 148–9
elections: 1734 36 n.; 1741 12 n., 34, 36 n., 37
Elizabeth I, Queen of England 9, 33, 74, 105–6, 150–84 *passim*, 193, 201, 208, 237; political uses of in 17th and 18th cent. 9–10, 150–66, 193; and William III 152; and Queen Anne 152; and George II 153, 163; and Prince Frederick 163, 197–8; Patriot and Court rivalry over in Walpole era 153–4; Armada spirit and war with Spain 9, 152–6; and empire 9–10, 157–61; and Commons 161–3; and 'royal favourites' 163–6; mid-18th cent. Elizabethan 'revival' 105–6; and the arts 53–4, 165–6; *see also* Cecil, William; Ralegh, Sir Walter; Spenser, Edmund
Elwin, J. W. 77 n.
empire, and trade 9–10, 15–16, 157
epic poetry, and Patriot poets 76–81
Erskine-Hill, Howard 16 n., 48 n., 69 n., 76 n., 83 n., 85, 87 n., 92 n., 114 n., 179 n., 185 n., 187, 205, 223 n., 231 n., 234 n., 237 n., 238
Essex, William, Capel, 3rd Earl of 41
Essex, Robert Devereaux, 2nd Earl of 164
Este, House of 118, 170
Etough, Revd Henry ('Parson Etoffe') 59
Evelyn, John 124
Examiner 168
Excise Crisis 6, 20, 25, 27, 41

Faerie Leveller, The 167
Farier, David 16 n., 73 n., 92 n., 151 n.
Fairy Prince, The 228
Farinelli (Carlo Broschi) 61, 65
Farley, F. E. 135 n.
Fénelon, François de Salignac de la Mothe, *Les Aventures de Télémaque* 186, 200
Fielding, Henry vii, 57 n., 62 n., 161, 176; and Patriot opposition 78–9; *Champion* 181;

Historical Register 161; *The Opposition: A Vision* 93; *Vernoniad* 176 n., 180

Fiske, Roger 120 n.

Fleetwood, Charles 89

Fog's Weekly Journal 38, 52 n., 169 n., 175, 239

Foley, Paul 5

Foord, Archibald 12 n., 21 n.

Fortescue, William 87, 91 n., 92 n.

forty-five, rebellion of, *see* Jacobite

Foster, Revd James 30, 31

Fountain Tavern meeting (13 Feb. 1742) 44

Foxe, John 100

France: British trade rivalry with 7; cultural rivalry with 48–51

Frederick Louis, Prince of Wales, *passim*; character and reputation of 58–60; education of 198–203; conflicts with George II and Caroline 40–2, 84; political role in Patriot opposition 14–16, 22, 44–5, 58, 81–4, 89, 189–92, 196–8, 203–5; in Patriot poetry 15–16, 50–1, 210–12, 215–229; and *Patriot King* 184–229; identification with City, trade, and commerce 14–17, 196–7; as patron of poets and the arts 46–7, 51, 53–4, 56–67, 245–6; portraits of 60, 212, 214–15; household finances of 40, 41, 61, 63–6; as Prince of Wales 107, 142, 212–15, 221–2; and princely image-making 192–8, 212–15; and Stuart dynasty 107, 194–5, 205–7, 223; as freemason 194 n., 233; as 'Germanicus' 54, 120–1; satire of 79 n., 83; death of 66

Frederick Wilhelm, King of Prussia 40

Frushell, Richard 167 n., 179 n.

Galliard, John 172 n., 215 n.

Garrick, David 57 n., 62, 226, 228–9

Garter, Order of 88, 107, 213, 216, 224–9

Gay, John vii, 17 n., 52, 69, 73; *Beggar's Opera* 72; *Fables* 205; *Shepherd's Week* 73, 168

Gentleman's Magazine 10 n., 31, 38, 46, 102, 103, 119 n., 169 n., 170, 172, 197, 203, 208, 237

George I, King of England 34, 40, 188, 199, 216, 224, 226, 234; idealized by Whigs 102–3, 118, 190, 208

George II, King of England: as Prince of Wales 19, 63, 199, 40, 83; public unpopularity 84, 118, 163, 192–3, 196; bad relations with Frederick 40–2, 61 n., 121, 196–7, 204; in Court panegyric 118–20, 153, 171–4; opposition criticism of 114–15, 176, 178, 237, 240–1; neglect of arts 48, 56, 63; hereditary right to the throne 188–9, 238–43; and Garter Order 88, 213, 225–6, 228; as hunter 216–17; and Windsor 229; mentioned 14, 15, 39

George III, King of England 14, 34, 45, 55, 62, 107, 199, 229

George IV, King of England 60, 228

George of Cappadocia, patron saint of England 137, 174, 225, 229

Germanicus, Nero Claudius, and Prince Frederick 54, 121–2

Gibbon, M. J. 68 n., 127, 128 n.

Gibbs, James 122, 128

Gibson, Edmund, Bishop of London 25–32, 35, 102, 118, 232

Giddings, Robert 245 n.

Giffard, William 119, 172–3, 220

Gilbert, M. 3 n.

Girouard, Mark 57 n., 229 n.

Glamorgan, Wales 29, 55, 222–3

Glory of Old England (print, 1738) 193

Glover, Richard viii, 17, 46, 63, 65, 80–1; *Admiral Hosier's Ghost* 17, 73; *Leonidas* 17, 73, 80–1, 211; *London* 10, 47, 73, 156, 232

Godolphin, Sidney 5

Golden, Morris 180 n.

Golden Rump, 'Festival of' (print, 1737) and 'Vision of' (essay) 39–40, 173 n., 175–6, 193; stage farce, 173 n.

Goldgar, Betrand, *Walpole and the Wits* vii, viii, 17 n., 24 n., 39 n., 47, 48, 52 n., 65, 71 n., 72, 74, 75 n., 93 n., 114 n., 136, 155 n., 168 n.

Goldie, Mark 24, 25, 188 n., 190

Goldstein, Malcolm 88 n.

Goodale, J. R. 6 n.

Goodman's Fields theatre 172

Gordon, Thomas 6, 8, 9, 22, 24, 28, 87, 93, 113; see also *Cato's Letters*

Gothic, the, 18, 103–5, 108–49 *passim*; opposition use of Gothic liberty and constitution 23, 103–5, 108–12; *translatio* theory 109, 137; merging of Gothic and Celtic 112–13, 136–7; and national identity 18, 104, 108; in Patriot drama 113–16;' and Hanoverian monarchy 116–21; and architecture 121–31; primitivism and poetic inspiration 131–6; *see also* Druids; Saxons

Gower, John Leveson, 1st Earl of 86, 91

Grand Tour 17, 177–80

Grant, Douglas 169 n.

Granville, George, Lord Lansdowne 86, 138 n., 173, 175 n.

Graves, Richard 34

Gray, Thomas 59 n., 120, 121, 132, 135, 146–9, 174 n.

Great Fire of London 196
Greene, Donald 180 n., 231, 243 n.
Greenwich, London 150, 196
Gregg, Edward 152 n.
Grenville, George 36, 45
Grenville, Richard 36, 37, 45
Greville, Fulke 151, 153
Griffin, Dustin 72 n., 80 n., 215 n.
Griffith, R. H. 75 n.
Grub-Street Journal 65 n., 167 n.
Grundy, Isobel 231 n.

habeas corpus 23
Hagley Hall, Worcs 83 n., 131, 226 n., 243
Hagstrum, Jean 156
Haig, Christopher 151 n.
Hales, Stephen 57
Hamilton, Newburgh 61
Hammond, Brean 91 n., 103 n., 185 n., 186 n.,
    203 n., 208 n.
Hammond, James 63, 245–6
Hampden, John 22, 191
Hampton Court, Herefordshire 126
Handasyde, Elizabeth 86 n.
Handel, George Frideric 52, 61, 196
Hanover Club 168
Hanover, House of 13, 33, 48; Hanoverian
    dynastic myths 102–3, 106–7, 117–21,
    142–3, 169–74, 220; White Horse of 53,
    118–20, 175, 239–41; *see also* Frederick,
    Prince of Wales; George II
Hardwicke, Philip Yorke, 1st Baron 42, 44
Harley, Edward 12, 26, 55
Harley, Robert 5
Harrington, James 9, 151 n.; neo-
    Harringtonianism 3 n., 5, 23, 151; *see also*
    civic–humanist tradition
Harris, George 42 n.
Harris, Michael 28 n., 31 n.
Harris, Robert 4 n., 11 n., 12 n., 15 n., 34 n.,
    40 n., 45 n., 64 n.
Harris, Tim 152 n.
Hart, Jeffrey 105 n., 198
Hatton, Ragnild 63, 188
Havens, R. D. 72 n.
Hawksmoor, Nicholas 126
Hawley, William 232
Haymarket theatre 62, 89
Hayton, David 5 n.
Haywood, Eliza, *Memoirs of Utopia* 176,
    181–2
Hedges, John 65
Hellfire Club 55 n.
Henry III, King of England 202
Henry V, King of England 102, 201, 214, 237
Henry VII, King of England 201–2
Henry VIII, King of England 171

Henry Frederick, Prince of Wales, compared
    with Prince Frederick 137, 157, 212–13,
    215
Hessian troops 20, 22
Hill, Aaron: and reformation of arts 49–54, 56;
    politics of 52 n.; and Pope 77–9, 87–8, 89;
    and the north 120, 133, 136; on
    Hanoverians 120–1, 163
  WRITINGS: *Advice to the Poets* 52, 72 n., 78,
    120; *Alzira* 53; *Athelwold* 136; *Caesar*
    52 n.; *Cleon to Lycidas* 136; *King Henry
    V* 214; *Muses in Mourning* 49–50; *Northern
    Star* 77 n.; *Progress of Wit* 77;
    Prompter 52, 220 n.; *Tears of the
    Muses* 53–4, 56, 120–1, 136, 170 n.;
    Zara 53
Hill, B. W. 5 n., 11, 21 n., 27, 44 n.
Hill, Christopher 109 n.
Hillarian circle 50–4, 233; *see also* Hill, Aaron
Histoire du Prince Titi [Themiseul de St
    Hyacinthe] 61–2
history: Court and opposition uses of 9–10,
    99–229 *passim*; historical scepticism 100–1;
    growing historical awareness 101–2; and
    national myth 101–3; *see also* Alfred the
    Great; cyclical view of history; Edward
    III; Elizabeth I; Gothic; Henry V; Henry
    Prince of Wales; myth; Windsor
Hoadly, Benjamin 25, 29, 31, 34
Hogarth, William 57 n.
Hollis, Thomas 22
Holmes, G. 21 n.
Holmes, Richard 232–3, 234 n., 237 n., 238
Horace 133
Hosier, Francis, Admiral 7, 155
Hudson, Revd Thomas 212 n.
Hume, David 201
Hume, Robert D. 42 n.
Hunt, J. D. 127 n.
Hunt, N. C. 26, 27 n.
Hussey, Christopher 127 n.

Independent Whig 24, 28
Irwin, Lady Anne 195 n., 196
Irwin, W. R. 211 n.

Jacobites and Jacobitism 13, 30, 32, 40, 41 n.,
    42, 154, 223; Jacobite uprisings: 1715 85,
    234, 1745 148, 194, 223, 232, 237; using
    language of Patriot opposition 13–14, 87
    n., 194–5, 234; and Bolingbroke 13, 70–1,
    85–7, 187–8, 205–7; and *Patriot King* 92,
    187–8, 205–7; and Frederick 194–5; and
    Pope 76, 85–7; and Savage 30, 232–8; and
    Johnson 231–2, 237–41
Jail Committee (1729) 27
Jamaica, capture of (1655) 9

James I, King of England 151, 157, 158, 159, 163, 164, 195, 212
'James III', *see* Stuart, James Francis Edward
Jekyll, Sir Joseph 22, 26
Jenkins, P. 194 n., 223 n.
Jenkins's Ear, War of vii, 7; *see also* Spain
Jesse, John Heneage 61 n., 63, 65 n.
Johnson, Michael 237
Johnson, Samuel viii, 10, 30, 31, 33 n., 38, 47, 68, 83, 100, 117, 132, 191; early political views 230–47
  WRITINGS: *Compleat Vindication of the Licensers of the Stage* 79 n., 231–2, 242–3; *Debates in the Senate of Lilliput* 243–4; *Lives of the Poets* 33 n., 63 n., 68, 83, 231, 233, 245–7; *London* 150, 156, 231, 232, 237–8; *Marmor Norfolciense* 231–2, 236–41; *Thoughts on Falkland Islands* 10; *Vanity of Human Wishes* 230, 231
Johnston, Arthur 105 n.
Jones, Clyve 5 n.
Jones, Ernest 100
Jones, J. H. 40 n.
Jones, Stephen 60 n., 195, 214
Jonson, Ben 216, 217
Jordan, Gerald 6 n., 9 n.
Jordanes 109

Kaminski, Thomas 102 n., 237 n., 243 n., 244 n.
Keener, Frederick M. 209
Kemp, Betty 3 n., 14 n., 58 n.
Kendrick, T. D. 137 n.
Kendrick, T. F. J. 26 n., 28 n.
Kent, William 60, 178 n., 195, 214, 215, 225 n.
Kenyon, J. P. 23 n., 188 n.
Ker, John 109 n.
Kew House (Richmond) 60, 214, 222
King, Bruce 11 n.
King, Ronald 60 n., 66 n.
King, William 122 n., 156, 223
kingship 12–14, 106–7, 162–3, 188–94; *see also* Patriot King
Klein, William 109 n.
Klemp, Paul 167 n.
Kliger, S. J. 104 n., 109 n., 115 n., 122–3, 130
Kneller, Sir Godfrey 60
Knevet, Ralph 167
Korshin, Paul 244 n.
Kramnick, Isaac 91 n., 100 n., 102 n., 104, 110, 162, 185, 190 n., 197, 203 n., 211 n.; and 'politics of nostalgia' theory 4, 16–17, 105 n.

Langford, Paul 221 n.
Langley, Batty 124–5
Last, B. W. 16 n.
Lechmere, Edmund 12, 34, 37, 38

Leibniz, Gottfried 170, 200
Leicester House 15, 46, 57, 58, 62, 204
Leicester House alliance 45, 186, 213, 221
Leicester House Diary, see Ayscough, Revd Dr Francis
Leigh, Theophilus 221
Leranbaum, Miriam 93 n., 94 n.
Levine, J. A. 11 n.
Lichfield, George Lee, 3rd Earl of 186
'Lilliput, Debates in Senate of' (*Gentleman's Magazine*) 46, 243–4; *see also* Johnson, Samuel
Lillo, George vii, 17; and Prince Frederick 46, 66
  WRITINGS: *Elmerick* 66; *London Merchant* and *Fatal Curiosity* 159–61; *Christian Hero* 211; *Britania and Batavia* 215 n.
Lipking, Lawrence 124–5, 132 n.
Lloyd, Christopher 60 n., 229 n.
Locke, John 33, 188, 191
Loftis, John 57 n., 78, 103 n., 114 n., 115, 155 n., 211 n., 235 n.
London, City of 5; Mayor and Aldermen's support for Prince Frederick 15, 206, 196–7
London Evening Post 153 n.
London Journal 153 n., 162, 189 n., 199 n.
London Magazine 30 n., 46, 170
Lonsdale, Roger 59 n., 105 n.
Louis XIV, King of France 50, 134
Lovejoy, A. O. 124 n.
Lucas, John 147–8
Lyttelton, Anne 34
Lyttelton, George, 1st Baron: personal qualities 39; political role in opposition 33–4, 36–7, 39–40, 41–51, *see also* 'Boy Patriots'; early anticlericalism 33–4; as literary patron 46–66, 62–7; and Frederick 41–5, 46–7, 62–4, 82–3; and Pope 68–74, 76–84, 87–95; Thomson on 184; Johnson on 47, 230–1, 243–7; and the Gothic 110, 129, 131; mentioned 10, 12 n., 17 n., 23, 105 n., 204, 228
  WRITINGS: *Considerations upon the Present State of Affairs* 156, 242; *Epistle to Mr. Pope* 77, 93–4; *History of Henry II* 82, 101; *Masque for Children* 226; 'Observations on Elizabeth' 150, 159, 163, 165–6, 208; *Persian Letters* 33, 34, 39, 110, 130, 162–3, 178–9, 189, 220; see also *Common Sense*
Lyttelton, Sir Thomas 37

McCarthy, Michael 124 n.
McDougall, Hugh 104 n.
McGuinness, R. 51 n.
Machiavelli, Niccolò, *The Prince* 190, 198, 201

Machiavellian theory 5, 75, 94, 110, 132–3, 162, 177, 182–3, 206

Mack, Maynard 16 n., 76, 79 n., 83 n., 99 n., 103 n., 176 n., 178 n.

McKendrick, Neil 3 n., 86 n., 104 n.

McKillop, A. D. 3 n., 27 n., 72, 74, 113, 117 n., 142 n., 192 n.

McMahon, Marie P. 24 n.

Macpherson, James 121

McQueen, John 181 n.

Madden, Samuel 56–7

Maecenas 46, 48, 53

Maffei, Scipione 51, 52–3, 61

Magna Carta 108, 227

Magnus, Olaus 111

Mallet, David vii, 15, 16, 34, 46, 185; and Hill 50, 52, 78 n.; and Prince Frederick 63–4, 88–9, Johnson on 231, 233, 245–6; *Eurydice* 78 n.; *Mustapha* 89, 211; *Alfred* 15

Manley, Delarivier 200

Marchmont, Alexander Campbell, 2nd Earl of 35, 36, 43

Marchmont, Hugh Hume, 3rd Earl of (styled Lord Polwarth, 1724–40) 10, 26, 36; Pope's admiration for 68, 70, 88 n., 90–1

Marchmont Papers 21 n., 41 n., 42 n., 64 n.

Marlborough, John Churchill, 1st Duke of 5, 8; wars of 35, 167

Marlborough, Sarah Churchill, Duchess of 93

Marples, Morris 58 n.

Martyn, Benjamin 55, 80, 211 n.

Marvell, Andrew 151 n.

masques, used by Patriot opposition 215, 225–6

Mawer, John 220

Maxwell, John 11 n.

May, Tom 23

Mead, Richard 55, 57

Meehan, Michael 123 n.

'Melissa', *see* Brereton, Jane Huges

Mercier, Philip 60, 62, 65, 214

Merlin 100; in Hanoverian propaganda 169–74; used satirically by opposition to Walpole 174–7; in Jacobite prophecy 175, 239

Merlin: Or, the British Inchanter (1735–6 version of Dryden's *King Arthur*) 119–20, 172–4, 209–10

Merlin's Cave, Richmond 106, 118, 128, 169–77, 184, 228, 239, 241

Merriman, James 100, 171 n.

militia, and Country party 5, 22

Millar, Andrew 9, 102

Millar, Oliver 60, 61 n., 83 n., 212 n., 214 n., 220 n.

Miller, James 136

Miller, Sanderson 127, 131

Milton, John 9, 23, 33, 53, 61, 121, 138, 141, 176

Miltonic verse 72–3

Mist's Weekly Journal 39, 224

Molesworth, Robert, 1st Viscount 23, 109, 111, 126

Molière 50, 134

Molloy, Charles 40

Monck, J. H. 56

Monmouth, Geoffrey of, *Historia Regum Britanniae* 94, 100, 101, 137, 138

Monod, Paul 188 n., 194, 232 n., 236 n.

Montesquieu, Charles de, *Lettres Persanes* 39

Montrose, James Graham, Duke of 35

Moore, C. A. 72–3

Moore, Robert E. 174

More, Thomas, *Utopia* 186

Morgan, David 206

Morgan, Joseph 213, 157

Morris, David 51

Mortmain Bill (1736) 12, 26

motion to remove Walpole (13 Feb. 1741) 43, 93, 231, 244

Motion, The (print series) 93

Moyle, Walter 23

Munby, A. L. N. 111 n.

Murdoch, Patrick 115

Murphy, Arthur 235 n., 244 n.

Murray, William 36, 70

myth: political creation of national 3–4, 9, 99–103; as opposed to scepticism 100–1; and opposition satire 103, 174–7; *see also* Arthur; Britannia; Brutus; Elizabeth I; Gothic; Hanover; Merlin; Troynovant; Windsor

Naked Truth, The (print) 8

Napoleon, Emperor 229

Nash, Richard, 'Beau' 90

Natan, A. 14 n., 58 n.

national debt 5, 8, 12

nationalism 7–8, 104, 108; *see also* patriotism

Newburgh, Brockhill 72 n.

Newcastle, Thomas Pelham-Holles, 1st Duke of 27, 44

Newman, A. N. 20 n., 64, 66 n., 221 n.

Newman, Gerald vii, 49 n., 104 n., 108 n., 146

Nicholl, Allardyce 215 n., 220 n.

Nichols, John, *Literary Anecdotes* 9 n., 55 n., 59 n.

Nickolls, John 9 n.

Nine Years War 5, 8

Nixon, John 48, 172 n.

Nixon, Robert 171, 239 n.

Norbrook, David 151 n., 167 n., 226 n.

Norfolk House 60
Norman Conquest 109
Norman Yoke 23; *see also* Saxons: Patriot use of liberty
Noyes, R. G. 228 n.
Nugent, Robert Craggs 90–1; *Political Justice* 38–9; *Ode to Mankind* 191

Observations on the Present Taste for Poetry (1739) 34, 76 n.
Odin, Norse god 116, 135
'oeconomical societies' 54, 56–7
Ogg, David 5 n.
O'Hehir, Brendan 216 n.
Okehampton, Devon 36 n., 64 n.
Old and Modern Whig Revived 45
Old Sarum 36 n.
Old Whig, political content of 22, 31–3, 35, 36, 121, 122, 130, 191, 202 n., 220
Oldmixon, John 101, 109, 237
Oldys, John 157–8
opera, and Prince Frederick 61
Opera of Nobility 61, 196
Oppian, *Cynegeuticks* 220
opposition poetry, diversity of vii, 16–17, 71–81; *see also* Patriot poetry
opposition to Walpole, composition and unity 10–12, 19–24; *see also* 'Patriot' title: Tories; Whigs
Ormonde, James Butler, 2nd Duke of 154, 205, 221, 223
Orrery, John Boyle, 5th Earl of 85, 86
Owen, A. L. 137 n., 141 n.
Owen, J. B. 192 n.
Oxford, University of 33, 34, 53, 57, 223

Pardo, Treaty of 7, 43, 129
Partridge, John, *Merlinus Liberatus* 150, 171
Paterson, William 55, 64 n., 184, 211 n.; *Arminius* 114–16
Patriot (ed. John Harris, 1714–15) 13 n.
Patriot drama: theory of 78–80; on stage 88–9, 113–16, 191–2
Patriot King: concept of 4, 12–16, 58, 91, 94–5, 106, 107, 162–3, 185–229 *passim*; Patriot King in Whig writings 198–203, 205, 208–12; Stuarts and 205–7; Defoe and 201–3; education of Patriot King 189–205; poetry depicting 210–12, 215–29; *see also* Bolingbroke: writings, *Idea of a Patriot King*; Frederick Louis, Prince of Wales
Patriot poetry 16–18; distinctive features and theory behind 71–8, 99
'Patriot' title: origins and political application 10–12, 19; Jacobite and Hanoverian use of 13–14, 125; distinct from

'patriotism' 4, 10–11; used by Dryden 11; Pope 12, 88; Johnson 10, 230; *see also* Whigs: dissident or Patriot
Patriotism: theories of 3–18 *passim*; as oppositional 'Country' doctrine 4–6; and Hanoverianism 13–16, 106–7, 171–4; and Jacobitism 13–14; Pulteney's betrayal of 44–5, 230–1; and war with Spain 6–10, 154–61; and xenophobic prejudice 7–8; and the arts 46–54; use of British history to create sense of 9–10, 99–229 *passim*, *esp.* 99–107; and Gothic racial origins 108–12; and nationalism 7–8, 104, 108; *see also* history; myth; 'Patriot' title; Patriot King; Whigs
patronage, literary: opposition view of 46–57, 133–4, 165–6; and Prince Frederick 58–67; Johnson on 47, 245–6
Patterson, Annabel 168 n.
Paulson, Ronald 103 n.
Peake, Robert 212
Pelham administration 45
Pelham, James 41, 63
Pemberton, Henry 80
Percival, Milton 224
'Persian Letter' (*Mist's*) 39 n., 62 n.
Persian Letters, *see* Lyttelton, George
Persian strip'd of his Disguise (1735) 33, 34, 189 n.
Peters, Marie 12 n., 13 n., 17 n.
Petrarch 198
Petyt, William 109
Philips, Ambrose 168
Philips, John 235 n.
Phillimore, Robert 41 n.
Phillips, Charles 60, 214
Phillips, Edward 215 n., 220
Phillipson, Nicholas 24 n., 109 n., 188 n.
Piggott, Stuart 137 n., 138, 144 n.
Pine, John 155
Pitt, Thomas 36
Pitt, William 10, 13 n., 23, 34, 70, 242; political role 35–7, 39, 45
Plato 186
Plumer, Walter 21 n., 22, 26
Pocock, J. G. A. 5 n., 6 n., 23 n., 100 n., 104, 109 n., 110 n., 133, 190, 205 n.
'politics of nostalgia', *see* Kramnick, Isaac
Pope, Alexander: relationship with Patriot Whigs 38, 67, 68–95 *passim*; and Prince Frederick 41, 68, 81–4, 204; and Aaron Hill 51–2, 77–8; and Bolingbroke 68, 69, 70–1, 85–94 *passim*; and Jacobitism 85–7, 180, 216, 222; definition of 'Patriot' 12, 88; sense of patriotism 95, 99; and *Patriot King* 92, 94–5, 180, 185, 204, 207; his satire contrasted with Patriot poetry vii,

Pope, Alexander (*cont.*):
71–81, 99; and the Gothic 112–13, 137;
and Spenser 176, 177, 179–82; as
Druid 141–2; on Garter Order 224–5;
Johnson on 68, 231, 245–6
WRITINGS: 'Bounce to Fop' 83–4; *Brutus* 68,
93, 140, 143–4; *Dunciad* vii, 48, 49, 50, 68,
74–5, 77, 86, 93, 99, 173 n., 176, 179–81,
224–5; *Epilogue to the Satires* 37, 75, 87,
99, 183, 224; *Epistle to Bolingbroke* 87;
Epistle to Cobham 69; *Epistle to Jervas* 77;
One Thousand Seven Hundred and Forty
76, 91–3, 99, 202 n., 207, 211; *Pastorals*
222; *Rape of the Lock* 219; *Temple of
Fame* 112–13, 138; *Windsor-Forest* 8, 73,
95, 99, 209, 215–18, 221, 222
Popple, William 52 n., 63 n.
Porteous Riots 240
Porto Bello 3, 7, 13
Potter, John 189 n.
Potter, Thomas 13 n.
Powney, Peniston 66 n., 221, 223
Powney, Richard 16, 46, 66, 217; *Stag Chace in
Windsor Forest* 16, 142, 221–3
Pretender, 'Old', *see* Stuart, James Francis
Edward
Prior, Matthew 106, 167–8, 169; *Ode, Humbly
Inscrib'd to the Queen* 167–8
Prompter, The 52, 78, 165, 220 n.
prophecy: political 170–4; satirical opposition
use of 174–7, 239–43; Jacobitism and 175,
239–43; *see also* Merlin
primitivism, conflict between political and
literary 131–6
Pulteney, William: political role 19–20, 21, 27;
Bolingbroke and 5, 70, 86; and
Carteret 41–5, 58; differentiated from
Cobhamite Patriots 35–8; their suspicion
of his principles 41–5, 89, 204; his
betrayal of patriotism 44–5, 230–1; Pope
and 12, 70, 71, 84, 88, 89, 91, 93; Johnson
and 241, 242; mentioned 10, 50, 155, 230
Purcell, Henry 174

Quadruple Alliance, war of 154
Quaintance, Richard 123 n.
Quaker Tithe Bill (1736) 26, 27, 35
Quakers 26
Quin, James 62, 154

Racine, Jean 50, 134
Rackett, Charles 86, 217
Radnar Lodbrog, 'death song of' 119, 135
Rainbow Coffee House 55
Ralegh, Sir Walter, opposition cult of 9, 10,
102, 157–61, 165–6, 213
Ralph, James 15 n., 55 n., 61 n., 164

Ramillies, Battle of (1706) 8, 167
Rapin de Thoyras, Paul 65, 101, 109, 111, 138,
154, 225
Ratchford, Fannie E. 185 n.
'Reafan Banner' 135
Remembrancer 15 n.
Reynolds, Sir Joshua 66
Richardson, Samuel 51
Richelieu, Cardinal 51, 52
Richmond, House 63; Gardens 128, 169–74,
217, 220, 240; Lodge (Freemasons) 233
Richmond, Rarities of, see Curll, Edmund
Rivers, Isabel 16 n., 79 n., 99
Rivers, Richard Savage. 4th Earl 233
Robbins, Caroline 5 n., 23, 111 n.
Robinson, Sir Thomas 28
Rogers, Nicholas vii, 6 n., 8 n., 9 n., 15 n.,
17 n., 152 n., 193 n.
Rogers, Pat 107 n., 193 n., 198
Rolli, Paolo 61, 65
Rolt, Richard 66, 212 n.
Rorschach, Kimerly 59–69, 196 n., 214 n.
Rosebery, Lord 36 n., 39 n.
Rothstein, Eric 72 n.
Rowe, Nicholas 62
Rowlands, Henry, *Mona Antiqua Illustrata*
138–9, 141, 144
Roxburghe Squadrone 36
Royal Academy 57
royal education 198–203
Royal Opera Company 61
Ruffhead, Owen, *Life of Pope* 83 n., 93 n., 143 n.
Rumbold, Valerie 76 n., 95 n., 113 n., 116 n.,
216 n., 241 n.
Rumpsteak Club 33
Rundle, Thomas 17 n., 27–31, 80–1, 141, 195,
232–3; and 'Rundle Crisis' 27–31, 232–3
Runnymede, Surrey 227
Rushout, Sir John 21 n.
Rysbrack, Michael 111 n., 128, 195

Sacheverell, Henry 30
Saddlers' Company, City of London 15
Saint-Hyacinthe, Themiseul de 61 n.
St Martin's Lane Academy 57
Sambrook, James 51 n., 63 n., 64, 81 n.,
114 n., 123 n., 211 n.
Sammes, Aylett 120 n., 135, 138
Samuels, Raphael 3 n., 104 n.
Sandys, Samuel 10, 12, 21 n., 26, 43, 91, 93,
231, 244–5
Saunders, J. S. 47 n.
Saussure, César de 224
Savage, Richard: political views of 30, 232–8;
and anticlericalism 30–1, 232–3; and
Jacobitism 13, 234–8; relations with
Johnson 231–8, 245

WRITINGS: 'Britannia's miseries' 234–5,
   Character of Rev. James Foster 30; *The
   Convocation* 235; *Of Public Spirit* 233; *On
   False Historians* 237; *Progress of a
   Divine* 30–1, 232–3; *The Wanderer* 234,
   235–6
Saxons and Saxonism 103–4, 108–49 *passim*;
   Saxon constitution 108–13; Hanoverian
   use of Saxon racial myths 102–3, 117–21;
   Patriot use of Saxon liberty 108–17;
   Bolingbroke and 108–12; at Stowe 111,
   112, 118, 119, 128–37; Johnson on 117,
   241; *see also* Alfred, Gothic
Schonhorn, Manuel 107 n., 169 n., 174,
   201 n.
Schutz, Augustus 127
Scott, George Lewis 55, 57
Scouten, Arthur 164 n., 173 n.
Scriblerus Club 69–70
Sedgwick, Romney 20 n., 64 n., 86 n., 191 n.
Septennial Act (1716) 23
Settlement, Act of (1702) 188–9
Seven Years War 13
Seville, Treaty of (1729) 7, 155
Sewell, George, *Tragedy of Sir Walter
   Raleigh* 154–5, 156
Seymour, Charles, 6th Duke of Somerset 55
Shaftesbury, 1st Earl of 11
Shaftesbury, 3rd Earl of 134, 141
Shakespeare, William 134; political uses and
   mid-18th cent. revival 105–6, 121
Shenstone, William 66 n.
Sherburn, George 90 n.
Sherwell, J. W. 15 n.
Shipley, William 54, 56–7
Shippen, William 91
Shotover Park, Oxon. 126–7
Sidney, Algernon 23, 191
Sidney, Sir Philip 134, 215 n.; *Arcadia* 166
Sitter, John 145, 148, 181 n.
Skerrett, Maria 59 n., 92
Skinner, Quentin 3 n., 24 n., 104 n., 109 n.,
   110, 111 n., 188 n.
Slaughter's Coffee House 57
Smith, R. J. 104 n., 61
Smith, Ruth 51 n, 61
Smithson, Hugh, 1st Duke of
   Northumberland 55
Smollett, Tobias 62, 129
Society of Arts 54, 57
Society for the Encouragement of
   Learning 54–6
Socinianism 24
Somervile, William 46, 48, 66; *Field Sports* 66,
   220; *The Chace* 74, 211, 217–20, 221
Sophia, Electress of Hanover (mother of
   George I) 200

Sophia, Princess of Prussia 40
South Sea Bubble 6, 133, 176
South Sea Company 5, 7, 33, 35
Spadafora, David 133 n.
Spain: War of Spanish Succession 8; British
   attacks on (1718–19) 154; war of 1727 and
   ministerial negotiations with 7, 155;
   Patriot campaign for war with 6–10, 105,
   153, 154–61; trade rivalry with 6–7,
   157–71; Cromwell's Western Design
   and 9–10; Elizabethan Armada spirit and
   anti-Spanish sentiment 154–61
Speck, W. A. 13 n., 16 n., 20 n., 21, 38 n.,
   74 n., 79 n., 194 n.
Spence, Joseph 83 n.
Spenser, Edmund: political use of in 17th and
   18th cent. 166–84 *passim*; mid-18th-cent.
   'romantic' revival 105–6, 121, 131, 184; in
   Queen Caroline's Cave 169–73; opposition
   use of 165–6, 174–84; Pope and 179–82;
   Thomson and 180–4; Gilbert West
   and 177–9; mentioned 27, 80, 134
   WRITINGS: *Faerie Queene* 122, 131, 166–70;
   Mother Hubberds Tale 180; *Ruines of
   Time* 177; *Teares of the Muses* 53–5, 170 n.
stag chase poems 215–33
Stage Licensing Act (1737) 55, 161, 176, 231,
   234, 242–3
Stair, John Dalrymple, 2nd Earl of 35
standing armies 5, 42
Stanhope, James, 1st Earl of 6, 19
Stature of a Great Man (1739 print) 156
Stebbing, Henry 28, 30
Sterling, James, *Ode on the Times* 210
Stevenson, John 6 n.
Stonehenge 138, 143, 145, 146, 172; *see also*
   Druids
Stowe House, Bucks: Cobham's political
   landscape gardening 35–6, 122–3, 127–9,
   169; Saxon Altar 111, 119, 137; Temple
   of Ancient Virtue 123; Temple of British
   Worthies 10, 33, 68, 117, 150, 158–9;
   Temple of Liberty 122, 125–9, 131;
   Temple of Venus 178 n.; *see also* Gothic:
   architecture
Strafford, Thomas Wentworth, 1st Earl of
   216
Straka, Gerald 152, 188
Strawberry Hill, Twickenham 123
Strong, Roy 212–13, 215 n.
Strutt, Samuel 55
Stuart, Charles Edward (Young Pretender)
   13 n., 194–5, 206
Stuart, James Francis Edward (Old Pretender,
   'James III') 40, 44, 76, 154, 237; *see also*
   Jacobites
Stukeley, William 136, 138, 141, 143–5

Suetonius Paulinus 138, 144
Sunderland, Charles Spencer, 3rd Earl of 6, 19
Swedenberg, H. T. 80 n.
Swift, Jonathan: and the Patriots 69–70, 81, 83; and Queen Anne 193–4; and Rundle 29; and the Gothic 101; and Bickerstaff hoax 171; other references vii, 8, 17 n., 46, 175, 224
    WRITINGS: *Conduct of the Allies* 8; *On Poetry, A Rapsody* 48, 225 n., *Gulliver's Travels* 72; *Windsor Prophecy* 171, 239
Sykes, Norman 24 n., 25, 26, 27 n.
'Sylvia' (Augusta, Princess of Wales) 61, 222

Tacitus: opposition use of 113–16; in Rowlands 139; in Pope 143
Talbot, Charles, 1st Baron Talbot of Hensol 27–9, 63, 222
Talbot, Charles Richard 17 n., 29
Talbot, William, Bishop 27
Talbot, William, 2nd Baron Talbot 29, 31, 34, 55, 221 n., 222
Tasso, Torquato 61
Taylor, Carole 61
Taylor, Stephen 26, 27 n.
Temple, Sir William: 'Of Poetry' 111, 135; 'Of Heroic Virtue' 111, 112, 135; *History of England* 138
Test Act, campaign to repeal 26, 31
Theobald, Lewis 63 n., 154, 158, 172 n.
Thompson, E. P. 86 n., 216–17, 221
Thomson, James: his patriotism 3, 15, 16–18, 48–51, 146; political views 17, 29–30, 55, 111; and Rundle 29–30; and Hillarian circle 51–4, 233; and Prince Frederick 34, 63–4, 190–1; and Patriot drama 88–9; and *Patriot King* 211; views on literary patronage 46–51; choice of genre 72–6, 80; member of Society for Encouragement of Learning 54–5; as freemason 233; and the Gothic 111, 116–17, 119, 122–5, 132–6; and Druids 139–45, 146–7; and Spenser 168, 177–84; influence on mid-cent. poets 146–9; Johnson on 245–6
    WRITINGS: *Agamemnon* 89; *Alfred, A Masque* 3, 135, 146, 150, 192, 226; *Britannia* 10 n., 17 n., 73, 74, 155–6, 183; *Castle of Indolence* 49 n., 50, 80, 132, 133, 140, 141–2, 146, 180–4; *Edward and Eleanora* 202 n., 211; *Liberty* 17 n., 49, 50–1, 52 n., 63, 74–5, 113, 119, 125, 132–5, 139–41, 211, 233; *Ode to His Royal Highness* 63; *Poem to the Memory of Talbot* 30, 233 n.; 'Rule, Britannia' vii, 3, 17 n., 95; *Seasons* 28, 51, 132, 141, 147, 159; *Tancred and Sigismunda* 230
Tiberius, Emperor 54

Tillyard, E. M. 105
Tindal, Nicholas 65, 101
Tipping, Avray 127
Toland, John 101 n., 138–9, 190
Tompkins, J. M. S. 139 n., 146 n., 147 n.
Torchiana, Donald T. 94 n.
Tories 4, 5, 12, 18; and 'Patriot' label 10–12; differentiated from Patriot Whigs in opposition 20–2; suspicion of Patriot Whigs 12, 26–7, 43, 84; attempted broad-bottom alliance with Patriots 42–4, 45, 89; relations with Prince Frederick 42, 195, 208, 221; and appeal of *Patriot King* 187, 207–8, *see also* Leicester House alliance; 'Tory satire' 72–3
Townesend, William 126
Townshend, Charles, 2nd Viscount 19, 45
Tracy, Clarence 30 n., 51 n., 235 n.
Trenchard, John 6, 8, 9, 23, 24, 190, 208; *see also* Cato
Troynovant myth 118, 167, 170; *see also* Brutus
Trumbull, Sir William 88 n.
Tyrell, James 22, 109, 111, 126–8
Tyrell, James (the younger) 111

Upton, John 125
Utrecht, Treaty of (1713) 6, 8, 73, 216

Vanbrugh, Sir John 126
Vane, Harriet 83 n.
Varey, Simon 4 n., 92 n., 185 n., 187 n., 205, 211 n.
Venn, William 28, 30
Vernon, Edward, Admiral 3, 7, 9, 13–14, 176
Verstegen, Richard 109, 136
Vertue, George 57, 59, 65 n., 66, 195
Victor, Benjamin 89 n., 230
Vigo (Spain) 35, 154
Virgil 77, 133, 209 n.
Vyner, Robert 22

Walkinshaw, Catharine 195
Waller, Edmund 73
Walmoden, Amelie von 192
Walpole, Horace 8, 13 n., 58 n., 59, 65, 131, 199, 224 n.; on the Gothic 123, 124–5
Walpole, Lady 52
Walpole, Sir Robert, later 1st Earl of Orford: in opposition 19–20; rise of 19; 'betrays' Whiggism 23; and church controversy 24–32; relations with City 15; Excise Crisis and aftermath 20, 35–6; foreign policy 6–8, 154–5; fall of 44–5; views on Boy Patriots 36–7; and literary patronage 48–50, 53, 168; and Garter Order 224–5; and hunting 216–17; opposition's satirical names and types

for 103, 163–6, 174–7, 180, 224–5;
  defended 164–5; *see also* Whigs
Warburton, William 90 n.
Warton, Joseph 70 n., 95, 121, 131, 135 n.,
  141, 145, 146
Warton, Thomas 121, 146, 147
Wasserman, Earl 105 n., 116 n., 138 n., 216 n.
Webster, William 28
Weekly Miscellany 28, 31
Weinbrot, Howard 49 n., 114 n.
West, Benjamin 229
West, Gilbert 33, 36, 46, 63, 69, 100 n., 122,
  246; and Pope 179–80; *Canto of the Fairy
  Queen* 177–80, 184; *Order of the
  Garter* 114, 122, 124, 144, 211, 224–9;
  Stowe 112, 118
West, Richard 65 n.
Wharton, Philip, Duke of 238; 'Persian
  Letter' 39 n.
Whateley, Stephen 101 n.
Whigs: Junto Whigs 5, 23; Court or ministerial
  Whigs 23–4, and their propaganda 104,
  110, 153, 162, 164–5; dissident or 'Patriot'
  Whigs 19–45 *passim*, and Whig 'Patriot'
  label 10–12; distinct from Tories in
  opposition 11–12, 20–2; content of
  Whiggism in Walpole era 21–4; and
  anticlericalism 24–34; and kingship 12–14,
  25, 107, 188–91; 'real Whig principles'
  defined by Molesworth 109, by Talbot,
  29, *see also* 'Patriot' title, Walpole; 'Whig
  aesthetics' 121–3; 'Whig panegyric' 69,
  72–3; 'Whig' verse forms 71–4
Whitehead, Paul: politics of 34, 55;
  Manners 55, 74, 75–6, 165, 211 n.; *State
  Dunces* 55

Whitehead, William 131
Wiggin, Lewis M. 36
Wilkite radicalism 23, 230
William, Duke of Cumberland 116 n., 195
William I, King of England 109
William III, King of England 5, 8, 85, 128,
  152, 174, 188
William IV, Prince of Orange 40, 193
Williams, Aubrey M. 75 n.
Williams, Sir Charles Hanbury, *Political
  Eclogue* 37–8, 230, 246
Wilson, Arthur 213
Wilson, Kathleen vii, 6 n., 8 n., 10 n., 14 n.,
  15 n., 17 n.
Wilson, Michael 60 n., 169 n., 178 n., 193 n.,
  195 n., 214 n., 225 n.
Wilson, Richard 196 n.
Windsor, Surrey 107, 215–29
wizards, in political satire 174–83; *see also*
  Spenser, Edmund
Wootton, Sir Henry 159
Wootton, John 212, 220, 222
Worcestershire, county election (1741) 12 n.,
  34, 37
World 122, 131
Wyndham, Sir William 55; and Pulteney 27;
  and Cobhamite Patriots 12, 22, 35, 41–3,
  86, 89, 91, 204; and Pope 12, 89, 91
Wynn, Sir Watkins William 43

Year of Wonders (1737) 239–41
Young, Edward 225; *Imperium Pelagi* 74, 155
Young, Sir George 58 n.

Zaller, Robert 104 n., 110